The author, Henry Jones Ford, taken from a photographic negative (*circa* 1910–15) by the Bain News Service and held as part of the George Grantham Bain Collection, Library of Congress Prints and Photographs Division (LC-B2- 2758-13)

THE
SCOTCH-IRISH
IN AMERICA

HENRY JONES FORD

PROFESSOR OF POLITICS AT PRINCETON UNIVERSITY

 BooksUlster

First published February 1915 by Princeton University

Second edition published 2016 by Books Ulster

Typographical arrangement © Books Ulster.

Cover image is from the painting *Climbing the Western Slope* by H. David Wright, with the artist's kind permission www.davidwrightart.com

ISBN: 978-1-910375-49-5

BIOGRAPHICAL NOTE ON THE AUTHOR

There was a heightened interest in Scotch-Irish history at the end of the nineteenth century and the beginning of the twentieth century on both sides of the Atlantic. This is evidenced by the formation of the Scotch-Irish Society of America, its congresses, and a plethora of publications extolling the role of the Scotch-Irish in American life.

The first Congress of the Scotch-Irish Society of America met in Columbus, Tennessee, in 1889. In his address, A. C. Floyd, the society's first secretary, observed:

> The Scotch-Irish people have been second to none in their influence upon civilization. Their impress upon American institutions has been especially strong. They have been leaders in every sphere of life, both public and private. They were the first to declare independence from Great Britain, and foremost in the revolutionary struggle; leaders in the formation and adoption of the Constitution, and its most powerful defenders; most active in the expansion of our national domain, and the hardiest pioneers in its development.

Books about the Scotch-Irish from this era include Charles A. Hanna, *The Scotch Irish: or, The Scot in North Britain, North Ireland, and North America* (1902); Whitelaw Reid, *The Scot in America and the Ulster Scot* (1912); James B. Woodburn, *The Ulster Scot: His History and Religion* (1914); and, not least, *The Scotch-Irish in America* (1915) by Henry Jones Ford.

Ford was born in Baltimore on 25 August 1851, the son of Franklin Ford and his wife Anne Elizabeth Ford (*née* Jones). Franklin Ford was a flour merchant of English stock whereas his wife's ancestry, as her surname suggests, was Welsh. Franklin died when Henry was only nine, leaving the family in straitened circumstances.

Henry attended public schools in Baltimore until he was 17 and then went to work in a wholesale dry-goods store, but such a job was evidently not commensurate with his talents and ability.

In due course he was to have three careers: as a newspaperman and journalist, as an academic and political scientist, and as a government official and public servant. Each of these gave him differing perspectives on what was to become his major preoccupation—the nature of government and politics, including the policy-making roles played by political parties and interest groups. Each career contributed to a very rounded understanding of government and the political process.

With respect to his career in journalism, between 1872 and 1905 he worked on a number of different newspapers in three cities: New York, Baltimore and Pittsburgh. In 1879 he was editorial writer on the *Sun* in New York. By 1883 he was the city editor of the *Sun* in Baltimore. Between 1885 and 1895 he was managing editor of the *Commercial Gazette* in Pittsburgh and of the *Chronicle-Telegraph* in the same city between 1895 and 1901. He was editor of the *Pittsburgh Gazette* (1901–5).

His academic career began in 1906 when he lectured in both the Johns Hopkins University and the University of Pennsylvania and attracted the attention of Woodrow Wilson, a factor which was to exert a significant influence on the shape of the rest of his life. In 1908 Woodrow Wilson, who at this stage was the President of Princeton University, invited him to become professor of politics.

It was Woodrow Wilson who launched Ford's career in public life. When Wilson became governor of New Jersey he appointed Ford commissioner of banking and insurance. After Wilson became president in 1913 he sent Ford on a mission to investigate and report on the governance of the Philippines, which the United States had assumed responsibility for after the defeat of Spain in the Spanish-American War of 1898. Towards the end of Wilson's presidency, he appointed Ford to the Interstate Commerce Commission. Ford's association with President Wilson gave rise to his book, *Woodrow Wilson, the Man and His Work: A Biographical Study* (1916), which was clearly a campaign biography written with the presidential election of 1916 in mind.

Woodrow Wilson was President of the American Political Science Association from 1910 to 1911. Ford followed in his footsteps and occupied the same position from 1918 to1919.

Ford was a prolific author, as the following list of publications more than amply demonstrates:

- *The Rise and Growth of American Politics: A Sketch of Constitutional Development* (1898)
- *The Cost of Our National Government: A Study in Political Pathology* (1910)
- *The Natural History of the State: An Introduction to Political Science* (1915)
- *Washington and His Colleagues: A Chronicle of the Rise and Fall of Federalism* (1918)
- *The Cleveland Era: A Chronicle of the New Order in Politics* (1918)
- *Alexander Hamilton* (1920)
- *Representative Government* (1924)

These books chart the political and constitutional history of the United States. In *The Scotch-Irish in America* Ford chronicles the important role that the Scotch-Irish played in the history of the American colonies, the American Revolution and the growth and evolution of the embryonic American republic. Two factors beyond the obvious—that the story of the Scotch-Irish in America makes for a riveting read—may have prompted him to embark upon this work. First, his time in Pittsburgh, the city of the Mellons and a very Scotch-Irish city, and, second, his admiration for Woodrow Wilson who not only played a central role in his career but was the greatest Scotch-Irish figure of his generation. It is not beyond the realms of possibility that Woodrow Wilson may even have suggested that he embark on the project.

Henry Jones Ford died on 29 August 1925, a few days after his 74th birthday, at Blue Ridge Summit, Pennsylvania. He was survived by his widow and four children. His legacy was an impressive body of work on American history, of which *The Scotch-Irish in America* forms a worthy part.

Gordon Lucy

PREFACE

Acknowledgment of the importance of Ulster emigration to America frequently occurs in the works of English and American historians dealing with the events of the eighteenth century, and a mass of literature has accumulated in both countries with regard to particular phases of the subject. A systematic treatise devoted to that special theme seemed to be desirable, and hence the book now before the reader.

This book tells the story of the Ulster Plantation and of the influences that formed the character of the people. The causes are traced that led to the great migration from Ulster and the Scotch-Irish settlements in America are described. The recital of their experiences involves an account of frontier manners and customs, and of collisions with the Indian tribes. The influence of the Scotch-Irish settlements upon American institutions is traced, particularly in organizing and propagating the Presbyterian Church, in spreading popular education, and in promoting the movement for American national independence. In conclusion, there is an appreciation of the Ulster contribution to American nationality.

The work is based upon original research. The State Papers of the period of the Ulster Plantation were examined, with the effect of throwing new light upon an undertaking over whose character and incidents there has been much controversy. Historical material on both sides of the Atlantic has been sifted, and pains have been taken to produce an authentic account of the formation and diffusion of a race stock that has played a great part in establishing and developing the American nation.

The author desires to express his thanks to the Rev. Professor James Heron, of the Assembly's College, Belfast, for permitting the reproduction of his analysis of the ethnic origins of the Scottish settlers of Ulster; to Mr. Albert Levin Richardson of Baltimore, for collections of historical material; to Professor Varnum Lansing Collins, of Princeton University, for help in the chapter on educational institutions; to Professor Harry Franklin Covington of

Princeton University for data respecting Scotch-Irish settlements in Maryland; to the Hon. W. U. Hensel of Lancaster and to Judge Harman Yerkes of Bucks County, Pennsylvania, for information; and to Charles L. McKeehan, Esq., Secretary of the Pennsylvania Scotch-Irish Society, for much kind assistance in reaching sources of information and in collecting material.

Princeton, February, 1915.

Note: The device stamped upon the front of the cover is the heraldic badge of Ulster. [*Editor's note*—in the original edition this was the red hand of Ulster on a white shield]

CONTENTS

CHAPTER I

The Ulster Plantation

In 1609, six years after the accession of James VI. of Scotland to the throne of England as James I. in its line of kings, a scheme was matured for planting Ulster with Scotch and English, and the following year the settlement began. The actual settlers were mostly Scotch, and the Ulster plantation took the character of a Scotch occupation of the North of Ireland. In that plantation was formed the breed known as Scotch-Irish, which was prominent in the struggle for American independence and which supplied to American population an ingredient that has deeply affected the development of the nation. It is the purpose of this work to give an account of this Scotch-Irish strain in the composition of the American people, tracing its history and influence.

The circumstances in which the Ulster plantation was formed had much to do with fixing the characteristics of the breed. The plantation was attended by an ouster of native Irish that is a staple subject of censure by historians who, from the point of view supplied by the ideas of our own times, hold that wiser arrangements might have been made in the interest of all parties. But that was not easy to see then. Francis Bacon is reckoned a wise man but he did not see it. In a letter written in 1601 to Cecil, Elizabeth's famous Secretary of State, Bacon referred to three roots of trouble in Ireland:

> "The first, the ambition and absoluteness of the chiefs of the families and septs. The second, the licentious idleness of their kernes and soldiers, that lie upon the country by cesses and such like oppressions. And the third, the barbarous laws, customs, their brehon laws, habits of apparel, their poets or heralds that enchant them in savage manners, and sundry other dregs of barbarism and rebellion."

The policy of making English settlements in Ireland was no new thing. It had been pursued fitfully from Norman times. Bacon did not question it, but he argued that further undertakings of the kind should not be left "as heretofore, to the pleasure of Undertakers and adventurers, where and how to build and plant; but that they do it according to a prescript or formulary." In this way the Government would be assured that the places would be selected "which are fittest for colonies or garrisons, as well for doubt of the foreigner, as for keeping the country in bridle." Bacon had the matter so much on his mind that in 1606 he presented to King James *Considerations Touching the Plantation in Ireland* written in the highest style of his stately eloquence. He said that among the works of kings two "have the supreme preeminence: the union, and the plantation of kingdoms." By a singular favor of Divine Providence "both these kinds of foundations or regenerations" had been put into the hands of King James: "the one, in the union of the island of Britain; the other in the plantation of great and noble parts of the island of Ireland." Adorning his periods with elaborate metaphors in which figured the harp of Ireland, the harp of Orpheus and the harp of David, Bacon expatiated upon the greatness of the achievement "when people of barbarous manners are brought to give over and discontinue their customs of revenge and blood, of dissolute life, and of theft, and of rapine; and to give ear to the wisdom of laws and governments."

At the time this discourse was written the property of the Crown in Ulster consisted chiefly of the abbey lands, and plans were under consideration for settling English and Scotch colonists upon these lands while the Irish lords retained their lands with English title and under English law. But so important did the plantation appear to Bacon, even although thus limited, that he suggested that the King, the better to express his "affection to the enterprise, and for a pledge thereof," should add the Earldom of Ulster to the titles of the Prince of Wales.

Bacon went on to discuss in detail the principles that should govern the enterprise. He thought that "the generality of Undertakers" should be "men of estate and plenty," not that they would go there themselves but that they would have means to engage in the business for the "advancement of their younger children or kinsfolks; or for the sweetness of the expectation of a great bargain in the end." As incentives the lands should be let to them on easy rates and large liberties. Upon the latter point Bacon promptly explains that he does not mean liberties of jurisdiction which "hath been the error of the ancient donations and plantations in that country." He means only "liberties tending to commodity; as liberty to transport any of the commodities growing upon the countries new planted; liberty to import from hence all things appertaining to their necessary use, custom-free." If this wise advice had been acted upon consistently the course of Irish and American history would have been different.

At this time the colonization of Virginia was appealing for support, but in comparison with the Ulster project the Virginia plantation seemed so visionary that Bacon referred to it as "an enterprise in my opinion differing as much from this, as Amadis de Gaul differs from Caesar's Commentaries." He struck the same note in 1617 when as Lord Chancellor of England he addressed the person called to be Lord Chief Justice of Ireland. Bacon remarked that "Ireland is the last *ex filiis Europae* which hath been reclaimed from desolation and a desert (in many parts) to population and plantation; and from savage and barbarous customs to humanity and civility." He commended the plantations to the special care of the new justice, with the admonition: "You are to be a master builder, and a master planter, and reducer of Ireland."

Bacon's views have been considered at some length because they illumine the ideas with which the statesmanship of the age approached such tasks, and also reveal the origin of some characteristic features of the Ulster plantation. To Bacon's view the tribal system of Ireland with its state of chronic disorder was a remnant of the same barbarism against which Caesar fought in Gaul and Charlemagne in continental Europe. The planting of trusty colonies among uncivilized peoples as garrisons to check their insubordination and as centers from which culture would be diffused was a practice that went back to the times of the ancient Roman commonwealth, had been adopted by many European rulers, and was generally regarded as a well-settled expedient of prudent statesmanship. Nothing in Bacon's remarks indicates any doubt in his mind as to the rightfulness of such a policy in Ireland, although it necessarily involved dispossession of natives.

His only concern was to adopt such measures as would make the policy efficacious. Moreover it should be borne in mind that in that time the feudal principle that the tenure of land is contingent upon personal service to the State had not been overborne by the notions of individual ownership and exclusive right that have since become dominant, although in our own times there are signs of reaction. It seemed altogether fitting that rebels and traitors should be ejected and that the land should be placed in charge of those upon whom the King could rely when he called for service. At the bottom of land tenure was a personal relation between the King and his liege. The State in its modern aspect as a sovereign authority deriving its revenues from systematic taxation and regulating rights and duties by positive law was in process of formation but it was not fully developed until long after the period of the Ulster plantation.

The effect of Bacon's advice in the Ulster arrangements is distinctly marked. To it seems to be due one of the existing orders of English nobility. Bacon deemed it so important "to allure by all means fit Undertakers" that in the memorial of 1606 he suggested that grants of knighthood, "with some new difference and precedence," might "work with many" in drawing them to the support of the cause. Action taken by the King early in 1611 accords with Bacon's advice. The order of baronets, officially described as "a new dignitie between Barons and Knights," was instituted, to consist of gentlemen who should bind themselves to pay a sum sufficient to maintain thirty foot-soldiers in Ireland for three years, the money thus obtained to be kept as a special fund so that it might be "wholly converted to that use for which it was given and intended." The first of these baronets was Bacon's own half-brother, and it appears that Bacon advised the King on points raised touching the dignity and precedence of the new order of nobility. There have been many flings at James I. in this matter of the institution of the order of baronet—it seems to have a special attraction for the sarcasm of writers of popular history—but the record shows that it was inspired by Bacon and was performed by the King as a utilitarian transaction quite in the modern spirit. A similar creation of baronets was planned by King James in 1624 in aid of the colonization of Nova Scotia, the fundamental condition being that each baronet of this class should maintain six colonists for two years. The two classes are still distinguished in their heraldry, all baronets having the right to bear the Red Hand of Ulster on their coat of arms, except those of the Nova Scotian creation who display the arms of Scotland. The order of baronet, although ranking below other orders of nobility in dignity and precedence, may justly claim to possess a distinctly imperial character.

Not long after Bacon's memorial to the King the possibilities in Ulster were enlarged by a series of events which at the same time emphasized the need of vigorous measures. These events serve also to illustrate the clash of cultures that was the underlying cause of Irish anarchy. The accession of James took place just as an uprising aided by Spanish troops had been subdued after more than four years of hard fighting. The submission of the Earl of Tyrone, the chief native magnate of Ulster, whose surrender ended resistance in that province, took place only a few days before James set out from Edinburgh to take possession of the throne of England to which he had just been called. The Irish situation presented an urgent problem to James and his counsellors. That problem, in addition to its chronic perplexities arising from internal conditions, was complicated by foreign influences. The Counter-Reformation was prosecuted with great vigor and success by Jesuit missionaries in Ireland and their plans of making the country an independent kingdom gained the sympathy of Pope Gregory XIII., who accepted the Crown of Ireland in behalf of a nephew. The movement

acquired serious importance when Philip II. of Spain gave support
to it. He was not inclined at first to have anything to do with the
Irish as he was embittered by the way in which crews of wrecked
galleons of the Armada had been robbed and murdered on the
western coast of Ireland. But English attacks on the coasts of Spain
and Portugal, and the support which Elizabeth extended to the
provinces of the Netherlands in revolt against his rule, reconciled
him to alliances with Irish insurgents, and twice during Elizabeth's
reign Spanish forces were landed in Ireland. Hugh O'Neill, the
Earl of Tyrone, took a leading part in the dealings with Spain,
and he received from the Pope a crown of peacock's feathers. In
making his submission he had stipulated for the retention of
his Earldom, with its territorial jurisdiction in Ulster, although
renouncing his Celtic chiefry. This was done before he had heard
of Elizabeth's death, and on hearing the news he is said to have
cried with vexation at not having held out for better terms. With
such an attitude on his part there was an instability in the Ulster
situation, soon to be displayed.

A difficulty with which the Government had constantly to
contend arose from the conflicts among the Irish themselves.
The chiefs argued that the land belonged to them; the occupants
protested that the land was theirs although the chiefs had a customary right to various services and dues in kind. The chiefs
quarreled among themselves as to their rights. Tyrone was incensed against his principal vassal, O'Cahan, who had made his
submission before Tyrone gave him leave. O'Cahan's feudal rent,
formerly fixed at 21 cows a year, was summarily raised to 200
cows. In support of this demand Tyrone took possession of a
large district belonging to O'Cahan. When O'Cahan made his
peace with the Government he had been assured that he should
in future hold his lands not from Tyrone but directly from the
Crown. O'Cahan appealed to the authorities at Dublin, but it
was difficult to get Tyrone to appear to answer the charges. When
he did so he insulted the Lord Deputy and Council by snatch-
ing the papers from O'Cahan's hand and tearing them to pieces.

Eventually the King decided to hear the case in England, but instead of obeying the summons Tyrone fled the country, never to return. This action was quite unexpected by the Government as Tyrone had been demanding that he be allowed to plead his cause before the King in person. The affair has never been fully cleared up but it is known that the Government had received information that arrangements were making for another rising with Spanish aid and that Rory O'Donnell, Earl of Tyrconnel, was in the movement. This information did not mention Tyrone; but his cousin, Cuconnaught Maguire, who was in the plot and who had just gone to Brussels on its business, heard there that it had been discovered. Maguire procured a ship with which he sailed to the North of Ireland and on September 4, 1607, took off both Tyrconnel and Tyrone. This was the famous Flight of the Earls by which a great part of Ulster was escheated to the English Crown. Those were times when the more strong and active spirits among the masses of the people preferred to live as fighting men and raiders rather than as industrial drudges, and bands began operations in various districts. O'Cahan himself became disaffected, owing to some claims of the Bishop of Derry to lands in O'Cahan's territory. He drove the bishop's tax gatherers off the disputed lands, defied writs of law and did not submit until a body of troops was about to march on his castle.

While these events were taking place a clash occurred between the English commander at Derry and a neighboring Irish lord that culminated in another insurrection. Sir George Paulet, commander at Derry, was a dull, incapable and arrogant person who had obtained the command by purchase. In one of the Lord Deputy's reports to the home Government it is said of him that "he was hated by those over whom he had command, and neither beloved nor feared by the Irish, his neighbors." O'Dogherty, lord of Innishowen, collected a number of his followers to fell timber. A rumor reached Paulet that O'Dogherty was out to await the return of Tyrone, and Paulet marched on O'Dogherty's castle. Although O'Dogherty was away, his wife refused to open the gates and showed such an undaunted spirit that Paulet had to choose between attempting a siege with an inadequate force or marching home again, and chose the latter. O'Dogherty wrote a sharp letter of complaint to Paulet, but it was in respectful language and was subscribed "your loving friend." Paulet sent a railing letter in reply, closing with the declaration: "So wishing confusion to your actions, I leave you to a provost marshal and his halter." Although O'Dogherty was greatly incensed he did not refuse to present himself at Dublin to answer for his conduct; and soon afterward he acted as foreman of the Donegal grand jury that found bills for high treason against the fugitive Earls. O'Dogherty, who was young and hot-headed, was worked upon by others so that at last he did engage in a plot that enabled him to take vengeance on Paulet. The details of this affair are particularly instructive from the revelation they make of the sort of experiences that colored Ulster traditions and stamped the character of the Ulster breed.

O'Dogherty's first task was to procure a supply of arms and ammunition to use against Paulet. He approached Captain Henry Hart, commander of the fort of Culmore guarding the entrance to the Foyle, with complaints that the attitude of the ladies of Derry deprived his wife of society suitable to her rank. He asked Captain Hart to set a good example of social intercourse by coming to dine with him bringing also Mrs. Hart and the children. The request accorded with the conciliatory policy of the Government and the invitation was unsuspectingly accepted. As soon as dinner was over O'Dogherty threatened Hart with instant death unless he would agree to surrender the fort. Hart, a man of the bull-dog breed, flatly refused. His wife and children were brought before him and threatened with death; his wife fell at his feet on her knees, crying and beseeching him to yield. It was urged that by so doing he would save the garrison too, as all would be killed if force had to be used whereas all would be spared if the post were quietly surrendered. O'Dogherty offered to take a solemn oath that he would carry out his promise. Hart reminded him that he was even then breaking the oath of allegiance he had taken not long before;

and bluntly declared that he "should never trust oath that ever he made again." But while O'Dogherty failed to budge Captain Hart, he gained his end by the aid of the Captain's wife. In her terror for her husband and her children Mrs. Hart entered into a scheme for betraying the garrison. Accompanied by O'Dogherty and his men, she went to the fort at nightfall, crying out that the Captain had fallen from his horse and had broken his arm. The little garrison ran out to help their commander and O'Dogherty rushed in and took possession.

These events took place on April 18, 1608. Having obtained the arms he needed, O'Dogherty set out at once to attack Paulet at Derry. Although that commander had been warned of danger, he had not taken any precautions and habitually neglected even such routine duty as the posting of sentries. O'Dogherty's men were inside the fortifications before the noise roused Paulet. He ran out of his own house and hid in one of the other houses where he was finally discovered and killed. The surprise was so complete that the garrison was not able to make much resistance, but Lieutenant Baker with about 140 persons, men, women, and children, took possession of two large houses and held out until noon on the following day. By that time provisions had run short and O'Dogherty had brought up a cannon from Culmore, so Baker surrendered upon the promise that the lives of all with him should be spared. This promise was fulfilled. O'Dogherty slew no prisoners and in the course of his short rebellion no blood was shed by his orders except in actual conflict.

As soon as the Government was able to throw troops into the country O'Dogherty's lieutenants abandoned Derry and Culmore, after setting them on fire. The rebellion was never really formidable although O'Dogherty's energetic movements carried it into several counties. His forces were finally routed and he himself was killed on July 5, 1608. In a report to the home Government Sir John Davies, Attorney-General of Ireland, noted that O'Dogherty's death "happened not only on the fifth day of the month, but on a Tuesday, but the Tuesday 11 weeks, that is 77 days after the burning of Derry, which is an ominous number being seven elevens and eleven sevens." The special mention of Tuesday in this collection of portents is an allusion to an old proverb that Tuesday is the day of English luck in Ireland.

* In consequence of these events vast areas were escheated to the Crown, including most of the territory now forming the counties of Donegal, Londonderry, Tyrone, Fermanagh, Armagh and Cavan. It was the good fortune of the Ulster plantation that the man then at the head of the Irish Government as Lord Deputy was an administrator of rare ability. Sir Arthur Chichester, the Lord Deputy, is a typical specimen of the class of proconsuls whose solid characteristics have been the building material of the British Empire. He was born in 1563, the second son of Sir John Chichester of Ramleigh, near Barnstaple, Devonshire. He was educated at Exeter College, Oxford; was an officer in one of the Queen's best ships in the fight with the Spanish Armada in 1588; in 1595 he was employed in a military command in Drake's unfortunate last expedition to the West Indies, and the next year he commanded a company in the expedition of Essex that captured Cadiz; in 1597 he was third in command of a force sent to the assistance of Henry IV. of France, was wounded at the siege of Amiens and was subsequently knighted. He afterward served in the Netherlands and was in garrison at Ostend when he was summoned to duty in Ireland, in command of a force of 1,200 men. The record shows that although only thirty-six when he began his distinguished career in Ireland, he was a veteran thoroughly seasoned by land and by sea.

A characteristic instance of his determination in all matters of discipline took place soon after Essex arrived in Ireland as head of its Administration by Elizabeth's personal favor. Having heard of the good order in which Chichester kept his force, Essex went to Drogheda to review it. Carried away by excitement the scatter-brain Earl led a cavalry charge against the pikemen. Chichester repulsed the horsemen as if they had been actual enemies, and the Earl himself was scratched by a slash from a pike that made him wheel about and retreat. Essex took the affair in good part and on April 28, 1599, appointed Chichester to be governor of Carrickfergus and the adjacent country. Chichester took an active but subordinate part in the war waged against Tyrone and his adherents. On April 19, 1603, shortly after the accession of James, Chichester was made a member of the Irish Privy Council; and on October 15, 1604, he was appointed Lord Deputy of Ireland, although not inducted into office until February 3, 1605. The appointment may be ascribed to the influence of a predecessor in that office, Mountjoy, who was now Earl of Devonshire and the King's chief adviser on Irish affairs, and who well knew the need there was for a strong hand and a cool head at the helm in Ireland. Chichester himself did not seek the office. About five months after assuming it he wrote to the home Government that it would be advisable to put a more eminent man at the head of affairs, "a man of his [Chichester's] estate and fortune being better fit to serve His Majesty in meaner places."

The perusal of Chichester's State Papers impresses one with his virtue in the Roman sense of hard manliness. His concern was always for the discharge of his professional duty; and that formed his moral horizon. He chose means with regard to their efficacy in attaining practical results, offering rewards for the heads of rebel chiefs, slaying their active partisans and wasting the land on occasion, but never indulging purposeless cruelty. He had a low opinion of the character of the native Irish, but he had no animosity and was more disposed to adopt conciliatory measures than the home Government. Indeed, his disapproval of measures to force the Roman Catholics into the Established Church eventually led to his retirement. While bent on repressing disorder and bringing the Irish chiefs under the rule of law, he was also vigilant against abuses in the administration and spared no one. He advised Montgomery, the Bishop of Derry, "sometimes to leave the care of the world, to which he thought him too much affected, and to attend to his pastoral calling and the reformation of his clergy." He showed great powers of sustained application to the literary tasks in which his position involved him, and his numerous State Papers are full, clear, and precise. In view of his previous career this side of his activity is remarkable, for he handles the pen with a readiness unusual in the captains of that age. In filing dispatches from the home Government he not only endorsed them with the date on which they were received but also added a summary of their contents, in a handwriting remarkably bold, clear and regular. The information gathered by his spies included stories of plots to make away with him by assassination or poisoning, but to alarms of that sort he appears to have been incredulous and callous. In the camp or in the office he was ever ready, clear-headed and sensible. In the plantation of Ulster he received a large grant of land and in 1613 he was raised to the Irish peerage as Lord Chichester of Belfast. He had no children and his estates devolved on his brother, Edward, father of Arthur Chichester, first Earl of Donegal.

Another official whose copious and vivid writings add greatly to our knowledge of this period is Sir John Davies. The modernized spelling of his name is here used although in the Irish Calendars it appears as Davys. He was born in Wiltshire, England, in 1569 and took his A.B. degree at Oxford in 1590. His poetical works hold an established place in English literature and his literary ability gives a distinctive lustre to his official papers, but in Ireland he figures as a hard-working administrator. He arrived in 1603 to assume the office of Solicitor-General. In 1606 he succeeded to the post of Attorney-General. From first to last he took an active and prominent part in the Ulster plantation. He was a man of high personal courage and of versatile ability, a fine poet, a voluminous essayist on legal, antiquarian and historical subjects, an eloquent speaker and a vigorous man of action. He held office in Ireland until 1619 and died in England in 1626, after he had been appointed Lord Chief Justice but before he had assumed the office.

The scheme adopted for the plantation of Ulster was not the invention of anyone but was the outcome of the statesmanship of the age. Just such ideas as Bacon expressed in his *Considerations* presented to King James run all through the State Papers of this period. So early as October 2, 1605, long before the Flight of the Earls, Chichester wrote that the situation "can only be remedied by planting of English and others well affected in fit places." Chichester held that none of the fields in which colonization was then projected equalled Ireland. He remarks that he "knows of many who endeavor the finding out of Virginia, Guiana, and other remote and unknown countries, and leave this of our own waste and desolate, which needs be an absurd folly or wilful ignorance." The allusion to Sir Walter Raleigh's projects is transparent. As a matter of fact both the Ulster and the Virginia plantations took root and bore abundantly, each deeply affecting the other's destiny. On September 17, 1607, less than a fortnight after the Flight of the Earls, Chichester advised the English Privy Council that to bring Ulster to any settled state of order it would be necessary either to plant strong "colonies of civil people of England or Scotland" or else drive out the wild Irishmen to the waste lands "leaving only such people behind as will dwell under the protection of the garrisons and forts which would be made strong and defensible." He strongly recommended the former course although he held the latter to be justifiable. At that period "civil" had a significance for which the term "civilized" would now be employed. The term "civilization" did not get into the vocabulary until long afterward, and so late as 1772 it was resisted by Dr. Samuel Johnson as an unnecessary innovation which he refused to admit into his dictionary. When Bacon and Chichester spoke of introducing civility into Ireland they had in mind substituting legally organized communities for the tribal groups.

The home Government was quite ready to act upon the suggestion and the response was prompt and decided. The Chief Secretary of State was Robert Cecil, a cousin of Francis Bacon. Cecil had served Elizabeth as Secretary of State and had been continued in the position with augmented power by James, who in 1605 conferred upon him the title of Earl of Salisbury. In advance of the action of the English Privy Council, Salisbury wrote to Chichester assuring him of support and on September 29, 1607, the ground plan of the Ulster plantation was thus formulated in a communication from the Privy Council to Chichester:

> "For the plantation which is to follow upon attainder, the King in general approves of his (Chichester's) project, being resolved to make a mixture of the inhabitants, as well Irish as English and Scotch; to respect and favor the Irish that are of good note and desert, and to make him (Chichester) specially judge thereof; to prefer English that are and have been servitors before any new men from hence; to assign places of most importance to men of best trust; and generally to observe these two cautions;—first, that such as be planted there be not needy, but of a reasonable sufficiency to maintain their portions; secondly, that none shall have a vast, but only a reasonable proportion; much less that any one of either nation shall be master of a whole country. But before this plantation can be digested and executed, much must be prepared by himself (Chichester), as His Majesty is to be better informed of the lands to be divided; what countries are most meet to be inhabited; what Irish fit to be trusted; what English meet for that plantation in Ireland; what offers are or will be made there; what estates are fit to be granted; and what is to be done for the conviction of the fugitives, because there is no possession or estate to be given before their attainder."

The tenor of official dispatches makes it clear that the Flight of the Earls was regarded as a good opportunity for radical treatment of the Ulster situation, "that those countries be made the King's by this accident," to use Salisbury's own words. By the term "servitors" is meant officers in the King's service in Ireland, who knew the country and had had experience in dealing with the natives. The need of careful management was appreciated by the Government, for in the preceding reign three attempts had been made at Ulster colonization, all ending in total failure. These had been in the nature of grants of territory to individual adventurers who undertook to take possession and bring in tenants, but who were unable to overcome the resistance of the native Irish, desperately opposed to the intrusion of individual holdings in their tribal territory. The Government was determined that the next attempt of the kind should be made in sufficient force.

The information demanded by the home Government was submitted under date of January 23, 1608, in "a project for the division and plantation of the escheated lands," etc., prepared by the Privy Council of Ireland. This is a long document in which for the first time the plantation scheme took definite form. It included a schedule of available lands in the six escheated counties, with a scheme of allotment. The different classes of Undertakers and the size of their holdings to be allowed to them were designated, and the main points of the scheme as finally carried into effect were set forth.

Not long after the transmission of this project the O'Dogherty rebellion broke out. With its suppression work on the project was resumed and in September, 1608, Chichester prepared a detailed statement entitled *Certain Notes of Remembrances Touching the Plantation and Settlement of the Escheated Lands in Ulster*, which he gave to Chief Justice Ley and Attorney-General Davies as their instructions in sending them to England to confer with the King and Privy Council. This was a soldier's review of the Ulster situation, county by county, noting the force and disposition of the natives, and mentioning the places that should be strongly occupied to guard the peace of the plantation.

The outcome of these reports and conferences was the publication of *Orders and Conditions To Be Observed by the Undertakers* issued by the King and Privy Council in March, 1609. The preamble sets forth that "many persons being ignorant of the conditions whereupon His Majesty is pleased to grant the said land are importunate suitors for greater portions than they are able to plant, intending their private profit only and not the advancement of the public service." The orders then set forth conditions of allotment and occupation similar in general to those proposed in the project of January 23, 1608, framed by the Irish Privy Council.

From now on the course of events spreads out in Ireland,

England and Scotland, and an attempt to follow chronological order would confuse the narrative. A chronology appended to this chapter gives the sequence of events, but comment upon them can be made most conveniently by a topical arrangement.

While the home Government was arranging to responsible Undertakers, the Irish Administration was busy getting the lands ready for occupation. On July 21, 1609, a new commission, with Chichester himself at the head, was appointed to survey the country and mark fit places for settlement. The letters of Davies, who was on this commission, give a picturesque account of its proceedings. It was accompanied by surveyors who worked under guard, for "our geographers," wrote Davies, "do not forget what entertainment the Irish gave to a map-maker about the end of the late rebellion." When he "came into Tyrconnell the inhabitants took off his head, because they would not have their country discovered." The thoroughness with which the commissioners did their work is attested by the completeness of their records. Abstracts of title were made, and detailed maps were prepared, for which there is still so much demand that the British Government issues facsimile copies, with the exception of the map of Donegal which has been lost. On June 5, 1610, Chichester received the King's warrant to prepare a new commission to put the settlers in possession and on August 28, 1610, this commission issued a proclamation that the allotted lands were open for occupation.

Meanwhile Court influence had been exerted to induce the City of London to take part in the enterprise. At that time London was still a medieval city, surrounded by walls the gates of which were shut at a certain hour. The population was less than 250,000, and even this number was regarded as overcrowding the area so as to invite outbreaks of the plague, deaths from which cause in London amounted to 30,561 in 1603. One of the arguments used in support of colonization projects was that they would, draw off surplus population and thus avert the periodical visitations of the plague. The importance of London was very much greater than the size of its population might suggest, for it was the privileged seat of great chartered companies, whose transactions ranged far abroad. In that period a municipal corporation was not so much a governing body in the modern sense as a mercantile body. It was interested in trade for the advantage of the burgesses far more than in administration of public affairs for the benefit of the inhabitants. Judicial and administrative functions were vigorously exercised as an incident of charter privileges and for their protection, but the conception of a public trusteeship for the general welfare was still undeveloped.

It was not until 1684 that the lighting of the streets was made a public function. The dirty and turbulent town was a mixture of squalor and magnificence, but its merchant princes were a recognized power in the State and the King and his Council were anxious to interest them in the Ulster project. One difficulty in the way was that schemes of American colonization were then attracting business adventure. Much was known about Ireland; it was a stale subject fraught with disagreeable associations. Little was known of America, and impressions originally derived from the East attached to it, as the term "West Indies" still bears witness, as also the common appellation of the American aborigines. The mention of Ireland called up notions of hard knocks and poor gains, while concerning America there were vague but alluring notions compounded of traditional belief in the gorgeous opulence of India, of genuine trade knowledge of the value of its products, and of rumors of vast treasure gained by the Spanish in America. Among the corporate powers of the London Company that founded Jamestown in May, 1607, was the right to search for mines and to coin money. No such golden lure could be held out in behalf of Ireland. It was felt that special efforts were necessary to impress upon the City magnates the business advantages to be derived from Irish colonization.

The King had a statement prepared for the purpose entitled *Motives and Reasons To Induce the City of London To Undertake Plantation in the North of Ireland.* An appeal is made to civic pride by citing "the eternal commendation" gained by Bristol, which city in the reign of Henry II. rebuilt and populated Dublin, and the hope is expressed that "this noble precedent were followed by the City of London in these times." The King desired that London do for Derry what Bristol did for Dublin, and he submits a detailed statement of the natural resources, industrial opportunities and commercial facilities of the north of Ireland, which in view of actual results does not seem to be much inflated. His assertion that materials for the linen trade are "finer there and more plentiful than in all the rest of the Kingdom" was eventually borne out by the establishment of the linen industry for which the North of Ireland has since been famous. This appeal together with the project of plantation as formulated in *Orders and Conditions To Be Observed by Undertakers*, was sent to the Lord Mayor, who, on July 1, 1609, issued a precept to the chartered companies requesting that they meet to consider the subject and also to nominate four men from each company to serve on a committee to represent the City in the negotiation.

The City companies were apparently reluctant to engage in the enterprise, and a few years later when some differences occurred as to the terms of the bargain, it was officially declared that the City had at last yielded to pressing importunity. The record shows that the companies did not move until a second and more urgent precept was issued, dated July 8, 1609. The companies then sent representatives to meet at Guildhall to discuss the King's proposals and deputies were appointed to answer for the City. Several conferences took place between these deputies and the Privy Council, hut the most that the City magnates would agree to do was to look into the matter. At a conference with the Privy Council held on Sunday, July 30, 1609, it was decided that the negotiations should he suspended until "four wise, grave and discreet citizens should he presently sent to view the place." They were to go at the City's charges and "make report to the City, at their return from thence, of their opinions and doings touching the same."

The official correspondence of that period reveals the solicitude of the King and Privy Council for the successful conclusion of the negotiation with the City. On August 3, 1609, the Privy Council wrote to Chichester notifying him that the City was sending out certain deputies to view the land and instructing him to provide such guidance as would impress upon them the value of the concessions, while "matters of distaste, as fear of the Irish, of the soldiers, of cess, and such like, he not so much as named." These citizens of London, John Brode, goldsmith, John Monroes, Robert Treswell, painter, and John Rowley, draper, doubtless found themselves much courted and flattered by the dignitaries to whom they bore letters of introduction. In a letter of August 28, written from camp in Coleraine, to Lord Salisbury of the Privy Council, Davies tells how they were all using "their best rhetoric" on the Londoners. He mentions that "one of the agents is fallen sick, and would fain return, but the Lord Deputy and all the rest here use all means to comfort and retain him, lest this accident should discourage his fellow-citizens."

However flattered the citizens may have been by these blandishments their business keenness was not impaired. On October 13, 1609, Chichester writes that "these agents aim at all the places of profit and pleasure upon the rivers of the Bann and Loughfole." He had endeavored to meet their demands "whereby he thinks they depart fully satisfied." But the soldier evidently does not repose entire confidence in the disposition of the civic bargainers, for he remarks that "he prays God they prove not like their London women, who sometimes long to-day and loathe to-morrow." But the citizens evidently made a favorable report to the City guilds for in the following January three conferences took place in London between the Government and the City in which the City's representatives showed an eager spirit. The City deputies that went to Ireland were present and the course of the proceedings showed that they had prompted demands beyond what the Government had thought of allowing. The minutes record that on some points there was "much altercation." The representatives of the Government showed an accommodating spirit and eventually an agreement was reached confirmed by articles signed January

28, 1610. In consideration of various privileges the City agreed to levy £20,000 in aid of the proposed plantation. The county of Coleraine, thereafter known as Londonderry, was allotted to the City for colonization, and it was stipulated that the city of Derry and the town of Coleraine should be rebuilt. The agreement is set forth in twenty-seven articles, concluding with the provision that "the City shall, with all speed, set forward the plantation in such sort as that there be 60 houses built in Derry and 40 houses at Coleraine by the first of November following, with convenient fortifications."

Although it was undoubtedly a wise stroke of policy on the part of the King to enlist the powerful City guilds in the enterprise, the mainstay of the Ulster plantation turned out to be the Scottish participation, which does not seem to have been originally regarded as important. Although from the first there was an understanding between Chichester and the English Privy Council that eventually the plantation would be opened to Scotch settlers, no steps were taken in that direction until the plans had been matured. If meanwhile any expectations of a share were entertained in Scotland there was no legal basis for them. Ireland belonged to the English Crown and although the King of Scotland was also King of England, the two kingdoms were then quite separate and distinct. The first public announcement of any Scottish connection with the Ulster plantation appears in a letter of March 19, 1609, from Sir Alexander Hay, the Scottish secretary resident at the English Court, to the Scottish Privy Council at Edinburgh. The tone of the letter shows that he was all agog with the news of the fine prospects opening up for the Scotch. Hay relates that he had been present by command at a meeting of the English Privy Council, at which he was notified that the arrangements for the Ulster plantation had been settled and that the King's Scottish subjects were to be allowed a share. Several members of the Privy Council put down their names in his presence, and the roll of the English Undertakers was already complete.

The articles required that every Undertaker for 2,000 acres

should build a castle of stone, which he feared "may effraye our people," but upon inquiry he learned that "nothing was meant thereby bot any litill toure or peill suche as are common in our Bordouris." He was also curious to know how great an area 2,000 acres would be, and was told that it meant a property two miles square of arable land and pasture, without counting attached wood and bog. He suggests to the Council that here is a great opportunity for Scotland, since "we haif greitt advantage of transporting of our men and bestiall in regard we lye so near to that coiste of Ulster." The Scottish Privy Council acted promptly. On March 28 orders were issued for public proclamation of the good things now available upon "certain easy, tolerable and profitable conditions," which the King had offered "out of his unspeikable love and tendir affectioun toward his Majesties subjectis"; and those of them "quho ar disposit to tak ony land in Yreland" were requested to present their desires and petitions to the Council. The King's ancient subjects responded so heartily that by September 14 the allotments applied for by seventy-seven persons amounted to 141,000 acres although Hay had reckoned the Scottish share at 90,000 acres. In the following year the matter of Scottish participation was taken over by the English Privy Council, and when the list of the Scottish Undertakers was finally revised and completed, the number had been reduced from seventy-seven to fifty-nine, and of these only about eighteen had been among the original seventy-seven. Instead of the 141,000 acres applied for, the final award allotted 81,000 acres to Scotch Undertakers.

Military considerations presided over arrangements for the plantation. Hence the scheme provided that the natives should have locations of their own, while the settlers should be massed in districts so that their united force would confront attack. Only the "servitors," a class of Undertakers restricted to officers in the public service in Ireland, were permitted to have Irish tenants. The design was that the servitors should have estates adjacent to the Irish reservations, to "defend the borders and fortresses and suppress the Irishry." This expression occurs in a letter of May,

1609, from the Bishop of Armagh urging a postponement of actual occupation until the following spring, one of his reasons being that it would be dangerous for the English Undertakers to start until the servitors were ready. The lands were divided into lots of 2,000, 1,500 and 1,000 acres, designated respectively as great, middle and small proportions. Each Undertaker for a great or middle proportion had to give bond, in £400 or £300 respectively, that within three years he would build a stone or brick house with a "bawn," fortified enclosure, and he was required to have ready in his house "12 muskets and calivers, 12 hand weapons for the arming of 24 men." The Undertaker for a small proportion had to give bond in £200 that he would build a bawn.

The Scotch and English Undertakers for great proportions were under obligation "within three years to plant or place upon the said proportion 48 able men, aged 18 years or upward, born in England or inward parts of Scotland." Applications for estates were open to three classes: (1) English or Scottish persons generally, (2) servitors, (3) natives of Ireland. The estates of 2,000 acres were charged with knight's service to the King *in capite*; those of 1,500 acres with knight's service to the Castle of Dublin; and those of 1,000 acres with the tenure of common socage. That is to say the larger estates were held by the military tenure of the feudal system, while the small proportions were simply held by perpetual lease at a fixed rent. The yearly rent to the Crown for every 1,000 acres was 5£ 6s 8d for Undertakers of the first sort, 8£ for the second and 10£ 13s. 4d. for the native Irish. If the servitors should plant their lands with English or Scottish tenants they should pay the same rent as the Undertakers of the first sort. No Undertaker or his assign had the right to "alien or demise any of his lands to a meer Irish, or to any who will not take the oath of supremacy" upon pain of forfeiture.

These particulars are taken from the Carew Manuscripts, which give a summary of the allotments as completed in 1611, making a total of 511,465 acres. Accompanying documents mention by name 56 English Undertakers holding 81,500 acres, 59 Scottish holding 81,000 acres, and 59 servitors holding 49,914 acres. The names of 277 natives are given as holders of allotments in the same precincts with the servitors, aggregating 52,479 acres. In addition Connor Roe Maguire received 5,980 acres and "several Irishmen" are scheduled as holding 1,468 acres, making a total of 59,927 acres allotted to natives. The Carew summary lumps together "British Undertakers and the Londoners" as holders of 209,800 acres. On deducting the 162,500 scheduled to English and Scotch Undertakers in the records accompanying the summary, the London allotments appear to have aggregated 47,300 acres. The remainder consisted of church endowments and lands reserved for public uses such as corporate towns, forts, schools, and hospitals. The College of Dublin received an allotment of 9,600 acres.

The total area appropriated in Ulster for the purposes of the plantation has been a controversial issue and estimates differ greatly, some writers putting it at about 400,000 acres while others contend that it amounted to nearly 4,000,000 acres. Such wide difference on a question of fact shows that passion has clouded the issue. The whole of the six counties includes only 2,836,837 Irish acres, or in English measure 3,785,057 acres. Just how much of this area was allotted to settlers it is impossible to determine exactly, notwithstanding the apparently precise statement made in the Carew records, for it seems that only cleared land was reckoned. The *Orders and Conditions* say that to every proportion "shall be allowed such quantity of bog and wood as the country shall conveniently afford." The negotiations with the City of London show that in that case large claims were made of privileges appurtenant to the acreage granted, among them woodlands extending into the adjoining county of Tyrone.

Nevertheless there is reason to believe that the Carew computation of 511,465 acres is a fair statement of the actual extent of the lands appropriated for the plantation. The principle upon which the plantation was founded was that the settlers should be massed in certain districts. It appears from a letter of Davies that the commissioners charged with making the surveys were in camp in Ulster nine weeks. In that period of time they could not have done more than to note and map areas suitable for tillage and pasture, and in a report of March 15, 1610, accompanying the transmission of the maps to the English Privy Council a summary is given of land available for the plantation aggregating 424,643 acres. There are also indications that appurtenant rights were strictly construed. The grant of woodlands to the City of London was made with the reservation that the timber was "to be converted to the use of the plantation, and all necessary uses in Ireland, and not to be made merchandize." It was afterward ordered that settlers in Donegal and Tyrone should be allowed to take supplies of timber from the Londoners' lands. The Carew computation of the area allotted exceeds by 86,822 acres the estimate of available lands made by the commission of 1610 which suggests that the Carew computation includes areas of every kind covered by the grants. This conjecture is strengthened by the fact that the articles of agreement with London in 1610 mention only 27,000 acres, whereas the Carew record made in 1611 of the actual distribution charges the Londoners with 47,300 acres.

Further confirmation is supplied by a report made in 1618 by Captain George Alleyne as muster-master of Ulster. It contains the names of all the landholders and the number of their acres, men, muskets, calivers, pikes, halberds and swords. The holdings of the English and Scottish Undertakers are returned as amounting to 197,000 acres, and of the servitors 51,720 acres, a total of 248,720 acres. The same items in the Carew summary aggregate 259,714 acres. So far as it is possible to test the Carew summary it appears to cover the total area appropriated for the occupation and use of the plantation. That is to say, about 18 per cent. of the total area of the six escheated counties, including however all the then desirable lands, was taken from the native Irish proprietors for the purposes of the plantation, but over 11 per cent. of these confiscated lands was allotted to Undertakers coming forward among the native Irish. However opinions may differ as to the morality of the scheme there can be no doubt of the success of the plantation. Ulster had been the most backward province of Ireland. It became the most populous and wealthy.

CHRONOLOGY

1605   October 2:—Chichester to Salisbury urging the need of "planting of English and others well affected" in Ulster.

1606   Bacon to James I:—"Considerations Touching the Plantations in Ireland."

1607   September 4:—Flight of the Earls.

September 17:—Chichester urges the need of bringing into Ulster "colonies of civil people of England and Scotland."

September 29:—Privy Council replies that the King is "resolved to make a mixture of the inhabitants, as well Irish, as English and Scottish."

1608   April 18:—O'Dogherty captures Derry.

July 5:—O'Dogherty killed.

September:—Chichester sends to the Privy Council "Certain Notes of Remembrances touching the Plantation and Settlement of the Escheated Lands."

1609   March:—The Privy Council issues "Orders and Conditions to be observed by the Undertakers."

March 19:—Letter from the Scottish Secretary of State in London to the Scottish Privy Council at Edinburgh announcing that Scots are to share in the Ulster Plantation.

March 28:—Proclamation of the Scottish Privy Council inviting applications for Ulster lands.

July 14:—Deputies chosen by the London Guilds to confer with the Privy Council on the matter of taking part in the Ulster Plantation.

July 21:—Commissioners appointed to make allotments and to mark fit places for settlement.

July 30:—Four citizens of London sent at the City's charge to view the country.

1610   January 28:—Articles of Agreement with the City of London for the rebuilding of Derry and the planting of Coleraine.

         June 5:—Chichester receives the King's warrant to appoint a new commission for Ulster to remove the natives and put the settlers in possession.

         August 28:—Proclamation from commissioners that allotted are open for occupation.

CHAPTER II

THE LAND AND THE PEOPLE

The feature of the physical geography of Ireland that has influenced its politics is the absence of mountain coverts or physical barriers capable of sheltering a native race after the manner of the Highlands of Scotland. No such demarcation of culture on physical lines as between the Highlands and the Lowlands of Scotland could be established. No such saying as that "the Firth of Forth bridles the wild Hielander" could become current. In Ireland there is no dominating mountain mass. Small clusters of mountains stud the rim of the island, almost encircling a central plain, but there is everywhere easy access from the coast to the interior by valley roads, and at some places the central plain comes clear to the coast. Narrow shallow seas separate Ireland from Great Britain and the strait between Ireland and Scotland at its narrowest point is only thirteen and a half miles wide.

During the period of barbarism in Europe, before races became united to the soil to form nations and while the State was still migratory, Ireland's openness to invasion invited descents upon the land. Extent and variety of invasion form the theme of the legendary history of early Ireland. Tribal successes figure as the founding of groups of kingdoms, the might and renown of which are so embellished by legend that it is well to remember that the island is only 302 miles in its greatest length with an average breadth of about 110 miles. It is a law of history that when cultures meet legends are apt to blend. One of the world's great epics is a monument of this process, Vergil's *Æneid*, in which the foundation of Rome is connected with the fall of Troy. This mythical relationship was not conceived until the expansion of Roman power had established close contact with the East. As Ireland entered the circle of European culture its own legendary history received strong tinctures from both classical and Biblical sources. According to some of the bards arrivals in Ireland before the deluge were numerous, and among other visitors three daughters of Cain are mentioned. A few weeks before the Flood a niece of Noah, named Cesara, arrived in Ireland with a party of antediluvians. After the Flood settlements were made by colonists from Greece, Scythia, Egypt and Crete. Before leaving the East the colonists intermarried with descendants of most of the heroes of Biblical history, and Judean princesses supplied sacred treasures for transmission to Ireland.

There are old Irish genealogies that extend without a break to Magog, the son of Japhet, the son of Noah. Lists are given of Kings of Ireland that were contemporary with the rulers of the Assyrians, the Medes, the Persians, the Greeks and the Romans. In like manner the legendary history of Poland tells how the ancient rulers of the land subdued Crassus, King of the Parthians, and inflicted severe defeats upon Julius Caesar. The curious mixture of myths in Irish legendary history is well illustrated by those which attach to the Lia Fail, or Stone of Destiny, preserved in the coronation chair of the Kings of England. It was brought into England by Edward I., who captured it in 1296 at Scone, where the Kings of Scotland were crowned. The legend runs that it was the stone on which Jacob pillowed his head at Bethel, and was handed down to his heirs, ultimately coming into the possession of Irish colonists, who carried the stone with them and set it up on the hill of Tara. Thence the stone was carried into Scotland, where its authentic history begins. It is a sacred stone of great antiquity, but geologists find it to be of local material and archæologists class it among the menhirs, or memorial stones of the period of barbarism, specimens of which are found in many countries.[1]

---

[1]   It appears from the following, in the weekly edition of the *London Times*, September 22, 1911, that the legendary history of the Coronation Stone still receives credence:

"Archdeacon Wilberforce, preaching at Westminster Abbey on Sunday, said that it fell to his lot during the preparations at the Abbey for the Coronation to guide to the Coronation Stone a well-known antiquary who had made a study of its history.

The barbarian culture that is found in Ireland when authentic history begins is commonly designated Celtic, and upon this classification much historical hypothesis has been set up. Some writers have predicated the existence in prehistoric times of a great Celtic Empire extending across Europe. The material upon which such conjectures are based is chiefly derived from references in Greek and Latin writers to the Keltoi or Celtae in different parts of Europe. But upon examination the terms are not found to possess a specific value, but are rather a general designation like our term "barbarians." The term "Keltoi" was first used to designate the barbarian neighbors of the Greek colony on the site of modern Marseilles in Southern France. According to Herodotus the country from the Danube to the Western Ocean was occupied by the Keltoi. Tribes later classed as German or Teutonic were once classed among the Celtae. Inferences as to the existence of Celtic empire, because ancient writers spoke of Keltoi in the

---

"The antiquary was convinced that it was the stone on which Jacob rested his head when he had the vision of angels at Bethel, and that from that night it was considered sacred and carried from place to place. He believed it was that stone that Moses struck, and that it was carried by the Israelites during their 40 years of wandering. He pointed to a big cleft in the back from which the water gushed out. He also indicated two rusted iron staples deeply sunk, one at each end, by which it was carried. He traced the stone to Solomon's Temple, and from thence, after the destruction of Jerusalem by Titus, to Spain, thence to Ireland, thence to Scone, and from Scotland to Westminster Abbey.

"Mr. E. S. Foot writes from 13, Marlboroughplace, St. John's-wood: 'The late Dean Stanley, in his *Memorials of Westminster*, pages 594-5-6, sets out the authorities, Professor Ramsay, Director of the Geological Survey of England, and his colleague, Mr. Geikie, who, after minute investigation, were satisfied that the stone is old red sandstone, exactly resembling that which forms the doorway of Dunstaffnage Castle, which exactly agrees with the character of the Coronation Stone itself. "The rocks of Egypt, so far as I know [Mr. Geikie], consist chiefly of mummulitic limestone, of which the Great Pyramid is built. I have never heard of any strata occurring there similar to the red sandstone, of the Coronation Stone." ' "

East and in the West, seem to be as little warranted as would be belief in the existence of an extensive empire among the American aborigines because of reports of encounters with Indian tribes in widely separated places.

Although as an ethnic term "Celtic" is a vague appellation, it is quite different as a philological term. It is applied to a well-defined group of the Indo-European family of languages, including Irish, Scottish, Gaelic, Manx, Welsh, Cornish, and Breton. The philological evidence is conclusive that these are all varieties of one language. Characteristics of Celtic speech are discerned by some philologists in specimens of the language of the ancient Gauls that have been preserved by classical writers, and indications of Celtic place names have been noted as far east as the Dniester River. But it is observed by the authorities that there is no evidence of any considerable Celtic infusion in either the Teutonic or the Romance languages, such as might be expected if dialect forms found in historic times had arisen on a basis of Celtic culture. Thus it would appear that Celtic names in Europe mark either stages in tribal migration westward or places whose Celtic inhabitants became subject to other peoples thus losing their own language and racial identity.

Thus, whether the matter be viewed in its ethnic or in its linguistic aspects, there appears to be no real support for the romantic conjecture still put forth in the name of history, according to which the Celtic peoples are relics of a once mighty nation spreading over Europe and contesting with Greece and Rome for the empire of the Western World. When the Celtic tribes appear in the full light of history they are all found in the west of Europe. They hold western parts of England and Scotland; they hold Ireland, the most western of the British Islands; and also Brittany, the most western part of France. The hypothesis that best fits the historic facts is that the Celtic tribes were the foremost wave of Indo-European migration westward, pressed to the remotest regions by succeeding waves. This hypothesis agrees with the well authenticated fact that Ireland did experience a

series of invasions. The process of migration is historically exhibited in the case of the Celts of Brittany, who migrated thither
from the Saxon invasions of England during the fifth and sixth
centuries. This hypothesis does not imply that the process would
not have widely separated stages, or that it may not have been
accompanied by long periods of settlement on the European
continent, or that the westward movement was necessarily the
result of the onslaught of other Indo-European tribes, although
ethnic collisions probably influenced the movement. It should
be remembered that early forms of the State are very migratory.
The crude technology of barbarians tends to exhaust the natural
resources of any locality occupied by them. The natural fertility
of Ireland, and particularly the richness and quick growth of its
natural pasture, would be very attractive to barbarians. Energetic,
roving peoples reaching the northern coasts of the mainland
would eventually reach Ireland.

The enthusiastic assiduity of Irish antiquarians has extracted from scanty material proofs that in Ireland Celtic character
developed its fairest flower and Celtic culture attained its finest
expression. The known facts do not discredit the claim. The name
of the country was associated with traditions of racial dignity
and culture. The archæological evidence harmonizes with these
traditions. Ancient gold ornaments, bronze weapons and articles of domestic use have been disinterred, giving evidence of
native acquaintance with the working of metals and of the existence of artistic crafts. Trade went on between Ireland and the
Mediterranean countries from the earliest times. Roman coins
both of the republican and of the early imperial period have
been found at a number of widely separated points. The fact that
Roman geographers regarded Ireland as midway between Spain
and Britain points to the existence of direct traffic between Irish
and Spanish ports. The escape of St. Patrick, when a youth, from
captivity in Ireland was made by the favor of a party of traders
who had among the merchandise they shipped from Ireland a
pack of Celtic hounds, a breed highly valued in Southern Europe.

It has been plausibly conjectured that Patricius owed his escape to the fact that he had learned to tend such hounds while in the service of his master. That the traffic should be going on at such a period shows that it was a thing of long custom, for the times were not such as to encourage new enterprise. The Vandals, Sueves and Alans entered Gaul at the end of A.D. 406, followed in a few years by the Visigoths. Barbarian bands ravaged the country, looting, slaying and burning, until considerable regions became a desolate wilderness. In his account of his journey with the traders through Southern Gaul after making a landing, Patricius says they journeyed as through a desert for eight and twenty days in all, in danger of dying from starvation.

Christianity must have entered Ireland through the intercourse of trade, its case in this respect being like that of Armenia and Abyssinia. The system of reckoning Easter employed by the Celtic church was obsolete in Rome and in the churches of Gaul before St. Patrick began his apostolic labors in Ireland in the fifth century. Professor Bury, who in his *Life of St. Patrick* has made an exhaustive examination of the evidence, concludes that this and some other typical differences between Ireland and the continent in Christian practice were due to the fact that an early form of Christianity had taken root before the arrival of St. Patrick. When Ireland made its appearance in European history it was as a center from which radiated a Christianity of a distinctly Celtic type. This implies that Christian doctrine found a cultural basis upon which to organize a native church. The specialist who supplied the *Encyclopaedia Britanica* [sic] article on the "Early History of Ireland" remarks: "The exalted position occupied by the learned class in ancient Ireland perhaps affords the key to the wonderful outbursts of scholarly activity in Irish monasteries from the sixth to the ninth centuries." That this scholarly activity was not an importation of classical learning is attested by evidence that prior to the seventh century the literary documents of the Irish church were composed in Irish. Professor Bury has pointed out that it was not until a later period that compositions in Latin began to appear alongside of literary productions in the vernacular.

The case of Ireland, when carefully considered, does not appear to be peculiar as regards ethnic origins. It is not disputed that the Irish are cognates of peoples that have founded highly organized States in England and on the continent. That the Irish did not do so is to be attributed to historical accidents. Of these, the most far-reaching in its effects was the fact that Irish tribal forms of social and political organization were never broken up by passing under the harrow of Roman law. Another important circumstance was that the spread of Christianity in Ireland retained and utilized tribal institutions that on the continent were broken down and discarded. When Charlemagne was hammering Christianity into the heathen Saxons in the eighth century he was smashing their tribal system at the same time. At that period Ireland had been a Christian country for centuries, and was famous as a center of missionary activity and yet it still retained its archaic pattern of social and political organization. The Irish kings, with some vicissitudes, successfully resisted invasions that were triumphant in England. In the first quarter of the eleventh century when the empire of Canute the Dane extended over England, Denmark, Norway, and part of Sweden, Ireland was under native princes whose historiographers could point to a succession of victories over the Northmen, destroying their settlements and uprooting their power.

It was not until the Norman invasion established a State in England with consolidated resources and centralized authority that the military inferiority of Irish institutions was manifested in the relations between the two countries. But while thereafter Ireland remained a prey to English invasion, her tribal polity displayed marked capacity for absorbing the invaders into the mass of native Irish. Irish nationality is a modern concept. Ancient and mediaeval Ireland was a country given over to internecine warfare. Foreign intervention in the aid of some native interest was sought and welcomed. A native chronicler, referring to the Anglo-Norman invasion beginning in 1169, says: "Earl Strongbow came into Erin with Dermod Mac Murrough to avenge his expulsion by Roderick, son of Turlough O'Connor; and Dermod gave him his own daughter and a part of his patrimony, and Saxon foreigners have been in Erin since then."

The Norman adventurers tried to carve the land into feudal fiefs, and the feudal system came into violent conflict with the Irish tribal system, but the latter showed greater endurance. The Anglo-Norman nobles found the vague, customary powers of Irish chiefry more favorable to their authority than the more explicitly defined rights and duties of a feudal lord. When Henry VIII. came to the throne of England in 1509, many old Anglo-Norman families had either disappeared or were merged into the Celtic mass. English polity was restricted to an area extending over a radius of about twenty miles from Dublin, known as the "Pale," and a still smaller area about Kilkenny. Over the greater part of the island Celtic tribal institutions still supplied the legal and political framework of society. It was not until after the accession of James I. that the division of the land into counties was completed, and Ulster the last province to be brought under civil jurisdiction. In Elizabeth's time a scheme of county organization for Ulster was adopted, but there was no machinery of government. Sir John Davies says of the period before Chichester's administration: "The law was never executed in the new counties by any sheriff or justices of assize; but the people were left to be ruled still by their own barbarous lords and laws."

The distinctive characteristics of Irish history may be attributed chiefly to the fact that an archaic type of polity was accidentally preserved to modern times. The struggles and sufferings that ensued from the clash of cultures were such as have always attended such a situation. It was with reference to this that Sir Henry Maine in his *Ancient Law* remarked: "The history of political ideas begins with the assumption that kinship in blood is the sole possible ground of community in political functions, nor is there any of those subversions of feeling which we emphatically call revolutions so startling and so complete as the change which is established when some other principle, such as that for instance of local contiguity, establishes itself for the first time as the basis of common political action."

When recorded history begins the Greek and the Latin tribes are discovered in the throes of this revolution from which civilization issued.

On the continent of Europe the change took place in the darkness of barbarism and left few records to history. The peculiarity of Ireland's case is that it was, as Lord Bacon observed, the last European country to pass from tribal status to civil polity. But that very circumstance now makes her native institutions specially interesting to scholars. What Bacon deplored as barbarous customs and habits that "enchant them in savage manners" are now the very things in which students are chiefly interested, for detailed knowledge of them would throw light upon the social and political organization of all the Indo-European tribes in the prehistoric period. An elaborate apparatus existed for the perpetuation of the customary laws and historical traditions of the tribe. There were brehons, who were repositories of tribal law; shanahs who were genealogists and incidentally recorders of titles of lands; rhymers who related the deeds of the heroes; and harpers, whose music celebrated the honor of the sept. Biographers of Thomas Moore tell us that his *Irish Melodies* are based upon Irish folk songs, a fact which must impress one with the variety and refinement of musical rhythms native to Ireland, and also serve to corroborate archaeological evidence to the effect that artistic culture was attained under native institutions.

In thus drawing upon native Irish sources Moore enriched the metrical resources of English verse and established his own best claim to fame. It seems to have been no more than a plain statement of the actual facts of the case when the poet wrote:

> "Dear Harp of my Country! In darkness I found thee,
> The cold chain of silence had hung o'er thee long,
> When proudly, my own Island Harp, I unbound thee,
> And gave all thy chords to light, freedom and song!"

The point at which the clash of Irish tribal status and English law was most acute was in the matter of land tenure. Although English law admitted various kinds of tenure in land it was exacting and insistent on the point of individual rights. Under the tribal system surviving in Ireland the individual had no rights as such defined by law, but as a tribesman he had certain traditional privileges in the common lands of the tribe conditioned upon customary dues and service to his chief, so vague that they might vary greatly according to the disposition and opportunity of the chief. The sort of tribal communism that existed in Ireland is exemplified in the following petition of one Neale O'Donnell to Chichester, October 9, 1613:

> "It is not unknown to your lordship that the Irish gentry did ever make their followers' purses their only exchequer. And I beseech your lordship (now anew) to take notice that mine ancestors left me as great an inheritance (in this kind) as any other man's did unto himself. Of which stock, as I never employed any part (of things given by myself) unanswerably claim as any Ulcestrian whatever. My humble suit, therefore, unto your honorable good lordship is, that as your honor has restored their commins unto all others, so you would… help me unto my commins also… I beseech your lordship, in regard to them, to cause my tenants (or if need be, force them) to bring up my children to school till I otherwise dispose of my commins at least."

These "comynes," for so the term usually appears in the State Papers, denotes a custom based upon the relations of the chief of a sept to his people. He claimed all the lands as his in trust for his people. It is a trusteeship that is merely customary and not legally defined, but it intermingles his private estate and the common wealth. His own exertions belong to his functions as ruler, judge and captain of his people. Instead of gathering wealth into his own possession, he distributes cattle or other goods among his people and in return they provide for his wants, rear his children and meet the expenses of their education. These dues are the chief's comynes. In instructions issued August 28, 1610, for settling claims of comynes, Chichester remarks that some of the tenants and followers of the Irish gentry "have by their customs of comynes gotten into their hands the greater part of those goods and chattels; and are, therefore, in far better estate than their landlords, except there be restitution made of some just portion thereof to him or them from whom the same have been received by way of comynes."

Such facts show how closely the interests of the native gentry were bound up with the maintenance of tribal custom in land tenure. The principal chiefs frequently showed themselves not averse to taking title from the English Crown for themselves, but they were bent on keeping their people in the position of tenants-at-will, their holdings subject to the disposition of the chief. It was the policy of the English Government to break up this dependence of the people upon the will of their chiefs. In one of his early letters from Ireland Sir John Davies pointed out that it was just by such control over tenants that the feudal barons of the Middle Ages were able to carry on rebellion:

> "Whereas, at this day, if any of the great lords of England should have a mind to stand upon their guard, well may they have some of their household servants and retainers, or some few light-trained fractious gentlemen to follow them; but as for those tenants who have good leases for years… those fellows will not hazard the losing of their sheep, their oxen and their corn, and the undoing of themselves, their wives and children, for the love of the best landlord in England."

Just such independence on the part of their tenants the Irish chiefs instinctively feared, and their obstinate resistance to surrendering their tribal sovereignty was the root from which rebellion kept growing. The collective right of the people to the soil, characteristic of Irish tribal polity, has received much praise from writers in our own times as an arrangement securing the individual against social degradation and the pressure of want. So judicial a historian as Lecky says of the Irish clansman: "His position was wholly different from and in some respects very superior to that

of an English tenant." His superiority consisted in the fact that
whereas the English tenant had to pay rent and in case of default
might be ejected, "the humblest clansman was a co-proprietor with
his chief." But in practice this co-partnership generally meant that
the clansman retained only what his chief chose to leave him. The
industrious could not possess for themselves the rewards of their
industry, and as invariably happens in all such cases industry did
not thrive. There was no motive for people to build and improve,
when their accumulations might be appropriated by the chiefs
and they themselves be shifted to other fields.

The system kept the people under primitive conditions of pastoral life. Some of the chiefs dwelt in clay houses; others of them
followed "creaghting," a term denoting the practice of moving
about the country with their live stock, chief and people living
in booths made of boughs coated with long strips of turf. Such
habitations could be easily run up and lightly abandoned. "Such
are the dwellings of the very lords among them," remarks an
English traveler who was in the country in 1600. What tillage
there was was carried on in the rudest fashion: several horses
were fastened each by the tail to a short plough with a man to
every horse to urge and direct the animal. In this way they raised
oats for their horses and barley for distilling into whiskey. The
principal flesh meat of the people was pork, while oatmeal and
herbs furnished vegetable food. There were also supplies of milk
and butter, chickens and rabbits. There must have been a rude
plenty, for it appears that wandering hawkers were familiar visitors
to the creaghts, bargaining for country produce. The chiefs passed
their leisure time hunting in the woods and coshering among
their tenants. "Coshering," from an Irish word meaning feasting
or entertainment, denotes the right of the chief to free quarters
and supplies for himself and his retinue. This mode of life had
such charms that even Anglo-Irish lords adopted it. At this time
equally primitive conditions existed among the Celtic peoples of
the Scottish Highlands and indeed continued there beyond the
eighteenth century. In Lockhart's *Life of Scott* it is related that on

Scott's first visit to the Highlands he found his host and three sons, with attendant gillies, all stretched half asleep in their tartans on the hearth, with guns and dogs, and a profusion of game around them. In an enclosure far below appeared a company of women actively engaged in loading a cart with manure. Scott was astonished to find that these industrious women were the laird's own lady and her daughters.

Some writers of our own times have idealized the pastoral conditions of Celtic Ireland. A good example of the process is given by a brilliant work on *Irish Nationality* by Alice Stopford Green. She holds that "in the Irish system we may see the shaping of a true democracy, a society in which ever broadening masses of the people are made intelligent sharers in the national life and conscious guardians of its traditions." This projects into the past the ideas of the present, for democracy by its terms is a late, elaborate, complex form of government. In every form of government power must exist and be vested somewhere. That the rule of the people shall actually exist, it must have appropriate institutions securing and defining the public trusteeship of the actual custodians of authority, and this requires a long course of political evolution. Upon close scrutiny all democratic government is found to rest upon apparatus of sovereignty originally formed on the basis of prerogative. Any inquiry into the origin of legal institutions discloses this fact.

The historical process by which modern society was prepared for democratic government through the growth of monarchical power has been accurately surveyed by Sidgwick in his *Development of European Polity*. The notion that any early form of the State possessed a democratic character is a belated piece of Rousseauism. All anthropological evidence is in agreement that political power in its earliest manifestations takes arbitrary forms. In the primitive form of the State, specimens of which have been detected among the Australian aborigines, political authority is of a piece with family authority, authenticating itself by its mere presence and power. The community commands and disposes of the lives of its units by transactions as instinctive and impulsive as the habits of bees or ants. The advance from primitive savagery into barbarism is marked by differentiations of tissue in the social organism. The formation of the priest class and the warrior class is an invariable concomitant of political evolution, and the development of class consciousness precedes the diffusion of public consciousness. The notion of individual rights is a late development of political evolution, marking a very advanced stage in the growth of the linguistic apparatus of thought. No such stage had been reached in Celtic Ireland. At the opening of the seventeenth century its institutions retained their barbarian pattern although those institutions were in their dotage.[2]

Authentic traditions indicate that in the pre-Christian period the priest class was a mighty power in the State, but that period had long passed away. The warrior class, however, still remained, its arrogance the greater because all social counterpoise had been removed. Its members are frequently referred to in the State Papers of the period as kerns, galloglasses or swordsmen. They had the typical characteristics of their class wherever found under tribal polity: disdain of labor, jealous guardianship of traditional privilege, fierce tenacity in adhering to their customary rights to public support. Everywhere as advancing civilization eliminates rapine from among the economic resources of the community, the pretensions of the warrior class have raised difficulties in the way of establishing public order. One of the early tasks of European kingship was to put down the robber knights; and the work was not fully performed until the invention and improvement of artillery had transferred the art of war from a hand-made to a machine-made basis. The Irish galloglasses—and their close kin, the moss-troopers of the Scottish Highlands—were survivals of a type that had long since been extirpated in the area of European civilization. Themselves proud of their rank and its adventurous

---

2   In Appendix A will be found an account by a contemporary observer of conditions just before the Ulster Plantation that gives the facts without romance.

activities, they were detested by the settled agriculturists of the Scottish Lowlands and of the Irish Pale as savage ruffians and cattle thieves. Blackmail was paid to the Rob Roys of Ireland as in Scotland. The Irish State Papers contain accounts of payments of tribute to the "wylde Iryshe" even by the King's officers as a regular charge in public accounts. Returns in the time of Henry VIII. show a yearly tribute amounting to 740 pounds paid as the price of immunity from molestation.

The seventeenth century antiquary William Camden has given us a picture of the Irish fighting-men, a company of whom accompanied Shane O'Neal when he visited the Court of Queen Elizabeth in the fifth year of her reign. Camden says the "axe-bearing galloglasses" were "bareheaded, with curled hair hanging down, yellow surplices dyed with saffron, long sleeves, short coats and hairy mantles." These hairy mantles were the pelts of wild animals, probably wolf skins. The dexterity and skill with which the galloglasses wielded the broad battle-axe are celebrated in English accounts of the Irish wars. A long sword, mailed tunic and iron helmet completed the equipment as formed on the military practice of the times, but the Irish never took well to armor, preferring to fight in their saffron coats. The kerns were light-armed footmen, who fought with a skean, or sharp-edged dagger, and a javelin.

The domination of these warriors was not compatible with conditions such as can properly be designated as democratic. They helped themselves as of right and the common people submitted with customary deference, but grudgingly. Any growth of individual ownership, privacy of habitation or enclosure of land was in derogation of their class privileges and made the offender a mark of attack. It is not necessary to offer evidence to support so obvious a proposition as that customs permitting an idle soldiery to rove about the lands of the clan quartering themselves on the people could not be favorable to morality. In urging upon Queen Elizabeth his claim to the Earldom of Tyrone, the succession to which was in dispute, Shane O'Neal remarked in his petition: "Being a gentleman, my father never refused no child that any woman namyd to be his." In a letter of May 4, 1606, Sir John Davies remarks that "by reason and impunity of the common use, the bastard is of as good reputation as the legitimate, and doth commonly share the inheritance with him."

The difficulties ensuing from the collision of civilized polity with tribal polity were aggravated by religious differences, and to this cause may be chiefly attributed the marked divergence between Celtic Scotland and Celtic Ireland in their modern history. The Reformation was a unifying influence in Scotland, a divisive influence in Ireland. When Henry VIII. began his war upon papal authority the ancient Celtic Church, which in its day had made Ireland a center of Christian activity, had long since disappeared, and the establishment that had absorbed it had become full of the abuses characteristic of the times. The Irish chiefs were as ready to share in the spoil of Henry's confiscations of church property in Ireland as the English nobles were in England. The English governors of Ireland at the time of the accession of James did not anticipate much trouble in securing conformity in matters of religion.

In a letter to the home Government, December 8, 1605, Sir John Davies remarks that "touching this work of reformation" he was strongly persuaded that "it would have a general good success, for the Irishry, priests, people and all will come to church" under official pressure. He mentions how the mass of the people in England had yielded to their rulers in the matter of religion, and remarks that "the multitude was ever made conformable by edicts and proclamations." This expectation was speedily disappointed. For one thing, the establishment of religion by English law was made odious by the character of bishops and clergy. There were illustrious exceptions, but at the time of the accession of James the general situation was base. In a report written some time in 1604, Chief Justice Saxey describes the bishops as "priests of Jeroboam, taken out of the basest of the people, more fit to sacrifice to a calf than to intermeddle with the religion of God." Writing in 1606, Sir John Davies says that he is informed that:

"The churchmen for the most part throughout the king-dom were mere idols and ciphers, and such as could not read; and yet the most of them, whereof many were serving men and some horseboys, were not without two or three benefices apiece. Nevertheless, for all their pluralities they were most of them beggars; for the patron or ordinary, or some of their friends, took the greater part of their profits by a plain contract before their institution... And what is the effect of these abuses? The churches are ruined and fallen down to the ground in all parts of the kingdom. There is no divine service, no christening of children, no receiving of the sacrament, no Christian meeting or assembly, no, not once a year; in a word, no more demonstration of religion than among Tartars or cannibals."

This religious desolation afforded a field for missionary labor, cultivated with such zeal and energy by the religious orders of the Roman Catholic Church that the people were gathered into that communion and confirmed in their attachment as never before. Whatever grounds for Sir John Davies' opinion of Irish pliability existed when it was uttered, they were soon conclusively removed. The friars who had been turned out of doors by Henry's suppression of the monasteries had in large numbers continued to work and preach among the people, and under the chastening influence of adversity the immoralities formerly charged against some of them tended to disappear. The restoration of discipline and the purification of morals were really facilitated by the pros-trate condition of the church. No legal obstacles would be raised against correctional measures taken by ecclesiastical authority that was itself outlawed. Among the Irish State Papers for 1613 there is a report on the work of a Franciscan friar that doubtless gives a faithful picture of activities characteristic of this period. At a meeting in the county of Londonderry the friar had before him all the priests of those parts to the number of fourteen. "He prayed long, exhorting them to reform their wicked lives, telling them of drunkenness, whoredom, and lack of devotion and zeal." The friar did not depend on exhortation alone but applied sharp discipline. The report goes on to say that he "compels all priests to put away their wives and whores, or else he deprives them of their living and makes them incapable to say mass or exercise their functions."

Such acts imply possession of large ecclesiastical authority. The State Papers afford plenty of evidence that persons described as wandering friars must in fact have been high dignitaries of the Church of Rome. Eventually the Government obtained lists of bishops that had been ordained and commissioned to the work in Ireland. The Jesuits, who flocked into Ireland in large numbers, displayed an energy and an activity that alarmed and incensed the Government officials. In a report sent to the home Government October 27, 1607, the Lord Deputy and Council say that priests and Jesuits land in every part, sometimes a dozen together and then disperse themselves:

> "... in such sort that every town and county is full of them, and most men's minds are infected with their doctrines and seditious persuasions. They have so gained the women that they are in a manner all of them absolute recusants. Children and servants are wholly taught and catechised by them... They withdraw many from the church that formerly had conformed themselves; and others of whom good hope had been conceived, they have made altogether obstinate, disobedient and contemptuous."

The movement that the Government officials describe with so much acrimony they found it impossible to arrest. The Reformation cut Scotland and England away from the papal see, but left Ireland more firmly united and more deeply loyal than before, but this religious divergence is to be attributed rather to historical circumstances than to any peculiarities of the Irish character. It is sufficiently accounted for by the Counter-Reformation by which abuses were corrected, morals were purified and faith was revived within the communion of the Church of Rome. This revival of spiritual energy was in full vigor at the time when the Irish people were practically unchurched. The situation afforded large opportunity to the missionary zeal then abounding and it was utilized with such energy and devotion as to stamp the national character. Within a decade there was a change for the better in the condition of the established church; but it came too late to recover lost ground, and the outlawed Church of Rome remained in secure possession of the loyalty of the Irish masses.

It is clear enough now that in dealing with this situation wise statesmanship would have sought to connect the interests of the masses of the people with the system of law and order which it was proposed to introduce. The conversion of tribal right into legal right should have been accompanied by an equitable distribution of the land among chiefs and people. Virtually this process is going on in our own times under the operation of the land laws, by schemes of purchase and re-allotment sustained by the public credit, and the ultimate effect will undoubtedly be a transformation of Irish social and political conditions. The time is approaching when it will appear that Irish character is no more inadequate to sustain orderly and efficient government than any other European stock. It is a matter of race discipline and race experience rather than of innate disposition. The qualities of shiftlessness and improvidence proverbially attributed to the Irish peasantry used to be imputed to the French peasantry before the changes in land tenure accomplished by the French Revolution. But such penetrating treatment of the situation was beyond the thought and capacity of statesmanship at the time of the Ulster plantation.

Sovereignty was too undeveloped, the State was too lacking in efficient organization to cope with such tasks as the equitable transfer of a people from a tribal to a legal status. Outside of the limited area known as the Pale there were no judges, no juries, no sessions of the courts in Ireland. The clansmen lived under the customary law of the septs, administered by their chiefs. The situation was something like that which confronted the English in India nearly two centuries later, when they acquired administrative authority over peoples among whom English law did not extend, and actuated by considerations of administrative convenience they set up a landlord system that disregarded the customary rights to the soil of the actual cultivators, converting them from co-proprietors into tenants-at-will. It eventually turned out that the arrangement perpetrated injustice, but at the time it presented itself as a public necessity.

It is easy to criticize the administrative shortcomings of one age from the mature knowledge and experience of a later age, but that is not the way to obtain insight. To appreciate the character of any age one must read down to it and not back to it. To understand the nature of events one must view them in genetic order. The English administrators in Ireland, working by the light of their own times, felt no scruples as to the wisdom and justice of their plans for reclaiming Ulster from barbarism. The lands were escheated to the Crown as the result of the treason of the lords. What more proper course to pursue than to do as had often been done in England itself, turn the lands over to the loyal lords, for occupancy by them and their retainers! No scruples as to the propriety of the course actually pursued appear to have been felt by anybody except Chichester, and his were based on practical and personal considerations. He thought it would have been wiser to make a more liberal provision for the native Irish and he feared that his own promise to the Irish had not been sufficiently respected.

Measures by which it was sought to break up Irish tribal institutions had long been pursued. In the time of Elizabeth severe laws were passed against bards and "shanachies," or historians of the clan. Soon after the accession of James the courts declared illegal the native system of inheritance known as tanistry and gavelkind, based upon the principle of collective ownership. This had been frequently recommended by English administrators in Ireland, who regarded it as a necessary reform. A State Paper of 1611 set forth among "Motives of Importance for holding a Parliament in Ireland" that "all the possessions of the Irish shall from henceforth descend and be conveyed according to the course of the common law of England, and not according to the barbarous customs of tanistrie or gavelkinde." Religious conformity was aimed at by a series of laws and proclamations against recusancy, which were futile save as sources of irritation and which Chichester came to regard as so troublesome and impolitic that eventually he resigned rather than administer them.

⁕ These measures belong to Irish history in general, and in view of the colonization which took place they were of less immediate importance in Ulster than elsewhere. The great administrative task in Ulster was to dispose of the warrior class. It was thought that since their trade was fighting the best thing to do was to send them into foreign service. Sweden then ranked as a powerful State aiming at empire, and her wars with Russia, Poland and Denmark attracted military adventurers, including many from Scotland. In 1609 it was arranged that 1,000 Irish fighting-men should be sent to Sweden. Writing from Fermanagh, September 18, 1609, Chichester says that he had accepted the submission of two chieftans in that county with their followers, "who so freely proffered themselves to this service for avoiding further danger by the prosecutions he made upon them." When ships arrived to transport them to Sweden Chichester had a different tale to tell. In a letter, October 8, 1609, he says that "idlers and swordmen everywhere (especially in the province of Ulster) now withdrew themselves into the woods." Before the end of that month, however, three ships sailed from Derry with 800 men. Another ship was about departing from Carlingford when the swordmen seized the ship and tried to run her ashore so that they might escape. Chichester acted with characteristic energy, mustering a force that attacked the ship with boats and put down the mutiny. Some of the ringleaders were hanged. This ship seems to have been doomed to disaster, for it was soon wrecked on the Isle of Man and had to put into a port of Scotland for relief. There another ship was hired, but this was driven into Newcastle where a body of the Irish escaped.

⁕ Chichester had a low opinion of swordmen. "To speak generally," he said in one of his reports, "they were all but an unprofitable burden of the earth, cruel, wild, malefactors, thieves." But he had the discernment to observe that it would be good policy to utilize their own native customs and habits of allegiance to their chiefs. Writing to the English Privy Council, October 31, 1609, he recommends that in making levies for foreign service he be allowed "to appoint the commanders, such as he in his knowledge and experience of them shall think most popular with the nation; for they will distaste and avoid all strange commanders." This anticipates the policy pursued by the elder Pitt a century and a half later when he extracted the spirit of turbulence from the Highland glens by forming the clansmen into regiments officered by their chiefs. In Chichester's day the regimental system did not exist, and armies were composed of casual levies. Chichester found that the swordmen did not like to enter the Swedish service, an antipathy readily accounted for when it is remembered that the King of Sweden was a Protestant champion and that the influence of the Roman Catholic missionaries was now active among the people. Chichester twice urged the Privy Council that the swordmen be employed in the service of Russia rather than of Sweden, but nothing appears to have come of the suggestion. Nevertheless, it appears from Chichester's own statement that he sent away 6,000 men for service in the Swedish wars.

The removal of so large a number of the warrior class seems to have aided in the pacification of the country. It appears that the common people were patient and submissive as the Undertakers and their followers made their entry upon the land. On September 24, 1610, Sir John Davies wrote to the home Government in a characteristic strain of cheerful optimism. He remarks that the natives were choosing to be tenants-at-will rather than receive land as freeholders "for which they would be compelled to serve in juries." Davies proceeds: "All the Irish (the chief lords excepted) desire naturally to be followers, and cannot live without a master, and for the most part they love every master alike, so he be present to protect and defend them." And therefore he is of opinion that, "if they were once settled under the servitors, the bishops, or others who may receive Irish tenants, they would follow them as willingly, and rest as well contented under their wings, as young pheasants do under the wings of a home-hen, though she be not their natural mother."

Chichester, the soldier, showed a more penetrating judgment of the situation than Davies, the jurist. Writing about the same time that expressed his confidence in the tranquility of Ulster, Chichester expressed doubts as to the prospects of the plantation:

> "But to hinder the same the natives of those countries will do what in them shall lie, for they are generally discontented, and repine greatly at their fortunes and the small quantity of land left them upon the division; especially those of the counties of Tyrone, Ardmagh and Colerayne, who having reformed themselves in their habit and course of life beyond others and the common expectation held of them (for all that were able had put on English apparel, and promised to live in townredes, and to leave their creaghting) had assured themselves of better conditions from the King than those they lived in under their former landlords: but now they say they have not land given to them, nor can they be admitted tenants, which is very grievous unto them."

Chichester complains that he himself has been discredited by the proceedings of the land commissioners, and "he prays that he may not be guided by any directions of theirs, for they know not Ireland so well as he does, especially Ulster." He points out that the grievances of the common people afford grounds upon which the priests can stir up disaffection. He remarks:

> "The priests now preach little other doctrine to them, but they are a despised people, and worse dealt with than any nation hath ever been heard or read of; for being received to mercy upon their humble submissions, their bodies, goods, and lands were taken into the King's protection, but now they are injuriously thrust out of their houses, and places of habitation, and be compelled, like vagabonds, to go they know not whither."

Chichester concludes that "how ill soever they be disposed, he sees not how they can rebel in any great numbers unless they have assistance of arms and munition from foreign parts." Nevertheless he suggests that it would be wise to treat them with more consideration. Chichester has been represented as a hard, ruthless soldier, whose policy in Ulster is marked by covetousness, but his own pen has unconsciously drawn for us his true portrait as a man who excelled his contemporaries in justice and discernment.

⁕ Before the Ulster plantation began there was already a considerable Scottish occupation of the region nearest to Scotland. These Scotch settlements were confined to Counties Down and Antrim, which were not included in the scheme of the plantation. Their existence facilitated Scottish emigration to the plantation, and they were influential in giving the plantation the Scottish character which it promptly acquired. Although planned to be in the main an English settlement, with one whole county turned over to the City of London alone, it soon became in the main a Scottish settlement.

CHAPTER III

THE SCOTCH MIGRATION TO ULSTER

The racial elements that have gone into the making of Scotland are matters upon which there are sharp differences among specialists in this field. The first chapter of Andrew Lang's *History of Scotland* gives a statement of the conflicting views that are expressed upon ethnic questions. The great question is: Who were the Picts? An eminent Celtic scholar, Professor Rhys, mainly upon philological grounds holds that they were members not of the Celtic but of some non-Aryan race, enmeshed by Celtic migration like the Basques of France. Mr. Lang himself concludes that they were simply a Celtic tribe, the ancestors in some degree of the present Highlanders. In Scotland as in England the historical data point to Teutonic and Scandinavian invasion pushing back the Celtic tribes. Mr. Lang points out that there is no marked difference in the racial composition of the people between the Scottish Lowlands and the adjacent parts of England. In both countries the people spoke a language now designated as Early English. The two regions were one geographically. Mr. Lang remarks: "Nothing in the topography of the country contains a prophecy of this separation of the Teutonic or English conquerors of Southern Scotland into a separate Scottish nation. The severance of the English north and south of the Tweed was the result of historical events."

Substantially the same view is taken in T. F. Henderson's history of *Scottish Vernacular Literature*. He holds that: "The Scottish vernacular is mainly a development of the Teutonic dialect of that Northumbria which embraces the more eastern portion of Britain from the Humber to the Firth of Forth. Here the Saxons obtained a firm footing early in the sixth century, the Cymri being, after a series of desperate struggles, either conquered or forced gradually westward until they concentrated in Cumbria or Strathclyde, between the Mersey and the Clyde, where for some centuries they maintained a fragile independence… The triumph of the Saxon element was finally assured by the great influx of Saxons during the period of the Norman conquest… The Teutonic speech and civilization gradually penetrated into every district of the Scottish Lowlands."

Mr. Henderson points out that "when it first emerges from obscurity toward the close of the fourteenth century, the literary language of the Scottish Lowlands is found to be practically identical with that of England north of the Humber." Early English exhibited three dialects, Northern, Midland and Southern. The Midland dialect became the sole literary language of England, the Northern and the Southern dialects "vanishing almost entirely from English literature." In the Scottish Lowlands the Northern dialect survived and from it the literary language of Scotland was fashioned. In support of these views Mr. Henderson points out that early Scottish, the Scottish of Barbour and Wyntoun (fourteenth century), "differs but slightly, if at all, from Northern English." At a later period the difference became marked.

The matter of ethnic origins has been touched upon, because some writers upon the Scotch-Irish have placed the Picts, the Caledonians and other early inhabitants of Scotland among the forebears of the Scottish settlers in Ulster. But as a matter of fact the settlers were almost as English in racial derivation as if they had come from the North of England. Occasional allusions in the State Papers show that the Government had in mind the English-speaking districts of Scotland and not the Gaelic regions as the source from which settlers should be drawn. Indeed, the conditions were such that the Ulster plantation appeared as part of the general campaign carried on to break down Celtic tribal polity and to extend civilized polity in both Ireland and Scotland. During the O'Dogherty insurrection Chichester wrote to the Scottish Privy Council advising that the sea-passage between Western Scotland and Northern Ireland be guarded to prevent the recruiting of the Ulster rebels by sympathizing fellow-Celts from Kintyre, Islay, Arran, and the neighboring islands. The Scottish Privy Council on the receipt of the news of O'Dogherty's rising had been quick to perceive the danger of sympathetic disturbance in Gaelic Scotland, and before they heard from Chichester they had issued a proclamation forbidding any aid from the southwestern shires to the Ulster rebels on pain of death. In later correspondence, after O'Dogherty's rising had been suppressed, Chichester referred to his own work in Ulster and the work which the Scottish Council had in hand against the Celts of the western Scottish islands as but two branches of one and the same service.

Irish history during this period has been kept under the spotlight so much as to create an impression that English policy in Ireland was somewhat singular in character and was actuated by special animosity. No support to this notion is found in the State Papers. In them the Ulster plantation appears as part of a general forward movement against barbarism. So far as treatment of the native inhabitants goes the measures taken in Ireland seem less severe than those taken in Scotland itself. The reign of James was marked by a determined effort to crush the marauding spirit of Gaelic Scotland and to suppress the feuds that were carried on in defiance of law. An armed expedition to the western islands was fitted out in 1608, and many castles were seized and dangerous chiefs were arrested both in the islands and the neighboring parts of the mainland. Andrew Stewart, Lord Ochiltree, who was in command of this expedition, became one of the Ulster Undertakers. His name did not appear in the original list, but on returning to Edinburgh, triumphant from his expedition, he was sent to London to make his report to the King. When the revision was made by the King and the English Privy Council of the list of applicants submitted by the Scottish Privy Council, the name of Lord Ochiltree appears as Undertaker for 3,000 acres in County Tyrone.

The steady pursuit of the Clan MacGregor in the main Highlands is an evidence of the determination to crush outlawry at any cost. They are described in proclamations as that unhappy race which has so long continued "in bluid, thift, reif and oppression." The members of the clan were proscribed and the use

of the very name was prohibited. The war on these wild clansmen went on for many years. In 1604 Alexander MacGregor of
Glenstrae, chief of the clan, and eleven of his principal kinsmen
and retainers, were hanged and quartered at the Market Cross
in Edinburgh. In August, 1610, a commission of fire and sword
against the MacGregors was issued to twenty-eight nobles and
lairds in territories surrounding the MacGregor country. By proclamation the King's lieges were warned not to assist any of the
clan, their wives, children or servants nor have any intercourse
with them. In 1611, after a preamble declaring that the clansmen
still persist in their "barbarous and wicked lyff," the Earl of Argyle
is commissioned to root out and extirpate all of that race, until,
says the King, "they be ather reducit to our obedience or ruitit
out of our kingdome." Notwithstanding these energetic measures
a report of 1613 says that remnants of the clan have again begun
to go about the country "sorning, oppressing, quarreling, where
they may be masters and commanders." "Sorning" is the Highland
equivalent of the Irish "coshering," the privilege claimed by the
warrior class of living on forced hospitality. The harrying of the
MacGregors went on by fits and starts for many years.

Besides these campaigns to introduce the King's law into Celtic
Scotland, the Government had to deal with the habits of rapine
which had been implanted by centuries of border warfare, and
which possessed something of a patriotic character when Scotland
and England were traditional enemies. Now that a Scottish King
had mounted the English throne the further continuance of border lawlessness became intolerable. It was put down with ruthless
energy. The English and Scottish shires which had formerly been
"The Borders" were rechristened by James in 1603 as "The Middle
Shires of Great Britain" and the administration was put into the
hands of ten commissioners, five for each side, each set of commissioners executing their orders through an appointed chief of
mounted police. The Scottish State Papers from April, 1605, to
April, 1607, contain abundant evidences of the activity of the
Scottish commissioners. Their chief of police was Sir William

Cranstoun, and with his force of twenty-five horsemen he scoured the Borders, arresting murderers and robbers and bringing them before justice courts held by commissioners from time to time at stated places. At the end of the first year the commissioners give the names of thirty-two persons hanged for their crimes, fifteen persons banished, and above seven score in the condition of fugitive outlaws, who should be pursued with hue and cry wherever they might be found. In October, 1606, fifteen more of these Border outlaws were hanged and by the end of the year the list of fugitives had increased to thirteen score, whose names were to be advertised on the market crosses of all towns and the doors of all parish kirks in all the "in-countrey." The Scottish Privy Council sustained this work with hard resolution. The commissioners reported periodically to the Council, asking instructions upon difficult points, sometimes referring a case in which they think there might be mercy, but in every such case the Council sent back word to "execute justice," which meant that the culprit should be put to death.

Besides hanging and banishing, the commissioners were active in breaking up the nests of outlawry. The houses of thieving families were searched for stolen goods, the iron gates that barred entrance were removed and dragged away to be turned into plough irons. The official record of those who were hanged doubtless fell short of the actual number put to death, for Sir William Cranstoun thought it necessary to obtain an act of indemnity, which was granted by the King, December 15, 1606. It sets forth as its occasion that he had been moved "often tymes summarlie to mak a quick dispatche of a grite mony notable and notorious thevis and villanes by putting thame to present death without preceiding tryall of jurye or assyse or pronunciatioun of ony conviction or dome."

Among the names of malefactors officially returned as having been hanged by order of the justice courts are such good patronyms as Armstrong, Gilchrist, Johnstone, Milburn, Patterson, Scott, and Wallis. This Scott may well have been a kinsman of the great author, for in times when Border lawlessness had been so long extinct as to be susceptible of romantic treatment Sir Walter was pleased to claim Border outlaws as among his forbears. *The Lay of the Last Minstrel* describes the stronghold of Auld Wat of whom the poet says:

> "But what the niggard ground of wealth denied,
> From fields more blessed his fearless arm supplied."

Of Auld Wat's bride, Mary Scott, "the Flower of Yarrow," Lockhart relates that "when the last bullock which Auld Wat had provided from the English pastures was consumed the Flower of Yarrow placed on her table a dish containing a pair of clean spurs; a hint to the company that they must bestir themselves for their next dinner." As the Flower of Yarrow married Auld Wat in 1567, the halcyon days of her predatory housekeeping were separated by little more than one generation from the stern suppression of such methods. The effect of the thorough work of King James' commissioners was very marked. The Borders were so tamed and disciplined that in 1610 Chancellor Dunferline was able to assure the King that they had been purged "of all the chiefest malefactors, robbers and brigands" as completely as Hercules had cleansed the Augean stables and that they were now "as lawful, as peaceable and quiet as any part of any civil kingdom in Christianity."

There is evidence that the chronic turbulence of the Borders was not so completely suppressed as would seem from the Chancellor's account, but the opening of safe land-passage for steady trade between the two kingdoms appears to date from that period. The memorials of the period of turbulence were eventually converted by the relieved people into materials for legend and song, but this poetry of the situation did not appear until the prosaic aspect had been established to which Dr. Johnson adverted when he remarked that the noblest prospect a Scotchman could see was the high road that led to England. The enlargement of commercial intercourse and the growth of business opportunity were essential features of the pacification of the Borders, as of all regions brought under the rule of law. Severe and terrifying punishment of crime is an indispensable agency in disciplining a people addicted to rapine, but in compelling them to live by honest industry the law must afford them opportunity.

To complete this account of the conditions in Scotland from which the Ulster settlers derived their habits of thought it should be added that the Ulster settlement was essentially a migration from the Lowlands. The elements of the population to whom the opportunity appealed are displayed by the first list of Undertakers. It was mainly composed of sons and brothers of lairds, sons of ministers, and burgesses or sons of burgesses in the shires south of the Firth of Forth, and nearly all were from the upper tier of those shires from Edinburgh to Glasgow. A few names appear from Border shires, among them Robert Stewart of Robertoun, a parish of Roxburghshire in which was situated Harden Castle, the seat of Auld Wat's power. This Robert Stewart received a grant of 1,000 acres in County Tyrone. A grant of 1,500 acres in the same county was made to Sir Robert Hepburn, a lieutenant of the King's Guard. This was a force employed in the general justiciary work of the Scottish Privy Council, outside of the special jurisdiction of the Border commissioners.

The Scots that flocked into Ulster carried with them prepossessions and antipathies implanted by centuries of conflict with predatory clansmen. The monkish writer Gildas, A.D. 560, describes the Picts as "a set of bloody free-booters with more hair on their thieves' faces than clothes to cover their nakedness." This might serve as well for a concise expression of Lowland opinion of the Celtic clansmen at the time of the Ulster settlement. The Lowlanders were accustomed to regarding the clansmen as raiders, pillagers, cattle-thieves, and murderers. The abduction and ravishing of women were crimes so frequent as to engage the particular attention of the Government. Hardened by perpetual contact with barbarism, the Lowlanders had no scruples about making merciless reprisals. The people were hard; the law was hard. It was an iron age. One of the acts of the Scottish Parliament at this period declared that every man and woman of the Gypsy race found in Scotland after a certain date should be liable to death and persons giving them accommodations should be liable to fine and imprisonment. Mention of arrests for sorcery and witchcraft is found in the records. The proceedings of the Privy Council for 1608 contain a report by the Earl of Mar of the burning of some witches at Breichin. "Sum of thame deit in dispair, renunceand and blasphemeand, and utheris half brunt, brak out of the fyre, and wes cast in quick in it agane quhill thay wer brunt to the deid." This horrible scene of human misery was evidently viewed with grim composure. There is not a word to indicate that the event was even deplored.

The greater avidity with which the Ulster opportunity was seized in the Scottish Lowlands than in England, which had the prior claim, is to be attributed to the chronic need of Scotland for outlets to the energies of her people. The migrating Scot was a familiar figure in continental Europe. In *Quentin Durward* Scott gives a romantic picture of the Scottish military adventurer, a type renowned throughout Europe for a shrewd head, a strong arm and a sharp sword. The Scottish trader was quite as well known. There were settlements of Scottish people living under their own laws and perpetuating their national customs in various countries of Europe. William Lithgow, a Scottish traveler who visited Poland in the seventeenth century, reported that there were thirty thousand Scots families in that country. When Sir William Alexander, afterward Earl of Sterling, [sic] was urging the colonization of Nova Scotia, an enterprise that came into competition with the Ulster plantation, he remarked that Scotland, "being constrained to disburden herself (like the painful bees) did every year send forth swarms." Many through stress of necessity had been compelled to "betake themselves to the wars against the Russians, Turks or Swedens." Alexander urged that this scattering of Scottish ability should be discontinued, saying:

> "When I do consider with myself what things are necessary for
> a plantation, I cannot but be confident that my own countrymen

are as fit for such a purpose as any men in the world, having daring minds that upon any probable appearance do despise danger, and bodies able to endure as much as the height of their minds can undertake."

Together with a long implanted migratory tendency operating to promote Scottish colonization of the territory opened to settlement in Ulster, another cause of Scottish forwardness was facility of access. The North of Ireland could be reached by ferries from the southwestern extremities of Scotland which had been purged of their dangerous elements by Lord Ochiltree's expedition. The Scotch settlers had quick transit for themselves and their chattels while the English settlers had to take the risks of a much longer sea-passage beset with pirates.

At this period piracy was a thriving trade, its range including both Atlantic and Mediterranean coasts. Among the outrages charged upon the pirates was that they associated with the Turks, to whom they sold captives, Tunis being a port at which this traffic was carried on.

In a report made to the English Privy Council, August 22, 1609, it is mentioned with satisfaction that John Ward, a pirate chief, had been captured by "the galliasses of the Venetians" with his ship and pinnace and their crews, "whereof thirty-six the next day were hanged in view of the town of Zante, the rest in other places, amongst which number were divers Englishmen." The Irish State Papers contain frequent references to the depredations of pirates on the southern and western coasts of Ireland. Chichester says in his despatches that it was their habit to move from the Spanish coasts to the Irish coasts during the fishing season, to revictual themselves at the expense of the fishing fleet. He mentions that in 1606 the pirates "hath robbed more than 100 sail and sent them empty home."

The traffic that sprang up as a consequence of the Ulster plantation attracted the pirates into the waters between Ireland and England. In a dispatch from Dublin Castle, June 27, 1610, Chichester says:

"The pirates upon this coast are so many and are become so bold that now they are come into this channel, and have lately robbed divers barks, both English and Scotch, and have killed some that have made resistance; they lay for the Londoners' money sent for the work at Coleraine, but missed it; they have bred a great terror to all passengers, and he thinks will not spare the King's treasure if they may light upon it."

Chichester had not the means of taking effective action against piracy, his frequent appeals for sufficient naval force failing of proper response from the home Government. This Scottish authorities acted with prompt decision and energy. An entry of June 27, 1610, on the Register of the Privy Council of Scotland notes that an English pirate had appeared on the coast of Ireland opposite Scotland, waylaying boats bound for the Irish plantation. Commission was given to the provost and baillies of Ayr to fit out an armed vessel to pursue the pirates. About the same time pirate ships were seen even in the Firth of Forth. Upon funds advanced by the City of Edinburgh three armed vessels were fitted out at Leith. The pirates had a depot in the Orkneys from which northern position their vessels could make excursions either to the eastern or western coasts of the mainland. An action was fought off the Orkneys in which one of the two pirate vessels was captured but the other escaped by fast sailing. Of the thirty pirates taken alive twenty-seven were put to death. They are constantly referred to in the State Papers as "English pirates" and their names are such as to justify the description. A feature of the official record that casts a curious light on the morals of the times is that the pirates had "one whome thay did call thair parsone, for saying of prayeris to thame twyse a day." This pirate chaplain furnished the Government with much useful information and he was not brought to trial. Piracy of such a serious-minded type must have been a relic of the time when marauding whether by land or by sea ranked as an honorable industry. This pious band perhaps regarded Scotland as a foreign country whose waters were as fair a field for spoils as the Spanish main in Elizabeth's time.

After this affair no notice appears in the Scottish records of any molesting of the sea-passage to Ulster, although mention is made of the presence of pirates in the Hebrides and the Orkneys. The probability is that the pirates found the narrow channel between Scotland and Ireland too tight a place in which to venture and they kept to safer and more profitable cruising grounds in the wide seas. Numerous references continue to appear in the Irish State Papers to their activity and audacity. They established a depot at Leamcon, a land-locked harbor, on the southern coast of Ireland, and at one time in the summer of 1611 they had there a fleet of nine sail together with four captured vessels. They were engaged in fitting up one of the captured vessels as an addition to their fleet, after which they were going to the Barbary coast where they had a market for their goods. They preyed upon the commerce of Holland, France and England impartially and defied the authority of all those Powers with remarkable success. The Dutch, who were particularly energetic in their efforts to crush the pirates, obtained permission from the English Government to pursue them into Irish waters. Three armed vessels were dispatched from Holland to the Irish seas in 1611, but the pirate fleet scattered at their coming to return when the coast was clear. Piratical depredations on the southern coast continued for many years thereafter, and the participation of the Barbary States in the business eventually led to a horrible affair. On June 20, 1631, a squadron of Algerine pirates sacked the town of Baltimore in County Cork, carrying off with their booty more than a hundred citizens of the place, mostly English colonists. Ulster, however, remained untroubled by the pirates after they had been driven out of the North Channel in the early days of the settlement. The South of Ireland was not delivered from the depredations of the pirates until about 1636 when Wentworth's energetic measures made the region too dangerous for them to visit.

In Appendix B will be found a complete list of the Undertakers as provisionally accepted by the Scottish Privy Council, and also the list as finally prepared by the English Privy Council. Although the two lists differ greatly, probably the class of immigrants was not to any corresponding extent affected by the change. It has already been remarked that the first list made up in September, 1609, was chiefly composed of sons or brothers of lairds and burgesses in the Lowlands. There is no name of a Scottish noble in the list of Undertakers. Lord Ochiltree appears as surety for four of the principals, but was not a principal himself at that time. The list as revised in England in 1611 contains the names of five Scottish noblemen, each receiving an allotment of 3,000 acres whereas in the first list the largest allotment was 2,000 acres. Only eighteen of the seventy-seven applicants enrolled in the first list appear in the final list. In view of the usual tenor of the King's proceedings in such matters favor doubtless played a part in those changes, but they cannot all be ascribed to favor.

According to the ideas of those times it was important to interest wealthy and influential noblemen in the success of the plantation. It is a point on which Chichester laid stress in his communications. Since it appears that Lord Ochiltree refrained from applying in his own behalf when the matter was in the hands of the Scottish Privy Council but is included in the list as made up in England it seems fair to presume that influence was brought to bear upon him. And it would also seem likely that the kinsmen and friends in the Lowlands for whom he had been willing to be surety when the first roll was made up might retain their connection with the enterprise under cover of his name. In a dispatch of July 29, 1611, Chichester mentions that Lord Ochiltree had arrived "accompanied with thirty-three followers, gent. of sort, a minister, some tenants, freeholders, artificers, unto whom he hath passed estates." Chichester notes that building and fortifying were going briskly forward, that horses and cows had been brought in and that ploughing had begun.

Other Scotch noblemen had thrown themselves with a will into the work of colonization. The Earl of Abercorn had brought in tenants with ploughs and live stock, and the Earl and his family were already in residence on their Irish estate. Sir Robert Hepburn was also resident, and was building and farming energetically. Mills and houses were going up and tools and live stock were being brought into the country. That there was a great bustle of intercommunication between Scotland and Ulster is evidenced by a petition to the Scottish Privy Council, October 27, 1612. The petitions set forth that in settling on their lands in Ulster they are "constrained and compellit to transporte frome this countrey thereunto, verie frequentlie, nomberis of men for labouring of the ground, and mony bestiall and cattell for plenisching of the same," so that passage between Scotland and Ulster "is now become a commoun and ane ordinarie ferrie," where seamen and boatmen are making rates at their own pleasure "without ony controlment." The public authority of Scotland was neither impotent nor irresolute in such matters. The Privy Council commissioned the justices of the peace along the west sea-coast to "reforme the said abuse in sic forme and maner as they sail hold fittest, and for this effect that they appoint and set down reasounable and moderat frauchtis [rates] to be tane for the transporte of men, bestiall, and goodis to and fra Yreland."

No further mention of this matter appears in the records but the severity with which unlawful exactions were repressed is evidenced by the entry in 1616 of an order that one Patrick Adair should be imprisoned in the Tolbooth of Edinburgh at his own expense during the pleasure of the Council for insolence in demanding custom on certain horses sent to Ireland by the Earl of Abercorn. There is however evidence that as communications became regular and ample criminals made use of the facilities. Entries of October, 1612, and November, 1614, refer to traffickers in stolen goods between Ireland and Scotland and orders are given to keep a strict watch of ports and ferries, "for apprehending of suche personis as in thifteous maner travellis to and fra Yreland, transporting the goodis stollin be thame furthe of the ane cuntrie to the uther."

The energetic scouring of the Scottish Border shires contributed some elements to Ulster plantation that did not make for

peace and order. Men proscribed in the Borders would take refuge in Ireland. A proclamation issued in 1618 orders the wives
and children of all such persons as have been banished or have
become voluntary fugitives into Ireland to join their husbands
with all convenient diligence, nor presume to return under pain
of imprisonment. To facilitate better control over travel between
Ireland and Scotland it was restricted to certain ports, and pass-
ports were required.

        The situation in the Borders which were the southern tier of
Lowland shires throws light upon a saying that is often quoted in
histories as indicative of a low state of morality among the Ulster
settlers. The authority for it is the Rev. Andrew Stewart, an Ulster
minister. He remarked: "Going to Ireland was looked upon as a
miserable mark of a deplorable person; yea, it was turned into a
proverb, and one of the worst expressions of disdain that could
be invented was to tell a man that 'Ireland would be his hinder
end.'" As one follows through the state papers accounts of the
measures taken by James to rid the Borders of "maisterles men
and vagabondis wanting a lawfull trade, calling and industrie"
and notes the terrible punishments inflicted, branding, drowning
and hanging, it is easy to understand how the popular imagination would be impressed. The severe attitude of the authorities
is strikingly displayed by the measures taken in August, 1612,
when some Scottish companies that had been in Swedish service returned home. It was ordered that "the said soldiers shall,
within two hours after landing, dissolve themselves and repair
peaceably to their homes, and that no more than two of them
shall remain together, under pain of death." To escape from such
rigor emigration to Ireland would be a natural impulse among the
restless and wayward, and an association of ideas was established
that became a text of warning in the mouths of sober-minded
people. But there is abundant evidence that both in Scotland and
Ireland the authorities were active in precautions against crime and
disorder. A frontier has a natural attraction for the misfits of old
communities but the evidence when analyzed does not warrant

the opinion that the Scottish migration into Ulster was so low in moral tone as has been averred by historians on the testimony of early Ulster divines.

The authorities upon whose word rests the charge of prevailing immorality are the Rev. Robert Blair, the Rev. Andrew Stewart, and the Rev. Patrick Adair. Blair, who arrived in Ireland in 1623, left an autobiographical fragment which was begun in 1663 when he was seventy. In it he gave this account of the early settlers:

> "The parts of Scotland nearest to Ireland sent over abundance of people and cattle that filled the counties of Ulster that lay next to the sea; and albeit amongst these, Divine Providence sent over some worthy persons for birth, education and parts, yet the most part were such as either poverty, scandalous lives, or, at the best, adventurous seeking of better accommodation, set forward that way... Little care was had by any to plant religion. As were the people, so, for the most part, were the preachers."

Stewart's account of early conditions is contained in a church history which was begun in 1670 and was left unfinished at his death in 1671. He was minister at Donaghdee from 1645 to 1671, so his account cannot be regarded as contemporary testimony as to original conditions although it has been cited as such. His account has been supposed to derive support from the fact that his father before him was a North of Ireland minister, but the elder Stewart himself did not arrive in Ireland until 1627, and the son was only ten years old when the father died. Even if the younger Stewart is to be credited with information derived from his father, his knowledge does not approach so close as Blair's to the first settlement but nevertheless he paints the situation in much darker colors. Stewart says:

> "From Scotland came many, and from England not a few; yet all of them generally the scum of both nations, who, from debt, or breaking and fleeing from justice, or seeking shelter, came hither, hoping to be without fear of man's justice in a land where there was nothing, or but little as yet, of the fear of God. Yet God followed them when they fled from Him. Albeit at first

it must be remembered, that as they cared little for any church, so God seemed to care little for them. For these strangers were no better entertained than with the relics of popery, served up in a ceremonial service of God under a sort of anti-Christian hierarchy... Thus on all hands atheism increased, and disregard of God, iniquity abounded with contention, fighting, murder, adultery, etc., as among people who, as they had nothing within them to overawe them, so their ministers' example was worse than nothing; for 'from the prophets of Israel profaneness went forth to the whole land.'"

Adair settled in Ireland, in charge of the parish of Cairn Castle, Antrim, May, 1646. He died in 1694 leaving unfinished *A True Narrative of the Rise and Progress of the Presbyterian Church in Ireland.* His account of the first settlers is simply a reproduction of Blair's, in almost the same language.

An examination of these several accounts shows that the purpose of the writers was hortatory rather than historical. The motive that set them all writing in their old age was to put on record edifying experiences. Literary composition of this sort instinctively avoids all colors except black and white. It needs strong contrasts to accomplish the desired effect. Hence Dr. Reid, in his *History of the Presbyterian Church in Ireland*, a work written in the genuine historical spirit, while he reproduces Stewart's account, gives the caution that it is "probably a little over-charged."

Doubtless to clergymen of strict opinions there was deplorable laxity of morals among the early settlers of the Ulster plantation, but if one's views are formed upon examination of the official records, it will not be thought that the people settling in Ulster were any worse than people of their class in Scotland or in England. If anything, the comparison is to the advantage of the Ulster settlers. As a matter of fact they showed far more regard for religious establishment than is usual among emigrants. It has already been noted that a minister accompanied the party of settlers brought over by Lord Ochiltree in 1611. By the close of 1625 seven ministers are known to have settled in the country. Neal's *History of the Puritans*, published in 1731–2, mentions the Ulster plantation

as a field in which Puritanism prospered. Referring to the work
of colonization carried on by the London companies, Neal said:

> "They sent over considerable numbers of planters, but were
> at a loss for ministers; for the beneficed clergy of the Church of
> England, being at ease in the enjoyment of their preferments,
> would not engage in such a hazardous undertaking, it fell there-
> fore to the lot of the Scots and English Puritans; the Scots, by
> reason of their vicinity to the northern parts of Ireland, transport-
> ed numerous colonies; they improved the country and brought
> preaching into the churches where they settled; but being of the
> Presbyterian persuasion, they formed their churches after their
> own model. The London adventurers prevailed with several of
> the English Puritans to remove, who, being persecuted at home,
> were willing to go anywhere within the King's dominions for the
> liberty of their consciences."

This reference to the Puritan complexion of the ecclesiastical
arrangements made along with the Ulster plantation accounts
for the acrimony with which pioneer ministers, writing in their
old age, described the situation in which they began their fruitful
labors. That situation did not exist however because the Ulster
settlers as a class were worse than the other people, but because
exceptionally high standards had been set up, measured by which
morals that elsewhere might have passed without much reproba-
tion were regarded as abominable. Such an epithet as "atheism"
when employed by religious zealots must be taken with allowance.
It may mean really no more than an indifference which however
culpable from the ministerial view-point was far from implying
actual atheism. It may be noted that Stewart couples the charge
of atheism with "disregard of God." That is to say the people
were atheists because they neglected the ordinances of the church
as construed by Puritan clergymen. Blair in his autobiography
mentions incidents that show that atheism could hardly have
been prevalent. He remarks that on the day after he landed in
Ireland he met some Scots with whom by way of conference he
discoursed the most part of the last sermon he had preached.

He speaks of finding several ministers in the field, and of hours spent "in godly conference and calling on the name of the Lord." Alongside of such fervor the behavior of the common people doubtless seemed cold and indifferent, and Blair describes them as "drowned in ignorance, security and sensuality." Yet he says the people were much affected by two sermons he preached on the same day, "one sermon on heaven's glory and another on hell's torments." It was suggested to him that as some of the people that dwelt far from the kirk returned home after the first sermon, he should thereafter preach of hell in the morning and of heaven in the afternoon. In fine, his autobiography gives such an account of successful ministry as to indicate that the people were not a bad sort when judged by ordinary standards, and that upon a fair scale of comparison with new settlements in any country they really stood high in their concern for religion and their attachment to ecclesiastical order.

They certainly were tractable, for the relations that have come down from this period show that the ministers were able to establish a strict discipline. Blair tells how he made evil-doers make public confession of their sins. The Rev. John Livingston who was called to Ireland in 1630 thus describes the process of church discipline in his time:

> "We [i.e. the session] met every week, and such as fell into notorious public scandals we desired to come before us. Such as came were dealt with, both in public and private, to confess their scandal in the presence of the congregation, at the Saturday's sermon before the communion, which was celebrated twice in the year. Such as after dealing would not come before us, or coming, would not be convinced to acknowledge their fault before the congregation, upon the Saturday preceding the communion, their names, scandals and impenitency were read out before the congregation, and they debarred from the communion; which proved such a terror that we found very few of that sort."

This was not an isolated case, for Livingston mentions that "there were nine or ten parishes within the bounds of twenty miles or little more, wherein there were godly and able ministers." Both Blair and Livingston speak of the extraordinary appetite of the people for religious exercise. Livingston says:

> "I have known them come several miles from their own houses to communions, to the Saturday sermon, and spending the whole Saturday's night in several companies, sometimes a minister being with them, and sometimes themselves alone in conference and prayer. They have then waited on the public ordinances the whole Sabbath, and spent the Sabbath night in the same way, and yet at the Monday's sermon were not troubled with sleepiness; and so they have not slept till they went home. In those days it was no great difficulty for a minister to preach or pray in public or private, such was the hunger of hearers."

All this, in less than twenty years after the colonization of Ulster began, certainly does not exhibit a community prone to atheism and immorality. It is evident that ecclesiastical control over the people was promptly applied and was speedily effectual, and it was a control of a strict Puritan type. The development of this characteristic was promoted not only by the fact that the North of Ireland served as a refuge for Puritan ministers harassed by episcopal interference in Scotland and England, but also by the fact that at this time the established church in Ireland had a strong Puritan tincture and the bishops there were friendly and sympathetic in their attitude toward the Presbyterians. The low state of the Established Church at the time of the accession of James had been somewhat retrieved by the appointment of good bishops and diligent pastors, trained under Puritan influence. During Elizabeth's reign Cambridge University had been a center of Calvinistic theology and Puritan doctrine. The famous Richard Cartwright, sometimes called the father of English Puritanism, was a fellow of Trinity College, Cambridge. Dublin University, founded in 1593, drew upon Cambridge University for its staff of professors and their influence upon the Irish Church was very marked. The articles of religion adopted by the Church of Ireland in 1615 are printed in full in Neal's *History of the Puritans* as a

Puritan document. Blair, Livingston and other Presbyterian ministers accepted Episcopal ordination after a form made to meet their approval. Neal says:

> "All the Scots who were ordained in Ireland to the year 1642, were ordained after the same manner; all of them enjoyed the churches and tithes, though they remained Presbyterian and used not the liturgy; nay, the bishops consulted them about affairs of common concernment to the church, and some of them were members of the convocation in 1634."

Looking back upon the situation in the plantation period from the standpoint of our own times, the remarkable thing now appears to be that the people were so spiritually minded. In the time when Blair used to preach his sermons on heaven's glory and hell's torments, both on the same day, it may have seemed deplorable indifference that some of the people were satisfied to hear only one; but what surprises one now is that there should have been so many willing to make long journeys to give whole days to hearing sermons. Such devotion is hardly intelligible until the general circumstances of the times are considered. Previous to the spread of popular education, the rise of journalism, and the diffusion of literature, the pulpit was in most places the only source of intellectual stimulus and mental culture. It was like the well in the desert to which all tracks converge, whereas now some sort of supply is laid to every man's house.

The nervous disorders that are apt to result from immoderate states of religious introspection and emotional fervor were early manifested in Ulster under the excitements of Puritan exhortation. In describing a revival under Blair's preaching Stewart says: "I have seen them myself stricken and swoon with the word—yea, a dozen in a day carried out of doors as dead, so marvellous was the power of God smiting their hearts for sin." Such scenes before long produced religious vagaries that gave trouble. Blair in his autobiography gives a long account of his dealings with Glendinning, described as "lecturer at Carrickfergus." Glendinning settled himself at Oldstone, near the town of Antrim, where "he began to preach diligently, and having a great voice and vehement delivery, he roused up the people and waked them with terrors." But Blair notes that he "was neither studied in learning, nor had good solid judgment." Indeed, it would appear that the man became deranged, judging from the strangeness of the doctrines he began to preach. "He watched much and fasted wonderfully, and began publicly to affirm that he or she after they had slept a little in bed, if they return themselves from one side to another, could not be an honest Christian." Blair gives a long account of a struggle he had with Glendinning to keep him from putting his foot in the fire to show that it would have no power to burn him. Glendinning professed to know when the Judgment Day was to come and he taught people to save themselves by "a ridiculous way of roaring out some prayer, laying their faces on the earth." Glendinning finally left the country, giving out that he had a call to visit the Seven Churches of Asia.

The educated clergy who directed the interests of early Presbyterianism of Ulster set themselves firmly against religious ecstasies that tended to folly and disorder. Blair described some manifestations at Lochlearn in 1630 as "a mere delusion and cheat of Satan." It seems that there were persons who "in the midst of the public worship fell as mourning, and some of them were afflicted with pangs like convulsions." Their case excited sympathy at first but as conference with them disclosed no spiritual value in such experiences they were before long sharply rebuked. Blair tells how a woman of his own congregation "in the midst of the public worship, being a dull and ignorant person, made a noise and stretching of her body." He forthwith denounced the exhibition as the work of the lying spirit and charged it not to disturb the congregation. Blair notes that after this rebuke nothing more of the kind occurred, "the person above mentioned remaining still a dull and stupid sot." One can hardly be mistaken in thinking that these early experiences had much to do with developing in Ulster Presbyterianism its characteristic insistence upon the importance of having an educated clergy. We may therefore descry here the initial impulse of important educational activities in the United States ensuing from Ulster emigration.

These accounts of early conditions by the pioneer clergy are tantalizingly curt in their references to the industrial situation. Blair remarks that when the plantation began "the whole country did lie waste; the English possessing some few towns and castles, making use of small parcels of near adjacent lands; the Irishes staying in woods, bogs and such fast places." After mentioning the influx from Scotland he observes: "The wolf and widcairn were great enemies to these first planters; but the long rested land yielded to the laborers such plentiful increase that many followed the first essayers." These brief references are all that Blair has to say about the conditions that the planters had to endure, but they cast a flashlight on the situation. A relief map of Ireland shows that elevations above 500 feet are more thickly clustered in Ulster than in any other part of Ireland except the southwestern extremity. Three highland masses whose general direction follows rather closely the sixth, seventh and eighth meridians of longitude stretch across Ulster from the north to the great central plain of Ireland. Between and about these highlands are lake basins and river valleys terminating in short coastal plains. At the time of the settlement forests and swamps occupied much of the country.

Ancient Ireland was a densely wooded country. State papers of 1529 represent the districts in which English law prevailed as being everywhere surrounded by thick forests. From time to time the Government had to cut passes and take measures for their maintenance. During the wars of Elizabeth it was a proverb that "the Irish will never be tamed while the leaves are on the trees," meaning that the winter was the only season in which the Irish could be descried and pursued in the woods. "Plashing" is mentioned as a great obstacle to the movement of the troops, by which was meant the interlacing of the tree trunks with underwood so as to render the forest paths impassable. The Government sought to reduce these woodland areas, with such success that by the time James succeeded to the throne the central plain of Ireland was nearly destitute of woods; but extensive forests still remained in Ulster, in the counties of Tyrone, Londonderry, Antrim and Down, particularly on the east and west shores of Lough Neagh, and the territories adjacent.

Almost everywhere the lands occupied by the planters were in reach of the "fast places" in which Blair speaks of the "Irishes staying." The planters had to pasture their cattle near coverts in which wolves prowled or marauding natives lurked. Blair speaks of the wolf as a great enemy. Its ravages were so great that so late as 1652 under Cromwell's Government a bounty of six pounds was offered for the head of every she wolf. Grand jury records mention payments for killing wolves as late as 1710, and they were not wholly extinct until about 1770. The "widcairn" mentioned by Blair is a corruption of wood kern. From the reference to this enemy it appears that although Chichester had shipped out of the country many of the fighting men many still remained behind, still trying to live their old lives as a privileged class to whom tribute was due. The planters thus lived in a state of siege. Thomas Blenerhassett, whose *Direction for the Plantation in Ulster* describes conditions at this period says: "Sir Toby Caulfield's people are driven every night to lay up all his cattle, as it were, in warde; and do he and his what they can, the woolfe and the wood kerne (within caliver shot of his fort), have oftentimes a share." Gainsford, another writer of this period, mentions that it was an Ulster practice in 1619 "to house their cattle in the bawnes of their castles where all the winter nights they stood up to their bellies in dirt."

Such hazards powerfully impelled the settlers to build securely. In the official survey made by Nicholas Pynnar in 1619 such entries appear as the following:

> "On the allotment of Lord Aubigny, held by Sir James Hamilton, is built a strong castle of lime and stone, called Castle Aubigny, with the King's arms cut in free stone over the gate. This is five storeys high, with four round towers for flankers; the hall is 50 feet long and 28 broad; the roof is set up and ready

to be slated. Adjoining one end of the castle is a bawn of lime and stone, 80 feet square, with two flankers 15 feet high, very strongly built."

―――――――

"John Hamilton has built a bawn of lime and stone, 80 feet square and 13 feet high, with round towers for flankers; he has also a stone house, now one storey high, and intended to be four, being 48 feet long and 24 broad; besides two towers, which are vaulted, flank the house. Also a village of eight houses adjoining the bawn, inhabited by British tenants, a watermill and five houses adjoining it."

Pynnar says that at that time there were in Ulster "in British families 6,215 men, and upon occasion, 8,000 men, of British birth and descent for defence, though the fourth part of the lands is not fully inhabited." Of buildings there were "107 castles with bawns, 19 castles without bawns, 42 bawns without castles or houses, 1,897 dwelling houses of stone and timber, after the English manner, in townredes, besides very many such houses in several which I saw not."

This estimate of the number of men able to bear arms of course implies a much larger population when the women and children are taken into the reckoning. The number of houses also points the same way. Inasmuch as the settlers took their families, and families were apt to be large in those days, the statistics given by Pynnar indicate that from 30,000 to 40,000 colonists were then settled in the country. Pynnar classes together English and Scotch as "British" but he gives details which show that the Scotch were much the more important element. He remarks that "many English do not yet plough nor use husbandry, being fearful to stock themselves with cattle or servants for such labors," and he goes on to say that "were it not for the Scottish, who plough in many places, the rest of the country might starve."

From the very first the Scotch took the lead in the settlement. In a report written in November, 1610, Chichester describes the English Undertakers as:

"For the most part, plain country gentlemen, who may promise much, but give small assurance or hope of performing what appertains to a work of such moment. If they have money, they keep it close; for hitherto they have disbursed but little, and if he may judge by the outward appearance, the least trouble or alteration of the times here will scare most of them away… The Scottish come with greater port and better accompanied and attended, but it may be with less money in their purse; for some of the principal of them, upon their first entrance into their precincts were forthwith in hand with the natives to supply their wants, or at least their expenses, and in recompense thereof promise to get license from His Majesty that they may remain on their lands as tenants unto them; which is so pleasing to that people that they will strain themselves to the uttermost to gratify them, for they are content to become tenants to any man rather than be removed from the place of their birth and education, hoping, as he conceives, at one time or other to find an opportunity to cut their landlord's throats; for sure he is they hate the Scottish deadly, and out of their malice toward them they begin to affect the English better than they have accustomed."

. Even apart from the ease of access enjoyed by the Scotch, Ulster opportunities were more attractive to the Scotch than to the English whose experience and habits did not fit them so well to endure the hardships. The Rev. Andrew Stewart dwells on this in his account of early conditions, remarking:

"It is to be observed that being a great deal more tenderly bred at home in England, and entertained in better quarters than they could find here in Ireland, they were very unwilling to flock hither, except to good land, such as they had before at home, or to good cities where they might trade; both of which in these days were scarce enough here. Besides that the marshiness and fogginess of this Island was still found unwholesome to English bodies, more tenderly bred and in a better air; so that we have seen in our time multitudes of them die of a flux, called here the country disease, at their first entry. These things were such discouragements that the new English come but very slowly, and the old English were become no better than the Irish."

By the "old English" Stewart means the descendants of English formerly settled in Ireland. In every age they have shown a marked tendency to melt into the general mass, making Irish nationality so composite in character that it would be hardly more accurate now to describe the Irish people as Celts than to describe the English people as Angles or Saxons. The conflicts of which Ireland has been the scene have been more political and religious than racial, and the political and religious differences have caused undue emphasis to be put upon racial differences. Even the preservation of the Celtic language and customs in some regions is no guarantee of race purity, for there is abundant evidence that descendants of early English settlers have adopted Irish speech and ways.

According to the original scheme only the class of servitors whose houses were to possess the character of military posts were to be allowed to have Irish tenants. It was the intention to remove the native Irish from the lands assigned to the Scotch and English Undertakers. But this part of the scheme, to which Chichester had always been opposed, proved to be impracticable. In a report made in July, 1611, the English Privy Council is informed that "experience tells the Undertakers that it will be almost impossible for them to perform the work they have undertaken, if the natives be removed according to the general project, for when they are gone there will be neither victuals nor carriage within twenty miles, and in some counties more." In view of this situation the removal had to be deferred and as time went on the obstacles increased. The Irish were willing to pay for the use of pasture lands and the newcomers found that the readiest way of turning their holdings to account was to let them out. Pynnar, writing in 1619, observes that "the British, who are forced to take their lands at great rates, live at the greater rates paid to them by Irish tenants who graze." He adds that "if the Irish pack away with their cattle the British must either forsake their dwellings or endure great distress on the sudden." Those considerations did not relax their force and the removal of the natives, although from time to time announced as settled policy, was never actually attempted.

. The practice by the Undertakers of letting the lands was particularly marked in the large tracts assigned to the London companies. Pynnar in his report made in 1619 says: "The greatest number of Irish dwell upon the lands granted to the City of London." He explains this by pointing out that the lands are "in the hands of agents, who, finding the Irish more profitable than the British, are unwilling to draw on the British, persuading the companies that the lands are mountainous and unprofitable, not regarding the future security of the whole."

The behavior of the London companies became the subject of an official inquiry, which incidentally produced a curious and beautiful record of the state of the plantation in the County of Londonderry in 1622. The survey was made under a royal commission to Sir Thomas Phillips and Richard Hadsor. The editors of the Calendar of State Papers, 1615–1625, say of the commission's report:

> "… in it the state of every building, public and private, is portrayed in colors, giving a picture of the liveliest kind. There are views of Londonderry and Coleraine, with all the houses in the streets and other buildings, the ramparts, etc. And on the proportions of the several London companies are drawn not only the several manor houses, but those of the freeholders and farmers, besides the cage-work houses in course of building, but yet unfinished."

In their report the commissioners call attention to the preponderance of natives and to the need of larger settlements of British "which would prevent many robberies and murders daily committed by the Irish, to the great terror of the few poor British already settled." Of one place the commissioners remark: "This plantation, albeit it is the strongest and most ablest of men to defend themselves, yet have they sustained great losses by the wood kerne and thieves." Of another place the commissioners report: "The few British that inhabit this proportion live so scattered that upon occasion they are unable to succor one another, and are daily robbed and spoiled and driven to leave the country." The military importance of the forests at that period is indicated by the urgent recommendation that there be "large passes cut through the woods to answer each several plantation."

In 1624 Sir Thomas Phillips made a petition to the King in which he charged the London companies with "defects and abuses … by which they have brought the country into an almost desperate case." He declared that "their towns and fortresses are rather baits to ill-affected persons than places of security, besides the few British now planted there be at the mercy of the Irish, being daily murthered, robbed and spoiled by them."

The London companies eventually incurred heavy penalties on conviction of default, but no great change took place in the general situation. The plantation instead of being a substitution of British for Irish, as originally intended, assumed the character of an incursion of British landlordism among the Irish. The mass of the natives were not displaced but became tenants and laborers upon the lands they used to regard as their own. And this appears to have been the case not only in Londonderry County but throughout Ulster. An official return made in 1624 gives the names of 629 Irish tenants in County Fermanagh alone.

The settlers thus lived surrounded by a hostile population, with almost daily risks from raiders and in almost constant alarm of a general rising. In 1615 a plot for the surprise and burning of Derry and Coleraine was formed, but was frustrated by the arrest of many of the conspirators. According to the cruel practice of the times torture was used to extort confessions. The authorities were too alert and the military precautions too extensive to admit any opportunity for a general rising at that time. But there appears to have been more or less marauding going on all the time. In an official report of March 27, 1624, the writer mentions that many thefts and robberies were being committed by bands operating in the counties of Tyrone and Londonderry. He adds: "I know well that this is a trifle to speak of in this kingdom, where such courses have been frequent, and where there are now many others in several counties upon their keeping, as we call it here."

The phrase "upon their keeping" may be taken to denote such as adhered to the old order, what had once been tribal privilege now taking the form of rapine.

A *Discourse upon the Settlement of the Natives in Ulster* which was submitted to the Government in 1628 gives this account of the situation at that time:

> "Whosoever doth know Ulster and will deal truly with His Majesty must make this report of it; that in the general appearance of it, it is yet no other than a very wilderness. For although in many of the proportions, I mean of all kinds, there is one small township, made by the Undertakers which is all, yet, the proportions being wide and large, the habitation of all the province is scarce visible. For the Irish, of whom many townships might be formed, do not dwell together in any orderly form, but wander with their cattle all the summer in the mountains, and all the winter in the woods. And until these Irish are settled, the English dare not live in those parts, for there is no safety either for their goods or lives, which is the main cause, though other reasons may be given, why they do not plentifully go thither, and cheerfully plant themselves in the province."

These perils and difficulties almost put an end to the settlement of English in Ulster. Their home conditions were not of such urgency as to force them out into such a field. It was different with the Scotch. More accustomed to emigration than the English of that period, more inured to hardships, more capable in meeting them, they held their ground, throve and spread, giving to the Ulster settlement a Scottish character.[3] Exact figures as to

---

[3] After this chapter had been written a valuable history appeared entitled *The Ulster Scot*, by the Rev. James Barkley Woodburn of Castlerock, County Derry, Ireland. This work may be commended as a fair and well-informed history of Ulster.

Mr. Woodburn, however, makes a statement in regard to racial origins with which I am unable to agree. He holds that there is little or no racial distinction between the Ulster Scots and the Irish people in general and that "the Ulsterman has probably as much

population are not attainable. No proper census of Ireland was taken until 1821; prior to that time there are only estimates. All authorities agree that Ulster increased rapidly in population, both in the native stock and in the planted stocks. Wentworth, who was Lord Deputy of Ireland from 1623 to 1640, estimated that there were at least 100,000 Scots in the North. The historian Carte, whose work although published in 1736 is based upon such diligent study of documentary sources that it still ranks as a leading authority, estimates that in 1641 there were in Ulster 100,000 Scotch and 20,000 English. When it is considered that Pynnar in 1619 reported only 6,215 men settled on the plantation, so great a growth in the next twenty years seems almost incredible. It is to be observed however that the estimates include not only the population of the six escheated counties covered by the plantation scheme, but also Antrim, Down and Monaghan in which settlements of Scotch and English took place before the plantation of 1610. After making all allowances for possible exaggeration, it is certain that within thirty years from the beginning of the plantation there was a large Scotch population in the country.

Celtic blood as the Southerner." In support of this averment he argues that the regions of Scotland from which the Ulster plantation drew settlers were predominantly Celtic. Mr. Woodburn's argument was the subject of thorough consideration by the Rev. Professor James Heron of the Assembly's College, Belfast, in an address delivered at that institution on April 9, 1910. This address, which makes a thorough and complete analysis of this intricate subject, will be found reproduced in Appendix C of this book.

CHAPTER IV

FORMATIVE INFLUENCES

Events of a kind that make or break character came hard and fast in Ulster. They belong to Irish history and they do not concern this work save as they operated in forming Scotch-Irish character, so for the present purpose it is necessary only to take some note of their nature and dimensions.

In 1625 Charles I. succeeded James I. In 1633 Thomas Wentworth, better known by his later title of Lord Strafford, was appointed Lord Deputy of Ireland. The career of this man remains a historical puzzle but of his ability there can be no question. He had been a leader of the parliamentary opposition to the absolutist policy of Charles and suddenly went over to the King's side as the energetic Minister of the policy against which he had previously contended. The same year that Wentworth became chief of the Government of Ireland, Laud became Archbishop of Canterbury. The two worked in hearty accord in asserting royal authority and in enforcing religious conformity. The Irish Established Church, under official pressure, discarded the articles of religion whose Puritan tone had facilitated working agreement with the Presbyterian ministers of Ulster.

In 1634 the Irish Church in convocation adopted the English articles, and it was ordered that they were to be subscribed by every minister and to be read by him publicly in church at least once a year. A high commission court was set up in Dublin, its purpose being, as Strafford wrote, "to support ecclesiastical courts and officers, to provide for the maintenance of the clergy and for their residence, either by themselves or able curators, to bring the people here to a conformity in religion, and in the way of all these to raise perhaps a good revenue to the Crown." Wentworth, whose motto was "thorough," knew perfectly well the significance of his policy. In a letter to Laud, describing the measures he had taken, he remarked: "So as now I can say, the King is as absolute here as any prince in the whole world can be."

To have a just appreciation of motives it should be observed that at that period, and indeed for over a century later, the weight of political theory was on the side of principle of absolutism in government. A good statement of opinion will be found in Chapter XXII of Sidgwick's *Development of European Polity*. He points out that the development of national unity, coherence and order, the suppression of the anarchical resistance of powerful individuals and groups, and the formation of sovereignty, all took place upon the basis of royal prerogative. Even so late as the middle of the eighteenth century "an impartial Continental observer ... would probably have regarded monarchy of the type called absolute as the final form of government to which the long process of formation of orderly country-states had led up; and by which the task of establishing and maintaining a civilized political order had been, on the whole, successfully accomplished, after other modes of political construction had failed to realize it."

Therefore it would be a great mistake to suppose that because a man held absolutist principles of government he was abject in his attitude toward kings or insensible to liberty. For the. King as an individual he might have contempt while valuing the office and its unrestricted authority as the essential principle of public order. Before the French Revolution absolutist principles in government were not considered inconsistent with liberalism. Indeed, on the Continent of Europe the two were traditionally associated. It was the tendency of kings to promote reforms for the benefit of the people while such organs of constituted authority as existed apart from royal authority were shelters of class privilege. Hence Voltaire, the great apostle of liberalism, was absolutist. He wrote to D'Alembert in 1765: "Who would have thought that the cause of kings would be that of philosophers? But it is evident that the sages who refuse to admit two powers are the chief support of royal authority." Again he said, "There ought never to be two powers in the State." This mode of thought was originally characteristic of British Toryism, and persisted in literature long after absolutism has been extinguished as a working scheme of government. In 1741 the Scotch philosopher Hume published an essay in which he held that the tendency to amass authority in the House of Commons may produce a tyranny of factions, and he concluded that "we shall at last, after many convulsions and civil wars, find repose in absolute monarchy, which it would have been happier for us to have established peacefully from the beginning." Considerations of this order supported the high Toryism of a thinker of such robust common sense as Dr. Samuel Johnson.

In his charming novel *The Vicar of Wakefield* Goldsmith argues the case at length through the mouth of one of his characters. It is in Chapter XIX, entitled "The Description of a Person Discontented with the Present Government, and Apprehensive of the Loss of Our Liberties." The gist of the argument is that by placing themselves under a king the people "diminish the number of tyrants and put tyranny at the greatest distance from the greatest number of people." He argues that the alternative to kingship is not liberty but oppression:

> "What they may then expect, may be seen by turning our eyes to Holland, Genoa or Venice, where the laws govern the poor and the rich govern the laws. I am then for, and would die for, monarchy, sacred monarchy: for if there be anything sacred among men, it must be the anointed sovereign of his people; and every diminution of his power, in war or in peace, is an infringement upon the real liberties of the subject."

When such views were still extant in the middle of the eighteenth century, it cannot surprise us that they should subsist along with sincere patriotism and genuine love of liberty in the middle of the seventeenth century. The issue was not intentionally one between despotism and liberty but between conflicting interpretations of liberty. To Wentworth and Laud the liberty proper to good Christians and good subjects was a particular state of civil and religious order which the Government prescribed and which it was its business to apply. Wentworth's conversion from the King's chief opponent to his chief agent is a puzzling circumstance but it is not unparalleled. A recent biographer, H. D. Traill, thinks the most plausible explanation is that his period of opposition was the familiar political expedient of making oneself such a nuisance to the Government that one has to be let into power. At any rate, Wentworth displayed such initiative, vigor and zeal in his administration as accords with sincere conviction and not with merely selfish calculation. His character was admired by Bismarck who too in his time acted as the champion of prerogative against parliamentary opposition. At a crisis in his career he declared he would persevere to the end even though it brought him Strafford's fate, but in his case it brought glory and honor; so much depends upon occasion and opportunity.

History has in a way vindicated the champions of absolutism as well as the champions of freedom, although it is the latter that naturally have the popular renown. The protagonists in the long drawn out battle between prerogative and popular rule that was not ended until the nineteenth century were both partly in the right. It is historically evident that the principle of the sovereignty of the State, which confers the power of volition essential to the discharge of the functions of modern government, was worked out on the basis of royal prerogative. What has happened is that the legal institution has been detached from the individual control of the incumbent of the kingly office. The custody has passed to the representatives of the people, but the institution itself is stronger than ever before, and it has become the cardinal principle of popular government. The great authority of the late Professor F. W. Maitland may be cited in support of this statement. In his *Constitutional History of England* (1908) he remarks:

> "We must not confuse the truth that the King's personal will has come to count for less and less with the falsehood (for falsehood it would be) that his legal powers are diminishing. On the contrary, of late years they have enormously grown. The principle being established that the King must govern by the advice of Ministers who are approved by the House of Commons, Parliament has entrusted the King with vast powers, statutory

powers. Many governmental acts, which in the last century would have required the passing of an act of Parliament, are now performed by exercise of statutory powers conferred on the King. Acts which give these powers often require that they shall be exercised by Order in Council. Thus in addition to his prerogative or common law powers the King now has statutory powers. All this, coupled with the delegation of other powers to this Minister and that, is the result of a new government which began about 1830."

Thus things may now be done in the King's name that involve larger claim of legal authority than would have been deemed conceivable in the time of the Stuarts or admissible even by so thoroughgoing an agent of prerogative as Wentworth himself. The difference is that now what is done in the King's name is done at the instance of the people constitutionally expressed, and it is done on the public business in the people's interest and for the general welfare. And the same remarks apply to the case of modern republics in which the term "the Crown" is superseded by the term "the People" as the source of authority. The apparatus of sovereignty used by modern democracy may be traced to institutions originally embodying royal authority. Thus in a way the champions of absolutism have contributed to the ultimate triumph of popular rule by their incidental service in developing the sovereignty of the State as a legal institution. Where the course of events has depleted sovereignty, popular government now suffers in its competency. The student of jurisprudence finds instances of such defect in the constitutional history of the United States, particularly in the government of the several States.

In the struggle over the constitution of government which began in the seventeenth century the legists of the period were so heavily on the side of prerogative that the opposition would have been fatally weak in the moral and intellectual force of its contention, had it not been able to offer on its side a principle of legitimacy and order. Religion supplied that principle. In opposition to the claims of royal prerogative it set up the paramount title of divine sovereignty. No one more strongly asserted the duty of obedience than John Calvin. With characteristically unflinching logic he insists upon passive obedience "if we are inhumanly harassed by a cruel prince; if we are rapaciously plundered by an avaricious or luxurious one; if we are neglected by an indolent one; or if we are persecuted on account of piety, by an impious and sacrilegious one." But he proceeds to make an exception which practically does away with his rule. The duty of obedience to magistrates is subordinate to one's duty to God. "If they command anything against Him, it ought not to have the least attention; nor in this case, ought we to pay any regard to all that dignity attached to magistrates."

Thus religious dissent contributed to constitutional progress. Mr. Figgis, who supplied to the *Cambridge Modern History* the article on "Political Thought in the Sixteenth Century," sums up the case by saying that religious liberty the parent of political liberty:

> "Religious liberty arose, not because the sects believed in it, but out of their passionate determination not to be extinguished either by political or religious persecution… The forces in favor of monarchy were so strong that, apart from a motive appealing to the conscience, making it a duty (even though a mistaken one in any individual case) to resist the Government, there would have been no sufficient force to withstand the tyranny of centralization which succeeded the anarchy of feudalism."

The mere assertion of this principle did not necessarily make for constitutional government. It was capable under individualistic interpretations of becoming an agency of social dissolution to counteract which the recourse would be to arbitrary power. This mode of thought received powerful expression in Milton's *Ready and Easy Way to Establish a Free Commonwealth* published in 1659–60. He argued from the experience of ancient republics that popular assemblies "either little availed the people, or else brought them to such a licentious and unbridled democracy as in fine ruined themselves with their own excessive power." That authority may be stable it should have a perpetual tenure.

Therefore he proposed that the people should elect their ablest and wisest men to sit as a grand council for the management of public affairs, holding office for life. "Safest therefore to me, it seems, and of less hazard and interruption to affairs, that none of the grand council be moved, unless by death or just conviction of some crime; for what can be expected firm or steadfast from a floating foundation." The "Long Parliament" was a sufficiently close approximation to this scheme of government to expose its characteristic quality. It remained in existence twenty years and until its behavior became so intolerable that Cromwell turned what was left of it out of doors.

In Ulster religion supplied not only a principle of legality in opposition to royal absolutism but also a principle of institutional order in the Presbyterian model of church discipline. The claims originally put forth in behalf of that model in Scotland and England were not such as can be reconciled with liberty of conscience, but no such object was professed, the only purpose being to establish what was regarded as true spiritual order, the duty of government being to repress violations of that order. The Scottish National Covenant of 1638 described the authority of the King as "a comfortable instrument of God's mercy granted to this country for the maintenance of His Kirk." But while the Presbyterian system did not aim at liberty it served the cause of liberty by supplying a principle of unity and coherence whose political strength was triumphantly displayed both in Scotland and Ulster. Presbyterian influence banded the people together in massive resistance to Wentworth's policy. Wentworth himself bore emphatic testimony to the fact that the Ulster Scots were the great obstacle to his plans for reducing Ireland to submission and conformity. He singled them out as the special objects of his care. In 1639 an oath of allegiance was proposed by which they were compelled to swear never to oppose the King's command and to abjure all covenants and oaths contrary to the tenor of this engagement. This imposition, which became famous in Ulster history as The Black Oath, was expressly designed to reach the

Ulster Scots, this purpose being set forth in the correspondence between Wentworth and the King with regard to the measure.

By proclamation of the Deputy and Council all the Scottish residents of Ulster above the age of sixteen, women as well as men, were required to take this oath. The only exception made was in favor of Scots who professed to be Roman Catholics. Commissioners were appointed to administer the oath, and to assist them the ministers and church wardens were required to make a return of all the Scots resident in their respective parishes. Then either the people named had to appear to take the oath, kneeling while the commissioners read it aloud, or else their names were reported as recusants liable to punishment. Wentworth's arrangements were so carefully made and so well backed up by military force that effective resistance was impossible, but the attitude of the people was such that later on he proposed "to banish all the under Scots in Ulster by proclamation," meaning by "under Scots" those who did not have large estates to incline them to submission to the policy of the Government. Nothing came of this notion for soon afterward his career was cut short by the impeachment that brought him to the scaffold. Wentworth, who became Earl of Strafford in 1640, was beheaded on May 12, 1641. Before parting with this remarkable man it should be observed that his energetic administration had its good side. His measures relieved the coasts of Ireland from the scourge of piracy and it was he that introduced the cultivation of flax which became and has remained a flourishing Ulster industry. In aid of that enterprise he imported flax seed from Holland at his own expense and induced expert workmen to come from France and the Low Countries. All historians of this period agree that under his six years of strong administration the country made great industrial progress. Reid's *History of the Presbyterian Church in Ireland* says: "At no former period had the country enjoyed so much real prosperity, and so long internal peace."

A tremendous change impended, the factors of which were concealed within that specious tranquility. A measure which more than any other of Stafford's actions drew down upon him the deadly hostility of the parliamentary party in England was his levy of an army in Ireland. At the outset he intended all the men to be Protestants, and of British extraction so far as possible. But his views on that point had to be modified when King Charles advised him that the army would be used "to reduce those in Scotland to their due obedience." After that Scots were carefully weeded out and preference was given to Irish Catholics, who, he told the King, might do good service for they hated the Scots and their religion. The headquarters staff were all Protestants, but among the regimental officers were men who afterward became prominent as leaders of rebellion. Strafford was perfectly well aware that in thus giving military organization to natives whose religion was proscribed by law he was taking serious risks. He wrote to the King that their training "might arm their old affections to do us more mischief, and put new and dangerous thoughts into them after they are returned home." So clear-sighted an administrator as Strafford would have taken precautions on this score, but after he had fallen a victim to the rage of the parliamentary party Charles precipitately ordered that the army be disbanded, with license to a number of officers to transport 8,000 foot "for the service of any prince or State in amity with us." At least seven of these officers were afterward active leaders of rebellion. One colonel by prompt work took over to the service of France one thousand picked men and engagements had been made also for shipments to Spain, when the English Parliament practically stopped the business by a resolution against transportation of soldiers by merchants from any part of the King's dominions. In the end the army, most of which was quartered in Ulster, was disbanded, the men giving up their arms and quietly dispersing.

The disbanding of the army seemed at the time to remove a great danger; what it actually did was to create a great danger, soon revealed by the outbreak of a civil war that lasted for eleven years. It was ushered in by massacres, the nature and extent of which has ever since remained a subject of controversy. In October, 1641, there was a sudden rising of the native Irish and a great slaughter of Protestants, attended by revolting atrocities. The seizure of Dublin Castle, in which Strafford had accumulated a great store of munition of war, was part of the plot, but this design miscarried. The number of persons who lost their lives in the October massacres is a matter about which there has been and still is great controversy. The number has been set as high as 200,000 and as low as 8,000. Gardiner, the latest historian to sift the evidence, concludes that four or five thousand were murdered, and about twice that number died of ill usage.

Woodburn, the latest historian of Ulster, accepts that computation as probably correct. An exact statement is not attainable but it is certain that thousands of Protestant settlers were massacred and that great atrocities were committed. The details as set forth in the depositions taken from survivors are revolting. A specification that frequently recurs is that the clothes were stripped from captives. But this would appear to be due rather to the fact that the poorer natives seized the opportunity to get clothes for themselves than that it was intended as a refinement of cruelty. Indeed some of the most horrible atrocities appear to have been committed by women and children, following after the raiding parties. At Kilmore in Armagh county, after a number of the leading Protestants had been murdered, a number of others were put as prisoners in a thatched house. A party headed by a woman set fire to this house, destroying all the inmates except two women who crept through a hole in the wall and feigning death waited until the murderers had gone when they escaped to the mountains. A letter of one of the leaders of the uprising is preserved in which he tells his correspondent that "as for the killing of women none of my soldiers dare do it, but the common people that are not under rule do it in spite of our teeth; but as for your people they killed of women and children above three score." Isolated acts of charity and mercy are recorded. The Rev. John Kerdiffe, a Protestant clergyman, in relating how he and his parishioners were made prisoners by the Irish under Col. Richard Plunket, said that "Col. Plunket treated us with great humanity and in like manner did Friar Malone at Skerry." It must be remembered that the uprising was carried on by local bands, subject to no regular discipline, throwing the country at once into a state of anarchy so that every ferocious instinct and evil passion had an opportunity of which horrible use was made. And there were horrible reprisals as soon as the Protestants got over the first surprise and were able to make a stand.

Ulster bore the brunt of this uprising but the English rather than the Scotch settlers were the chief victims of the first onslaught. The Rev. Dr. Reid, himself an Ulsterman, says in his history:

> "As a body, the Presbyterians suffered less by the ravages of the rebellion than any other class. The more influential of their ministers, and the principal part of their gentry, had previously retired to Scotland to escape the tyranny of Strafford and the severities of the bishops, and were thus providentially preserved. Those who remained in the country were at first unmolested by the Irish, in conformity with the royal commission. This temporary preservation gave them time to procure arms, and to take other necessary measures to protect themselves against the storm which they saw approaching. When the rebels, therefore, abandoned their professed neutrality, and fell upon them, as furiously as upon the English, they were prepared for the attack. When they associated together in sufficient numbers, they were generally enabled to maintain their ground, and frequently repulsed their assailants with loss."

The "royal commission" mentioned by Dr. Reid refers to a document published by the insurgents as coming from King Charles authorizing them to seize and disarm the English Protestants, but to spare the Scots. This document is generally regarded by historians as a forgery. So far from being any advantage to Charles the Irish insurrection was a most untoward event. He exerted himself to bring about a cessation of hostilities, so that he might draw upon Ireland for aid in his struggle with the English Parliament.

In 1645 he instructed Ormonde, his deputy, "to conclude a peace with the Irish, whatever it cost; so that my Protestant subjects there may be secure, and my regal authority preserved." The articles of peace concluded by Ormonde under this instruction contain one article which affords remarkable evidence of persistence of savage customs. One of the engagements exacted of the King was that the law "prohibiting the ploughing with horses by the tail" should be repealed.

The civil war opened by the massacres of October, 1641, was not ended until during the year 1653. During its course the Ulster Scots formed a distinct interest at variance with all parts and in danger from all. Throughout they had to encounter the steady enmity of the native Irish who regarded them as intruders and usurpers. They occupied a middle position between the royalists and the parliamentarians, between whose military operations they were caught as between upper and nether millstones, and if they were not ground fine that was because they were unusually hard material and the grindstones were defective in power and application. In Strafford's time they were on the parliamentary side and thus became a mark of royalist hostility. But when the Presbyterian leaders were ejected from the English House of Commons the Ulster Scots turned against the Rump Parliament and denounced its members as sectarians. The beheading of Charles I. brought out an indignant protest from the Belfast Presbytery to which John Milton, then beginning his career as Latin secretary of Parliament, made a tart reply, in which he described the Ulster ministers as "blockish Presbyters" living in "a barbarous nook of Ireland." In 1649 General George Monk, who was in command of the parliamentary forces in Ulster, actually formed a temporary alliance with the Irish rebel chief O'Neill and furnished him with military supplies so that he could keep the field against the royalists and the Presbyterians.

When Cromwell's campaign had reduced Ireland to submission the Ulster Scots were again in jeopardy of deportation, this time not at the hands of the royalists but from the agents of

Parliament. As a part of the Cromwellian settlement it was proposed that the Presbyterians should be cleared out of Down and Antrim, whose proximity to Scotland was thought to make the situation dangerous. What is known as the engagement of 1650, an instrument binding those taking it to support a Government without King or House of Lords, was pressed upon the people of Ulster by military force. The Presbyterian ministers as a class refused to take the engagement, and they were strongly upheld by the people. To break the resistance a plan was formed to transplant the leading Presbyterians in the counties of Down and Antrim to Kilkenny, Tipperary and the seacoast of Waterford, all districts in the extreme south of Ireland, and thus remote from Scotland. A list of 260 persons was made up and a proclamation ordering transplantation was issued on May 23, 1653. This transplantation was part of a general scheme for repeopling the parts of Ireland that had been desolated by the long civil war, and consideration was shown for property rights. The persons transplanted were to be compensated for the estates which they lost, including payment for the crops, and were to be allowed over a year's remission of taxes on lands occupied by them in the districts where they should be settled. It was expressly provided that:

> "The said persons shall and may enjoy the freedom of their religion, and choose their own ministers: provided they shall be such as shall be peaceable minded men toward the authority they live under, and not scandalous: and such ministers shall be allowed a competence for their subsistence, suitable with others in their condition."

This scheme got so far forward that some of the leading men among those proclaimed for deportation visited the south of Ireland to examine the allotted lands, and other steps were taken by the people to make ready for the transplantation. The Scots of Antrim and Down who had successfully held out against the arbitrary power of the King were on the point of succumbing to the arbitrary power of Parliament, when absolutism intervened in the person of Oliver Cromwell to end factious tyranny. In April,

1653, Cromwell turned the Rump Parliament out of doors and that event made an end of the transplantation scheme. The Irish Government continued to be hostile to the Ulster Scots. An entry of February 14, 1656, on the minutes of the Council of State sets forth a scheme of driving out of Ulster and County Louth "all such of the Scottish nation" as bore arms against the Commonwealth in England, Scotland and Ireland, together with all who had arrived in Ulster or County Louth subsequent to June 24, 1650. It was further proposed that "others of the Scottish nation desiring to come into Ireland" should be prohibited from settling in Ulster or County Louth. This scheme of repressing the Scottish occupation of Ulster did not go into effect. It was Cromwell's policy to maintain public order without denominational preference. The Presbyterian ministers of Ulster were no longer vexed by oaths of fidelity or political engagements, and officiated without restraint.

The Cromwellian epoch marks the end of the pioneer period of the Scottish settlement of Ulster. It had survived persecution, massacre and war. It emerged from the years of trial scarred but vigorous, straitened in circumstances but undaunted in temper. Its vitality was promptly exhibited in the rapid growth of its characteristic institution, the Presbyterian Church, in the seven years of mild political climate that now ensued. Reid says:

> "It was during this period that Presbyterianism struck its roots so deeply and extremely throughout the province, as to enable it to endure in safety the subsequent storms of persecution, and to stand erect and flourishing, while all the other contemporary scions of dissent were broken down and prostrated in the dust. In the year 1653, the church possessed scarcely more than the half dozen of ministers who had ventured to remain in the country; now, however [that is in 1660], she was served by not less than seventy ministers regularly and permanently settled, and having under their charge nearly eighty parishes or congregations, comprising a population of probably not far from one hundred thousand souls."

This period may be taken as that in which the Scotch-Irish

type of character was definitely fixed. The Cromwellian settlement marks the end of the old era and the beginning of a new era, with its own social and economic base distinct from the foundations previously existing. Old Ireland had been a pastoral country and a meat diet predominated. At the close of the civil war meat had to be imported. During this period the potato rose to the prominence in Ireland that it has since preserved as a staple foodstuff. Not long after the civil war, Sir William Petty, a statistician of the period, found that the people were living on potatoes, their practice being to dig out the tubers just as they were wanted. That is to say, potatoes were a concealed crop to which the people could resort, although grain might be easily cut or burned by enemies and cattle still more easily driven off.

The potato crop seems to have been the mainstay of the people against the famine that followed the civil war and, accompanied by an outbreak of plague, increased the desolation caused by war. According to Petty, out of a population of 1,446,000, 616,000 had in eleven years perished by the sword, by famine or by plague. According to this estimate 504,000 of those who perished were Irish, and 112,000 were of English extraction. According to some calculations the number of victims was even greater, but Petty's estimates are generally regarded as the most trustworthy. Moreover, there were extensive deportations of native Irish to the West Indies and great numbers went into European exile. It is estimated that from 30,000 to 40,000 men left the country to enlist in foreign service. The details of this tremendous social revolution do not come within the province of this work. Probably the most dispassionate and trustworthy account is that given by Lecky in the sixth volume of his *England in the Eighteenth Century*. But from what has been stated it will readily be inferred that the tribal organization of society that had heretofore shown such tenacious vitality was destroyed root and branch. According to Petty about two-thirds of the good land had been possessed by Catholics before 1641; in 1660, more than two-thirds had passed into the possession of the Protestants. The mass of the people had been converted from clansmen into a tenant peasantry.

The Ulster breed was formed during these terrible vicissitudes of Irish history. It had still to pass through severe trials, but the permanence of the type was now secure. An amusing instance of the thoroughness with which Ulster had been Scotticized is supplied by a document in the Irish State Papers for 1660, entitled "A Short Memorandum What is to be Looked unto in the North of Ireland." The writer says that "There are 40,000 Irish and 80,000 Scots in Ulster ready to bear arms, and not above 5,000 English in the whole province besides the army." It is suggested that the Scotch should be made to wear hats instead of bonnets, which the writer calculates would remove from Scotland to Ireland a trade of about £10,000 a year. Moreover, the change would help the English "who in all fairs and markets see a hundred bonnets worn for one hat, which is a great prejudice and doth wholly dishearten the English there and those who would come out of England."

The Presbyterian Church of Ulster was the first to suffer from the proceedings against nonconformity after the restoration of Charles II. to the throne. In 1661 sixty-one Presbyterian ministers of Ulster were ejected from their benefices, and it was not until the following year that the non-conforming ministers of England and Scotland were ejected. But the Ulster Presbyterians were not called upon to endure such severe persecution as befell non-conformists in England and Scotland. As a general thing the ministers were able to keep on officiating although shut out of parish endowments. Ormonde, then head of the Irish Administration, was disposed to be indulgent. Reid remarks: "On the whole, the general mildness of his administration, which continued during seven years, presented a remarkable contrast to the unprecedented severity with which the non-conformists and Presbyterians were treated at this period both in England and in Scotland."

The most famous chapter of Ulster history was that which opened with the English revolution of 1688 and the Catholic rising in Ireland in support of James II. The Ulster Presbyterians were prompt to declare their allegiance to William and Mary, and the

Presbyterian ministers took the lead in organizing the people for defense against the adherents of James. Ireland, outside of Ulster, was in the hands of Tyrconnel, the deputy of James, and Tyrconnel moved promptly to reduce Ulster to submission. But the invaders were decisively repelled at Enniskillen in the west of Ulster and at Londonderry in the north. Londonderry successfully resisted attack for 105 days. The siege supplied a theme admirably suited to Macaulay's powers as a literary artist and the account he has given in his *History of England* is a masterpiece of scenic writing.

The war ended in 1691 with the complete overthrow of the Jacobite interest and the entire submission of Ireland to William and Mary. Fresh confiscations of land followed together with the exile of many thousands of native Irish. The famous Irish brigade of Louis XIV. of France dates from this period, and it was kept up by a stream of recruits from Ireland. With the opening of the eighteenth century Protestant ascendance was securely established in Ireland, and yet it was during the period now begun that the causes that promoted Ulster emigration became powerful and influential. These will be dealt with in the next chapter, but before leaving the formative period of Ulster it should be observed that its history is not seen in its proper setting unless it is viewed as an episode in the wars of religion. The Scotch settlement of Ulster began before the Thirty Years' War in Germany (1618–1648). Dreadful as were the sufferings of Ireland, they were on a smaller scale than the misery and depopulation of Germany; and Germany was far more advanced than Ireland in civilization when the war began. The Peace of Westphalia was a political reorganization from which the Europe of today takes its start, and prior events now possess only an antiquarian interest. But Ulster history is unbroken in its continuity and it has transmitted to our own times feelings, interests, prepossessions and antipathies derived from the sixteenth century. This has tended to obscure appreciation of the work accomplished in the Scotch settlement of Ulster. It is still too much involved in political controversy to obtain fair treatment, consideration of the theme being marred by prejudice for or against the actors in events. The ardent partisanship that is apt to characterize treatises upon Irish history is in marked contrast with the scientific detachment that marks historical works dealing with the contemporaneous periods of European history.

An incident of this continuity of Ulster history is the constancy of the Ulster type. Scotch-Irish character has such depth of root and the growth has been so durable that its fibre is singularly hard and strong and it retains this nature wherever it is planted. The specific qualities of the breed cannot be accounted for unless the influence of the Presbyterian discipline is taken into consideration. Influence of this order has become so lax in our own times that no idea of its original stringency can be obtained unless the nature of church government during the formative period is considered.

The essential principle of government is the subordination of the individual to the community. That principle was not abandoned by the Presbyterian reformers in their revolt against the Established Church. They did not conceive of liberty as the absence of restraint but as a state of order repressing brute propensity and developing the moral sanctions that distinguish human life from animal existence. That state of order the Church should institute and the State should protect. This principle they applied by a discipline which enfolded individual life and subjected it to guidance and control. In describing social conditions in Ulster while the Plantation was in the making, it has been mentioned that public penitence was exacted of evil doers. The affairs of each congregation were presided over by the session composed of the minister and the elders and deacons representing the congregation. This body took jurisdiction of the morals of the members of the congregation, and inflicted penalties for misconduct. The rules of the Session of Templepatrick adopted in 1646 provided:

> "That all complaints come into the Session by way of bill: the complaintive is to put one shilling with his bill, and if he proves not his point, his shilling forfeits to the session book. This is done to prevent groundless scandal.

"That all beer sellers that sell best beer, especially in the night time, till people be drunk, shall be censured.

"That if parents let their children vague or play on the Lord's Day, they shall be censured as profaners of the Sabbath.

"All persons standing in the public place of repentance, shall pay the church officer one groat.

"That no children be baptized till the parents who present them come to some of the elders and get their children's names registered, that the elders may testify of them to the minister."

The character of the penalties imposed in the exercise of this jurisdiction will appear from the following record:

"That John Cowan shall stand opposite the pulpit, and confess his sin, in the face of the public, of beating his wife on the Lord's Day."

The rule respecting baptism looks to securing the publicity of that rite. The early Presbyterian ministers strongly condemned the administering of baptism or marriage in private. An overture considered by the Ulster synod at its meeting in Belfast, June 17, 1712, sets forth that "the ancient and laudable custom of publishing Marriage-Banns three several days of publick worship, whereof two at least shall be Lord's days, ought to be carefully observed." Any minister marrying persons without the consent of their parents or guardians was to be suspended from office for six months and "afterward to make a full and ingenuous confession of his sin, and express unfeigned repentance for the same before his Presbytery."

The ministers themselves were subject to strict supervision, for which purpose there was a process known as "privy censures" following a custom that formed part of the Presbyterian discipline in Scotland and France. The form of procedure is thus described:

"In every Presbytery, at least twice a year, on days for prayer, as should be dune in sessions likeways, there ought to be privy censures, whereby each minister is removed by course, and then enquiry is made at the pastors and elders, if there be any known scandal, fault, or negligence in him, that it may be in a brotherly manner censured; after the ministers, the Presbytery clerk is to pass these censures likeways."

Reid, writing in 1837, remarks that these censures "were laid aside at the general relaxation of discipline in the last century but they ought to be revived." In the early days the authority claimed by the church was freely and vigorously exercised, and its discipline was a school of morals for the people that made a deep and permanent impress upon the character of the Scotch-Irish—a term, which by the way, they were slow to accept. They used to describe themselves as of "the Scottish nation in the North of Ireland," and they resented the adjunct appellation "Irish" as an abatement of their proper nationality. But common usage gradually overcame the early antipathy.

From this training school came the stream of American immigration that has been so distinctive an ingredient of American society and so potent in its influence upon American history. The diffusion of the Scotch-Irish breed in the United States will occupy the remainder of this work. But before leaving Ulster, completeness of treatment requires the statement that in Ulster it is not only the Presbyterian Church that affords a signal instance of the value of institutional order in perpetuating national life. The case of the native Irish is even more significant. Nothing more strongly attests the institutional efficiency of the Catholic Counter-Reformation than the way in which the wasted and impoverished native Irish were sustained and recuperated by their church. The work was carried on under a heavy ban of law backed up by extremely severe penalties, but there seems to have been no lack of missionaries willing to meet all hazards. In 1747 the Primate of the Established Church of Ireland estimated that there were more than 3,000 Roman Catholic priests in the country while the Established Church had incumbents and curates to the number only of about 800. At the present time Ulster itself is more Catholic than Presbyterian, the Roman Catholics numbering 44 per cent., the Presbyterians 27 and the Episcopalians 23. In

Ireland as a whole these three bodies have respectively 74, 10 and 13 per cent. of the population. While Catholic discipline must be acknowledged to be the main factor in producing this result, yet a powerful accessory has been the drain of Protestantism from the country through the effect of the legislation of the eighteenth century, and of this drain the most important part was the Ulster emigration now to be considered.

CHRONOLOGY

The period covered by this chapter was marked by such sharp vicissitudes of government that the following chronology may be of service in enabling readers to keep track of events:

1625   Accession of Charles I.
1633   Wentworth is appointed Lord Deputy.
1636   Introduction of linen manufacture.
1640   Wentworth created Earl of Strafford.
        The Long Parliament opens.
        Impeachment of Strafford.
1641   Execution of Strafford.
        Rising and massacres in Ulster.
1642   Civil War begins in England
        Parliamentarians, Royalists and Catholic Confederates, each struggling for ascendancy in Ireland.
1644   Ormonde, Lord Lieutenant.
1645   Battle of Naseby in England.
1646   Charles surrenders to the Scots.
1647   Presbyterianism established in England.
        The King seized at Holmby.
1648   Scottish army invades England and is defeated at Preston and Wigan.
        Col. Pride expels the Presbyterian majority from the House of Commons.
1649   Execution of King Charles.
        The Commonwealth proclaimed.
        Cromwell arrives in Ireland.

1650   Cromwell returns to England.
1652   Act for the settlement of Ireland.
1653   Cromwell expels the Rump Parliament and establishes the Protectorate.
1654   The first Protectorate Parliament. Thirty members sit representing Ireland.
        The Cromwellian settlement of Ireland.
1656   Henry Cromwell, Lord Lieutenant of Ireland.
1658   Death of Cromwell.
1659   Monk marches from Scotland.
1660   He declares for a "free Parliament."
        The Restoration. Charles II. seated on the throne of England.
1662   Act of Uniformity.
1663   Ireland excluded from the Navigation Act.
1664   The Conventicle Act.
1666   Prohibition of export to England of Irish cattle and provisions.
1685   Accession of James II.
1688   William lands at Torbay.
        Flight of James.
        Closing of the gates of Derry and Enniskillen.
1689   Siege of Derry and Enniskillen.
1690   Battle of Boyne.
1691   William III. seated on the throne.
1696   Navigation Act unfavorable to Ireland.
1699   English Act prohibiting export of Irish wool.
        Irish Parliament lays prohibitive export duties on wool.
1702   Accession of Anne.
1704   Penal Act against Roman Catholics, with a test clause excluding Presbyterians from public office.
1711   Persecution of the Presbyterians.
1714   Accession of George I.
1725   Potato famine.
1727   Accession of George II.

1740–1741   Famine years in Ireland.
1760   Accession of George III.
1761   Agrarian disturbances in the North of Ireland.
1765   Passage of the Stamp Act for American Colonies.
1771   Decline of linen manufacture.
         Extensive emigration to America from Ulster.
1776   American Declaration of Independence.

CHAPTER V

Emigration to America

The beginnings of the Ulster Plantation coincided with the beginnings of the American plantation, so that migration across the Atlantic was from the first a known recourse if conditions in Ulster became too hard. When the Presbyterian ministers in Ulster began to suffer from Strafford's vigorous measures against nonconformity a start was made that but for a mischance might have set in motion at that early period the stream of Scotch-Irish emigration to America. In 1635 work was begun on the building of a ship of 115 tons burden at Groomsport, on Belfast lough. The ship was called the Eagle Wing in allusion to the text, Exodus XIX., 4: "I bare you on eagles' wings, and brought you unto myself." A number of Presbyterian ministers, among them Livingston and Blair, were interested in this enterprise. On September 9, 1636, a company of 140 persons set sail for New England, the number being increased on the voyage by the birth of a child who named Seaborn. After some hindrance at the start, the ship had fair weather until more than half the distance had been traversed when severe storms were encountered and the ship became leaky, so that it was decided to put back to Ireland.

In reading the account of this voyage as given in the *Life of Robert Blair* by his son-in-law one gets the impression that signs and omens had more to do with the failure than the weather. The account says that when the storm struck the vessel they were "nearer the bank of Newfoundland than any part of Europe." The decision to return was reached after "Mr. Livingston proposed an overture," which was that if in twenty hours the Lord "were pleased to calm the storm and send a fair wind, they might take it for an approbation of their advancing, otherwise they should return." But the storm grew worse, and the matter was then put to Mr. Blair to decide, whereupon he did "fall into a fit of fainting or a kind of swarf [Scot for swoon], but shortly recovering, he was determined to be of their mind." They made their way without further mishap, arriving on November 3 in the harbor whence they had started. Mr. Blair took the affair as a sign against emigration to America, "seeing the Lord, by such speaking providences and dispensations, had made it evident to them that it was not His will they should glorify Him in America, He having work for them at home." What troubled them most about the affair was that "they were like to be signs and wonders, and a very mockery to the wicked, who did laugh and flout at their enterprise."

There is remarkably little of organized exodus on religious grounds from Ulster. There were times when it seemed that one was about to take place, but before it actually started conditions were relieved sufficiently to cause action to be deferred. Instead of seeking refuge in far places the habitual inclination of the Presbyterians of Ulster was to stand their ground and abide results in common with the Presbyterians of Scotland. The Ulster settlers regarded themselves as being Scotch Presbyterians just as much as though resident in Scotland. The short sea-ferry between the two countries made intercourse easy and there was close ecclesiastical fellowship. Scotland was a regular source of ministerial supply to Ulster and Presbyterian ministers harassed in Ulster could count upon welcome and favor in Scotland. Among the Independent sects ecclesiastical influence could readily tend to emigration by groups and companies, but among the Ulster Presbyterians it tended to knit the community together and to hold them to their place.

Ulster emigration upon any important scale is to be attributed to economic and not to religious causes. While the conditions were taking form that eventually produced a great migration of Ulster Scots, facilities of transportation were developed that familiarized the people with the possibilities of emigration and acquainted them with the means. After the first difficulties of planting colonies in America had been overcome and the settlements had taken root, popular appreciation of the New World as the land of opportunity spread rapidly. The State Papers of so early a date as

1649 contain a petition from Captain John Bayley setting forth that he has a scheme for ship building in Ireland, in connection wherewith he will be able to plant in Virginia "100 poor people yearly with all necessary provisions." He says he has already done much work in explaining the scheme and interesting people in it, and asks permission to collect funds for it in all parishes of England and Ireland.

The first notice in the State Papers of any considerable emigration from Ulster to America appears in May, 1656. A letter written from Lisnegarvy says: "We are very full of soldiers come from all parts to ship at Carrickfergus and where eight or ten are appointed out of a company commonly three times as many are offering and desiring to go." The soldiers referred to presumably belonged to the Cromwellian army in Ireland which the Government was endeavoring to disband. Land in Ireland was offered to them but they showed no disposition to settle on it, though it appears from the letter quoted that a chance to get to America was eagerly seized. But emigration of this character could not be properly described as a movement of Ulster Scots. The true beginning of that probably took place in connection with the growth of the trade between Scotland and America, in which Ulster naturally participated. Scotch mercantile enterprise which had long been noted for its bold activity and wide range was not likely to neglect such a promising field as America, and there are many indications that a brisk trade between Scotland, America and the West Indies was established the latter half of the seventeenth century. The English State Papers record urgent complaints from English merchants that Scotch ships were spoiling their trade with the American plantations.

In 1695 Edward Randolph, a Maryland official, recommended that in order to check Scotch trade the three lower counties of Delaware should be annexed to Maryland, West Jersey to Pennsylvania, East Jersey to New York and Rhode Island to Massachusetts. The obnoxious trade must have been going on a long time before it could have acquired such extent and importance as to provoke such sweeping measures. Scotch predilection for American adventure was strikingly illustrated by the unfortunate Darien expedition of 1698. Three quarters of a million sterling were subscribed with the idea of establishing a New Caledonia on the Isthmus of Darien. Fleets carrying first 1,200 men and later 1,500 men were sent out to occupy the country, the result being disastrous failure and complete abandonment.

The first distinctively Scotch-Irish settlements known to have taken place in America were on the Eastern Shore of Maryland. That colony, granted to Lord Baltimore in 1632, was prior to that time chiefly known for its trade in beaver skins obtained from the Indians. St. Mary's, the first capital of Maryland, was located on the site of a trading post. Religious toleration was one of the inducements to settlers offered by the Proprietors. It was hoped by this means that people would be attracted from other colonies as well as from Europe. In 1643 Lord Baltimore wrote to Captain Gibbons of Boston describing the land grants Maryland was offering to settlers, "with free liberty of religion."

The records are silent as to when and how the Scotch-Irish entered Maryland but it was a natural consequence of the large inducements which the Maryland Proprietary was offering to settlers. In 1648, when commissioning William Stone as Governor of Maryland, Lord Baltimore set forth that Stone "hath undertaken in some short time to procure five hundred people of British or Irish descent to come from other places and plant and reside within our said province of Maryland for the advancement of our colony there." Stone, a Protestant, who had himself come into Maryland from the Eastern Shore of Virginia, is known to have promoted a Puritan emigration from that section into Maryland. In 1649 Lord Baltimore offered 3,000 acres of land for every thirty persons brought in by any adventurer or planter. The influx of settlers that resulted from such measures is doubtless accountable for the beginnings of Scotch-Irish settlement in Maryland. The known facts all harmonize with this supposition. The earliest notice of an American minister from Ireland appears in a letter of

April 13, 1669, from Matthew Hill, an English non-conformist minister, to Richard Baxter, on whose advice Hill had gone to Maryland. Describing the situation in Maryland, Hill remarked: "We have many also of the reformed religion who have a long time lived as sheep without a shepherd, though last year brought in a young man from Ireland who hath already had good success in his work."

The Irish minister thus referred to has never been identified. Dr. Briggs in his *American Presbyterianism* thinks he may have been one of those driven into exile from Ireland by the persecutions beginning in 1663. This is quite likely but the fact cannot be established. The first Presbyterian minister of whom there is certain knowledge was William Traill, who, in 1672, was ordained pastor of the Presbyterian congregation at Lifford, in the Presbytery of Laggan, Ireland. He was clerk of the Presbytery and was one of five ministers prosecuted in 1681 for observing a special fast appointed by the Presbytery. The ministers were sentenced to pay a fine of twenty pounds each and on their refusal were sentenced to prison. Reid says: "They were confined in Lifford, though not very rigorously, for above eight months, when they were released by the sheriff, and their fines afterward remitted by the court of exchequer on payment of their fees." It is probable that upon his release from prison in 1682 Traill went directly to Maryland where he knew he would be among friends. The records of Somerset county, Maryland, show that he acquired 133 acres on the Pocomoke River near Rehoboth on May 8, 1686, and it is probable that he was the founder of the Presbyterian Church at Rehoboth. He was evidently held in marked esteem as he received bequests from John White in 1685 and from John Shipway in 1687. In November, 1689, he was one of the signers of a petition to William and Mary asking "protection in securing our religion, lives and liberty under Protestant Governors." Somerset County records show that in February, 1690, he gave a friend a power of attorney to convey land, which was doubtless done as an incident of his return to Scotland, where on September 17, 1690, he became pastor of the church of Borthwick, near Edinburgh.

It is highly probable that Thomas Wilson, another minister known to have been in Somerset County at this period, was also from the Laggan Presbytery. The Presbytery records have several entries in regard to Thomas Wilson between 1674 and 1678. It appears that he was pastor of Killybegs, a parish on the western coast of Donegal, where he was having great difficulty in getting a living. An entry of July 3, 1678, notes that Killybegs has paid him only twelve pounds a year for the past two years, with no prospects of improvement. From 1681 to 1691 there is a blank in the Presbytery minutes, but when they resume there is no further mention of Killybegs or Wilson. But a Thomas Wilson appears in the Maryland land records as acquiring from Colonel William Stevens on May 20, 1681, a parcel of land called Darby, containing 350 acres. He was the first pastor of the Presbyterian Church at Manokin, and as its pastor is mentioned in the will of John Galbraith, 1691, and the will of David Brown, 1697.

Samuel Davis, another Maryland minister at this period, is supposed to be an Irishman, as it seems probable that he is meant by a reference made in 1706 to "an Irish Presbyterian" who preached in Delaware for some years. A "Samuel Davies," who was residing in Somerset County in 1678, may have been the same person. In 1684 a marriage was celebrated by the Rev. Samuel Davies in Somerset County, and in September of that year he received from Colonel Stevens a warrant to have laid out a tract of 500 acres upon St. Martin's Creek, southeast side of the Pocomoke River. He was pastor of the Presbyterian Church at Snow Hill in 1691, remaining there until 1698 when he removed to Hoarkill, now Lewes, Delaware, where he resided and preached for a number of years.

The Colonel Stevens who appears in the records as a conveyer of land to the early Presbyterian ministers of the Eastern Shore of Maryland seems to have been active in promoting immigration in pursuance of Lord Baltimore's policy. He was one of the earliest settlers in Somerset County, and was for 22 years a judge of the county court. In 1684 he was appointed by Lord Baltimore Deputy Lieutenant for the province. He died on his plantation near Rehoboth December 23, 1687, aged 57 years. The interest he took in procuring Ulster ministers for the Eastern Shore of Maryland indicates the existence of Scotch-Irish settlements there. An entry of December 29, 1680, on the minutes of the Laggan Presbytery says:

> "Collonell Stevens from Maryland beside Virginia, his desire of a godly minister is presented to us, the meeting will consider it seriously and do what they can in it. Mr. John Hoart is to write to Mr. Keip about this and Mr. Robert Rule to the meetings of Route and Tyrone, and Mr. William Traill to the meetings of Down and Antrim."

No action in response to this application is recorded, the minutes discontinuing in 1681 and not resuming until 1690. But the removal of Traill to Maryland, and the subsequent removal of Makemie is doubtless to be ascribed to this call. Francis Makemie, famous as a pioneer organizer of the Presbyterian Church in America, was born near Ramelton, Ireland, and was educated at the University of Glasgow. When the letter from Colonel Stevens arrived, Makemie had been for some time preparing for the ministry under the supervision of Laggan Presbytery. The minutes for 1681 note that he submitted a homily which was approved, and presumably he was licensed soon thereafter. Owing to the discontinuance of the minutes there is no official record of the date, but it must have been prior to April 2, 1682, as it is known that on that date he preached at Burt, Ireland. He is next heard of in Maryland, whither he went probably in 1683. He did not settle permanently for some years, but carried on an itinerant ministry in Maryland, Virginia and the Barbadoes. A letter of July 22, 1684, mentions that he was then on the Elizabeth River, Virginia (near the present site of Norfolk), ministering to a congregation "who had a dissenting minister formerly from Ireland until the Lord was pleased to remove him by death in August last." The name of this Irish minister has not been discovered, and no reference to him has been found other than that made by Makemie.

Reid says that during 1684 the greater part of the ministers composing the Presbytery of Laggan intimated their intention of removing to America "because of persecutions and general poverty abounding in those parts, and on account of their straits and little or no access to their ministry." But it does not appear that they put that design into effect, for with the death of Charles II. the following year the pressure relaxed. The persecutions to which the Ulster Presbyterians were exposed were less severe than those from which the Scotch Presbyterians were then suffering. There can be no doubt that the religious motive was an important factor in Scotch emigration at this period. In 1684 and 1685 bodies of Scotch people fleeing from persecution landed in East Jersey. George Scot, Laird of Pitlochie, who was active in the movement, gave as his reason for the enterprise that "there are several people in this kingdom, who, upon account of their not going that length in conformity required of them by the law, do live very uneasy; who, beside the other agreeable accommodations of that place may there freely enjoy their own principles without hazard or trouble." In a volume which he published in Edinburgh describing conditions and opportunities in East Jersey, he made this mention of the Scotch-Irish in Maryland:

> "I had an account lately from an acquaintance of mine, that the Province of Ulster, where most of our nation are seated, could spare forty thousand men and women to an American plantation, and be sufficiently peopled itself. The gentleman who gave me this information is since settled in Maryland; the account he sends of that country is so encouraging that I hear a great many of his acquaintances are making for that voyage."

It is evident from this that there was a particularly close connection between Ulster and the Chesapeake Bay settlements at this period. Additional evidence of this is furnished by the fact that the congregation on Elizabeth River, Virginia, to which Makemie ministered for a time, obtained his successor from the bounds of Laggan Presbytery. He was Josias McKee, son of Patrick McKee, of

St. Johnstone, County Donegal. He probably began his ministry in 1691 and he continued pastoral work in the Elizabeth River country until his death in November, 1716.

These particulars, which we owe to the minute research made by historians of the American Presbyterian Church, afford conclusive evidence of the existence of distinctively Scotch-Irish settlements on the Eastern Shore of Maryland and Virginia considerably prior to 1680, and probably dating back to the immigration started in 1649. Doubtless, in view of the intimacy between Scotland and Ulster, there was some Ulster ingredient in Scotch trade and Scotch settlements in other American colonies during the seventeenth century but no record has been discovered of distinctively Scotch-Irish settlements at this period except in the Chesapeake Bay region. The records of ministerial supply are of themselves enough to show that the Scotch-Irish community was well established. Moreover, this supposition is confirmed by records preserved in the State Papers. In a report of July 19, 1677, Lord Baltimore gave this account of religious conditions in Maryland:

> "That there are now four ministers of the Church of England residing there who have plantations of their own, and those who have not are maintained by voluntary contributions of their own persuasion, as others are of the Presbyterians, Independents, Anabaptists, Quakers and Romish church. That there are a sufficient number of churches and meeting houses for the people there which are kept in good repair by voluntary contributions… That three-fourths of the inhabitants are Presbyterians, Independents, Anabaptists and Quakers, the rest being of the Church of England and Romish church."

The Presbyterians mentioned as maintaining ministers "of their own persuasion" may be taken to include the Scotch-Irish settlers. A more distinct reference appears in a later report made by Lord Baltimore, which was received by the Board of Trade on March 26, 1678. Replying to interrogatories from the English Government, Lord Baltimore says:

"All the planters in general affect the style of merchants, because they all sell tobacco, and their chief estate is the number of their servants, who serve generally five or six years, and then become planters and call themselves merchants... Can give no probable guess of the number of masters or servants, nor of the number imported for any time, but are generally English and Irish."

We are not left to inference as to whether these "Irish" included Ulster Scots, for some years later we find the same Chesapeake Bay settlements appearing in the State Papers as distinctively Scotch-Irish. In the course of a long report, June 25, 1695, from Sir Thomas Laurence, Secretary of Maryland, the following occurs:

"In the two counties of Dorchester and Somerset, where the Scotch-Irish are most numerous, they almost clothe themselves by their linen and woolen manufactures and plant little tobacco, which learning from one another, they leave off planting. Shipping, therefore, and the bringing in of all manner of English clothing is to be encouraged, and if they be brought in at easy rates, the planter will live comfortably and will be induced to go on planting tobacco."

Laurence says that cotton weaving has begun in Virginia and that some few have begun to grow cotton in Maryland. He suggested that it be taken into consideration "whether an act of Parliament should not be passed to prevent the planting of cotton in these countries." This mention of the Scotch-Irish exhibits them as a community so long established that linen and woolen manufactures had attained considerable development. This circumstance tallies with the fact that so early as 1680 the community was large enough to issue a call for ministerial supply. There is no record of any other Scotch-Irish settlement in America at that time. The most likely place then would have been Massachusetts, but a report of Governor Bradstreet of May 18, 1680, on conditions in that colony says that very few English, Scots, Irish or foreigners had arrived there for seven years; that there were there then about 120 negroes "and it may be as many Scots bought and sold for merchants in the time of the war with Scotland … and about half so many Irish."

᛭ All accessible data indicate that the Chesapeake Bay settlements were the first distinctively Scotch-Irish settlements made in America. But these settlements left in the wake of the tobacco trade do not appear to have been important as a stage in the Scotch-Irish occupation of America. When the emigration from Ulster began on a large scale in the eighteenth century it turned chiefly to Pennsylvania. The Maryland settlements, however, possess much importance in connection with the planting of the Presbyterian Church in this country, as will appear when that branch of the subject comes up for consideration in the course of this history.

The economic conditions that occasioned a genuine exodus from Ulster early in the eighteenth century were the outcome of the narrow views of commercial policy that then inspired governmental action. Colonies and plantations were valued simply as a convenience to home interests and it was considered intolerable that they should develop industries of a competitive character. The anxiety which Sir Thomas Laurence expressed over the linen and woolen manufactures of the Scotch-Irish on the Eastern Shore of Maryland is quite typical. Strafford during his lieutenancy of Ireland showed genuine solicitude for the development of industry and yet his correspondence shows that he held that Irish enterprise in such an important English industry as woolen manufacture was reprehensible. After the Restoration, when Ireland began to recover from the Cromwellian wars, Irish exports of cattle excited the alarm of English landowners who complained that the competition of the Irish pastures was lowering English rents. Laws were accordingly enacted in 1665 and 1680 absolutely prohibiting the importation into England from Ireland of all cattle, sheep and swine, of beef, pork, bacon and mutton and even of butter and cheese.

This attitude was not peculiar to the Government of England but was just as strong in Scotland at that period. The Government of Scotland complained of the effect of English laws on Scottish industry and obtained some concessions, but meanwhile it subjected Ireland to worse treatment than that of which it complained when it was the sufferer. In February, 1667, on the urgent representation of Scottish traders, an embargo was laid on the importation of Irish cattle, salt beef, meal and all kinds of grain; and subsequently horses were added to the list. This embargo was probably more detrimental to Ulster than the English prohibition, and it explains "the general poverty abounding in those parts" mentioned as one of the reasons that in 1684 caused a general disposition toward emigration among the ministers of the Laggan Presbytery. One marked effect of this sort of legislation was to build up a smuggling trade that long abounded in Ulster and on the neighboring coasts of Scotland.

In addition to shutting Irish produce out of English markets, English commercial selfishness was as urgently solicitous that Irish enterprise should not invade the colonies and interfere with English trade there. They were England's colonies and it was held that Ireland had no right to participate in colonial trade. Acts passed in 1663, 1670 and 1696 excluded Irish vessels from the American trade and prohibited any importation directly from the colonies to Ireland. In the presence of such restraints upon the commerce of the country in its natural products, the industrial activity of the people sought an outlet in manufactures. Woolen manufacture, whose beginning in 1636 Strafford had discouraged, now revived. The quality of Irish wool was excellent and the cloth obtained such a reputation that industrial prospects became bright. Although shut out of Scotland, England and America, Ireland might trade with the rest of the world and in that way establish her prosperity. The Irish woolen trade became so important that it attracted capital and manufacturers from Scotland, England and even Continental Europe. But there was an important woolen industry in England whose loud complaints were soon voiced in Parliament. The House of Lords and the House of Commons both made urgent representations to King William that the English woolen manufacture was menaced by the Irish industry.

The memorial of the House of Commons urged William "to enjoin all those you employ in Ireland to make it their care, and use their utmost diligence to hinder the exportation of wool from Ireland, except it be imported hither, and for discouraging the woolen manufacture." The King promised to comply with the request and the Irish Parliament itself was submissive. At a session begun in September, 1698, the Irish House of Commons pledged its hearty endeavors to establish linen and hempen manufacture in Ireland, with the hope that there might be found "such a temperament" in respect to the woolen trade as would prevent it from being injurious to that of England. It then proceeded to impose heavy duties on the export of Irish woolen goods. But even this was not enough to satisfy the English woolen manufacturers. By existing laws Irish woolen manufactures were already excluded from the colonial market, and were virtually excluded from England by prohibitory duties. In 1699 the work of exclusion was completed by a law enacted by the British Parliament prohibiting the Irish from exporting manufactured wool to any other country whatever.

The main industry of Ireland was thus destroyed. Even the promise that encouragement would be shown to other manufactures was only partially and grudgingly fulfilled. It was not until 1705 that, at the urgent petition of the Irish Parliament, the Irish were allowed to export white and brown linens to the British colonies, but checked, striped and dyed linens were absolutely excluded, and no colonial goods could be brought directly to Ireland. Efforts to build up linen manufacture met with opposition in England on the ground that the competition of Irish linen with Dutch linen might hurt the Dutch market for English woolen manufactures, and would therefore be indirectly injurious to England. It was only after a hard struggle that the linen manufacture escaped the fate of the Irish woolen manufacture. Hempen manufacture was discouraged until it ceased. Indeed for a long period no exactions seemed too great to make upon Ireland. There was even agitation in favor of measures to prohibit all fisheries on the Irish shore except with boats built and manned by Englishmen.

After the Revolution of 1688 Scotch migration set strongly toward Ulster. Land was offered on long lease at low rents and for some years a steady stream of Scotch Presbyterians poured into the country. In 1715 Archbishop Synge estimated that not less than 50,000 Scotch families had settled in Ulster since the Revolution. In 1717 and 1718 as the leases began to fall in, the landlords put up the rents double and often treble, and the smaller farms tended to pass from Protestant hands to Catholic tenants who were ready to bid higher terms. And while the tenant farmers were rackrented by their landlords they had to pay tithes for the support of the Established Church whose ministrations they did not desire or receive. Such conditions, introduced at a time when the commercial legislation of England was uprooting Irish industry, created an intolerable situation. Moreover, fresh religious disabilities were put upon the Presbyterians. The penal act of 1704 against the Roman Catholics had a test clause which excluded Presbyterians from all civil and military office. Presbyterian ministers were legally liable to penalties for celebrating marriages, and cases occurred of prosecutions although as a rule the Government was more tolerant than the laws. Entries on the Ulster Synod records show how solicitous the ministers were that none of their communion should provoke the authorities by marrying members of the Established Church.

To escape from such conditions the people began to flee the country in great numbers, often accompanied by ministers. An instance of emigration under pastoral care is supplied by an entry on the records of the General Synod of Ulster, June 15, 1714, which at the same time illustrates the care exercised as to ministerial qualifications in such cases. It appears that John Jarvie had been a probationer under the Presbytery of Down, but had received ordination from the Presbytery of Belfast, and the Synod called for explanations. The Belfast Presbytery replied that:

> "Mr. Jarvie having a great inclination to go to some of the
> Plantations in America, Down Prebry having signified that to the

late Synod of Belfast, and gave a very good character of him—
Mr. John Jarvie bringing testimonies from the Prebry of Down
to the Prebry of Belfast, which was abundantly satisfying—he
readily subjected to the Prebry of Belfast; that Mr. Robert Wilson,
mercht in_Belfast, wrot to Mr. Kirkpatrick, to be comunicate
to the Prebry of Belfast, that there was a ship in the Logh of
Belfast bound for South Carolina; that the seamen and passengers
amount to the number of 70, that it was earnestly desir'd that
they may have a Chaplain on board, and if ordain'd, so much
the better for the voyage, and also for the person to be ordain'd
and the Country whither they are bound."

It was further explained that before ordaining Mr. Jarvie the
Belfast Presbytery had obtained the consent of Down, and examined him "in Extemporary Questions, Cases of Conscience,
Church History, Chronolog: Questions" to all of which he "gave
satisfying answers." Furthermore, Mr. Jarvie "had an '*Exegesis de
Perfectione Scripturae contra Papistes*,' and sustain'd his Thesis, delivered a popular sermon, in all of which he acquit himself with
approbation."

In the spring of 1718 a minister in Ulster writing to a friend
in Scotland said: "There is likely to be a great desolation in the
northern parts of this Kingdom by the removal of several of our
brethren to the American plantations. No less than six ministers
have demitted their congregations, and great numbers of their
people go with them; so that we are daily alarmed with both
ministers and people going off."

The original sympathy between the Puritan settlements in
Ulster and the Puritan settlements in New England naturally
had the effect of directing emigration to New England when
the Scotch-Irish began to remove from Ulster. As in the abortive
attempt of 1635, ministers appear as leaders of the first systematic
movement. The Rev. William Homes, born in 1663 of an old
Ulster family, came over to Martha's Vineyard about 1686, and
obtained a position as a school teacher. He returned to Ireland,
studied for the ministry, and was ordained December 21, 1692,
as pastor of a church at Strabane, in the Presbytery of Convoy. On

September 26, 1693, he married Katherine, daughter of the Rev. Robert Craighead of Londonderry. The Rev. William Homes and his brother-in-law, the Rev. Thomas Craighead, decided to move to New England, and they sailed from Londonderry on the ship Thomas and Jane, arriving in Boston the first week in October, 1714. The settling in New England of these two ministers with extensive family connections in Ulster opened a channel into which immigration soon began to flow.

Homes's eldest son, Robert, born July 23, 1694, in Stragolan, County Fermanagh, became captain of a ship engaged in transporting emigrants to America. He married Mary Franklin of Boston, a sister of Benjamin Franklin. Captain Homes appears to have been the agent by whom people at Strabane, Donoghmore, Donegal and Londonderry were apprised of opportunities of removing to New England. It is recorded that Captain Homes sailed for Ireland April 13, 1718, and his ship returned "full of passengers about the middle of October."

The regular intercourse between Ulster and New England thus established led to movements on a scale approaching the transportation of communities. The congregations in the valley of the Bann became so interested that the Rev. William Boyd, pastor of Macosquin, went to New England as their agent to see what arrangements could be made for settling there in a body. Mr. Boyd was well received and having finished his mission, preached a valedictory sermon, on March 19, 1718. It was published with an introduction by the Rev. Increase Mather in which occurs the following reference to Boyd's mission:

> "Many in that Kingdom [Ireland] having had thoughts of a remove to this part of the World, have considered him as a Person suitably qualified to take a voyage hither, and to make Enquiry what Encouragement or otherwise they might expect in case they should engage in so weighty and hazardous an undertaking as that of Transporting themselves & Families over so vast an Ocean. The issue of this Affair has a great dependence on the conduct of this Worthy Author. The Lord direct him in it."

Boyd brought with him a petition to Governor Shute of New England, certifying that Boyd had been appointed "to assure his Excellency of our sincere and hearty Inclinations to Transport ourselves to that very excellent and renowned Plantation upon our obtaining from his Excellency suitable incourragement." As well as can be made out from the faded writing there were 322 signers of this petition, all but thirteen of them in fair autograph. Only eleven made their marks, a remarkably low percentage of illiteracy. Among the signers were the Rev. James Teatte of Killeshandra, County Cavan; the Rev. Thomas Cobham of Clough, County Antrim; the Rev. Robert Neilson, a superannuated minister, formerly of Kilraughts in the Presbytery of Route; the Rev. William Leech of Ballymena, County Antrim; the Rev. Robert Higginbothan of Coleraine, the Rev. John Porter of Bushmills, the Rev. Henry Neill of Ballyrashane (the last three, all members of the Presbytery of Coleraine); the Rev. Thomas Elder of County Down; the Rev. James Thomson of Ballywillan, near Coleraine. Three of the signers, Samuel Wilson, Alexr. Dunlap and Arch. McCook,—have the degree M.A. appended to their names, which was then often a clerical dignity, but they are not known as belonging to the Presbyterian ministry of Ulster. The ministers who signed the petition have appended to their names the initials V.D.M. a contraction for *Verbi Dei Minister*—Minister of the Word of God. The ministers who signed did not all emigrate. Boyd himself, the agent of the emigrants in obtaining assurances of lands for settlement, remained in Ireland.

Through those various influences there was an active emigration from Ulster to New England, during the period from 1714–1720 inclusive, of which precise details have been obtained by the research of Mr. Charles K. Bolton. The list given by him in his *Scotch-Irish Pioneers in Ulster and America*, shows that five ships arrived in New England from Ireland in 1714, two in 1715, three in 1716, six in 1717, fifteen in 1718, ten in 1719 and thirteen in 1720.

So far as the disposition of the Ulster people was concerned

New England would have been their American home, but their reception and experiences were such that the main stream of Ulster immigration soon turned toward Pennsylvania. The immigration to New England was from the first regarded with anxiety and distrust by the leading people there. In the letters of Thomas Lechmere to John Winthrop at the period there is a mention of Irish immigration in 1718 with the remark: "20 ministers with their congregations in general, will come over in Spring; I wish their comeing so over do not prove fatall in the End." Even such an ally of the Irish as Cotton Mather was apparently not free from anxiety although hopeful of good results and friendly to the movement. In his diary for August 7, 1718, he wrote: "But what shall be done for the great number of people that are transporting themselves thither from ye North of Ireland: Much may be done for ye Kingdom of God in these parts of ye World by this Transportation."

The records of the General Synod of Ulster make frequent references to the departure of ministers for America and to the difficulties experienced in providing subsistence for the ministers who remained. Representations of the necessitous condition of ministers or their widows and children formed a staple topic at meetings of the Synod and the difficulty of raising funds is shown by the frequency with which reiterated appeals are made for help in particular cases. At the meeting of Belfast, June 21, 1720, it was decided that "a moving letter be writ by this Synod" to all the people of the church. The letter approved by the Synod began by saying:

> "Dearly Beloved.
>
> You cannot be Ignorant of the deplorable circumstances that many of our Brethren are in, and how exceedingly deficient that fund which was design'd for their support has prov'd, in so much, that to some scarce can a third part of what was promist be obtain'd. Many of our Congregations who us'd to contribute, are not now in condition to maintain their own Minister, and far less give anything for the relief of others. It is melancholly to

hear that many of our Brethren are wanting ev'n the necessaries of life; others are forc'd to lay down their charge; and others to transport themselves to America. The Credit of the Synod sinks from an inability to perform what they promist; and notwithstanding all the pains that have been taken time after time to get this remedy'd, it grows every year worse and worse."

Many went not only to America but also to the West Indies. Archbishop Boulter, Primate of Ireland, in a letter written in 1728, said:

"Above 4,200 men, women and children, here have been shipped for the West Indies within three years, and 3,100 this last summer… The whole North is in a ferment at present, and people every day engaging one another to go next year to the West Indies. The humor has spread like a contagious disease… The worst is that it affects only Protestants and rages chiefly in the North."

Writing in March, 1729, Archbishop Boulter said further:

"The humor of going to America still continues, and the scarcity of provisions certainly makes many quit us. There are now seven ships at Belfast that are carrying off about 1,000 passengers thither."

The alarm of the authorities over this drain of population caused letters of inquiry to be sent to the Presbyteries as to the causes. The reply of the Presbytery of Tyrone has been preserved. It gives as the chief cause the religious test that excluded Presbyterians from all places of public trust and honor, and then goes on to say:

"The bad seasons for three years past, together with the high price of lands and tythes, have all contributed to the general run to America, and to the ruin of many families, who are daily leaving their houses and lands desolate."

The authorities showed themselves incapable of action going to the root of the trouble. All that seemed to occur to them was to extend the policy of prohibition from the industries of the people to the movements of the people. The records of the English Privy Council contain the following entry of December 4, 1729:

> "Reference to a Committee of a letter from the Lords Justices of Ireland to the Lord Lieutenant, Lord Carteret, dated 23 Nov., with a memorial from several noblemen and gentlemen on behalf of themselves and others of that kingdom, relating to the Great Numbers of Protestant Subjects who have lately transported themselves from the North of Ireland to the Plantations on the Continent of America, and that Twenty Thousand have declared their Intentions of transporting themselves the ensuing Spring to the great prejudice of the Linnen Manufacture, and lessening the Protestant Interest in those parts, and also relating to the great Quantities of Corn which have been lately bought up for Exportation to Foreign ports, and proposing the issuing of Proclamations to restrain the Exportation of Corn, and to prohibit the Subjects leaving the Kingdom. And likewise to prohibit the carrying Money or Bullion out of the Kingdom."

Some particulars of the way in which emigration was obstructed are given in a letter, written some time in 1736, preserved among the Penn manuscripts of the Historical Society of Pennsylvania. The writer, John Stewart, a sea captain, says:

> "As you are the Proprietor of Pennsylvania, and being informed of your being in London, I would beg liberty to inform your Worship of some of the difficulties of the poor people who are flying from the oppression of landlords, and tithes, (as they term it) to several parts of America, viz:—When last our Irish Parliament was sitting, there was a bill brought in respecting the transportation of America; which made it next to a prohibition. The said bill greatly alarmed the people, especially in the North of Ireland, and lest a second should succeed, greater numbers than usual made ready. But when said landlords found it so, they fell on with other means by distressing the owners and masters of the ships, there being now ten in the harbor of Belfast. The method they fell in with, first, was that when any of said ships advertised that they were bound for such a port, and when they

would be in readiness to sail, and their willingness to agree with the passengers for which, and no other reasons, they issued out their warrants and had several of said owners and masters apprehended and likewise the printers of said advertisements, and bound in bonds of a thousand pounds, to appear at Carrickfergus assizes, or thrown into a loathsome gaol, and for no other reason, than encouraging his Majesty's subjects, as they were pleased to call their indictment, from one plantation to another. But even after all this, when the assizes came on, they were afraid of their enlargement, and begged very earnestly of the judges to have them continued upon their recognizances, the consequence of which may easily be seen. Most of said ships being strangers, this would have effectually ruined them. But the Judge was pleased to discharge them. Nay one of the Justices got up in court and swore by God, if any came to Lisburn the town in which he lived, to publish an advertisement he would whip him through the town. To which the Judge very mildly replied, to consider if they deserved it and if he whipped any person, to do it according to law. Money had been offered by some of them to swear against some of said ships and rewards actually given, but yet a more hellish contrivance has been thought of and is put in practice by the Collector George Macartney of Belfast. He will not now, when said ships and passengers were just ready to sail, so much as allow the poor people to carry their old bedclothes with them, although ever so old, under pretence of an Act of the British Parliament."

Captain Stewart goes on to say that an appeal had been made to higher authority but meanwhile ten ships are detained and more than seventeen hundred people are in distress.

Such an attitude of mind only gave additional impetus to emigration. The authorities might harass but could not prohibit the movement of people, for nothing short of measures reducing them to the condition of serfs bound to the soil would have been sufficient to stay the exodus. A marked increase above the ordinary volume occurred from time to time owing to bad harvests and acute industrial distress. The famine years of 1740 and 1741 gave a great impetus to the movement. It is estimated that for several years the emigrants from Ulster annually amounted to 12,000. After the first run to New England the main stream of Scotch-Irish emigration set toward Pennsylvania, a destination frequently mentioned in the reports made to the Ulster Synod of ministers demitted. Edmund Burke, in his *Account of the European Settlements in America* published in 1761, says:

> "And as for the province ... there is no part of British America in a more growing condition. In some years more people have transported themselves into Pennsylvania, than into all the other settlements together. In 1729, 6,208 persons came to settle here as passengers or servants, four-fifths of whom at least were from Ireland."

Burke further mentions Pennsylvania as the center from which Scotch-Irish occupation of America proceeded. He says:

> "The number of white people in Virginia is between sixty and seventy thousand; and they are growing every day more numerous by the migration of the Irish, who, not succeeding so well in Pennsylvania as the more frugal and industrious Germans, sell their lands in that province to the latter, and take up new ground in the remote counties in Virginia, Maryland and North Carolina. These are chiefly Presbyterians from the northern part of Ireland, who in America are generally called Scotch-Irish."

Holmes's *American Annals*, a collection of historical data, first published in 1829, repeatedly mentions the large immigration from the North of Ireland. The annalist notes that in 1729 there arrived in Pennsylvania from Europe 6,208 persons with the purpose of settling in America. Of these 1,155 were designated as "Irish passengers and servants," and it was further stated that there "arrived at New Castle government alone passengers and servants chiefly from Ireland about 4,500."

Among the entries in the Annals for 1737 is the following:

> "About this time multitudes of laborers and husbandmen in Ireland oppressed by landlords and bishops, and unable to

procure a comfortable subsistence for their families embarked for Carolina. The first colony of Irish people, receiving a grant of land near Santee River, formed a settlement, which was called Williamsburgh township."

Among the events of 1764 it is noted that "besides foreign Protestants, several persons emmigrated from England and Scotland, and great multitudes from Ireland, and settled in Carolina." Two townships, each containing 48,000 acres, had been laid out for occupancy by settlers, one named Mecklenburg, the other Londonderry.

Among the events of 1773 it is noted that "there were large migrations from Ireland and other parts of Europe to America." In the first fortnight of August 3,500 passengers arrived in Pennsylvania from Ireland. In the same month 500 arrived in North Carolina from Ireland. In September a brig arrived at Charleston from Ireland, with above 120 settlers. A sad reminder of the risk of sea travel in that period is contained in the announcement that a Scotch brig that brought 200 passengers to New York lost about 100 on the passage. Although those immigrants from Ireland are not designated as Scotch-Irish there can be no doubt that generally they came from Ulster.

In 1760 the exodus to America seems to have almost ceased. The author of an *Essay on the Ancient and Modern State of Ireland* written in that year remarks that in the region of George II.:

> "the North of Ireland began to wear an aspect entirely new; and, from being (through want of industry, business and tillage) the almost exhausted nursery of our American plantations, soon became a populous scene of improvement, traffic, wealth and plenty, and is at this day a well planted district, considerable for numbers of well affected useful and industrious subjects."

In less than a decade distress and discontent were again general and emigration to America was resumed on a large scale. A note to Killen's *History of the Presbyterian Church in Ireland* computes that in 1773 and the five preceding years the North of Ireland was "drained of one-fourth of its trading cash, and of a like proportion of the manufacturing people." Killen remarks:

> "Not a few of the Presbyterian ministers of the northern province had now to struggle against the discouragements of a slender and decreasing maintenance. Some of the members of the Synod of Ulster resigned their pastoral charges, and joined the stream of emigration to America."

The movement was greatly stimulated by the decadence of linen manufacture which set in about 1771. The principal cause assigned for it was the interruption of commerce due to the disturbed relations with the American colonies. Investigation by a Committee of the House of Commons in 1774 brought out official statements that one-third of all the weavers had been thrown out of work and that not less than 10,000 had within the last two or three years emigrated to America.

Arthur Young, the shrewdest observer of agricultural conditions at that period, made his *Tour in Ireland* in the years 1776 to 1779. He was in Belfast in July, 1776, and he notes that for many years emigration from that port was at the rate of about 2,000 annually. In 1772 the decline of the linen manufacture caused an increase which brought the number up to 4,000 in 1773, but in 1775 emigration ceased. In Derry he noted that "the emigrations were very great from hence, of both idle and industrious, and carried large sums with them." At Lurgan he was informed that "if the war ends in favor of the Americans, they will go off in shoals." Young notes that in 1760 the shipping of Derry consisted of sixty-seven sail, from thirty to three hundred and fifty tons. For eighteen to twenty years the emigrants numbered 2,400 annually.

As a result of his investigations Young concluded that emigration was closely connected with the vicissitudes of the linen trade. He says that for forty years "the passenger trade had been a regular branch of commerce, which employed several ships and consisted in carrying people to America... When the linen trade was low the passenger trade was always high." Young remarks that

the ordinary recourse of factory hands thrown out of employment
is to enlist, but in the North of Ireland the linen manufacture
"is not confined, as it ought to be, to towns, but spreads into all
the cabins of the country. Being half farmers, half manufacturers, they have too much property in cattle, etc., to enlist when
idle; if they convert it into cash it will enable them to pay their
passage to America, an alternative always chosen in preference to
the military life."

As a result of his inquiry Young concluded:

> "The spirit of emigration in Ireland appears to be confined
> to two circumstances, the Presbyterian religion, and the linen
> manufacture. I heard of very few emigrants except among man-
> ufacturers of that persuasion. The Catholicks never went; they
> seemed not only tied to the country but almost to the parish in
> which their masters lived."

Young, although an unsympathetic was an acute observer, and
he pointed out unsparingly the evil nature of England's commercial policy. He drily observed that "emigration should not,
therefore, be condemned in States so ill governed as to possess
many people willing to work, but without employment."

Young's range of vision did not extend beyond economic factors. There are unmistakable indications that apart from the decay
of the linen industry, motive for emigration was supplied by the
spirit of social revolt then prevalent. Intercourse with America had
become so close and knowledge of conditions there had become
so general that the whole attitude of popular thought on political
and social arrangements had been affected. A spirit was abroad
that made the old grievances of rackrents and tithe payments seem
more odious and intolerable. There were agrarian disturbances
that were repressed with severity, but whose effect in promoting
emigration could not be repressed. In the years preceding the
American Revolution a wave of discontent with existing conditions swept over not only Ireland but Scotland as well. At this
period there was a great migration to America from the western
islands and the Highlands of Scotland. Dr. Samuel Johnson's tour

to the Hebrides under the guidance of Boswell was made in 1773 and Boswell's account of it makes frequent reference to emigration. An episode of their stay on the Isle of Skye affords a curious bit of evidence as to the way in which emigration to America had seized the popular imagination. Under date of October 2, 1773, Boswell noted in his diary:

> "In the evening the company danced as usual. We performed, with much activity, a dance which, I suppose, the emigration from Skye has occasioned. They call it *America*. Each of the couples, after the common involutions and evolutions, successively whirls round in a circle, till all are in motion; and the dance seems intended to show how emigration catches, till a whole neighborhood is set afloat. Mrs. M'Kinnon told me, that last year when a ship sailed from Portree for America, the people on shore were almost distracted when they saw their relations go off; they lay down on the ground, tumbled and tore the grass with their teeth. This year there was not a tear shed. The people on shore seemed to think that they would soon follow. This indifference is a mortal sign for the country."

A suggestion of the hardships to which passengers were then exposed in the American voyage is made by an anecdote related by Boswell. In the Isle of Ulva he met a Captain McClure, master of a vessel belonging to the port of Londonderry. Boswell says:

> "The Captain informed us that he had named his ship the Bonnetta out of gratitude to Providence; for once, when he was sailing to America with a good number of passengers, the ship in which he then sailed was becalmed for five weeks, and during all that time, numbers of the fish Bonnetta swam close to her and were caught for food; he resolved therefore, that the ship he should next get should be called the Bonnetta."

Long delays through contrary winds or calms frequently occurred in the days of dependence on sails. Robert Witherspoon, who emigrated to South Carolina with his father's family in 1734, left an account of early experiences in which he said:

"We went on shipboard the 14th of September, and lay wind-
bound in the Lough at Belfast fourteen days. The second day of
our sail my grandmother died, and was interred in the raging
ocean, which was an afflictive sight to her offspring. We were
sorely tossed at sea with storms, which caused our ship to spring
a leak: our pumps were kept instantly at work day and night; for
many days our mariners seemed many times at their wits end.
But it pleased God to bring us all safe to land, which was about
the first of December."

The case of "the starved ship" was famous among the New
England settlers. In voyaging to America in 1740 the provisions
ran out, and the starving crew and passengers finally resorted
to cannibalism. Samuel Fisher, a ruling elder of the West Parish
Church of Londonderry, N. H., came out on that ship, and had
been picked for slaughter when a ship was met that gave relief.
Piracy was also a risk to be encountered. Among the early settlers of Londonderry, N. H., was a Mrs. Wilson who was one of
a company captured by pirates. Their captain appears to have
been remarkably goodnatured for one of that occupation. While
a captive Mrs. Wilson gave birth to a daughter, and the captain
was kind and sympathetic. Upon her promise to name the child
after his own wife, he gave Mrs. Wilson a silk dress and other
articles, and allowed the whole party of Scotch-Irish emigrants to
proceed on their way. A granddaughter of this Mrs. Wilson was
Mrs. Margaret Woodburn, the maternal grandmother of Horace
Greeley, to whose instruction and influence he attributed his intellectual awakening.

Eighteenth century conditions were such that the hardy, the
energetic, the resolute went to the making of America. Emigration
was then a sifting process, to the advantage of America. Arthur
Young, a thoroughly prosaic and unimaginative observer, remarked: "Men who emigrate are, from the nature of the circumstance, the most active, hardy, daring, bold and resolute spirits,
and probably the most mischievous also."

Every writer on Ulster emigration notes its bearing upon the

American Revolution. Killen, a Belfast minister, in his church history says: "Thousands of them [the Ulster tenant farmers] sought a home on the other side of the Atlantic, and a few years afterward appeared in arms against the mother country as asserters of the independence of the American republic."

Lecky, the historian who has given the most complete and impartial account of the circumstances of the emigration from the English standpoint, says: "They went with hearts burning with indignation, and in the War of Independence they were almost to a man on the side of the insurgents. They supplied some of the best soldiers of Washington."

CHAPTER VI

Scotch-Irish Settlements

At the time the stream of Scotch-Irish immigration became particularly noticeable in America, the country under English occupation was a narrow strip along the seaboard, extending south as far as the Spanish province of Florida. Actual settlement did not extend far from the coast, and the interior of the country was in the possession of Indian tribes with whom hostilities occurred checking colonial expansion. At the opening of the eighteenth century, although the colonies were firmly established, they were not vigorous in their growth. The early hopes of rich mines and vast treasure, such as the Spanish were reputed to have found everywhere in America, had been dispelled. It had become generally known that in English territory America was not a land of golden adventure, and that such gains as it afforded came as the result of laborious industry. Add to this that the desirable lands along the coast had been taken up and the movement of the population to the interior could be effected only by thrusting back the Indians, and it will be seen that there was a situation that tended to check colonial development. Thomas Hutchinson, in his *History of Massachusetts*, written in this period, says:

> "In 1640 the importation of settlers now ceased. They, who then professed to be able to give the best account, say that in 298 ships, which were the whole number from the beginnings of the colony, there arrived 21,200 passengers, men, women and children, perhaps about 4,000 families, since which more people have removed out of New England to other parts of the world than have come from other parts to it, and the number of families to this day [1670] in the four Governments [of New England] may be supposed to be less, rather than more, than the natural increase of 4,000."

Conditions were apparently not so slack in the middle and southern colonies, but in them also at this period there was a decline in colonizing energy. Accurate statistics of population are lacking, but on the accession of George I., in 1714, the English Board of Trade, on the basis of such data as were afforded by muster rolls and returns of taxables, estimated that the entire population of the American colonies, including Nova Scotia, consisted of 375,750 whites and 58,850 negroes. This estimate is the only one available as to the population of the colonies at the time Scotch-Irish immigration began. That immigration not only gave an impulse to national expansion that has operated ever since but it also cleared the way for that expansion by opening the interior of the country to occupation. In the seven years 1714–1720 inclusive fifty-four vessels arrived in Boston harbor from Ireland with companies of immigrants. Although details of arrivals at other ports are less minute, it is known that they were much larger at the ports of the Delaware. The mass of the Scotch-Irish arrivals everywhere moved on to the frontier. They constituted the border garrisons; they were the explorers, the vanguard of settlement in the interior. Their Ulster training had inured them to hostile surroundings, and their arrival in the colonies marks the beginning of a period of vigorous expansion, the effect of which is plainly visible in the Board of Trade returns. In 1727, on the accession of George II., the population of the American colonies was estimated at 502,000 whites and 78,000 negroes; in 1754 the estimated numbers were 1,192,896 whites and 292,738 negroes.

There was a Scotch ingredient of colonial population from the earliest times, and also Scotch-Irish, although not usually distinguishable as such. Josselyn, in his *Two Voyages to New England*, published in 1665, says: "It is published in print that there are not less than 10,000 souls, English, Scotch and Irish, in New England." The Scotch-Irish settlements in the Chesapeake Bay region probably had begun at this period, but taking the earliest distinct mention of Scotch-Irish settlements as the safest guide, their chronological order appears to be as follows: 1. Maryland, 1680; 2. South Carolina, 1682; 3. Pennsylvania, 1708; 4. New England, 1718.

Of these the Pennsylvania settlements were the most numerous and the most important in their bearing upon American national development. Consideration of them will be reserved until after some account has been given of all the other settlements.

No record has yet been discovered of the departure from Ireland of the founders of the Maryland settlements. In default of any positive information, it may be plausibly conjectured that the settlers formed part of the migration to Barbadoes and Virginia that ran strong in the middle of the seventeenth century. There was a close trading intercourse between the Barbadoes and Virginia, one evidence of which is the fact that Makemie, although settled in Maryland, extended his pastoral care to Barbadoes. The Scotch-Irish settlers in Virginia were doubtless among those non-conformists against whom the acts of 1642 and 1644 were passed, forbidding any person to officiate in a church who did not conform to the Book of Common Prayer. Some of the non-comformists were fined and three of their ministers were banished. Thus Virginia was made uncomfortable at a time when Lord Baltimore was offering the large inducements noted in the preceding chapter; and hence there was an exodus to Maryland where a policy of toleration then prevailed. It can hardly be doubted that the Scotch-Irish settlements in Maryland date from this period. The illustrious Polk family dates from these settlements. The founder of the family was Robert Polk who emigrated from Ulster in the second half of the seventeenth century and settled in Somerset County, Maryland. A grandson, William Polk, removed from Maryland to Pennsylvania. Two sons of William became famous in North Carolina, to which State they removed from Pennsylvania. One of them was Thomas Polk, the leading man of Mecklenburg County, member of the legislature, an officer of the militia, chairman of the famous Mecklenburg convention, and Colonel of the Fourth Regiment of North Carolina. His brother, Ezekiel Polk, was captain of a company of rangers. Ezekiel's grandson, James Knox Polk, born at Mecklenburg, November 2, 1795, was the eleventh President of the United States. Leonidas

Polk, Bishop of the Protestant Episcopal Church, and also a distin-guished Confederate General, was among the many descendants of the Somerset County immigrant that have achieved distinction. Effective occupation of the Carolinas did not take place until 1665. At that time popular interest in colonization had greatly declined in England, and proprietors of American lands had to look elsewhere for settlers. Their main resource was to draw them from the other colonies. New England, Virginia and Barbadoes each contributed to the population of the Carolinas. The most populous and prosperous of the early settlements was that made at Cape Fear, upon a tract purchased by a company of Barbadoes planters in August, 1663. The actual settlement took place in 1665, and within a year it numbered 800 inhabitants, but the location was so unwholesome that eventually the site was aban-doned and the remaining settlers removed to Charleston, where in 1670 a settlement had been started with emigrants drawn from England and Ireland. This settlement eventually grew into the State of South Carolina.

The first distinct instance of emigration from Ireland to South Carolina is mentioned in Chalmer's *Political Annals*, published in London in 1780. Referring to liberal arrangements made by the Proprietors in 1682, Chalmers goes on to say: "Incited by these attentions, Ferguson not long after conducted thither an emigration from Ireland which instantly mingled with the mass of the inhabitants."

George Chalmers, the author of this statement, was born in 1742, and practiced law in Maryland prior to the Revolution, when he returned to England and became clerk of the Board of Trade, which office he held until his death. His information was doubtless accurate, and although he gives no particulars it is safe to infer that this Ferguson drew emigrants from Ulster. There is on record the will of Richard Newton, dated September 9, 1692, in which he makes a bequest to his brother, Marmaduke Newton, of Carrickfergus, County Antrim, Ireland.

Notwithstanding the early beginning of Scotch-Irish

emigration to South Carolina, it was not marked in extent or influence. The sultry climate and the malarial fevers of the swampy lowlands in which the first settlements were made were peculiarly trying to people of Scotch blood and habit. There was at one time a disposition to regard the Carolinas as an asylum from persecution, but it was practically extinguished by the disastrous experience of the Scotch colony at Port Royal, which was wiped out of existence by a force from the Spanish posts in Florida. It was not until half a century later, when white settlements had penetrated to the uplands, that emigration from Ulster became noticeable. In 1732, in response to a petition from James Pringle and other Irish Protestants, the Council of South Carolina granted a township twenty miles square to Ulster colonists, which they named Williamsburgh, in honor of William of Orange. There was a considerable movement from the North of Ireland to this new settlement, and by the end of 1736 the inhabitants were sufficiently numerous to send to Ireland for a minister, the Rev. Robert Heron coming out and remaining for three years. Among the Williamsburgh settlers were John Witherspoon, James McClelland, William Syne, David Allan, William Wilson, Robert Wilson, James Bradley, William Frierson, John James, William Hamilton, Archibald Hamilton, Roger Gordon, John Porter, John Lemon, David Pressly, William Pressly, Archibald McRae, James Armstrong, the Erwins, Plowdens, Dickeys, Blakelys, Dobbinses, Stuarts and McDonalds.

When, by the treaty of 1763, France yielded to England all her possessions east of the Mississippi, South Carolina received a large share of the heavy emigration from Ireland which then set in. An account of it is given in the earliest history of South Carolina, written by the Rev. Alexander Hewatt, a Presbyterian clergyman and a resident of Charleston. He went to England at the outbreak of the Revolutionary War and published his history in 1779. In it he says:

> "Besides foreign Protestants, several persons from England and Scotland resorted to Carolina after the peace. But of all

other countries, none has furnished the province with so many inhabitants as Ireland. In the northern counties of that kingdom, the spirit of emigration seized the people to such a degree, that it threatened almost a total depopulation. Such multitudes of husbandmen, laborers and manufacturers flocked over the Atlantic, that the landlords began to be alarmed, and to concert ways and means for preventing the growing evil. Scarce a ship sailed for any of the plantations that was not crowded with men, women and children. But the bounty allowed new settlers in Carolina proved a great encouragement, and induced numbers of these people, notwithstanding the severity of the climate, to resort to that province. The merchants finding this bounty equivalent to the expenses of the passage, from avaricious motives pursuaded the people to embark for Carolina, and often crammed such numbers of them into their ships that they were in danger of being stifled during the passage, and sometimes were landed in such a starved and sickly condition, that numbers of them died before they left Charleston...

"Nor were these the only sources from which Carolina at this time, derived strength, and an increase of population. For, notwithstanding the vast extent of territory which the provinces of Virginia and Pennsylvania contained, yet such was the nature of the country, that a scarcity of improvable lands began to be felt in these colonies, and poor people could not find spots in them unoccupied equal to their expectations. Most of the richest valleys in these more populous provinces lying to the east of the Alleghany Mountains were either under patent or occupied, and, by the royal proclamation at the Peace, no settlements were allowed to extend beyond the sources of the rivers which empty themselves in the Atlantic. In Carolina the case was different, for there large tracts of the best land as yet lay waste, which proved a great temptation to the northern colonists to migrate to the South. Accordingly, about this time above a thousand families, with their effects, in the space of one year resorted to Carolina, driving their cattle, hogs and horses overland before them. Lands were allotted to them on the frontiers, and most of them being only entitled to small tracts, such as one, two or three hundred acres, the back settlements by this means soon became the most populous parts of the province."

North Carolina, which grew out of a settlement from Virginia
on Albemarle River, remained in obscurity until 1729, when
the inefficient Proprietary government came to an end and the
country became a Crown colony. About the year 1736 a body of
emigrants from Ulster settled in Duplin County, founding Scotch-
Irish families whose progeny is scattered through the South. But
in the main the Scotch-Irish settlements of the South and West
were derived from the overland emigration that had its main
source in Pennsylvania. While there is abundant evidence that
this was large, it is impossible to give statistics even approximately.

The classification of Scotch-Irish has never figured in official
computations of American population. The first national census
was taken in 1790. The law provided for lists of free white males
under sixteen and also above sixteen, of white females, free blacks
and slaves. The Census Bureau in 1909 published an analysis of
the returns obtained by the first census, and a chapter was devoted
to "Nationality as Indicated by Names of Heads of Families."
The following was given as the proportion of total population
formed by each nationality: English, 83.5 per cent.; Scotch, 6.7;
German 5.6; Dutch, 2.0; Irish, 1.6; French, 0.5; Hebrew, less
than one-tenth of 1 per cent.; all other 0.1. Despite this show
of statistical precision, a little consideration will show that the
exhibits are fallacious and untrustworthy. Many Ulster names are
also common English names. There is nothing in such names as
Boyd, Brooks, Brown, Clark, Cornwall, Dunlop, Gray, Holmes,
Long, Little, Miller, Smith, Young and others to suggest that they
did not in all cases belong to English families, and doubtless the
English proportion as given above includes many Scotch-Irish
families. Names classed as Scotch or Irish were probably mostly
those of Scotch-Irish families. There was very little emigration
from Ireland, outside of Ulster, until after the War of 1812. Mr.
James Mooney of the Bureau of American Ethnology in a paper
published in 1913 on racial elements of population, said that
"the Irish immigration to the American colonies previous to the
Revolution was mainly of the alien Scotch and English element,

known sometimes as Scotch-Irish." The proportions given in the Census Bureau publication are admittedly vague and conjectural, and they are remote from known facts. The probability is that the English proportion should be much smaller, and that the Scotch-Irish, who are not included in the Census Bureau's classification, should be much larger than the combined proportions allotted to the Scotch and the Irish.

CHAPTER VII

ON THE NEW ENGLAND FRONTIER

The early ties of religious sympathy and common purpose of the two countries were such that it was natural for Ulster emigration to set strongly toward New England. But when the Scotch-Irish began to arrive in Boston in large numbers, they were not entirely welcome. Their ministers were received with marked courtesy by such leading citizens as Cotton Mather and Samuel Sewall, but in general the large arrivals of 1718 appear to have been viewed with anxiety. In July and August Scotch-Irish arrivals in Boston numbered between five and seven hundred. On August 13 the selectmen chose an agent to appear in court, "to move what he shall think proper in order to secure this town from charges which may happen to accrue or be imposed on them by reason of the passengers lately arrived here from Ireland or elsewhere." In the course of the winter a number were warned to leave or find sureties for their support. If one had to depend upon such records alone it would be natural to infer that emigration from Ulster was throwing paupers upon the community, but there is ample evidence that such was not the case. The Surveyor-General of Customs at Boston, Thomas Lechmere, was a brother-in-law of John Winthrop of Connecticut, who requested him to get a miller from among the immigrants. John Winthrop, son of Governor John Winthrop of Massachusetts, acquired an extensive estate in Connecticut in 1646, at a place then known as Pequot and later as New London. John Winthrop, the younger, was Governor of Connecticut in 1657–58, and again in 1659–76. The John Winthrop who corresponded with Lechmere in 1718 was a grandson of this John Winthrop the younger, and he was interested in developing the family estate at New London. Writing about this business on August 11, 1718, Lechmere remarks:

> "Whoever tells you that servants are cheaper now than they were, it is a very gross mistake, & give me leave to tell you your

informer has given you a very wrong information about ye cheapness thereof, for never were they dearer than now, there being such demand for them, & likewise pray tell him he is much out of the way to think that these Irish are servants. They are generally men of estates, & are come over hither for no other reason but upon encouragement sent from hence upon notice given that they should have so many acres of land given them gratis to settle our frontiers as a barrier against the Indians."

In another letter Lechmere says: "There are none to be sold; have all paid their passages sterling in Ireland." Nevertheless there were doubtless some among them who had exhausted their means in scraping up their passage money, or who had come upon agreement to pay for their passage by sale of their services, as was the custom of the times. Shortly after the arrival of a shipload of immigrants the Boston *News-Letter* contained an advertisement offering for sale, together with linen and woolen, "sundry boys' times by indentures, young women and girls by the year." This, with great probability, is taken to refer to some of the Scotch-Irish immigrants, but such indigent persons were comparatively few in number. The great mass were not adventurers, but were people of settled character, seeking a new field of labor. In departing from Ulster they brought testimonials of their good standing in the places where they had lived. Frequent mention of such testimonials is made in New England records of this period. The usual style is exhibited in this one brought over by one of the defenders of Londonderry:

"The bearer, William Caldwell, his wife, Sarah Morrison, with his children, being designed to go to New England and America—These are therefore to testifie they leave us without scandal, lived with us soberly and inoffensively, and may be admitted to Church priviledges. Given at Dunboe, April 9, 1718, by JAMES WOODSIDE, JR., Minister."

The explanation of the antipathy excited by Scotch-Irish immigration lies not in the character of the arrivals but in the character of the economic system of the community. It was then an ordinary duty of public authority to look after supply and prices of food. There was anxiety about provision of grain before the Scotch-Irish began to arrive, and the selectmen had made purchases on public account. Before the ensuing winter was over the town authorities had to purchase grain in Connecticut to supply the needs of the community. In his letter of August 11, 1718, Lechmere remarked: "These confounded Irish will eat us all up, provisions being most extravagantly dear, & scarce of all sorts." The alarm seems to be justified, as the stock of provisions was so closely adjusted to the ordinary needs of the community, then only a few thousand in number, that the arrival of over 500 immigrants was enough to excite fear of famine. Despite the efforts of the selectmen to import grain and to moderate prices, provisions became scarce and dear. On December 18, 1718, the selectmen ordered that the public granaries should be opened for the sale of Indian corn, not exceeding one bushel to each buyer, at the rate of five shillings a bushel. Wheat went up in price from six shillings to ten shillings a bushel. The price of small fruits and vegetables, however, showed no material advance. Kitchen garden products in and about a country town are generally so ample that increase of demand can ordinarily be met by more thorough harvesting than usual.

⋅   In carrying out the design mentioned by Lechmere of sending the Scotch-Irish to the frontiers, "as a barrier against the Indians," arrangements were made for a settlement at Worcester. Although only about fifty miles west of Boston, it was then a frontier outpost. Everywhere in the English colonies at that period Indian territory lay so close to the coast settlements that any movement of settlers to the interior was apt to produce race conflict. At the end of the seventeenth century Massachusetts was slackening in growth of population owing to the desertion of frontier towns. Acts were passed prohibiting removals without leave from the Governor or Council; but nevertheless they went on, to the advantage of Connecticut and Rhode Island, whose comparative security from Indian attack was a great attraction. An official estimate made in 1702 reckons the total population of Massachusetts as being then only 50,000.

It was a matter of importance to the Massachusetts authorities to strengthen the frontier towns, and particularly the fertile regions of central Massachusetts, in which Worcester is situated.

The country was attractive to settlers, but in 1675 and again in 1709 Worcester was abandoned because of Indian hostilities. The place was again occupied in 1713, and at least five garrison houses were erected, one of them a block fort. About 200 people were living in some fifty log cabins when the Scotch-Irish began to arrive. They soon became active and prominent in the affairs of the settlement, whose population was probably doubled by their arrival. It was not long before the military value of the Scotch-Irish was drawn upon. In 1722 an Indian war broke out, and as part of the measures of defense two Scotch-Irishmen, John Gray and Robert Crawford, were posted as scouts on Leicester Hill, west of the settlement. In September of the same year a township organization was effected, and that same John Gray was chosen one of the selectmen. In 1724 James McClellan was chosen to be town constable. He was the direct ancestor of General George B. McClellan.

Numerous families of the name of Young in western Massachusetts are descended from John Young, probably the oldest immigrant that ever arrived in this country. He was born in the island of Burt, near Londonderry, and he was ninety-five when he landed in Boston. He lived in Worcester twelve years before he died, June 30, 1730, aged 107. His son, David Young, who also was an old man when he landed, lived to be ninety-four. At least two of the settlers in Worcester, Abraham Blair and William Caldwell, took part in the defense of Londonderry in 1689, and other survivors of that famous siege participated in the Scotch-Irish settlements in New England at this period. These men and their heirs were made free of taxation by acts of the British Parliament, and their holdings were known as "exempt farms" in New England until the American Revolution. The lands occupied by the Scotch-Irish at Worcester, like those of their English neighbors, were generally obtained by direct grant of the General Court of Massachusetts.

As the frontier was pushed back and Indian perils were removed religious differences and probably racial differences created antipathies between the English and Scotch-Irish elements of Worcester, and these led to some migrations. In 1738 a company consisting of thirty-four families was organized to purchase and settle a new town, and this movement originated Pelham, about thirty miles west of Worcester. The principal motive of this migration is indicated by a provision of the contract under which the land was purchased. It was stipulated that "families of good connection be settled on the premises who shall be such as were the inhabitants of the Kingdom of Ireland or their descendants, being Protestants, and none be admitted but such as bring good and undeniable credentials or certificates of their being persons of good conversation and of the Presbyterian persuasion."

John Clark, whose name appears first upon a petition for himself and fellow signers for exemption from taxation for support of the Congregational Church of Worcester, was among the first settlers of the Scotch-Irish town of Colerain, fifty miles to the northwest of Worcester. This settlement, begun about 1740, was participated in by the Morrisons, Pennells, Herrouns, Hendersons, Cochranes, Hunters, Henrys, Clarks, McClellans, McCowens, Taggarts and McDowells, many of whom had previously been settlers in Worcester.

In 1741 Western (now Warren), in Worcester County, and Blandford, in Hampden County, were incorporated by Scotch-Irish from Worcester. The families of Blair, Boise, Knox, Carnahan, Watson, Wilson and Ferguson were prominent in Blandford, and some of the same names, especially the Blairs, together with Reeds and Crawfords, appear in the early records of Western. Notwithstanding these removals a strong Scotch-Irish element remained in Worcester, such family names continuing there as McClellan, Caldwell, Blair, McFarland, Rankin, Gray, Crawford, Young, Hamilton, Duncan, Graham, Forbush, Kelso, Clark, Ferguson, McClintock, McKonkey, Glassford and McGregor.

From the Scotch-Irish centers established in central and western

Massachusetts, in the first half of the eighteenth century, Scotch-Irish blood was diffused throughout western Massachusetts. From western Massachusetts the Scotch-Irish spread into Vermont, along the west shore of the Connecticut River, forming strong settlements in the sections now comprised within Windsor, Orange and Caledonia Counties, and also east of the Connecticut River in the section now designated as Rockingham County, New Hampshire. The Worcester settlement was the fountain head of a distribution of Scotch-Irish blood all through the western parts of New England, and many distinguished American families trace their ancestry to this source. Matthew Thornton, a signer of the Declaration of Independence, belonged to a Worcester family. He was a lad of four in 1718 when his father landed in Boston. Professor Asa Gray, the famous botanist, was a great-great-grandson of the first Matthew Gray who settled in Worcester.

Next to Worcester in point of time was probably the Scotch-Irish settlement at Casco Bay, Maine, then belonging to Massachusetts. A company of about 300 persons sailed from Boston in the autumn of 1718 to explore the coast northward for a good place of settlement with a promise from Governor Shute of land grants in any unoccupied territory. Numerous attempts had been made to establish settlements on the Maine coast, but the Indian wars had been particularly violent and desolating in this region, and there was little left of former colonizing ventures at the time Scotch-Irish emigration began. The ship which bore the first company appears to have been the brigantine Robert, which had arrived in Boston from Belfast on the fourth of August, James Ferguson, master. They sailed as far north as Casco Bay, where the ship went into winter quarters. A town was already in existence there, known as Falmouth. From a petition sent to the Government in Boston by John Armstrong and others, it appears that about thirty families landed in November, 1718, and began to build shelters for the winter. They asked allotments of land and supplies of provisions. The latter request was backed up by a petition from the town authorities, desiring that the provincial

Government should consider "the deplorable Circumstances of the said Place by reason of the great Number of poor Strangers arrived amongst them and take some speedy & Effectual Care for their supply." In response orders were issued that 100 bushels of corn meal should be forwarded. Some of these settlers eventually went to the Kennebec country, or to Londonderry, New Hampshire, but enough remained to form a settlement in Falmouth township known as Pooporduc, now included in the city of Portland. Among those who remained and founded Portland families were John Armstrong, Thomas Bolton, Robert Means, William Jameson, Joshua Gray, William Gyles, Randal McDonald and Bruce McLellan. Among the Scotch-Irish settlers arriving at a somewhat later period was John Motley from Belfast, from whom descended the historian, John Lothrop Motley.

Andrew and Reuben Gray, sons of the above-mentioned Joshua Gray, took part in the expedition which Governor Pownall of Massachusetts fitted out in 1759 to capture from the French the mouth of the Penobscot River, and the Grays were in the guard of twenty men who accompanied the Governor when he occupied an abandoned French fort and hoisted the King's colors. The place is now known as Castine, on the east side of Penobscot Bay. A strong fort was erected and settlement began in this region, the two Gray brothers being among the first to take up land. Several other brothers followed them, and eventually their old father and mother joined them. The Grays are now in large numbers in the lower Penobscot country, and other Scotch-Irish families abound, such as the Wears, Orrs and Doaks. The town of Belfast now stands on the west shore of Penobscot Bay, opposite Castine, and up the river, about thirty miles north, is Bangor, the State capital. Bangor in Ulster is on the southern shore of Belfast Lough, about twelve miles east of Belfast.

Professor Perry, who has made a careful study of all accessible data, thinks it probable that of the company that sailed up coast on the brigantine Robert a larger number were deposited at or near Wiscasset on the Kennebec than were left at Portland. If this be the case, the Kennebec settlement was the third Scotch-Irish settlement in New England, antedating that at Londonderry, N. H., which also was founded by emigrants belonging to the company on the Robert. Nothing is certainly known as to the extent of the first Kennebec settlement, or the number of the original settlers. The population was soon augmented by the arrival of another company of emigrants. The MacCallum, James Law, master, from Londonderry, Ireland, arrived in Boston on or about September 6, 1718.

The MacCallum was originally bound for New London, Conn., but having had a long passage, Captain Law put in to Boston. In Lechmere's correspondence it is remarked that the MacCallum brought "twenty odd familys." The arrivals at once became the object of colonizing overtures. Captain Robert Temple, who had been an officer in the English army, had come to America with the view of establishing himself as a large landed proprietor, a purpose which naturally excited the interest of those who had lands for sale. It would seem that he was shown the Winthrop holdings at New London, for he had recently returned to Boston from a trip to Connecticut when the MacCallum arrived, and it appears from Lechmere's correspondence that at first he tried to induce the emigrants to settle at New London. But more attractive inducements were offered by the Gentlemen Proprietors of Eastern Lands, a company with holdings in the Kennebec country. Writing to Winthrop about this competition Lechmere said, "The method they go in with the Irish is to sell them so many acres of land for 12 pence an acre and allow them time to pay it in. I know land is more valuable with you, and therefore 'twill be more difficult to agree with them."

The Gentlemen Proprietors succeeded in interesting Captain Temple himself in the Maine lands. Lechmere, writing under date of September 8, 1718, tells Winthrop that Temple had rejected the Connecticut proposals, and had made arrangements by which the MacCallum would take her Scotch-Irish passengers to Merrymeeting Bay, at the mouth of the Androscoggin.

These arrangements can have consumed only a few days, as the MacCallum both arrived and cleared at Boston in the week September 1–8, 1718. Temple became an active colonizer of the Kennebec country. Within two years he chartered five ships to bring over families from Ulster, and by 1720 several hundred families were settled on the Kennebec or the Androscoggin which unites with the Kennebec near its mouth. The MacCallum's passengers settled at Merrymeeting Bay in the region now known as Bath, but then called Cork, or Ireland. Many of the settlers brought in by Temple settled in and about Topsham, so named from the Devonshire port from which Temple left England on his first voyage.

The Kennebec settlements were made in such force and had such influential support that their prosperity seemed assured; but Indian wars broke out with disastrous results. A number of settlements were abandoned, some of the people going to Londonderry, N. H., but the greater number removed to Pennsylvania. In 1722 nine families belonging to the Merrymeeting Bay settlement were captured by the Indians. A striking recital of the experience of the settlers is contained in the petition of the Rev. James Woodside to the English Crown in June, 1723. It sets forth:

> "That he with 40 Familys, consisting of above 160 Persons, did in the year 1718 embarque on a ship at Derry Lough in Ireland in Order to erect a Colony at Casco Bay, in Your Majesty's Province of Main in New England."
>
> "That being arriv'd they made a settlement at a Place called by the Indians Pegipscot, but by them Brunswick, within 4 miles from Fort George, where (after he had laid out a considerable sum upon a Garrison House, fortify'd with Palisadoes, & two large Bastions, had also made great Improvements, & laid out considerably for the Benefit of that Infant Colony) the Inhabitants were surpris'd by the Indians who in the Month of July, 1722, came down in great Numbers to murder your Majesty's good Subjects there.
>
> "That upon this Surprize the Inhabitants, naked and destitute of Provisions, run for shelter into your Pet.ⁿ House (which is still

defended by his sons) where they were kindly receiv'd, provided for, & protected from the rebel Indians.

"That the S^d Indians being happily prevented from murdering Your Majesty's good Subjects (in revenge to your Pet.^r) presently kill'd all his Cattel, destroying all the Movables, & Provisions they could come at, & as Your Pet.^r had a very considerable Stock of Cattel he & his Family were great sufferers thereby."

* Captain Temple, who received a military commission from Governor Shute, remained in the country with many of the people he induced to settle there, and in this region are now found such Scotch-Irish names as McFadden, McGowen, McCoun, Vincent, Hamilton, Johnston, Malcolm, McClellan, Crawford, Graves, Ward, Given, Dunning and Simpson.

* After leaving some of her company in Casco Bay and some in the Kennebec, the Robert turned back to the Merrimac and ascended that river as far as the town Haverhill. They did not receive a cordial welcome, as the townspeople were not pleased to see the Irish coming there. But the emigrants learned of a fine tract of land about fifteen miles north called Nutfield, because chestnut, walnut and butternut trees were unusually thick in that region. A party under the lead of James McKeen, grandfather of the first president of Bowdoin College, visited the place and decided that it would be a good site for a settlement. It was doubtless a joyful decision to passengers on the Robert as they had passed the winter in Maine and were anxious to find some place to stay. The settlement at Nutfield was begun in April, 1719, and among those taking part in it were James McKeen, John Barnett, Archibald Clendenin, John Mitchell, James Sterrett, James Anderson, Randall Alexander, James Gregg, James Clark, James Nesmith, Allen Anderson, Robert Weir, John Morrison, Samuel Allison, Thomas Steele and John Stewart, with their families. The settlers at the time supposed the place to be in Massachusetts but it turned out to be in southern New Hampshire. As a frontier post, it was exposed to Indian incursions, and two stone garrison houses were built the first season as places of refuge.

The dwelling houses were of course log cabins, and for the better protection of the community they were placed in a definite order which became known as the Double Range. The houses were on each side of West Running brook, on home lots thirty rods wide, and extending back until they enclosed sixty acres each. Sawmills were built and in a few years good frame houses began to go up, the first one for the Rev. James McGregor, and the second for John McMurphy, who bore a commission as Justice of the Peace, issued in Ireland. The settlement was never attacked by the Indians, and through the influence of Pastor McGregor a valuable resource was discovered through information obtained from the Indians. He was told of a place some nine miles distant where fish were abundant. With the help of his compass the pastor was able to mark a course to Amoskeag Falls, where the city of Manchester now stands. The Merrimac at this point abounded in salmon, and shad at some seasons, and the stores of salted fish laid in by the settlers were an important source of food supply.

The original settlers were soon joined by others, and it appears from a petition for incorporation as a township, subscribed on September 21, 1719, that the inhabitants then numbered seventy families. In June, 1722, Nutfield was incorporated as a town containing ten square miles, laid out so as to extend to the fishing station at Amoskeag Falls, that portion becoming known as Derryfield, and now as Manchester. At its incorporation the town was entitled Londonderry after the famous Ulster city in whose defense some of the settlers had taken part. Pastor McGregor was one of these. He used to tell how he had himself fired a gun from the cathedral tower to announce the approach of the ships up the Foyle to relieve the besieged garrison. After the death of McGregor his pastoral duties were for a time discharged by the Rev. Matthew Clark, then seventy years old, who came direct from Ireland. He wore a black patch over the outer angle of the right eye to cover a wound that refused to heal, received in one of the sallies of the besieged at Londonderry. When he died in January, 1735, at the age of 76, it was in compliance with his deathbed request that his remains were borne to the grave only by those who were survivors of the Londonderry siege.

An authentic account of the manners and customs of the Scotch-Irish settlers is preserved in the Rev. Edward L. Parker's *History of Londonderry*. The author, born in 1785 in Litchfield, N. H., was for a time a student at the academy in Londonderry, and in 1810 became pastor of the Presbyterian church in the East Parish of Londonderry, remaining until his death in 1850. Thus he spent his life in and about Londonderry and was in the best possible position to acquaint himself with its history, to which he devoted such painstaking investigation that he died before the final completion of the work. It was in such shape that his son was soon able to prepare it for publication. The work itself testifies to its accuracy by its transparent honesty of statement. The following account is given of early customs:

> "The bridegroom selected one of his intimate friends for the 'best man,' who was to officiate as master of the ceremony, and the bride likewise one of her companions, as 'best maid.' The morning of the marriage day was ushered in with the discharge of musketry, in the respective neighborhoods of the persons who were to be united. This practice it seems originated in Ireland, in consequence of the Catholics having been, after the Revolution, deprived of the use of firearms. The Protestants, proud of the superior privilege which they then enjoyed, made a display of their warlike instruments on all public occasions. Seldom was a respectable man married without his sword by his side. At the appointed hour, the groom proceeded from his dwelling with his select friends, male and female; about half way on their progress to the house of the bride, they were met by her select male friends; and, on meeting, each company made choice of one of their number to 'run for the bottle' to the bride's house. The champion of the race who returned first with the bottle, gave a toast, drank to the bridegroom's health, and, having passed round the bottle, the whole party proceeded, saluted by the firing of muskets from the houses they passed, and answering these salutes with pistols. When arrived at the bride's residence, the bridegroom's company were placed in an apartment by themselves, and it

was considered an act of impoliteness for any one of the bride's company to intrude. When the ceremony was to commence the 'best man' first introduced the bridegroom; then, entering the bride's apartment, led her into the room, and, placing her at the right hand of her 'intended,' took his station directly behind, as did the 'best maid.' The minister commenced the marriage service with prayer; on requesting the parties to join hands, each put the right hand behind, when the glove was drawn off by the best man and maid. Their hands being joined, the marriage covenant was addressed to them, with appropriate remarks on the nature and responsibilities of the connection thus formed. Having concluded with another prayer, he requested the groom to salute his bride, which being done, the minister performed the same ceremony, and was immediately followed by the male part of the company; the female in like manner saluted the bridegroom.

"The ceremony being concluded the whole company sat down to the entertainment, at which the best man and best maid presided. Soon after the entertainment, the room was cleared for the dance and other amusements, 'and the evening,' remarks our aged informant, kindling at the recollection of bygone scenes, 'was spent with a degree of pleasure of which our modern fashionables are perfectly ignorant.'

"Their funeral observances were of a character, in some respects, peculiar. When death entered their community, and one of their number was removed, there was at once a cessation of all labor in the neighborhood. The people gathered together at the house of mourning, and during the earlier periods of the settlement, observed a custom which they had brought with them from Ireland, called the 'wake,' or watching with the dead, from night to night, until the interment. These night scenes often exhibited a mixture of seriousness and of humor which appear incompatible. The Scriptures would be read, prayer offered, and words of counsel and consolation administered; but ere long, according to established usage, the glass, with its exhilarating beverage, must circulate freely; so that, before the dawn, the joke and the laugh, if not scenes more boisterous, would break in upon the slumbers of the dead.

"At the funeral, whatever might have been the age, the character, or condition of the deceased, the assemblage would be large.

Every relation, however distant the connection, must surely be present, or it be regarded as a marked neglect; and it was expected that all the friends and acquaintances of the deceased, within a reasonable distance, would attend. Although funeral sermons were seldom if ever delivered on the occasion, yet there would be usually as large a congregation as assembled on the Sabbath. Previous to the prayer, spirit was handed around, not only to the mourners and bearers, but to the whole assembly. Again, after prayer, and before the coffin was removed, the same was done. Nearly all would follow the body to the grave, and usually the greater number walked. Processions, from a third to a half a mile in length, were not unfrequent. At their return, the comforting draught was again administered, and ample entertainment provided. Many a family became embarrassed, if not impoverished, in consequence of the heavy expenses incurred, not so much by the sickness which preceded the death of one of its members, as by the funeral services as then observed, and which as they supposed respect for the dead required.

"Their diversions and scenes of social intercourse were of a character not the most refined and cultured; displaying physical rather than intellectual and moral powers, such as boxing matches, wrestling, foot races, and other athletic exercises. At all public gatherings, the 'ring' would be usually formed; and the combatants, in the presence of neighbors, brothers, and even fathers, would encounter each other in close fight, or at arms length, as the prescribed form might be; thus giving and receiving the well directed blow, until the face, limbs, and body of each bore the marks of almost savage brutality. All this was done, not in anger, or from unkind feeling toward each other, but simply to test the superiority of strength and agility."

Parker could speak from his own knowledge of the arrangements in the meetinghouses as they were still in force when his pastorate began. He remarks:

"The construction of the pulpit with its appendages, in Presbyterian communities corresponded with their form of ecclesiastical government. As you entered the pulpit, you first came to the deacons' seat, elevated like the pews, about six inches from the floor of the aisles, or passages. In the deacons' narrow slip usually sat two venerable men, one at each end. Back of the deacons' seat and elevated ten or twelve inches higher, was the pew of the ruling elders, larger than that of the deacons and about square. Back of the elders' pew, and two or three feet higher, and against the wall, was the pulpit."

The town grew so fast that in 1734, only fifteen years after the first settlement, the church records note 700 communicants present at the sacrament. Londonderry was a source from which Scotch-Irish blood was diffused throughout Rockingham, Hillsboro, and Merrimack counties in New Hampshire. At least ten distinct settlements were made by emigrants from Londonderry during the quarter of a century preceding the Revolution, all of which became important towns. An emigration spread into Vermont, joining with that which moved northward from the Worcester settlement. Numerous families moved northward and westward and over the ridge of the Green Mountains. The Scotch-Irish were active in the French and Indian War, and participated in the Conquest of Canada in 1759. Major Robert Rogers, commander of three companies of rangers raised in New Hampshire in 1756, was a native of Londonderry and most of his men were from that place. John Stark, who commanded one of these companies, was in 1777 commander of the American troops that won the battle of Bennington. Robert McGregor, a grandson of the Londonderry pastor, served on Stark's staff. Col. George Reid, who served throughout the entire war of the Revolution in command of the New Hampshire forces, was a native of Londonderry. Col. James Miller, who led the decisive charge at Lundy's Lane in the War of 1812, was of Londonderry stock, although his people were settled at Peterborough, N. H., at the time of his birth in 1776. He became Territorial Governor of Arkansas, and on retiring from that post an invalid in 1823 he was appointed collector at Salem and Beverly, Mass., where he had as a subordinate Nathaniel Hawthorne, who in his writings made some appreciative notices of the Scotch-Irish veteran. Parker mentions that from Londonderry stock came six Governors of New Hampshire, nine members of Congress and five justices of the Supreme Court of the State.

A decade after the first Scotch-Irish settlements in New England an Ulster colonization of eastern Maine was begun by the activity of a stout hearted adventurer who had a romantic career. David Dunbar, a native of Ulster who had been a colonel in the British army and had served in Spain, was in 1728 appointed Surveyor of the Woods. It was the policy of the English Government to make forest reservations for the use of the navy, and there had been much complaint about the way these reservations had been plundered. The attitude of colonial juries was such that it was practically impossible to convict or punish for such offenses in Massachusetts or New Hampshire. Dunbar conceived the idea of making the country east of the Kennebec a distinct province which he undertook to settle from Protestant Ireland. In 1729 he obtained an order appointing him Governor of the Province of Sagadahock, which was placed at his disposal upon condition that he should preserve 300,000 acres of the best pine and oak for the use of the Crown. With the aid of troops sent from Nova Scotia Dunbar took possession, ignoring the Massachusetts claim of jurisdiction. He rebuilt the fortification at Pemaquid, naming it Fort Frederick, and with it as the seat of his Government he addressed himself energetically to the work of planting and set-tling the country. His career was brief. Jonathan Belcher, who was appointed Governor of Massachusetts in 1730, pressed the claims of Massachusetts so effectively that in 1732 orders were issued revoking Dunbar's powers. Dunbar obeyed orders like a good soldier. His enterprise had involved his finances so that on returning to England in 1737 he was imprisoned for debt; but his friends were able to obtain his release. In 1743 he was appointed Governor of St. Helena. Brief as was Dunbar's career in Maine, he brought in about 150 families, some coming from Massachusetts or New Hampshire, and some direct from Ireland.

Incidentally, Dunbar's enterprise led to another Ulster col-onization of eastern Maine. Samuel Waldo, who was active in

London as an agent of Massachusetts in the proceedings against Dunbar, was himself holder of a grant to lands between the St. George and the Penobscot Rivers. Impressed by the vigor and capacity of the settlers brought in by Dunbar, Waldo sought to get some of the same sort on his lands. The first company consisted of twenty-seven families, who arrived in 1735, each family receiving 100 acres of land on the bank of the St. George in the present town of Warren. Among them were Alexanders, Blairs, Kilpatricks, Pattersons, McLeans, McCrackens and Morrisons.

These successive settlements in Massachusetts, Maine and New Hampshire were the original centers from which the Scotch-Irish strain spread through New England. The Ulster men amply fulfilled all that was expected of them as frontier barriers for the protection of the older settlements. They were the chief colonizing agency in Maine, in which State the infusion of Scotch-Irish blood was greatest, but the strain was also strong in western Massachusetts, New Hampshire and Vermont. It spread into Connecticut and Rhode Island but is not so marked in those States. It was borne in the current of emigration from New England as the settlement of the interior of the country progressed and many western families of Scotch-Irish derivation have New England antecedents. The main stream of Scotch-Irish influence in the growth of the nation was, however, that which issued from the settlements in Pennsylvania, in which the characteristic institutions of the race were better preserved than in New England.

CHAPTER VIII

In New York and the Jerseys

When the Dutch colony of New Netherlands became the English colony of New York by the Peace of 1674 there was a movement of population thither from the older English colonies. The Rev. John Livingston, whose ineffectual attempt to go to America on the Eagle Wing has been narrated, became progenitor of an illustrious American family through an immigrant who settled in New York at this period. Robert Livingston, born in 1654 while his father was pastor of Ancrum, Scotland, emigrated to Massachusetts in 1673. The next year he removed to New York and proceeded to Albany, then a frontier settlement doing a large trade with the Indians. Livingston had lived several years in Holland, while his father was a religious exile there, and his knowledge of the Dutch language was now of great service. He obtained employment as clerk to the Board of Commissaries which then governed the Albany district, and thus began a prosperous official career in the course of which he acquired an extensive tract of land still known as the Livingston Manor. He had numerous descendants and it is doubtful whether any other family in the Revolutionary period contributed so many of its members to the army and navy. There were certainly seven and probably eight Livingstons of his blood among the officers of General Gates' army at Saratoga, three of them in command of regiments. Among his descendants are William Livingston, Governor of New Jersey throughout the Revolutionary War, and a framer of the Constitution; Chancellor Livingston, a member of the committee that framed the Declaration of Independence, who administered the oath to Washington as first President of the United States, and who as Minister to France began the negotiations which resulted in the cession of Louisiana; and Edward Livingston, United States Senator from Louisiana, Secretary of State under Jackson and a jurist of international celebrity.

About 1682 a Scotch migration to East Jersey set in, promoted by a group of eminent Scots who had acquired Proprietors' shares in that Province. George Scot, of Pitlochie, whose colonizing activity has been heretofore noted, was one of the movers in this enterprise. Samuel Smith, the first historian of the Province, says: "There were very soon four towns in the Province, viz., Elizabeth, Newark, Middletown and Shrewsbury: and these with the country round were in a few years plentifully inhabited by the accession of the Scotch, of whom there came a great many." It is quite probable that this Scotch immigration had Ulster ingredients, but this is a matter of inference and not of positive knowledge.

It is not until the great wave of Ulster emigration in 1718 that Scotch-Irish settlement in New York and New Jersey becomes distinctly noticeable. In 1720 Scotch-Irish settlers in the vicinity of Goshen, Orange County, New York, were numerous enough to form a congregation. In the succeeding decade some forty families from the North of Ireland settled in the country west of the Hudson in what became Orange and Ulster counties. A congregation was formed at Bethlehem, Orange County, and one also at Wallkill, Ulster County; and in 1729 a call for ministerial supply was sent to the Philadelphia Synod. These settlements, which were in the valley of the Wallkill River, were augmented in 1731 by a body of emigrants from the North of Ireland in whose number were Charles Clinton and his sister, Christiana Clinton Beattie. Clinton was the founder of the New York family of that name, that produced two Revolutionary generals and two of the early Governors of New York. Mrs. Beattie was the mother of two noted Presbyterian clergymen. In 1742 another company of Scotch-Irish families arrived in Orange County, settling in Monroe Township. In 1740 sixteen families from Ulster made a settlement as far north as Glen Township, Montgomery County, but the danger from Indian attack was so great that the settlement was eventually abandoned.

A marked infusion of Scottish blood in New York came through settlements made in response to a proclamation issued in 1735 by the Governor, inviting "loyal Protestant Highlanders" to settle the lands between the Hudson and the Northern Lakes. Attracted by this offer, Captain Lauchlin Campbell of the Island of Islay brought over eighty-three families of Highlanders by November, 1740, but his expectations in regard to land grants were disappointed, and some of the people left the country. It was not until 1764, after Lauchlin Campbell's death, that tardy justice was done to these emigrants by grants of land in Washington County. This county borders on western Massachusetts, from which at this period Scotch-Irish emigration had . penetrated New York. Scotch-Irish settlements were made in Salem Township, Washington County, in 1762. The lands granted to the Highlanders were in the township immediately west of Salem.

A strong addition to this Scotch-Irish settlement made in 1765 illustrates the motive of religious freedom that operated so strongly on American colonization. The Rev. Thomas Clark of Scotland had been called to Cahans, near Ballybay, County Monaghan, Ireland, as the result of a split in the Presbyterian congregation there. Clark ministered to the seceders, and had to encounter much opposition. In 1754 he was arrested through the agency of some elders of the rival Presbyterian church at Ballybay. He lay in Monaghan jail for ten weeks, meanwhile preaching to as many of his people as could attend. The charge against him was eventually dismissed. In 1763 he received calls from America which he was inclined to accept. An emigration movement ran through his congregation and when he went to sail from Newry, on May 16, 1764, some three hundred persons were ready to go with him. They arrived in New York, whence some removed to the Abbeville district of South Carolina. The majority went to Stillwater on the Hudson, pending arrangements for their permanent settlement. At Stillwater James Harshaw, one of the elders, died during the summer of 1765. From him descended at least ten Presbyterian ministers, among them the Rev. Dr. William W. Harsha, professor of systematic theology in the Presbyterian Seminary of Nebraska.

Clark procured a grant of twelve thousand acres of land in Washington County, New York, free of charge for five years after which there was to be paid an annual rent of one shilling an acre. The congregation removed thither in 1766, settling at a place variously known as White Creek or New Perth, but which in 1786 became definitely known as Salem. An interesting feature of this settlement was that it was the transplantation of a congregation. The pastoral relation between Clark and his people remained unbroken. There was little if any interruption in the regular services, and when the congregation was settled in Salem Clark was pastor of eight ruling elders and 150 communicants who had come with him from Cahans. The first church building was the usual log cabin; in use only three years, it then became a school house and finally, in 1777, its timbers were used in building a block house as a defense against attack by the Indians. The second meeting house, built in 1770, has also disappeared, but the third one, built in 1797, is still standing, much altered and enlarged, with a congregation including some eighty families of the original stock. Among names connected with the original congregation are Adams, Armstrong, Beatty, Boyd, Carswell, Crozier, Cruickshank, Graham, Harshaw, Henderson, Lytle, Matthews, McClelland, McDougall, McCrea, McFarland, McMillan, McMurray, McNish, McWhorter, Reid, Rowan, Steele, Stevenson, Stewart, Williams.

Dr. Clark severed his relation with the Salem congregation in 1782, owing to difficulties in which he was involved because he was in a way landlord as well as pastor. He had made himself responsible for the shilling an acre rent and in making collections he pressed tenants in arrears, causing hard feelings that made his position uncomfortable. It is said that the congregation voted, with only two dissenting voices, that he should remain, but he resolved to leave. He appears to have resided at Albany for several years and then he removed to the Abbeville district in South Carolina, where a portion of his original flock had settled. He organized the Cedar Spring and Long Cane congregations over which he was installed pastor in 1786. The records of these early congregations have perished. Dr. Clark died on December 26, 1792, and was buried at Cedar Spring.

Washington County, New York, became a strong Scottish centre through repeated colonizations both from Scotland and Ulster. From 1764 to 1774 the township of Hebron, lying north of Salem, was largely granted to the officers and men of Montgomery's Highlanders, who had served in America for seven years and had received their honorable discharge. In 1761 Cambridge Township in the southern part of the county became the scene of Scotch-Irish settlement, the emigrants coming probably from Massachusetts and Connecticut. The settlement of all of the country east of the Hudson was largely due to immigration from New England. Central New York was first occupied by settlers moving up the Hudson River valley. Emigrants from Scotland, with some from Ulster, settled in Albany in such numbers that in 1760 a Presbyterian Church was organized there. A Presbyterian settlement was begun in Boston township, Saratoga County, in 1770, by the Reverend Eliphalet Ball and some members of his congregation who removed from Bedford, New York. Emigrants went to this settlement from New Jersey, New England, Scotland and Ulster. Stillwater Township, in the same county, was settled largely by Scotch-Irish emigration from New England.

In pursuance of the same design of garrisoning the frontier by Scotch-Irish settlements as was pursued in New England, a tract of 8,000 acres in what is now Otsego County was granted in 1738 to John Lindesay and three associates. The grant covered the present township of Cherry Valley in the upper watershed of the Susquehanna. Lindesay, a Scottish gentleman of some fortune, bought out his associates and addressed himself to the work of attracting settlers. While in New York City he became acquainted with the Rev. Samuel Dunlop, a minister of Ulster birth, and pursuaded him to take part in the enterprise. Mr. Dunlop visited Londonderry, N. H., and induced some of his friends there to accompany him to Cherry Valley, where, about 1743, he opened a classical school in his home. People came from both Scotland and Ulster to settle in this region. Middlefield was established by Scotch-Irish families in 1755, but the settlements grew slowly because of their exposed position on the frontier. In 1765 there were about forty families at Cherry Valley, and there were also some small settlements in the vicinity along the valley of the upper Susquehanna. The fears that retarded settlement were sadly justified by the Cherry Valley massacre, on October 11, 1778, when many of the inhabitants were killed, others carried off as prisoners, and all the buildings in the settlement were burned in an attack by Tories and Indians. It was not until 1784 that people began to return and rebuild.

Ulster participation in the settlement of New York, although distinctly marked, seems to have been inferior in extent to that of Scotland, from which country schemes of New York colonization were actively promoted. It seems probable that emigration from Ulster to the interior counties of New York was incidental to emigration from Scotland, which usually took in Ulster ports on the way. To this day Londonderry is a regular port of call in the voyage between America and Scotland. At one time it looked as if New York was about to become New Scotland. Sir William Johnson, an Ulster man, belonging to an English family that took part in the Plantation and settled in County Down, came to America in 1738. For his services in the French and Indian War he received from the Crown a grant of 100,000 acres north of the Mohawk River in what is now Fulton County. Sir William induced over 400 of the Highland Clan MacDonnell to settle on his lands, coming from the districts of Glengarry, Glenmorison, Urquhart and Strathglass. It was a complete transplantation, the Highland families going out under four chiefs, the MacDonnells of Aberchalder, Leek, Collachie and Scotas. The settlement, which was made in and about the present town of Gloversville, was after the feudal pattern, with tenantry grouped about the lord of the manor. These Highlanders strongly attached themselves to the interests of Sir William Johnson and when he died in 1774 their allegiance was transferred to his son, Sir John Johnson.

When the Revolutionary War broke out they followed him into the British army, the majority of them serving in the first and second battalions of the King's Royal Regiment of New York. In recognition of their loyalty and as a compensation for their losses the British Government granted them lands in Canada. They settled in districts of Ontario, which still remain intensely Gaelic. The Scotch element in Canada eventually became proportionately larger than in the United States. The colonies of Highlanders once established were augmented by emigration from among friends and neighbors in the home country. Nova Scotia, which as its name implies originated as a Scotch colony, has been even more retentive of the folk ways of old Scotland than modern Scotland itself. The Scotch settlements in Canada attracted emigrants even from the United States. Emigrants from Londonderry, N. H., took part in a settlement at Truro, Nova Scotia, in 1760, while on the other hand there was some migration from Nova Scotia to New England. But in general the Canadian provinces became and still remain a favored field for Scottish emigration while Ulster has always favored the United States.

CHAPTER IX

PENNSYLVANIA—THE SCOTCH-IRISH CENTRE

If one examines the relief map of the United States issued by the Geological Survey, it will appear that the leading position taken by Pennsylvania in Scotch-Irish settlement has a physical basis. In the color scale of the map the tint which indicates elevation from 0 to 100 feet is a narrow fringe in New England, but south of New York it becomes a broad belt, the greatest width being in the Carolinas, where it averages about 75 miles. During the period of colonization there were numerous swamps in this coast belt of low land, abounding with the germs of malarial fever. This belt does not extend into Pennsylvania, and emigrants arriving in that State had immediate access to salubrious uplands. Moreover, in Pennsylvania the Appalachian Range lies farther from the coast than it does north of Pennsylvania, and at the beginning of the eighteenth century this meant that the French were not such close neighbors as they were to New York and New England. From central Pennsylvania broad valleys stretch to the southwest along the eastern side of the Appalachians and toward the south convenient gaps occur in the mountain barrier. The tints on the relief map indicating elevation from 100 to 1,000 feet broaden from Pennsylvania southward and narrow from Pennsylvania northward. It was along these broad terraces that emigration first moved to the interior of the United States, its trend being southwest. Kentucky became a State in 1792; Tennessee in 1796; while Ohio, immediately west of Pennsylvania, did not become a State until 1803. It was owing to her situation and not because of any favor or encouragement from the authorities that Pennsylvania became the Scotch-Irish centre in the United States, and the chief source from which the race was diffused through the South and West.

The province was so accessible either by New York harbor and across the narrow width of New Jersey, or by the Delaware Bay and River, or by Chesapeake Bay and the Susquehanna River, that it is impossible to determine exactly where the first Scotch-Irish settlement took place. The grant of the country west of the Delaware River to William Penn was made in 1681. Emigrants usually landed either at Lewes or at Newcastle in Delaware, or in Philadelphia. There were Presbyterian congregations in all these ports before 1698. From any of them sections of Pennsylvania are in easy reach, a circumstance which a glance at the map makes plain at once. The earliest record that points to Scotch-Irish settlement relates to the triangular projection between Delaware and Maryland that now belongs to Chester County, Pennsylvania. In 1683 a tract on the east side of Elk Creek, Cecil County, Maryland, was surveyed for Edwin O'Dwire and "fifteen other Irishmen." This tract was known as New Munster, which together with the name of the principal grantee would indicate that this group of settlers came from the South of Ireland. Nevertheless, the New Munster district received so many settlers from the North of Ireland that they founded two Presbyterian churches, "Head of Christiana" and "The Rock." The church at the head of Christiana Creek was organized before 1708. The Rock church, subsequently known as East Nottingham, was at the head of Elk Creek. In the records of the Presbytery of Newcastle, May 18, 1720, the following minute occurs:

> "A certain number of people, lately come from Ireland, having settled about the branches of the Elk River, have by Thomas Reed and Thomas Caldwell, their commissioners, supplicated this Presbytery, that, at what time this Presbytery think convenient, they would appoint one of their number to come and preach among them, and then to take such note of their circumstances and necessities as by his report made to this Presbytery at their next session, the Presbytery may the more clearly know how to countenance their design of having the Gospel settled among them."

The Rev. Samuel Young was sent by the Presbytery and made such a favorable report as to the ability of the people to support a minister that the Presbytery voted in favor of organizing the congregation at the head of Elk.

The genesis of this Scotch-Irish settlement, while not definitely known, is readily explained. The grant to Penn overlapped the previous grant to Lord Baltimore. The boundary lines between Maryland and Pennsylvania were not finally settled until 1774. The New Munster tract was claimed by both Maryland and Pennsylvania, but the Maryland authorities were in possession. The opening of lands for settlement in that region drew Scotch-Irish families, among them four that bore the name of Alexander. John McKnitt Alexander, who was active in the Mecklenburg (N. C.) convention of 1775, was descended from one of these New Munster settlers. The Scotch-Irish immigrants, in seeking new lands, moved north of the older Maryland settlements, entering Pennsylvania. The early date at which a congregation is known to have existed there is a strong indication that the first Scotch-Irish settlement in Pennsylvania took place in this region, which is only about thirteen miles west of Newcastle, a port at which emigrants frequently debarked, and which was originally supposed to be in Pennsylvania territory. It was to this section of the country that Scotch-Irish immigration first turned. Writing to the Penns in 1724, James Logan, Secretary of the Province, said that the Ulster emigrants had generally taken up lands on the Maryland line. He refers to them as "bold and indigent strangers, saying as their excuse when challenged for titles, that we had solicited for colonists and they had come accordingly." In a letter of November 23, 1727, Logan says: "The Irish settle generally toward the Maryland line, where no lands can honestly be sold till the dispute with Lord Baltimore is decided."

In this same letter Logan gives some particulars that indicate the great volume of migration from Ulster to Pennsylvania. He says: "We have from the North of Ireland great numbers yearly. Eight or nine ships this last Fall discharged at Newcastle." In 1729 Logan writes: "It looks as if Ireland is to send all its inhabitants hither, for last week not less than six ships arrived, and every day, two or three arrive also." It appears that from December, 1728, to December, 1729, the immigrants numbered 6,208, of whom 5,605 were Scotch-Irish. Later on the arrivals exceeded 10,000 in the year. Proud's *History of Pennsylvania*, written before 1776, mentions that in 1749 about 12,000 immigrants arrived from Germany, and he adds that there are "in some years nearly as many annually from Ireland." He says that "Cumberland County is mostly settled by the Irish, who abound through the whole province." In 1735–1736 there was a great rush of emigration from Ireland through fear of restrictive legislation. In 1749 it was estimated that the Scotch-Irish population of Pennsylvania was one-fourth of the whole, and in 1774 Benjamin Franklin computed the proportion as one-third in a total of 350,000.

The early emigration followed the river valleys. One stream moved up the Delaware River and it could not have been much, if any, later than 1720 that Scotch-Irish settlers began to arrive in Bucks County. In 1726 there was quite a settlement of Scotch-Irish in Warwick, Warrington, Warminster and Northampton. Among the earliest arrivals were the families of Craig, Jamison, Baird, Stewart, Hair, Long, Weir, Armstrong, Gray, Graham and Wallace. A venerable monument of this settlement is Neshaminy Church, established about 1726 in Warwick Township.[4] The northern expansion of the Scotch-Irish settlements on the western bank of the Delaware River is marked by the organization of two churches in Northampton County in 1738, one the East Alien Church in the township of that name, the other at Mount Bethel. This stream of Scotch-Irish settlement lay between the Quaker settlements in and around Philadelphia and the Quaker settlements in West Jersey. To the northward there was great risk

---

[4]   The founding of Neshaminy Church has been dated as far back as 1710 by church historians. The evidence has been examined by William W. H. Davis, president of the Bucks County Historical Society, and he concludes that the church could hardly have been in existence much before 1726 when William Tennent became pastor. The assertion that the church dates to 1710 rests upon the fact that Bensalem church, of which Paulus van Vleck was pastor in 1710, had a branch at Neshaminy; but Mr. Davis holds that this branch had no connection with the Warwick Township church, of which Tennent became pastor. See Davis, *History of Bucks County*, Vol. I, pp. 300, 302.

of Indian incursion. The Gnadenhutten massacre took place in 1755 not far west of the Northampton County line.

* The principal field of Scotch-Irish occupation and settlement was the valley of the Susquehanna. From the original settlements on the Maryland line the Scotch-Irish moved into the interior along the east side of the Susquehanna, settling by the side of the creeks whose waters they used for their mills. Marks of these early settlements are Upper Octorara Church, organized in 1720; Donegal, in 1721; Pequa, in 1724; Middle Octorara, in 1727; Derry, in 1729; and Paxtang, in 1729. Thus large Scotch-Irish settlements were made in Chester, Lancaster and Dauphin Counties in the first third of the century. From Dauphin County the stream of settlement crossed to the west side of the Susquehanna. This region was at that time Indian country, and was known as Kittochtinny, a beautiful valley lying between the Susquehanna River and the Tuscarora Mountains, extending southward into western Maryland and Virginia. It is a natural thoroughfare between the North and the South, a fact which during the Civil War made it the scene of the manoeuvres culminating in the Battle of Gettysburg. The upper portion, now Cumberland County, was the scene of the first settlements. The provincial authorities acquiesced in the Scotch-Irish occupation after title had been obtained from the Indians by a treaty concluded in 1736. Under date of 1743, Watson's *Annals* contains the following note:

> "The Proprietaries, in consequence of the frequent disturbances between the Governor and Irish settlers, after the organization of York and Cumberland Counties, gave orders to their agents to sell no lands in either York or Lancaster Counties to the Irish; and also to make advantageous offers of removal to the Irish settlers in Paxton and Swatara and Donegal townships to remove to Cumberland County, which offers, being liberal, were accepted by many."

* From Cumberland County emigration turned southward. Cumberland County was organized in 1750; Franklin County, to the southwest, in 1764; Adams County, to the southeast, not

until 1800. The main stream of Scotch-Irish emigration to the interior moved northwest up the valley of the Susquehanna to the junction with the Cumberland valley, and thence moved southwest, following the trend of the mountain ranges. Scotch-Irish pioneers penetrated the country west of the mountains at an early date, and in 1750 there were sixty-two inhabitants of this outlying settlement. Their presence there was such a provocation to the Indians that the provincial authorities compelled them to remove, and their dwellings were destroyed. This withdrawal was undoubtedly wise; even the Cumberland Valley settlements were such advanced outposts that they suffered severely by Indian incursions after Braddock's defeat in 1755.

· All the Presbyterian congregations organized in Pennsylvania before 1760 were either in the valley of the Delaware or in the arc formed by the junction of the Cumberland valley with the valley of the Susquehanna. From 1766 onward Scotch-Irish emigration pressed further up the valley of the Susquehanna, the familiar place names now making their appearance in the records. The congregations of Tyrone and Toboyne in Perry County were organized in 1766; Derry, Mifflin County, in 1766. Juniata County has a Fermanagh township with a congregation organized in 1766. The Scotch-Irish settlement of western Pennsylvania did not take place until after the stream of Ulster emigration had reached the southwest. The oldest trans-Alleghany congregations date from 1771. The greater number of the first settlers of the southwestern counties of Pennsylvania came from Maryland and Virginia, over what was then known as Braddock's Trail. This trail extended from Cumberland, Maryland, to the valley of the Youghiogheny, crossing the country now included in Somerset and Fayette counties. At Uniontown, Fayette County, where there was a settlement as early as 1767, there was a trail westward to the valley of the Monongahela, along which settlers moved into Greene and Washington Counties. There was another trail, farther north, from Fort Bedford in what is now Bedford County to Fort Ligonier, and thence northwesterly to Fort Pitt. This was known as General

Forbes's Route. This trail traversed Westmoreland County, and many Scotch-Irish families settled in this region. Emigration was so heavy that the organization of counties made rapid progress, the most remote of all, Greene County, dating from February 9, 1796, at which time some of the present counties in the eastern section of the State were as yet unorganized. It is a general rule that outside of the original counties the oldest counties lie along the track of Scotch-Irish emigration.

A letter has been preserved written by Robert Parke, in 1725, to his sister in Ireland, giving an account of the conditions which settlers then encountered. He was living in what is now Delaware County, west of Philadelphia. His sister had written to him that report had reached Ireland that emigrants thence to Pennsylvania were dissatisfied. This prompted him to go into details. He declares it is:

> "The best country for working folk & tradesmen of any in the world... Land is of all Prices, Even from ten Pounds to one hundred Pounds a hundred, according to the goodness or else the situation thereof, & Grows dearer every year by Reason of Vast Quantities of People that come here yearly from Several Ports of the world."

He mentions that the rate for passage between Philadelphia and Ireland is nine pounds. Supplies are plentiful, the market price for beef, pork or mutton being two and one-half pence a pound. The country abounds with fruit.

> "As for chestnuts, wallnuts, & hasel nuts, strawberrys, bilberrys, & mulberrys, they grow wild in the woods and fields in Vast Quantities. ... A Reaper has two shills. & 3 pence a day a mower has 2 shills. & 6 pence & a pint of Rum, beside meat & drink of the best; for no workman works without their victuals in the bargain throughout the Country. A Laboring man has 18 or 20 pence a day in winter."

He advises his sister to bring plenty of clothes, shoes, stockings and hats, for such things are dear. Stockings cost four shillings and a pair of shoes, seven shillings.

"A saddle that will cost 18 or 20 Shills. in Ireland will cost here 50 Shills. or 3 pounds & not so good neither."

The writer remarks that notwithstanding high prices for manufactured articles, "a man will Sooner Earn a suit of Cloths here than in Ireland, by Reason workmen's Labour is so dear."

The reference to the increasing price of land of course applies chiefly to the region between the Delaware and the Susquehanna first opened to settlement. Scotch-Irish immigration flowed around the Quaker settlements and poured into the interior with a force that annoyed provincial authorities. Writing in 1730, Secretary Logan complains that the Scotch-Irish in an "audacious and disorderly manner" settled on the Conestoga Manor, a tract of 15,000 acres reserved by the Penns for themselves. Logan says the settlers alleged that it "was against the laws of God and nature, that so much land should be idle while so many Christians wanted it to labor on and to raise their bread."

It was, however, Logan himself who introduced them into that country, which took its name from the Susquehannock town of Conestoga, lying northwest of the creek of the same name. The title of the Indians was extinguished by the treaty concluded by Penn in 1718, but Indian towns were still so thick along the valley of the Susquehanna that it was deemed advisable to use the Scotch-Irish as a frontier garrison. In a letter dated November 18, 1729, Logan says:

"About that time [1720] considerable numbers of good, sober people came in from Ireland, who wanted to be settled. At the same time, also, it happened that we were under some apprehensions from ye Northern Indians. ... I therefore thought it might be prudent to plant a settlement of such men as those who formerly had so bravely defended Londonderry and Inniskillen, as a frontier, in case of any disturbance. Accordingly, ye township of Donegal was settled, some few by warrants at ye certain price of 10s. per hundred [acres] but more so without any. These people, however, if kindly used will, I believe, be orderly, as they have hitherto been, and easily dealt with. They will also, I expect, be a leading example to others."

It was the policy of Penn and his associates to make large reservations for themselves. Penn sold nearly 300,000 acres to persons in England who had never seen the land but who acquired it with a view to its prospective value. If their desires had been gratified there might have developed in Pennsylvania a tenant system with absentee landlords like that from which Ireland is now extricating herself. The chief instrument by which this system was frustrated appears to have been the Scotch-Irish. As the available lands in Donegal Township were taken up these people spread into the manor, and the Proprietors had to make terms with them.

Logan's successor, Richard Peters, had a similar experience in what is now Adams County. The Penns had reserved for themselves a tract of some 40,000 acres including the site of Gettysburg and the land southward to the Maryland line. Scotch-Irish emigrants settled in this country, and in 1743 Peters undertook to dispossess them. Seventy of the settlers confronted Peters, who had with him a sheriff and a magistrate, and strongly protested. Peters had brought surveyors to plat the region but the settlers would not allow them to proceed. A number of indictments were brought, but in the end the cases were compromised, the Scotch-Irish settlers being left in possession of their holdings with titles from Penn for a nominal consideration.

The Proprietors, while thus reserving to themselves large manors, and quite willing to use the Scotch-Irish to ward off Indian incursions, were unwilling to help bear the public burdens. This was a chronic issue between the Governor and the Assembly, the Governor importuning the Assembly to lay taxes for the public defense, and yet rejecting all bills that did not exempt the Proprietary estates. In his *Autobiography* Benjamin Franklin mentions a bill which set forth "that all estates, real and personal, were to be taxed; those of the Proprietaries not excepted." The Governor agreed to approve the bill, with the change of only a single word. His amendment was that "only" should be sustituted for "not." Franklin says that the account of these proceedings, transmitted to England, "raised a clamor against the Proprietaries for their meanness and injustice in giving their Governor such instructions; some going so far as to say, that, by obstructing the defense of their province, they forfeited their right to it."

That was a view of the case upon which the Scotch-Irish were inclined to act. It is noted as a racial characteristic that they were opposed to paying any rent, however small. This aversion is amply explained by their experience in Ulster, where rents had been raised after they had settled the country and made the lands valuable by their industry.

In habits and mode of living there was little to distinguish the Scotch-Irish from other settlers, except their attachment to Presbyterianism. There were some Scotch-Irish among the Quakers, James Logan himself was one of these, but the proportion was very small. Many of the Irish Quakers who emigrated to Pennsylvania were natives of England who had lived only a few years in Ireland. The Scotch-Irish who settled in America had to adapt their ways of life to the new conditions. Their style of dress was that which was common among the backwoodsmen, and in general they fell into the folkways of the frontier. Particular information about their manners and customs is meagre. Journals kept by pioneer ministers have been preserved, but they rarely contain any descriptive matter. In the *Diary* of the Rev. David McClure there is an entry under date of October 17, 1772, when he was in the Youghiogheny region:

> "Attended a marriage, where the guests were all Virginians. It was a scene of wild and confused merriment… The manners of the people of Virginia, who have removed into these parts, are different from those of the Presbyterians and Germans. They are much addicted to drinking parties, gambling, horseracing and fighting. They are hospitable and prodigal."

These Virginia customs have been sometimes exhibited as Scotch-Irish. An account which has been drawn upon for that purpose is one written by the Rev. Joseph Doddridge, whose father settled in Washington County in 1773. His *Notes* which were prepared for publication in 1824 give a vivid and authentic account of pioneer society. Mr. Fisher, in his *Making of Pennsylvania*, refers to it as "the best description we have of the colonial Scotch-Irish." But Doddridge did not describe the Scotch-Irish. The people with whom he was reared came from Maryland and Virginia, and he expressly disclaims any particular knowledge of the Scotch-Irish settlers. He says:

> "With the descendants of the Irish I had but little acquaintance, although I lived near them. At an early period they were comprehended in the Presbyterian Church, and were, therefore, more reserved in their deportment than their frontier neighbors, and from their situation, being less exposed to the Indian warfare, took less part in that war."

The reference is to the outbreak of Indian hostilities in 1774, known as Dunmore's War. Doddridge attributes to the Presbyterians the introducing of religious worship and the founding of educational institutions in the western country. There is no denominational bias in his testimony, as he was reared in the Methodist Church, entered its ministry and eventually became an Episcopal clergyman. Writing to Bishop White in 1818, to give an account of religious conditions, Doddridge declared:

> "To the Presbyterians alone we are indebted for almost the whole of our literature. They began their labors at an early period of the settlement of the country, and have extended their ecclesiastical and educational establishments so as to keep pace with the extension of our population; with a Godly care which does them honor."

Doddridge was educated at a Presbyterian institution, Jefferson College, at Canonsburg, Pa., and he never forgot his indebtedness to it. The account he gives of frontier conditions doubtless describes dress, home crafts and customs which the Scotch-Irish adopted in common with other settlers. They may have made some contribution to the stock, a possible allusion to which is Doddridge's mention that among the dances was one called the "Irish trot." In general frontier customs reflected frontier conditions. The dress of the men showed the influence of Indian example. In colonial times this style of dress prevailed throughout the interior. It should be remembered that the frontier was for a long period close to the coast. There were Indian camps even in Bucks County, the oldest section under European occupation. Doddridge's account, although made from observations in western Pennsylvania in the last quarter of the century, may be taken as characteristic of frontier conditions everywhere before the growth of factories and the construction of railroads transformed living conditions. He says:

> "The hunting shirt was universally worn. This was a kind of loose frock, reaching half way down the thighs, with long sleeves, open before, and so wide as to lap over a foot or more when belted. The cape was large and sometimes handsomely fringed with a ravelled piece of cloth of a different color from that of the hunting shirt itself. The bosom of this dress served as a wallet to hold a chunk of bread, cakes, jerk, tow for wiping the barrel of the rifle, or any other necessary for the hunter or warrior. The belt, which was always tied behind, answered several purposes besides that of holding the dress together. In cold weather the mittens, and sometimes the bullet bag, occupied the front part of it. To the right side was suspended the tomahawk, and to the left the scalping knife in its leathern sheath. The hunting shirt was generally made of linsey, sometimes of coarse linen, and a few of dressed deerskins. These last were very cold and uncomfortable in wet weather. The shirt and jacket were of the common fashion. A pair of drawers, or breeches and leggins, were the dress of the thighs and legs; a pair of moccasons answered for the feet much better than shoes. They were made of dressed deerskin. They were mostly made of a single piece with a gathering seam along the top of the foot, and another along the bottom of the heel, without gathers as high as the ankle joint or a little higher. Flaps were left on each side to reach some distance up the legs. These were nicely adapted to the ankles and lower part of the leg by thongs of deerskin, so that no dust, gravel or snow could get within the moccason.
>
> "The moccasons in ordinary use cost but a few hours labor to make them. This was done by an instrument denominated a

moccason awl, which was made from the back spring of an old clasp knife. This awl with its buck's horn handle was an appendage of every shot pouch strap, together with a roll of buckskin for mending the moccasons. This was the labor of almost every evening. They were sewed together and patched with deerskin thongs, or whangs, as they were commonly called. In cold weather the moccasons were well stuffed with deers' hair or dry leaves, so as to keep the feet comfortably warm; but in wet weather it was usually said that wearing them was 'a decent way of going barefooted,' and such was the fact, owing to the spongy texture of the leather of which they were made.

"The women usually went barefooted in warm weather. Instead of the toilet, they had to handle the distaff or shuttle, the sickle or weeding hoe, contented if they could obtain their linsey clothing and cover their heads with a sunbonnet made of six or seven hundred linen. The coats and bedgowns of the women, as well as the hunting shirts of the men, were hung in full display on wooden pegs round the walls of their cabins, so while they answered in some degree the place of paper hangings or tapestries, they announced to the stranger as well as neighbor, the wealth or poverty of the family in the articles of clothing.

"The fort consisted of cabins, block houses and stockades. A range of cabins commonly formed one side at least of the fort. Divisions 6r partitions of logs separated the cabins from each other. The walls on the outside were ten or twelve feet high, the slope of the roof being turned wholly inward. A very few of these cabins had puncheon floors; the greater part were earthen. The block houses were built at the angles of the fort. They projected about two feet beyond the outer walls of the cabins and stockades. Their upper stories were about eighteen inches every way larger in dimensions than the under one, leaving an opening at the commencement of the second story to prevent the enemy from making a lodgment under the walls. In some forts, instead of block houses, the angles of the fort were furnished with bastions. A large folding gate made of thick slabs, nearest the spring, closed the fort. The stockades, bastions, cabins and blockhouse walls were furnished with portholes at proper heights and distances… The whole of this work was made without the aid of a single nail or spike of iron, and for this reason—such things were not to be had. In some places less exposed, a single blockhouse, with a cabin or two, constituted the whole fort. Such places of refuge may appear very trifling to those who have been in the habit of seeing the formidable military garrisons of Europe and America; but they answered the purpose, as the Indians had no artillery. They seldom attacked, and scarcely ever took one of them."

The settlers were naturally loath to leave their own cabins, abandoning their live stock and other possessions, until absolutely compelled to do so, and usually they did not repair to the fort until actual bloodshed showed that the Indians were on the ground. Doddridge gives a vivid account of his own experience. He says:

> "I well remember that, when a little boy, the family was some-times waked up in the dead of night, by an express with a report that the Indians were at hand. The express came softly to the door, or back window, and by a gentle tapping waked the family. This was easily done, as an habitual fear made us ever watchful and sensible to the slightest alarm. The whole family were instantly in motion. My father seized his gun and other implements of war. My stepmother waked up and dressed the children as well as she could, and being myself the oldest of the children, I had to take my share of the burdens to be carried to the fort. There was no possibility of getting a horse in the night to aid us in removing to the fort. Besides the little children, we caught up what articles of clothing and provision we could get hold of in the dark, for we durst not light a candle or even stir the fire. All this was done with the utmost dispatch, and the silence of death. The greatest care was taken not to awaken the youngest child. To the rest it was enough to say *Indian* and not a whimper was heard afterward. Thus it often happened that the whole number of families belonging to a fort who were in the evening at their homes, were all in their little fortress before the dawn of the next morning. In the course of the succeeding day, their household furniture was brought in by parties of the men under arms."

Doddridge's account of the domestic crafts of his region is doubtless applicable to all the backwoods settlements. It depicts conditions that were once general outside of the coast settlements where supplies could be obtained from Europe. In colonial times society in such centres as Boston, New York, Philadelphia, Annapolis, Richmond and Charleston was ornate and even luxurious among the well-to-do, but the people who tamed the wilderness and gave the nation its continental expansion lived in the style Doddridge describes, and these include the mass of the Scotch-Irish immigrants. Some extracts from his account will exhibit living conditions:

> "The hominy block and hand mills were in use in most of our houses. The first was made of a large block of wood about three feet long, with an excavation burned in one end, wide at the top and narrow at the bottom, so that the action of the pestle on the bottom threw the corn up the sides toward the top of it, from whence it continually fell down into the centre. In consequence of this movement, the whole mass of the grain was pretty equally subjected to the strokes of the pestle. In the fall of the year, while the Indian corn was soft, the block and pestle did very well for making meal for Johnny cake and mush, but were rather slow when the corn became hard…
>
> "A machine, still more simple than the mortar and pestle, was used for making meal, while the corn was too soft to be beaten. It was called a grater. This was a half circular piece of tin, perforated with a punch from the concave side, and nailed by its edges to a block of wood. The ears of corn were rubbed on the rough edges of the holes, while the meal fell through them on the board or block to which the grater was nailed, which being in a slanting direction, discharged the meal into a cloth or bowl placed for its reception. This to be sure was a slow way of making meal; but necessity has no law…
>
> "The hand mill was better than the mortar and grater. It was made of two circular stones, the lowest of which was called the bedstone, the upper one the runner. These were placed in a hoop; with a spout for discharging the meal. A staff was let into a hole in the upper surface of the runner near the outer edge, and its upper end through a hole in a board, fastened to a joist above, so that two persons could be employed in turning the mill at the same time. The grain was put into the opening in the runner by hand…

"Our first water mills were of that description denominated tub mills. It consists of a perpendicular shaft, to the lower end of which an horizontal wheel of about four or five feet diameter is attached, the upper end passes through the bed stone and carries the runner after the manner of a trundle-head. These mills were built with very little expense, and many of them answered the purpose very well.

"Instead of bolting cloths, sifters were in general use. These were made of deerskin in a state of parchment, stretched over an hook and perforated with a hot wire. Our clothing was all of domestic manufacture. We had no other resource for clothing, and this, indeed, was a poor one. The crops of flax often failed, and the sheep were destroyed by the wolves. Linsey, which is made of flax and wool, the former the chain and the latter the filling, was the warmest and most substantial cloth we could make. Almost every house contained a loom, and almost every woman was a weaver.

"Every family tanned their own leather. The tan vat was a large trough sunk to the upper edge in the ground. A quantity of bark was easily obtained every spring, in clearing and fencing the land. This, after drying, was brought in and in wet days was shaved and pounded on a block of wood with an axe or mallet. Ashes were used in place of lime for taking off the hair. Bear's oil, hog's lard and tallow answered the place of fish oil. The leather, to be sure was coarse; but it was substantially good.

"Almost every family contained its own tailors and shoemakers. Those who could not make shoes, could make shoe packs. These like moccasons, were made of a single piece of leather, with the exception of a tongue piece on the top of the foot. This was about two inches broad, and circular at the lower end, to this the main piece of leather was sewed, with a gathering stitch. The seam behind was like that of a moccason. To the shoe pack a sole was sometimes added. The women did the tailor work. They could all cut out and make hunting shirts, leggins and drawers."

Such were the living conditions to which the Scotch-Irish subjected themselves as they poured into the country. They were not at all repelled by them, as they were inured to privation, and skilled in self-help through their Ulster training. The abundance

of game and wild fruits made the basis of subsistence more ample
and varied than they had been accustomed to in Ulster. That they
took to backwoods life with relish is shown by the alacrity with
which they moved forward wherever lands could be obtained for
settlement. The rapid expansion of the United States from a coast
strip to a continental area is largely a Scotch-Irish achievement.

The practices peculiar to them as a class belong to their religious system, which was a culture and a discipline whose effects
upon American national character have been very marked. From
old church records that have been preserved some idea may be
obtained of the thoroughness with which religious instruction was
diffused through Scotch-Irish settlements. Big Spring congregation, in the western part of Cumberland County, was organized
not later than the spring of 1737, for in June of that year a minister was called. This congregation had a succession of pastors,
either natives of Ulster or born of Ulster parents. One of these
early pastors was the Rev. Samuel Wilson. He was born in 1754
in Letterkenny township, now included in Franklin County, was
graduated from Princeton in 1782, licensed by Donegal Presbytery
on October 17, 1786, and was installed pastor of the Big Spring
Church, June 20, 1787. Some records of his pastorate have been
preserved, and they give an instructive view of the workings of
the system, the details showing that Ulster traditions were still
vigorous after the lapse of over half a century. He used a form of
address in the marriage ceremony which illustrates the plainness
and directness of speech then still in vogue. After searching inquiry
whether or not objections to the marriage existed Mr. Wilson
proceeded to address the couple as follows:

> "The design of marriage is, that fornication may be avoided,
> and as our race is more dignified than the lower creations, so
> then, our passions should be regulated by reason and religion. It
> is likewise intended for producing a legitimate offspring, and a
> seed for the church. There are duties incumbent upon those who
> enter this relation, some of them are equally binding upon both
> parties, some upon one party, some upon the other.

"First, it is equally binding upon you both to love each other's persons, to avoid freedom with all others which formerly might have been excusable, to keep each other's lawful secrets, fidelity to the marriage bed, and if God shall give you an offspring, it will be mutually binding upon you both, to consult their spiritual, as well as their temporal concerns.

"Secondly, it will be particularly binding upon you, Sir, who is to be the head of the family, to maintain the authority which God hath given you. In every society there must be a head, and in families, by divine authority, this is given to the man, but as woman was given to man for an helpmeet and a bosom companion, you are not to treat this woman in a tyrannical manner, much less as a slave, but to love and kindly entreat her, as becomes one so nearly allied to you.

"Lastly, it is incumbent upon you, Madam, who is to be the wife, to acknowledge the authority of him who is to be your husband, and for this, you have the example of Sarah, who is commended for calling Abraham, Lord. It seems to be your privilege in matters in which you and he cannot agree, that you advise with him, endeavoring in an easy way by persuasion to gain him to your side; but if you cannot in this way gain your point, it is fit and proper that you submit in matters in which conscience is not concerned. It will be your duty in a particular manner, to use good economy in regard to those things which may be placed in your hands. In a word, you are to be industrious in your place and station."

The congregation was regimented under the elders, John Carson, John Bell, William Lindsay, John McKeehan, David Ralston, Robert Patterson, Robert Lusk, Samuel M'Cormick, Hugh Laughlin and John Robinson. One of the elder's duties was to visit the members in his district and catechize them upon questions prepared by the minister, whose duties included not only the conduct of religious worship, but also the systematic instruction of the people; and the elders discharged among other functions, that of district examiners. Lists of questions used by the elders of Big Spring Church in 1789 have been preserved. Here is a specimen:

John Bell's District

1. What do you understand by creation? Is it a work peculiar to God?

2. How will you prove from Scripture and reason in opposition to Aristotle and others, that the world is not eternal?

3. How will you defend the Mosaic account, which asserts that the world has not existed 6,000 years, against ancient history, which tells us of Egyptian records for more than thirteen thousand years, and the Babylonians speak of things done four hundred and seventy thousand years before, and the Chinese tell of things still longer done?

The third chapter of the Confession of Faith also to be examined upon.

The elders did not use the same set of questions, although some questions appear in more than one paper, particularly the following:

What are those called who do not acknowledge divine revelation? What objections do they offer against Moses and his writings, and how are their arguments confuted?

Is the doctrine of the saints' perseverance founded on Scripture? If so, how will you prove it, and defend the doctrine against those who deny it?

What do you understand by the law of nature?

The extracts make a fair exhibit of the range of the questions. The papers were prepared by the pastor, and in view of the large size of parishes in those days it is to be presumed that the elders were coached by the pastor and made the medium of instruction supplementary to his pulpit discourses. It is plain that the questions assume a considerable degree of knowledge on the part of the people. In considering such records the historian feels that he is peering into the source of the extraordinary zeal for education displayed by the Scotch-Irish, which made them as a class superior in literacy and knowledge to the general run of American colonists.

CHAPTER X

The Indian Wars

A trait frequently attributed to the Scotch-Irish is that of cruelty to the Indians. Accusation of this nature goes back to the beginnings of Scotch-Irish settlement. In a letter of James Logan, written in 1729, he remarks that "the Indians themselves are alarmed at the swarms of strangers and we are afraid of a breach between them, for the Irish are very rough to them." In 1730 Logan wrote that "the settlement of five families from Ireland gives me more trouble than fifty of any other people." At a later period the Scotch-Irish are charged with provoking Indian outbreaks, and atrocious massacres of friendly Indians are laid to their account. Such charges are so inveterate and so general that a detailed examination is desirable.

When the planting of English colonies in America began the Indians were everywhere thick along the coast, and accounts of collision between the two races appear in the history of all the early settlements. The Massachusetts Bay colonists had less difficulty of this kind to encounter, because not long prior to their landing some epidemic sickness swept away the Indians. Cotton Mather remarks in his *Magnalia*: "The woods were almost cleared of those pernicious creatures, to make room for a better growth." The attitude of thought manifested by this Puritan divine is typical of the sentiment which close contact with the Indians has inspired at every stage of the settlement of the country. Throughout the world's history, when peoples of different culture systems are brought into contact, the instinct of self preservation naturally operates to produce conflict. The white settlers in America impaired the natural basis of subsistence of the Indian tribes by their clearings and homesteads, and while they thus instilled a deep sense of grievance, at the same time they aroused cupidity by their possessions. Out of such a situation hostilities have always emerged, be the scene America on one side of the world, or Australia on the other.

There are early stages of Australian history that equal in atrocity anything that American history can show. The Tasmanians, whose habit of regarding all animals as their natural prey made it hard for them to discriminate in favor of sheep or cattle belonging to a settler, came to be regarded as so much vermin, to be extirpated by the handiest means, and it is charged that even poison was used for the purpose. The American Indians, a race of much higher grade than the Australian black-fellows, had a sense of law and public obligation that could be availed of in the negotiation of treaties and the purchase of titles; and as a rule arrangements of this character either preceded or closely attended the advance of white settlement. The superior knowledge and astuteness of the whites enabled them to get the better of the Indians in such negotiations, and dealings between the two races were to the disadvantage of the Indians who from time to time made bloody reprisals for their wrongs.

The conflict of race interest was aggravated by personal antipathy. Accounts of the Indian tribes with which the colonists came in contact describe them as filthy in their persons and licentious in their behaviour. The account given by William Penn is a sharp exception to the general tenor. He believed the Indians to be derived from the ancient Hebrews, and he idealized their persons, their living and their manners to an extent that makes his account read more like a rhapsody than a description. No doubt Penn was enabled to hold such idyllic beliefs by the fact that he was an absentee landlord. Those who lived in the colonies and knew what the Indians were through familiar observation had a very different opinion. "More dirty, foul and sordid than swine," says the early New England historian Hutchinson, "being never so clean and sweet as when they were well greased." The common charge that they had no more sense of decency in the relations of the sexes than so many brutes is now known to be an error, due to inability to apprehend the classificatory system upon which the domestic institutions of the Indians rested. Lewis H. Morgan, whose work on *Ancient Society* first delineated the archaic types of family organization, based his theories upon minute study of the customs of the American Indians. He pointed out that by Indian law the husband of the eldest daughter of a family was entitled to treat her sisters also as wives. This polygamy appears to have been originally part of a system of group marriage.

Champlain, who lived a whole winter about 1615 among the Algonquins, is quoted by Hutchinson as saying that "the young women, although married, run from one wigwam to another, and take what they like; but no violence is offered to the women, all depending upon their consent. The husband takes like liberty, without raising any jealousy, or but little between them; nor is it any damage or loss of reputation to them, such being the custom of the country." Group relations of this kind have been found among savages in many parts of the world, and they are really regulated by a stringent system of tribal morality, although on the surface they appear as abominable promiscuity.

Early New England historians say that the Indians did not make advances to white women. Hutchinson remarks that "the English women had nothing to fear as to any attempt upon their honor." The families of settlers who were made captives in the French and Indian wars in New England seem to have been on the whole well treated. This was probably due to the influence of the French in Canada to which country the captives were taken. It was different in the Indian wars in the middle colonies and the South; women captured by the Indians might suffer the worst indignities. The victims, if they eventually escaped, were naturally reticent upon such matters, but it was common knowledge that they occurred, and this intensified frontier hatred of Indian character. A well known case on the Virginia frontier was that of an Indian child born to a married woman who had been an Indian captive. The child was reared as a member of the family, but resisted efforts to educate him, and after enlisting in the Revolutionary Army was never heard from again.

The cruelty of the Indians is remarked by all observers of their characteristics. They displayed a positive enjoyment of the spectacle of suffering, so that children would be put to the torture for their amusement. A family named Fisher were among the captives made by an Indian raid in 1758 in what is now Shenandoah County, Virginia. After the band reached its village Jacob Fisher, a lad of twelve or thirteen, was set to gathering dry wood. He began to cry, and told his father that he was afraid they were going to burn him. His father replied "I hope not," and advised him to obey. When a sufficient quantity of wood was gathered the Indians cleared a ring around a sapling to which they tied the boy by one hand; the wood was arranged about the boy in a circle and then fired. The boy was compelled to run around in this ring of fire until his rope wound him up to the sapling, and then back again until he was in contact with the flames. Meanwhile he was prodded with long, sharp poles whenever he flagged, and thus the child was tortured to death before the eyes of his father and brothers.

Doddridge, who is a careful narrator, and who does not write in a spirit of animosity toward the Indians, gives the following account of the experience of settlers in what is now Greenbrier County, West Virginia:

> "Before these settlers were aware of the existence of the war, and supposing that the peace made with the French comprehended their Indian allies also, about sixty Indians visited the settlement on Muddy Creek. They made the visit under the mask of friendship. They were cordially received and treated with all the hospitality which it was in the power of these new settlers to bestow upon them; but on a sudden, and without any previous intimation of anything like a hostile intention, the Indians murdered in cold blood all the men belonging to the settlement, and made prisoners of the women and children. Leaving a guard with their prisoners, they then marched to the settlement in the Levels, before the fate of the Muddy Creek settlement was known. Here, as at Muddy Creek, they were treated with the most kind and attentive hospitality at the house of Mr. Archibald Glendennin, who gave the Indians a sumptuous feast of three fat elks which he had recently killed. Here, a scene of slaughter similar to that which had recently taken place at Muddy Creek, occurred at the conclusion of the feast.

"Mrs. Glendennin, whose husband was among the slain, and herself with her children prisoners, boldly charged the Indians with perfidy and cowardice, in taking advantage of the mask of friendship to commit murder. One of the Indians, exasperated at her boldness, and stung no doubt at the justice of the charge against them, brandished his tomahawk over her head, and dashed her husband's scalp in her face. In defiance of all his threats, the heroine still reiterated the charges of perfidy and cowardice against the Indians. On the next day, after marching about ten miles, while passing through a thicket, the Indians forming a front and rear guard, Mrs. Glendennin gave her infant to a neighbor woman, stepped into the bushes, without being perceived by the Indians, and made her escape. The cries of the child made the Indians inquire for the mother. She was not to be found. 'Well,' says one of them, 'I will soon bring the cow to her calf,' and taking the child by the feet, beat its brains out against a tree. Mrs. Glendennin returned home in the course of the succeeding night, and covered the corpse of her husband with fence rails. ... It was some days before a force could be collected in the eastern part of Botetourt and the adjoining country, for the purpose of burying the dead."

These are typical cases of Indian outrages that occurred along the track of Scotch-Irish settlement. There were like incidents on the frontier at every stage in the settlement of the country, and they produced everywhere an inveterate hatred of the Indians. It was not a Scotch-Irish characteristic but a frontier characteristic, and while the Scotch-Irish settlers certainly evinced this feeling, it was not peculiar to them as a class. Everywhere in colonial annals, whether the scene be in New England, or in Pennsylvania or in the South, there is the same story of the mutual hatred and ferocity of the two races. At the same time to those who became accustomed to it the Indian mode of life seems to have had a decided charm, for there are many instances of captives becoming genuinely incorporated in the tribe. A noted case is that of a young daughter of the Rev. John Williams, pastor of Deerfield, Mass. She married an Indian, and although she eventually returned to Deerfield to visit her family and early friends, she could not be induced to return to civilized life.

The Indian wars were not systematic military operations, but a succession of guerilla raids. The colonial Governments were so poorly organized, so deficient in resources and so crude in their methods, that they were apparently incapable of any steady exertion of public authority for the protection of the frontier. In the early wars of the New England settlements Indian methods were adopted. The attitude of the authorities and the state of public opinion in that period are instructively displayed in Penhallow's *History*. Samuel Penhallow was a native of Cornwall, England, who arrived in Massachusetts in 1686 originally with a view of becoming a missionary to the Indians. He married a wealthy heiress, by whom he acquired property at Portsmouth, N. H., where he settled. He was appointed a member of the Provincial Council, was Treasurer of the Province for several years, and for many years before his death in 1726 he was Chief Justice of the Superior Court. His *History* was published in 1726 with an introduction by the Rev. Dr. Benjamin Colman, of Boston, who likened the experience of the New England settlers with the Indians to that of the children of Israel with the Canaanites. Judge Penhallow's *History* is a document of the highest value, as it is a first-hand record of events. He gives a detailed account of massacres committed on both sides along the border, whither Scotch-Irish immigration to New England was directed. His account shows that all the provincial authorities did ordinarily was to incite reprisals upon the Indians. Referring to the year 1706 he says:

"The state of affairs still looking with a melancholy aspect, it was resolved for a more vigorous prosecution of the war, to grant the following encouragement, viz.:

To regular forces under pay £10
To volunteers in service 20
To volunteers without pay. 50   } per scalp
To any troop or company that go to the
    relief of any town or garrison 30

"Over and above was granted the benefit of plunder, and captives of women and children under twelve years of age, which at first seemed a great encouragement, but it did not answer what we expected."

The bounty was later raised to £100 a scalp to volunteers serving at their own expense, and £60 to soldiers drawing pay. The war was therefore carried on principally by expeditions of scalp hunters. On one occasion a party of them paraded the streets of Boston with ten scalps stretched on hoops and borne aloft on poles. Sullivan, in his *History of Maine*, published in 1795, mentions that in 1756 James Cargill was charged with the murder of two of the Norridgewock tribe of Indians, "but was acquitted and drew a bounty of two thousand dollars from the treasury for their scalps."

This method of making war was as inconclusive as it was expensive. In 1706 Penhallow estimated that every Indian killed or taken "cost the country at least a thousand pounds." Of the three years war, 1722 to 1725, he says: "The charge was no less than one hundred and seventy-five thousand pounds, besides the constant charge of watching, warding, scouting, making and repairing of garrisons &c, which may modestly be computed at upward of seventy thousand pounds more." And yet after all, the Indians were never really formidable in numbers or resources. Penhallow remarks that "it is surprising to think that so small a number of Indians should be able to distress a country so large and populous to the degree we have related."

, In Pennsylvania the customary inertia of the Government was aggravated by the positive unwillingness of the Assembly to permit the use of force. Benjamin Franklin in his *Autobiography* speaks of the unwillingness of "our Quaker Assembly to pass a militia law and make other provisions for the security of the Province." He relates that even when they did yield to stress of public necessity they would use "a variety of evasions to avoid complying, and modes of disguising the compliance when it became unavoidable." He gives as an instance that when an appropriation was needed for purchasing supplies of gunpowder the Assembly would not make the grant, but did make an appropriation "for the purchase of bread, flour, wheat, or *other grain*," the Government construing "other grain" to cover the purchase of gunpowder, and the Assembly not objecting to that interpretation. The usual situation was, however, that the Governor and Council were left without adequate funds for public defense.

This state of affairs should be kept in mind when the events are considered that have made a deep stain upon the record of the Scotch-Irish settlers in Pennsylvania. The Province was peculiarly exposed to Indian incursion through the easterly course of the mountain ranges. The Kittatinny mountain range or Blue Ridge, which was the western boundary of white settlement up to 1758, extends from Western Maryland to Northern New Jersey. After Braddock's defeat, on July 9, 1755, there were Indian raids all along this extensive frontier. By November 1, 1755, the magistrates of a region so far southeast as York County were calling for help to resist an Indian band moving down the Susquehanna. On the 24th of the same month the Indians struck into the region now included in Carbon, one of the easternmost counties of Pennsylvania, and massacred the inhabitants of the Moravian settlement of Gnadenhutten. Reports of Indian atrocities poured in upon the Government from every part of the frontier.

The settlers in Cumberland County, who were mainly Scotch-Irish, suffered greatly owing to their exposed position. Upon August 22, 1756, the Rev. Thomas Barton wrote to the Provincial Secretary relating that Indians had ambushed and killed a number of people at the funeral of a young woman "and what is unparallel'd by any Instance of Brutality, they even open'd the Coffin, took out the Corpse, and scalp'd her." Petition after petition went up from Cumberland County for help from the Government, particularly in the way of ammunition. The plight in which the people were left through the supineness of the Government is set forth in the following statement from the magistrates of York County, whose action cannot be imputed to Scotch-Irish prejudice as in that region the German element predominated:

> "We believe there are Men enough willing to bear Arms,
> & go out against the Enemy, were they supplied with Arms,

Ammunition & a reasonable Allowance for their Time, but without this, at least Arms, and Ammunition, we fear little to purpose can be done.

"If some Measures are not speedily fallen upon, we must either sit at home till we are butcher'd without Mercy, or Resistance, run away, or go out a confused Multitude destitute of Arms & Ammunition & without Discipline or proper Officers or any way fixed to be supplied with Provisions."

The then Governor of the Province, Robert Hunter Morris, was alive to his duties, but he lacked means to discharge them; and the situation tried his temper. He wrote to Governor Shirley of Massachusetts, August 27, 1756: "I am unfortunately linked with a set of men that seem lost to all sense of duty to their Country, or decency to their Superiors, who will oppose whatever I recommend, however beneficial to the public." The Assembly was opposed to creating a militia, and argued that the way to deal with the situation was by friendly overtures to the Indians, inquiring into their grievances, appeasing their complaints, and thus winning them from their alliance with the French. The imminence of the danger did not prevent the raising of the old issue, the Assembly insisting upon taxing the lands of the proprietors, and the Governor, acting under their instructions, pertinaciously resisting it. This issue was eventually compromised, the Penns agreeing to make a contribution in lieu of taxes, and means were obtained to erect forts along the frontiers to which the people could resort for protection. Lacking an organized force to repel the Indians, the New England policy of offering bounties for scalps was adopted. On April 9, 1756, the following schedule was proclaimed:

"For every Male Indian prisoner above ten years old,
that shall be delivered at any of the Government's
Forts, or Towns. $150
"For Female Indian Prisoner or Male Prisoner of
Ten years old and under, delivered as above. $130
"For the Scalp of every Male Indian of above Ten
years old $130
"For the Scalp of every Indian woman . . . .$ 50"

Such measures disgraced the Provincial Government by adopt-ing the methods of savages and were quite futile as a means of public defense. They made the war just such a game as the Indians liked to play. To give and take in the matter of scalps was what they expected. The outrages committed by them were as a rule the work of small parties who would surprise the settlers in the fields or at their homes, slay and scalp, and then make off. The alarm would crowd the forts for a while, but the settlers could not permanently abandon their fields and crops and would eventually leave the fort to become exposed to another raid. Thus the war dragged along for years attended by inconceivable misery. The cry of distress was heard across the ocean, and on June 24, 1760, the Ulster Synod authorized a collection for the relief of the afflicted Presbyterian ministers in Pennsylvania and New York. The number of refugees gathered about the forts of Shippensburg in July, 1763, is computed at 1,384—301 men, 345 women, and 738 children. Every shed, barn or possible place of shelter was crowded with people who had been driven from their homesteads, losing their live stock and harvests and reduced to beggary.

There was persistent complaint that aid and comfort to Indian incursions were given by the Indians still resident in the area of white settlement. An official report was made to the Assembly in October, 1763, that the Moravian Indians in Northampton County were supplying the hostiles with arms and ammunition. It was ordered that these Indians should be brought in from the frontier. Similar complaints were made against the Conestoga Indians in Lancaster County, and it was strongly urged that they, too, should be removed to some other place where they would be out of the way of frontier events, but nothing was done until there was a terrible catastrophe.

Among a number of companies organized for frontier defense was one under the command of the Rev. John Elder, which was recruited from the Scotch-Irish of the Paxtang district, now in Dauphin County. The outrages from which the settlers were now suffering were the work not of war bands but of a few Indians moving furtively, who would ambuscade and kill some traveler or attack some one working in the fields, and only by finding mutilated bodies would the settlers know that Indian marauders were about. It was generally believed that such acts were facilitated by the existence of Indian villages in which the stray hostiles could find shelter. It was charged that strange Indians were seen going to and coming from the village of the Conestoga Indians. Under date of September 13, 1763, Colonel Elder wrote to the Governor: "I suggest to you the propriety of an immediate removal of the Indians from Conestoga, and placing a garrison in their room. In case this is done, I pledge myself for the future security of the frontiers." The reply to this letter was written by John Penn, who about this time became Governor of the Province. He said that "The Indians of Conestoga have been represented as innocent, helpless, and dependent upon the Governor for support. The faith of this Government is pledged for their protection. I cannot remove them without adequate cause."

At last the people decided to act for themselves. On December 13, 1763, a party of frontiersmen moved upon the Conestoga Indians. According to one version the intention was to apprehend some prowling Indians who had taken refuge in Conestoga, and the massacre that ensued was due to a show of resistance by some Indians who rushed out, brandishing their tomahawks. According to Governor Penn the affair was "barbarous murder," committed "in defiance of all Laws & Authority," by "a party of Rioters." Colonel Elder, in a letter to Governor Penn, under date of October 16, 1763, gave this account:

> "On receiving intelligence the 13th inst. that a number of persons were assembling on purpose to go & cut off the Connestogue Indians, in concert with Mr. Forster, the neighboring Magistrate, I hurried off an Express with a written message to that party, entreating them to desist from such an undertaking, representing to them the unlawfulness & barbarity of such an action, that it's cruel & unchristian in its nature, & wou'd be fatal in its consequences to themselves & families; that private persons

have no right to take the lives of any under the protection of the Legislature; that they must, if they proceeded in that affair, lay their accounts to meet with a Severe prosecution, & become liable even to capital punishment; that they need not expect that the Country wou'd endeavour to conceal or screen them from punishment, but that they would be detected & given up to the resentment of the Governm't. These things I urged in the warmest terms, in order to prevail with them to drop the enterprise, but to no purpose; they push'd on, & have destroyed some of these Indians, tho' how many, I have not yet been certainly informed; I, nevertheless, thought it my duty to give your Honour this early notice, that an action of this nature mayn't be imputed to these frontier Settlem'ts. For I know not of one person of Judgm't or prudence that has been in any wise concerned in it, but it has been done by some hot headed, ill advised persons, & especially by such, I imagine, as suffer'd much in their relations by the Ravages committed in the late Indian War."

That the affair was indeed an outburst of mob cruelty inspired by race hatred is shown by the sequel. The Indians killed in the attack on Conestoga were six in number. The survivors were now removed to Lancaster, where they were lodged in the workhouse. On December 27 a party of men from Paxton and Donegal stormed the workhouse and killed the Indians. One version is that the original intention was to seize one of the Indians, who was charged with murder, and take him to Carlisle jail where he would be held for trial; but as resistance was encountered, shooting began and did not cease until every Indian was killed. The dead numbered fourteen, among whom there were three women, eight children, and only three men. Such facts do not support the pretext that the massacre was occasioned by resistance to arrest. Colonel Elder wrote at once to Governor Penn deploring the affair which he attributed to the failure of the Government to remove the Indians as had been frequently urged. "What could I do with men heated to madness," Elder went on to say. "I expostulated, but life and reason were set at defiance."

Public sentiment in the Scotch-Irish settlements strongly

condemned the mob outbreak. Writing to the Governor from Carlisle on December 28, Col. John Armstrong said: "Not one person of the County of Cumberland so far as I can learn, has either been consulted or concerned in that inhuman and scandalous piece of Butchery—and I should be sorry that ever the people of this County should attempt avenging their injuries on the heads of a few inoffensive superannuated Savages, whom nature had already devoted to the dust." Cumberland was more strongly Scotch-Irish in population than any other county in Pennsylvania. Colonel Armstrong, of Ulster nativity, was an elder in the Presbyterian Church.

Under date of December 31, 1763, Governor Penn received an anonymous letter from Lebanon, advising him that "Many of the Inhabitants of the Townships of Lebanon, Paxton & Hanover are Voluntarily forming themselves in a Company to March to Philadelphia, with a Design to Kill the Indians that Harbour there." This view of the situation was at once adopted by the Governor in his official announcements. On January 3, 1764, he sent a message to the Assembly notifying it of "the cruel Massacre of the Indians" at Lancaster, and adding that "the party who perpetrated this outrage do not intend to stop here, but are making great additions to their numbers, and are actually preparing to come down in a large Body and cut off the Indians seated by the Government on the Province Island; and it is difficult to determine how far they may carry their designs, or where the mischief may end."

The provincial records of this period contained much about this threatened attack upon friendly Indians. But what was really impending was a popular revolt against the supine, nerveless and bewildered rule of the narrow oligarchy that controlled the policy of the Assembly. The Government made extensive preparations to repel attack. General Gage, who was in chief command of the British forces in America, supplied a detachment of regulars to guard the barracks in which the Indians were lodged. Cannon were posted and the place was strongly fortified. If an attack upon the Indians had been the controlling purpose of the frontiersmen they would now have desisted, as such an undertaking was plainly hopeless, but they were not deterred from continuing their march toward Philadelphia, as their main object was a redress of grievances. At Germantown they were met by commissioners with promises of a hearing of their complaints. Col. Matthew Smith and James Gibson went forward with the commissioners to meet the Governor and the Assembly, and the body of frontiersmen now dissolved, most of them returning at once to their homes. The statement of grievances presented to the provincial authorities is of such value as an historical record, and is so illuminative of the ideas of the times, that it is given in full in Appendix D.

The Assembly did nothing to the point. The petitions were referred to a committee which recommended a conference with representatives of the back counties, the Governor to take part. The Governor sent a pedantic message declining to participate, and declaring that he "doubts not but the House will take into Consideration such parts of the Remonstrance as are proper for their Cognizance, and do therein what in their Wisdom and Justice they think Right, as he will with Regard to such other parts as Relate to the executive Branch of the Government." The Assembly proceeded no further with the matter of the petitions. An act providing for removing the trial of persons charged with killing Indians in Lancaster County was passed despite the remonstrance, but no convictions were obtained under it.

Contemporary opinion among the Scotch-Irish themselves, while deploring the occurrence, was inclined to make excuses on the score of the exigencies of the case. The Rev. John Ewing, D.D., writing to Joseph Reed at London in 1764, gave the following account:

"There are twenty-two Quakers in our Assembly, at present, who, although they won't absolutely refuse to grant money for the King's use, yet never fail to contrive matters in such a manner, as to afford little or no assistance to the poor distressed frontiers; while our public money is lavishly squandered away, in supporting a number of savages, who had been murdering and scalping us for many years past. This has enraged some desperate young men who had lost their nearest relatives by these very Indians, to cut off about twenty Indians, that lived near Lancaster, who had, during the war, carried on a constant intercourse with our other enemies; and they came to Germantown to inquire why Indians, known to be enemies, were supported, even in luxury, with the best that our markets afforded, at the public expense, while they were left in the utmost distress on the frontiers, in want of the necessaries of life. Ample promises were made to them, that their grievances shall be redressed, upon which, they immediately dispersed and went home. These persons have been unjustly represented as endeavoring to overturn the Government, when nothing was more distant from their minds. However this matter may be looked upon in Britain, where you know very little of the matter, you may be assured that ninety-nine in a hundred of the Province are firmly pursuaded that they are maintaining our enemies, while our friends, who are suffering the greatest extremities, are neglected; and that few, but Quakers, think that the Lancaster Indians have suffered anything but their just deserts."

It is now known that Dr. Ewing's letter correctly describes the state of public opinion, but the opponents of the Scotch-Irish secured a lasting advantage in getting historical authority on their side. The first history of Pennsylvania was written by Robert Proud, an English Quaker, who arrived at Philadelphia in January, 1759. At the time of the march of the frontiersmen he was teaching Greek and Latin in the Friends' Academy. His *History* is a dry, colorless narrative of events, except when he describes the approach of the frontiersmen, and then the heat of his language reflects the alarm and excitement felt in the section of the community to which Proud himself belonged. He says that "This lawless banditti advanced, in many hundreds, armed, as far as Germantown, within about six miles of the city, threatening death and slaughter to all who should dare to oppose them."

Proud's *History* stood alone in its field until Thomas F. Gordon's work was published in 1829. Gordon wrote in a judicial spirit, and

in an appendix he gave a list of Indian outrages that had exasperated public sentiment, but he treats the march to Philadelphia as
of a piece with the riots at Conestoga and Lancaster, and declares
that "nothing but the spirited measures of the inhabitants of the
city, saved it from the fury of an exasperated armed multitude,
who would not have hesitated to extend their vengeance from the
Indians to their protectors." Gordon also declares that "there is
every reason to infer, from the profound veneration the Indians
entertained for the Quakers, and the attention they paid to their
messages, that had the Friends been permitted to follow out their
plans of benevolence, the Indian War would never have existed
or would have been of short duration."

The verdict of history as thus pronounced by Proud and
Gordon was generally accepted until Dr. William H. Egle's *History*
appeared in 1876, in which there was a weighty presentation of
the case in behalf of the Scotch-Irish, and it was shown by cita-
tions from the private correspondence of Governor Penn that he
was really of the opinion that the frontier complaints were well
founded, although he was so situated that he did not feel able to
act on that belief.

The ground upon which Quaker policy toward the Indians
rested, from which nothing could budge it, was that by it the
Province had escaped the Indian wars from which other colonies
had suffered, and peaceful relations had been maintained until
the breaking out of hostilities with the French and Indians in
1754. This is an impressive fact that has been much remarked
by historians. The circumstances however indicate that the success of this policy was due more to particular conditions than
to its intrinsic merit. At the time the settlement of Pennsylvania
began the Indians living in that Province had been so broken
and humbled by wars with other tribes that they were ready for
peace on any terms. In submitting themselves to the conquering
Iroquois they even accepted the humiliation of declaring themselves to be women, and putting on women's dress. In 1742,
when Governor Thomas had some trouble with a tribe of the

Delawares, he solicited the influence of the Six Nations. That powerful Indian confederacy sent a delegation whose spokesman gave the Delawares a scolding that cowed them at once. One of the delegates, Canassatego, a Mengwe chief, addressing the Delawares in the presence of Governor Thomas said:

> "We conquered you; we made women of you; you know you are women, and can no more sell land than women; nor is it fit you should have the power of selling lands, since you would abuse it. This land that you claim is gone through your guts; you have been furnished with clothes, meat and drink, by the goods paid you for it, and now you want it again, like children as you are."

In conclusion Canassatego bade them talk no more about their claims but to depart at once, as he had some business to transact with the English. The Delawares meekly complied, leaving the council at once, and soon thereafter removing from the region to which they had been laying claim. These broken spirited tribes were ready enough to hold peace conferences and receive presents, and they became artful in practicing upon the inexhaustible pacificism of the Quakers. This policy of tribute was condemned by the settlers both as a drain upon the public treasury and as an incentive to aggression. Even Gordon admits:

> "Their hostility has been rewarded rather than chastised by Pennsylvania; every treaty of peace was accompanied by rich presents, and their detention of the prisoners was overlooked upon slight apologies, though obviously done to afford opportunities for new treaties and additional gifts."

The policy of soft words and tribute, while tolerably successful so long as only the Indians of the Province had to be dealt with, was entirely futile when the French were stirring up the Indians, and the entire frontier was in a blaze. The notion of the Quaker oligarchy at Philadelphia that the Pennsylvania situation could be localized and the Indians be pursuaded to be good within that area was grotesquely inept, and its practical effect was to facilitate Indian outrages by paralyzing the Government.

Gov. John Penn took office in November, 1763, when frontier exasperation over the supineness of the Government had reached a maddening pitch. A grandson of William Penn, he was born in the Province and lived there for ten years before taking office; so he was personally familiar with conditions. His father, Richard Penn, and his uncle, Thomas, were at that time the Proprietors as heirs of William Penn, and his commission as Governor came from them. Soon after taking office he wrote as follows to Thomas Penn, under date of November 15, 1763:

> "I have had petitions every day from the Frontier Inhabitants requesting assistance against the Indians, who still continue their ravages in the most cruel manner, and as they say themselves, are determined not to lay down the Hatchet till they have driven the English into the Sea. We had news yesterday of two families being murdered near Shippensburg. I have not yet heard the particulars, but the fact may be depended upon. We have been obliged to order the Moravian Indians down to Philadelphia to quiet the minds of the Inhabitants of Northampton County, who were Determined either to quit their settlements or take an opportunity of murdering them all, being suspicious of their having been concerned in several murders in that County. These Indians came down two days ago & were immediately sent to the Pesthouse, where they were quartered."

But with regard to the Conestoga Indians Governor Penn pursued an altogether different policy, and yet it appears from his private correspondence that he did not believe the Conestogas to be so innocent as they were represented to be. Why then did he refuse to remove them, although he did remove the Moravian Indians? It is a reasonable conjecture that he was trying to avoid difficulties with the controlling element in the Assembly. Moravian missionaries and Quakers were suffering from the Indian incursions into Northampton County, and about their welfare there was more concern than about the Scotch-Irish of Lancaster County. It may be noted that he does not himself undertake to exonerate the Conestoga Indians, but merely says that they "have been represented as innocent." In the following letter to Thomas Penn, the manuscript of which is undated, he expresses a different opinion:

"... You will see by the commotion the Province has been in for a long time past, the Impossibility of apprehending the murderers of the Conestoga Indians. There is not a man in the County of Cumberland but is of the Rioters' Party. If we had ten thousand of the King's troops I don't believe it would be possible to secure one of these people. Though I took all the pains I could, even to get their names, I could not succeed, for indeed nobody would make the discovery, though ever so well acquainted with them, & there is not a magistrate in the County would have touch'd one of them. The people of this Town are as Inveterate against the Indians as the Frontier Inhabitants, for it is beyond a doubt that many of the Indians now in Town have been concerned in committing murders among the back settlers; & I believe, were it not for the King's troops, who are here to protect them, that the whole power of the Government would not be able to prevent their being murder'd. Nothing can justify the madness of the people in flying in the face of Government in the manner they have done, although what they have suffer'd from these cruel savages is beyond description. Many of them have had their wives and children Murder'd and scalped, their houses burnt to the ground, their Cattle destroy'd, and from an easy, plentiful life, are now become beggars. In short this Spirit has spread like wildfire, not only through this Province, but the neighboring governments, which are to the full as Inveterate against the Indians as we are. The 14th of this month we expect two thousand of the Rioters in Town to insist upon the Assembly's granting their request with regard to the increase of Representatives, to put them upon an equality with the rest of the Counties. They have from time to time presented several petitions for that purpose, which has been always disregarded by the House; for which reason they intend to come in person."

It may be argued that the passage in the above referring to the complicity of the so-called friendly Indians in the outrages on the frontier does not necessarily include the Conestoga Indians. Dr.

Egle in his *History* cites a letter from John Penn to Thomas Penn in which the Governor says:

> "The Conestoga Indians, but also those that lived at Bethlehem and in other parts of the Province, were all perfidious—were in the French interest and in combination with our open enemies."

Another circumstance, significant as indicative of Governor Penn's own opinion, is that he transmitted to Thomas Penn a pamphlet entitled *The Conduct of the Paxtons Impartially Represented*, with the information that it is by a Mr. Barton, for whom he vouches as a sensible and honest man. Writing under date of June 16, 1764, Governor Penn mentions that Barton's authorship "is a secret; for it seems the Assembly have vow'd vengeance against all who have ventur'd to write anything, that may have a tendency to expose their own iniquitous measures." The Assembly took very high views of prerogative and regarded any comment upon its behavior as a breach of privilege to be severely punished. The pamphlet transmitted by Governor Penn was published anonymously in March, 1764, and it is a very severe arraignment of Quaker policy, holding that upon it the guilt of bloodshed chiefly rests. The pamphlet is loaded with classical erudition and Scriptural citation to an oppressive extent, but it contains some sharp home thrusts, as in the following:

> "When a Waggon Load of the scalped and mangled Bodies of their Countrymen were brought to Philadelphia and laid at the State House Door, and another Waggon Load brought into the Town of Lancaster, did they rouse to Arms to avenge the Cause of their murder'd Friends? Did we hear any of those Lamentations that are now so plentifully poured for the Connestogoe Indians?—O my dear Friends! must I answer—No? The Dutch and Irish are murder'd without Pity."

The author of this pamphlet was the Rev. Thomas Barton, a native of Ireland belonging to an English family which settled there in the reign of Charles I. He was graduated at Dublin University, went to America and was for a time a tutor in the Philadelphia

Academy that was the germ of the University of Pennsylvania. In 1754 he received Episcopal orders in England, and returned as a missionary for the Society for the Propagation of the Gospel. He accompanied General Braddock's expedition as a chaplain, and later settled in Lancaster as rector of St. James parish, where he remained until his Tory principles made his position untenable and caused his removal to New York. He was a resident of Lancaster at the time of the riots, and as an Anglican clergyman he was not likely to have any partiality for the Scotch-Irish Presbyterians. He disclaims approval of the acts of the rioters, but he contends that the blame chiefly rests upon the policy of the Provincial Assembly, which in view of all the evidence now appears to be a just verdict.

The light of history at times has the effect of coming from a bull's eye lantern, bringing its object into unnatural relief. Such has been the case with the affair of the Conestoga Indians, which is only one, and that far from being the greatest, among the innumerable cases of lynch law which have resulted from the weakness and incompetence of American public authority.

NOTE—The letters of John Penn quoted in this chapter were copied by the writer from the original manuscripts in the archives of the Historical Society of Pennsylvania, Philadelphia, with the exception of one letter, which is not in the Philadelphia collection, but is given on the authority of Dr. W. H. Egle, who cites it in his *History of Pennsylvania*. Dr. Egle was for twelve years State Historian of Pennsylvania, and availed himself of manuscript collections at Harrisburg.

CHAPTER XI

Planting the Church

Although all the church historians recognize the important influence which Scotch-Irish emigration exerted in introducing and spreading Presbyterianism in the American colonies, yet owing to the usual mode of treatment which regards Presbyterianism as a phase of the Puritan movement, the architectonic character of the Scotch-Irish influence does not stand out with the distinctness that is its due. Thus Dr. Briggs in his *American Presbyterianism* first mentions the Puritan settlements in New England. A much older *History* by the Rev. Richard Webster gives a more correct view of genetic order, by taking Ulster as the starting point of the history of the Presbyterian Church in America. The still older *History* by the Rev. Charles Hodge regards the beginnings of American Presbyterianism as involved in Puritan emigration to America. All these historians have solid grounds for the positions they have taken, but for a clear understanding of the matter certain distinctions should be borne in mind. We must distinguish between Puritanism and Presbyterianism; between Presbyterianism and the Presbyterian Church in the United States of America.

The use of the term "Puritan" has been traced to the year 1564. Fuller, in his *Church History*, says that in that year "the English Bishops, conceiving themselves empowered by their canons, began to show their authority in urging the clergy of their dioceses to subscribe to the liturgy, ceremonies and discipline of the Church, and such as refused the same were branded with the odious name of Puritans, a name which, in this nation, first began in this year." Archbishop Parker, in his letters of this period, uses the terms "Precision," "Puritan" and "Presbyterian" as nicknames for the reforming party in the Church. In 1574 Dr. Thomas Sampson, who was himself one of those that sought to purify the order and discipline of the Church, wrote to Bishop

Grindal, protesting against the use of the odious epithet "Puritan" to designate "brethren with whose doctrine and life no man can justly find fault." This repugnance to an appellation that later was accepted as honorable was due to the fact that as originally used it carried with it an imputation of schism, whereas the early Puritans considered themselves loyal Churchmen, seeking to rid the Church of abuses and corruptions.

The Puritan movement in its inception had a marked infusion of the joyous spirit of the Renaissance, of which indeed it was intellectually a derivative. The Puritan gentry united the elegance of Elizabethan culture with a keen appreciation of the Biblical scholarship that was exposing as unwarranted the episcopal jurisdiction against which there were strong practical grievances. Hallam's *Constitutional History* remarks that "the Puritans, or at least those who rather favored them, had a majority among the Protestant gentry in the Queen's [Elizabeth] days," and "they predominated in the House of Commons." Puritanism was a spirit of resistance to current pretensions of high prerogative in both Church and State, in natural association with demands for such reforms in both those spheres of government as would establish constitutional order. There was originally nothing narrow or ascetic in Puritanism, The strength of the movement that thwarted the strivings of James I. toward absolute dominion in Church and State was in the country gentry, a pleasure-loving class. The biography of Colonel Hutchinson gives the portrait of a Puritan gentleman of the original type. He was fond of painting, sculpture and all liberal arts; was devoted to gardening and gave much attention to the improvement of his grounds; he had a great love for music, and often played upon the violin.

"Presbyterian" was originally synonymous with "Puritan," because the term denoted the historical theory which Puritanism advanced in opposition to the current claims of episcopal authority. The theory asserted the parity of presbyters and denied that the bishopric was a distinct and superior order. Originally this doctrine was advanced as a principle of reform within the Church, and not as the mark of a particular denomination, as it has since become. In Chapter III. of this work it was noted that the early Presbyterian preachers in Ulster accepted a Presbyterian form of episcopal ordination, and sat in convocation with the clergy of the Church of Ireland. At that time one could be a Puritan, a Presbyterian and a Churchman. At a later period, when the Presbyterian order had been overthrown by the Independents, the Presbyterian clergy of Ulster denounced the revolution and became a mark for the scurrilous invective of John Milton. The Independent sects which through Cromwell's military supremacy obtained a temporary control of the Government of England also took to themselves the term of "Puritan," associating it with austere behavior, while "Presbyterian" became the title of a particular Church, which was Established in Scotland, but which in England and Ireland was a form of dissent from the Established Church.

Puritanism then originally signified hardly more than the championship of constitutional order and opposition to absolutism in Church and State. Like all opposition parties it embraced various elements that in course of time came to differ in their particular aims and methods. The intellectual ferment of the times produced doctrines and principles at variance with Presbyterianism, and eventually sects claimed the name of "Puritan" that had little in common with original Puritanism. The term has become so amplified that now any denomination that dates from the Puritan period is apt to lay claim to Puritan ancestry and include Puritan achievement in its denominational history.

Puritanism as a doctrine of Church polity had a following that extended far beyond the bounds of English Puritanism. As is well known, the doctrine received its most logical and authoritative exposition from the French theologian John Calvin, who was settled in Geneva, Switzerland. Presbyterian sentiment flowed into America from many sources, so that an examination of the beginnings of American Presbyterianism must consider many elements. But if the inquiry be narrowed to the question of the corporate derivation of the Presbyterian Church of the United

States, the evidence points unmistakably to Ulster as the source.

In Chapter V. some account was given of the reasons why Puritan migration to America took place more readily among the Independents than among the Presbyterians. Hence that particular element among the Puritans heavily predominated in the settlement of New England; but there was a Presbyterian element in Puritan migration, and it was strongly evident even in New England. It is estimated that about 21,200 emigrants arrived in New England before 1640, and according to Cotton Mather about 4,000 of them were Presbyterians. Calvinists from Holland and France brought Presbyterianism with them to America, as well as the immigrants from Ireland, Scotland and England. Germs of Presbyterianism were strewn throughout the colonies as far south as the Carolinas, and some isolated congregations were formed at a very early date. But while Presbyterianism was thus diffused by many rills the organization of the Presbyterian Church of the United States was the particular achievement of the Scotch-Irish element.

Although evidence of record is meager, there is enough to establish a direct connection between Ulster and the formation of the first American Presbytery. In Chapter V. mention was made of the Scotch-Irish settlements on the Chesapeake Bay in the last quarter of the seventeenth century, and of their call to Ulster for ministerial supplies. Francis Makemie, who went to Maryland in response to this call, organized the first American Presbytery. About that time the Presbyterians were hard pressed by an energetic movement started in 1701 to build up the Church of England in the colonies. Makemie, who had been long in the American field, went to London in the summer of 1704, and appealed to the Presbyterian and Puritan leaders for men and funds to sustain them. Support was pledged for two missionaries for two years, and Makemie returned to America with two young ministers, John Hampton, who like Makemie himself prepared for the ministry under the supervision of Laggan Presbytery, and George McNish, who was doubtless a Scotsman as no nationality is specified in the record of his admission to the University of Glasgow and that was the custom in case of students from Scotland. The three arrived in Maryland in 1705, and in the spring of 1706 they united with Jedediah Andrews, John Wilson, Nathaniel Taylor and Samuel Davis, four ministers already at work in Pennsylvania, Delaware and Maryland, to form the Presbytery of Philadelphia. Andrews came to Philadelphia from Boston in 1698 and appears to have been ordained in Philadelphia in 1701. Wilson came from Boston to Newcastle, Del., in 1698. Taylor was minister to the Presbyterians on the Patuxent River, Md. The date when his ministry began and his derivation are uncertain, but Dr. Briggs thinks it most likely that he came from New England. Davis was settled at Lewes, Del., prior to 1692, and was probably an Irish Presbyterian.

The membership of the Presbytery was therefore pretty evenly divided between Irish Presbyterians and New England Presbyterians, but the formative influence undoubtedly proceeded from the Scotch-Irish missionary Makemie. The organization affected was Scotch-Irish in type. The analysis made by Dr. Briggs brings this out clearly. After describing the organization of the Ulster Presbyteries, he observes: "The first American classical Presbytery was such an Irish meeting of ministers, but without subordination to a higher body. ... It was very different from a Westminster classical Presbytery, or a Presbytery of the Kirk of Scotland." Makemie writing about the Presbytery said that among its rules was one "prescribing texts to be preached on by two of our number at every meeting, which performance is subject to the censure of our brethren." Dr. Briggs remarks: "This also was an Irish custom. The records of the early Irish Presbyteries contain frequent references to it."

At that time Presbyterianism was weak in Philadelphia, and it remained so until the great Scotch-Irish immigration poured Presbyterianism into the country and the preaching of George Whitefield gave a marked impetus to religious zeal. When the Presbytery of Philadelphia was organized only one member was settled in Philadelphia, and so far as the composition of the membership was concerned the Presbytery might well have had another location and another name. But sound strategic reasons controlled the choice. George Keith, once a zealous Quaker, but who had become quite as zealous a Church of England man, had made Philadelphia the base of a controversial activity that took a wide range. In 1692 Keith visited Makemie's parish on the Eastern Shore of Virginia and challenged him to a public disputation. There was a forward movement on the part of the Church of England all along the line, and Puritans of every sort, Presbyterian or Congregational, were impressed with the necessity of energetic action for the common defense. New England Congregationalists and English, Scotch and Irish Presbyterians cooperated in this crisis. The organization of the Presbytery of Philadelphia was a stroke in the Puritan interest. Soon after the first meeting of the Presbytery Makemie wrote to Dr. Benjamin Coleman of Boston, March 28, 1707: "Our design is to meet yearly, and oftener if necessary, to consult the most proper measures for advancing religion and propagating Christianity in our various stations." The results of this action were of profound importance. Dr. Briggs says of the work of Makemie and his associates:

> "They organized an institution which was a rallying point for Presbyterianism in the Middle States. It enabled them to license and ordain their ministers in a regular manner; it enabled them to cooperate with the organized forces of Puritanism and Presbyterianism in all parts of the world; it was a master stroke of wise policy which now gave Presbyterianism an advantage over Episcopacy, in spite of the strong influences and active oppression by the authorities in Church and State."

An incident occurring immediately after the first meeting of the first American Presbytery showed that organization for the common welfare was the urgent need of the non-conformists. After the adjournment of the Presbytery, October 27, 1706, Makemie and John Hampton set out on a journey to Boston, probably to consult with the Puritan ministers there. On the way they stopped in New York, and preached in that city and on Long Island. Both were arrested on a charge of preaching without license. The charge against Hampton was not pressed, but Makemie had to sustain trial. He was defended by three of the ablest lawyers in the Province, and was acquitted on the ground that he had complied with the Toleration Act; but the costs of the trial were thrown upon him, amounting to £83, 7s., 6d. The affair outraged Puritan sentiment on both sides of the Atlantic. Feeling against Governor Cornbury of New York was so strong owing to this and other arbitrary action that in April, 1707, the New York Assembly made a strong indictment of his administration. He was eventually recalled by the home Government and his successor took office in 1709.

The Presbytery of Philadelphia was the centre from which the organization of American Presbyterianism proceeded. In 1716 the Presbytery had grown so that it divided itself into subordinate meetings or Presbyteries, three in number at first, with expectations soon realized of a fourth, organized on Long Island. These Presbyteries were represented in the first American Synod, which met in 1717. At the first meeting of this Synod a "fund for pious uses" was founded, and Jedediah Andrews was appointed treasurer. Dr. Briggs remarked that "this was the basis of all the schemes of missionary enterprise which have arisen from time to time in the American Presbyterian Church."

An instance of Scotch-Irish pugnacity is furnished by the struggle of 1741 over some points of doctrine, discipline and practice which it does not lie within the province of this work to discuss. From the accounts given by Church historians it appears that an energetic minority, only twelve in number, got control of the Synod, the membership of which was four times their number. Dr. Briggs says that the twelve were all Irishmen with the possible exception of one, whose nativity is uncertain. Seven belonged to the Presbytery of Donegal. One result of this struggle was the organization of the Synod of New York, with three Presbyteries, New York, New Brunswick and New Castle. The two Synods remained separate until 1758, when they were united as the Synod of New York and Philadelphia. In 1788 this great Synod organized the General Assembly of the Presbyterian Church, the first session of which was held in Philadelphia in May, 1789. This was the consummation of the work of organization begun by the Scotch-Irishman Francis Makemie in 1706.

Thus it appears that both in historical connection and in nature of organization the Presbyterian Church in the United States was a Scotch-Irish enterprise. Still another mark of Scotch-Irish influence is the name borne by early Presbyteries. In or about 1729 the first New England Presbytery was organized, and was named Londonderry. In 1732 Donegal Presbytery was formed, with such an extensive area in Pennsylvania and Maryland that from it other large Presbyteries eventually issued, Carlisle in 1765 and Baltimore in 1786. From place names alone, the historian could infer that Scotch-Irish influence was active in the American colonies from about 1715, but fortunately many records remain of ministerial supplies furnished by Ulster, that were of illustrious service in planting religion and in spreading learning and culture.

CHAPTER XII

ON STONY GROUND

Some account has already been given of the earliest arrivals of Scotch-Irish ministers, in connection with the Chesapeake Bay settlement. Ministerial activity next becomes noticeable in New England immigration. In October, 1714, the Rev. William Homes and his brother-in-law, the Rev. Thomas Craighead, with their families arrived in Boston from Londonderry. Mr. Homes was born in 1663 of an old Ulster family, and went to New England about 1686 as a school teacher. A desire to enter the ministry caused him to return to Ireland, and at the meeting of Laggan Presbytery in 1692 he was reported as "on trial to ordination." He was ordained December 21, 1692, as pastor at Strabane. He received the M.A. degree from the University of Edinburgh in 1693. On September 26, 1693, he married Katherine, daughter of the Rev. Robert Craighead of Londonderry. When he emigrated to America he was over fifty years old, and had had ten children. He was a man of note and consequence in the Irish Church and was elected Moderator of the General Synod that met at Belfast in 1708. His knowledge of administration incited him to publish *Proposals of Some Things to be done in our Administring Ecclesiastical Government*, printed at Boston in 1732. Mr. Homes settled at Chilmark, in Martha's Vineyard, where he remained until his death, June 27, 1746, in his eighty-fourth year.

The Rev. Mr. Craighead came of distinguished Scotch-Irish stock. He was graduated at the University of Edinburgh as *Scoto-Hibernus*, December 10, 1691, and became pastor of Dearg, in the Presbytery of Convoy, Ireland. On May 3, 1715, the Presbytery approved his demission from the congregation of Dearg, and gave him a testimonial to go to America. The Synod censured the Presbytery for not acting with greater deliberation. This minister, whom the Scotch-Irish church was so loath to lose, did not at first meet with favorable acceptance in America. He settled at

Freetown, Mass., where the support he received was so inadequate that he petitioned the General Court for assistance. In June, 1718, he was allowed ten pounds for six months services. In 1719 he appealed to the Justices of the Peace for Bristol County, and at the Court of General Sessions the town was ordered to lay a rate for his support. There was a violent resistance to this measure, many refused to pay, and some were imprisoned. A petition went up to the General Court, which on June 19, 1719, ordered that the prisoners should be liberated, the rate be annulled and Craighead's election as minister of Freetown should be void. Craighead then petitioned for relief, setting forth that he had served for four and a half years, and had received no pay for three years. In December the General Court granted him twenty pounds. Craighead then left Freetown, but was unable to settle himself in New England. He joined New Castle Presbytery, January 28, 1724. This was the opening of a new career whose lustre made amends for his unfortunate New England experience. On February 22, 1724, he was installed pastor of the church at White Clay Creek, in Delaware. He labored in that region for seven years greatly promoting the spread of Presbyterianism by his eloquence and zeal. In 1733 he moved to Lancaster, Pa., and joined Donegal Presbytery. He was pastor of the church at Pequea from October 31, 1733, thence he went to Hopewell, within the bounds of the present town of Newville, a few miles west of Harrisburg. It was a frontier settlement, presenting a difficult post for an old man to fill, but he was now at the close of his career. He died in the pulpit in April, 1739, just as he had pronounced the benediction.

Father Craighead, as he was generally known in Pennsylvania, was progenitor of families prominent in southern and western Presbyterianism. One son, Thomas, born in 1702, married Margaret, daughter of George Brown, Londonderry, Ireland, and coming to America, became a farmer at White Clay Creek, Del. Another son, Alexander, became an eloquent minister whose stirring activities were exerted in Pennsylvania, Virginia and North Carolina. Jane, a daughter of the Rev. Thomas Craighead, married,

October 23, 1725, the Rev. Adam Boyd, pastor of a church at the Forks of the Brandywine.

The difficulties which Mr. Craighead experienced in Massachusetts are said to have been largely due to a contentious disposition, but it is difficult to reconcile this opinion with the judgment of him expressed by Cotton Mather in a letter written July 21, 1719, to a leader of the opposition to Craighead. Mather said: "Mr. Craighead is a man of singular piety and humility and meekness, and patience and self denial and industry in the work of God. All that are acquainted with him, have a precious esteem of him."

While this particular controversy may have been aggravated by personal differences (John Hathaway, a kinsman, was conspicuous among the minister's enemies) yet the underlying causes were such as to make it symptomatic of conditions unfavorable to Scotch-Irish Presbyterianism in New England. The Independents were virtually an Established Church. Notwithstanding the common Puritanism of both Independents and Presbyterians, and the sympathetic attitude of leading clergymen in both parties, the differences in order and discipline were bound to tell. The seat of authority in the Presbyterian polity is the council of presbyters and elders of the member congregations. This implies the existence of ecclesiastical units as a condition precedent. An isolated body is practically a Congregational church, and as Presbyterianism entered New England it found a Congregational field in which its adherents could feel at home. On the other hand, attempts at separate organization would raise practical difficulties as regards the support of the Church. At that time it was considered entirely proper to levy taxes for ecclesiastical use. Originally among the New England Puritans the town meeting was virtually the congregation in session upon public business, an integral part of which was care of the meetinghouse and the support of the minister. So the planting of a Presbyterian Church would raise the question for the Congregationalists whether provision for its support should be included in the town rates, and for the Presbyterians, whether they should have to pay a town rate for public worship while providing for themselves at their own expense. It is pretty clear that difficulties of this nature inflamed the situation with which Craighead had to deal at Freetown, and were too much for him, notwithstanding his eloquence, zeal and fortitude. Removed to Pennsylvania, his qualities were such as to secure for him an illustrious and fruitful career.

At the same time that Craighead was having his troubles at Freetown there was an event at Worcester significant of the clash of interests that retarded Presbyterianism in New England. The Scotch-Irish immigrants who settled in Worcester were accompanied by the Rev. Edward Fitzgerald, whose antecedents have not been traced. They began to erect a building of their own, but one night a crowd of townspeople destroyed the framework. According to local historians Deacon Daniel Heywood of the Congregational Church encouraged the attack, and the "best people in town" were present. The explanation of this outburst is that the people did not want to have to support two Churches when one would suffice for all. The affair was a crushing blow to the Presbyterian interest. The settlers clung to their own form of worship, some going to Sutton to be under the Rev. John McKinstry, who began his ministry there about 1720; some removing to Londonderry in New Hampshire. The Rev. Mr. Fitzgerald departed when it was found that no regular place of worship could be had, but he returned occasionally to preach, and there is mention of his presence as late as 1729.

Some years later another attempt was made to establish a Presbyterian Church and a call was sent to the Rev. William Johnston of Mullaghmoyle, County Tyrone, a graduate of the University of Edinburgh. In 1737 John Clark and nine others petitioned the town to free them from taxation for religious purposes. It is recorded that "ye Irish petition" was voted down by "a grate majority." The point of the application was that the petitioners wanted to be rid of the burden of contributing to the support of the established Congregational Church, in addition to supporting their own Presbyterian Church. Johnston, unable to maintain himself in Worcester, removed to Windham, N. H., where in July, 1742, he became the first minister of the town. In July, 1752, the poverty of the parish forced him to withdraw, and he went into the State of New York, where he held a number of charges and gave years of service before his death, May 10, 1782, in Florida, Montgomery County.

A still more violent clash between Presbyterian tendency and the established Congregationalism occurred in Connecticut in or about 1741. In Milford, New Haven County, some people revolted against the doctrinal views of the town minister, and formed a Presbyterian congregation which sent a call to the Rev. Samuel Finley, For the offense of preaching to them, Mr. Finley was arrested and sentenced to be transported out of the colony as a vagrant and a disturber of the public peace. Mr. Finley eventually became President of the College of New Jersey.

Although Presbyterianism was checked in New England, there were no theological barriers to the incorporation of the Scotch-Irish in the Congregational Church, and that is what generally took place. The seating lists of the Worcester Congregational Church for 1733 have been preserved and show many Scotch-Irish names. What probably happened is that the Scotch-Irish became enrolled in the local Puritan congregation and as such were members of the Church and of the town meeting, although gathering for church services of their own when some Presbyterian minister visited the community. A like process doubtless went on in other places. For instance, James Smith, who settled in Needham, Mass., is thus mentioned in the record of the Congregational Church of that town:

> "Jan. 9, 1726—James Smith & Mary his Wife, admitted into the Church, came from Ireland A. D. 1718, & Brought a Testimonial with them from Mr John Stirling, Minister of the Congregation of Ballykelly in the County of Londonderry."

Thus Scotch-Irish emigration to New England tended

rather to furnish recruits to Congregationalism than to spread Presbyterianism. The ministers, too, apparently found it hard to preserve their Ulster type of organization in a land without Presbyteries or Synods, and they allowed themselves to be converted into Congregational ministers, a process that not only was without theological shock but made little practical difference in the status of a particular congregation.

It has already been noted that Ulster immigration to New England in 1718 was promoted and attended by ministers. The five ships that arrived in August, 1718, brought among their passengers the Rev. William Boyd, of Macosquin, Londonderry, and the Rev. James McGregor, of Aghadowey, a neighboring village. Boyd came rather as a guide than as an emigrant and he returned to Ireland; McGregor intended to remain. His charge at Aghadowey was unable to support him, and eighty pounds were due him at the time of his departure. Little is known of Mr. McGregor's antecedents, but it is thought that he came from the Scotch Highlands, inasmuch as he had such a knowledge of Celtic that he took a leading part in missions organized for work among Celtic speaking people. He was ordained at Aghadowey June 25, 1701. He arrived in Boston August 4, 1718. The records show a blot upon his career of a sort likely to occur at that period. It was an age of hard drinking among all classes of people. In 1704 McGregor was admonished before the Ulster Synod for his behavior in having taken several cans of ale at Coleraine, when, as he admitted, "less might have served." But the charge of drunkenness was declared to be not proven, and except for that one affair he appears to have led an exemplary life.

Cotton Mather, after two months of intercourse, exerted himself to obtain employment for McGregor, writing of him as "a person of a very excellent character: and considerably qualified for the work of ye ministry as well for his ministerial abilities, as his Christian piety, serious gravity, and as far as we have heard, every way unexceptionable Behaviour." Upon Mather's recommendation the town of Dracut, a little north of the present city of

Lowell, gave McGregor a trial. It makes rather a strong suggestion that even at that early period the ministerial profession was overcrowded when it appears that McGregor was chosen from among some fifteen candidates for the place. In town meeting on October 15, 1718, it was voted that Mr. McGregor should be invited "to settle in Dracut to preach the Gospel and do the whole work of a settled minister" at a stipend of £65 a year, rising to £70 after four years, and until there should be fifty families in the town, when the amount should be increased to £80. McGregor accepted the call and in addition to his work as pastor taught the village school.

In this there is no mark of gain to the Presbyterian Church. A Scotch-Irish Presbyterian minister had been settled as a Congregationalist minister in a Massachusetts town; that appears to be all. There is no evidence that any of the Scotch-Irish who landed in Boston with McGregor accompanied him to Dracut. The mass of them were at that time looking forward to a collective occupation of new territory, and this desire was before long realized in the settlement of Nutfield subsequently known as Londonderry. This place, although in New Hampshire, is not very far north of Dracut, and a number of the Scotch-Irish settlers stopped at Dracut on their way. They induced McGregor to go with them, and the first religious services in the new settlememt were conducted by him. It says much for McGregor's constancy to his people that as soon as they were thoroughly established in their new home he gave up his secure position at Dracut to join them. He settled in Londonderry in May, 1719, and died there on March 5, 1729, leaving a widow and seven children. One of the sons, David, became famous as a Presbyterian leader, through his ability as a preacher and as a controversialist. The widow, Mary Ann McGregor, was married, January 9, 1733, to the Rev. Matthew Clark, McGregor's successor at Londonderry. Clark came to America from Ireland in 1729 with credentials from the Presbytery of Coleraine.

In 1719, the Rev. James Woodside arrived in Maine with some Ulster emigrants who settled at Merrymeeting Bay, but Woodside remained behind in Falmouth with his family, probably awaiting more settled conditions. The people at Brunswick, Me., at a town meeting November 3, 1718, called him as pastor at a stipend of forty pounds a year. Apparently he did not get on well with his parishioners. In May, 1719, the town meeting voted to continue his services for six months "provided those of us who are Dissatisfied with his Conversation (as afore Said) Can by Treating with him as becomes Christians receive Such Satisfaction from him as that they will Heare him preach for ye Time Afores^d." The town voted on September 10, 1719, to dismiss him, and not long thereafter he returned to Boston. In a letter of January 25, 1720, Cotton Mather writes that "poor Mr. Woodside, after many and grievous calamities in this uneasy country, is this week taking ship for London."

There is a local tradition to the effect that Woodside was disliked by some for not being sufficiently Puritanical, and this appears to have been a reproach brought against the Scotch-Irish clergy as a class. In a letter written to a friend in Scotland Cotton Mather spoke of them as having an "expression full of levity not usual among our ministers." It is evident that Puritanism had by this time come to connote austere manner and repressed behavior. That Puritanism should take this turn among the Independents instead of among Presbyterians exemplifies the familiar principle that custom is more exacting than law. Presbyterians had a systematized authority within whose bounds they were at ease. The Independents rejected systematized authority but custom established a formal pattern of behavior, from which it was dangerous for ministers to deviate.

The Rev. James Hillhouse was born about 1688 at Freehall, County Londonderry. He studied divinity at Glasgow and was ordained by Derry Presbytery October 15, 1718. He came to America in 1720 and in 1722 was called to a church in the second parish at New London, Conn., where he died December 15, 1740. Hillhouse came of a distinguished Ulster family, and he founded a distinguished American family. His grandfather,

Abraham Hillhouse of Artkill, Londonderry, was in the famous siege. His father, John Hillhouse, was owner of a large estate known as Freehall. James, an uncle of the emigrant, was Mayor of Londonderry in 1693. A son of the Rev. James Hillhouse was a member of the Continental Congress, a grandson was a member of the United States Senate, and a great-grandson was the James Abraham Hillhouse who was famous as a poet in the first third of the nineteenth century.

Mrs. Hillhouse was a Mary Fitch of a family that was among the earliest settlers of New England. Her second husband was the Rev. John Owen of Groton, Conn., whom also she survived, and she married the Rev. Samuel Dorrance, who like her first husband, was an Ulster clergyman. Dorrance was registered as Scotch-Irish, of Glasgow University in 1709. He was licensed by Dumbarton Presbytery in Scotland and in 1719 was received by the Presbytery of Coleraine. He came to America and settled at Voluntown, now Stirling, Conn., together with several brothers and friends. He was installed as town pastor in 1723, and served until March 5, 1771. He died November 12, 1775, at the age of ninety, leaving a large family.

The early arrivals of Scotch-Irish appear to have gone into the country, but later the flow made deposits in Boston and in connection with these a notable pastorate was created. The Rev. John Moorhead, son of a farmer at Newton, near Belfast, was born there in 1703. He was educated at the University of Edinburgh, and upon his return to Newton was influenced to go to America. He came to Boston in 1727 and soon began services, gathering about him a congregation which was known as the "Church of the Presbyterian Strangers." He was ordained as its pastor, March 30, 1730. John Little, a market gardener, was a member of the congregation, and for several years services were held in his barn. Eventually Mr. Little conveyed this barn and some land to the church, and in 1744 a building was erected which later became known as the Federal Street Church. Mr. Moorhead was an assiduous pastor, making periodical visits to each family under his care, to converse with the parents, catechize children and servants, and pray with the household. He died December 2, 1773. The funeral sermon was preached by the Rev. David McGregor of Londonderry.

The Scotch-Irish settlements on the Maine coast attracted a number of ministers of whom Woodside and Cornwall have already been mentioned. The Rev. Hugh Campbell, who obtained his M.A. degree at Edinburgh in 1714, spent a year at Scarboro, Me., in 1720, and was succeeded by the Rev. Hugh Henry in June, 1722. The Rev. Robert Rutherford came over in 1729 and preached at Bristol, Nobleboro, and Boothbay, Me. He was minister at Brunswick from about 1735 to 1742, and died at Thomaston, October 18, 1756, aged sixty-eight. The Rev. Robert Dunlap was born in County Antrim in August, 1715. He received his M.A. degree at Edinburgh about 1734 and emigrated to America in 1736. In December, 1746, he was called to Brunswick and preached there until October, 1760. He died June 26, 1776.

It would seem that so large a migration accompanied by so many ministers should have made an extensive planting of Presbyterianism in New England, and so it did; only Presbyterianism did not seem to take root and thrive, except at Londonderry where the Scotch-Irish had the field to themselves. As the settlement grew, it sent out colonies and in this way a church was planted at Windham in 1747 and at Bedford in 1757. Another colony went to Antrim and in 1775 formed a congregation that was organized into a church in 1778. The Scotch-Irish settlements on the Maine coast were not so fruitful. Between 1745 and 1791 churches were formed at Georgetown, Newcastle, Brunswick, Boothbay, Bristol, Topshew, Warren, Gray, Canaan, Turner and other places, all of which either died out or became Congregationalist.

From the Londonderry settlement appears to have issued the first New England Presbytery, constituted in or about 1729, by James McGregor of Londonderry and Edward Fitzgerald, together with LeMercier, pastor of the Huguenot Church at Boston, and some others. The career of Londonderry Presbytery affords another illustration of the difficulties occasioned by the contact of such diverse disciplines as Presbyterianism and Independency. On March 30, 1730, it ordained John Moorhead to the charge of the Presbyterian congregation in Boston. Thompson, a probationer of the Presbytery of Tyrone, Ireland, was received and ordained October 10, 1733. In 1736 the Presbytery was disrupted by a struggle over the admission of the Rev. James Hillhouse, who although a Presbyterian, was pastor of the Congregational Church at New London, Conn. Only five ministers were present when he was admitted by a majority of one vote. At the same meeting the Presbytery ordained David, son of the Rev. James McGregor. Three of the ministers present protested against the proceedings as unlawful. At the next meeting of the Presbytery there was a large attendance and the majority refused to recognize Hillhouse and McGregor and suspended Joseph Harvey and John Moorhead, who had voted for their admission. The effect was to break up the Presbytery.

On April 16, 1745, Boston Presbytery was constituted through the efforts of John Moorhead, David McGregor and Robert Abercrombie. They represented the party that had been excluded from the Presbytery of Londonderry in 1736. In 1768 they had grown to a body of twelve members. The original Presbytery of Londonderry appears to have died of inanition through the scattering of its members and inability to hold sessions. So late as 1771, however, there is record of an appeal to this Presbytery with reference to the organization of a Synod. Nothing appears to have come of it, and the Presbytery was probably then dead, although its name had survived. The Presbytery of Boston, however, developed such strength that on June 2, 1775, it organized as a Synod, composed of three Presbyteries: Newburyport with six ministers, Londonderry with four, and Palmer with six; in all, sixteen ministers and twenty-five churches. This Synod declined to receive the Presbytery at the Eastward, started by the Rev. John Murray of Boothbay, Me., who had been a member of the Presbytery of

Philadelphia but had been deposed by that body. There was another independent Presbytery of Grafton, N. H., constituted by Eleazar Wheelock and others. The strength of Presbyterianism of New England at the outbreak of the Revolutionary War was one Synod of three Presbyteries and two independent Presbyteries. Dr. Briggs computes that these five had in all thirty-two ministers, at a time when the Synod of New York and Philadelphia had 132 ministers and the total number of Presbyterian ministers in the colonies was 186. This number is exclusive of the Dutch, German and French Reformed Churches, having the same polity but maintaining their separate organization. It is computed that these Reformed Churches had sixty-one ministers in 1775.

It therefore appears that notwithstanding the early start of Presbyterianism in New England it did not thrive there. Independency, which had overthrown the Presbyterian order in England, clogged its introduction in New England, and although New England obtained increase of population from Ulster, Congregationalism was a greater gainer thereby than Presbyterianism. While Presbyterianism was rapidly spreading in the West and South, the New England field was for the most part resigned to the Congregational variety of Puritanism. The common ancestry of the two denominations was however kept in remembrance, and served as a basis for fraternal association. Through the efforts of the Synod of New York and Philadelphia a convention was held at Elizabethtown, New Jersey, in November, 1766, attended by delegates from the Synod and from the Consociated Churches of Connecticut. It was decided that an annual convention should be held to which all the Congregational, Consociated and Presbyterian Churches in North America should be invited to send delegates. The following year the convention met at New Haven, and at that convention two delegates from Boston Presbytery were present. Thereafter the convention was exclusively composed of delegates from the Synod and the churches of Connecticut. The chief motive for the formation of this convention was opposition to the creation of an

American episcopate. Hodge observed that this was "the great and almost the only subject which occupied their attention." The meetings of the convention were held alternately in Connecticut and at Elizabethtown, N. J., but were discontinued during the Revolutionary War.

When the General Assembly of the Presbyterian Church was constituted in 1789 no New England Presbytery or ministerial association was represented, and New England was without any representation whatever, save for the fact that the Synod of New York and Philadelphia had some ministers under its jurisdiction in Connecticut. The General Assembly at its meeting in 1790 unanimously adopted the following:

> "Whereas there existed, before the late revolution, an annual convention of the clergy of the Congregational Churches in New England, and of the ministers belonging to the Synod of New York and Philadelphia, which was interrupted by the disorders occasioned by the war;—this Assembly, being peculiarly desirous to renew and strengthen every bond of union between brethren so nearly agreed in doctrine and forms of worship, as the members of the Presbyterian and Congregational Churches evidently are, and remembering with much satisfaction the mutual pleasure and advantage produced and received by their former intercourse,—did resolve that the ministers of the Congregational Church in New England, be invited to renew their annual convention with the clergy of the Presbyterian Church."

A committee was appointed through whose efforts a plan was adopted of fraternal association through delegates. The General Assembly seated as members delegates from the general association of Connecticut, and from the general convention of Congregational and Presbyterian ministers from Vermont; and in its turn elected delegates to those New England bodies. Associations in Vermont, New Hampshire, Massachusetts, Maine and Rhode Island were eventually included in these arrangements; but this intercourse languished, and by 1837 or 1838 had almost declined. In 1840 it was revived, but embarrassments through differences in discipline occurred, and the slavery controversy also made trouble. In 1857 the General Assembly decided not to send delegates to any of the Congregational bodies of New England.

CHAPTER XIII

The Source of American Presbyterianism

The foregoing review of the situation in New England brings out more clearly the importance of Pennsylvania in the planting of Presbyterianism in America. The Presbytery of Philadelphia, founded by Makemie, was the tap root from which the institutional growth of Presbyterianism proceeded. Presbyterianism in New York City and vicinity, which early became an important factor in the development of the Church, was an offshoot from the Presbytery of Philadelphia. The first movement for the organization of a Presbyterian church in New York City dates from the visit of Makemie and Hampton in 1707. The first regular congregation was constituted in 1717, and the Rev. James Anderson, a native of Scotland and a member of the Presbytery of Philadelphia, was the first pastor. In 1718 a lot was purchased in Wall Street, and the following year a meetinghouse was erected. Owing to its inability to obtain a charter, and alarmed for the security of its property, the congregation eventually vested the fee of its lot and building in the General Assembly of the Church of Scotland. The property was reconveyed to the trustees of the church after the Revolution.

Notwithstanding legal hindrances, Presbyterianism throve so that, in 1738, New York Presbytery was constituted through the action of the Synod of Philadelphia, which ordered that the Presbytery of Long Island and the Presbytery of New Jersey should be united and thenceforth known as the Presbytery of New York. When erected it consisted of sixteen ministers and fourteen churches—Woodbridge, Hanover, Elizabethtown, Westfield, Newark and Connecticut Farms, in New Jersey; Wallkill, Bethlehem, and Goshen in and about the Highlands of the Hudson; Jamaica, Newtown, Setauket and Mattituck, on Long Island; together with the church in New York City. The churches of Elizabeth and Newark and those on Long Island were originally Congregational in their government, so it appears that in this section Presbyterianism gained at the expense of Congregationalism, although having no advantage in legal position. Probably we shall not err if we attribute the early prosperity of Presbyterianism outside of New England to the early formation and vigorous activity of the Presbytery of Philadelphia.

The fountainhead influence of that Presbytery is distinctly manifested when the ecclesiastical antecedents of the original membership of New York Presbytery are considered. The oldest and most distinguished member of the new Presbytery was Jonathan Dickinson. Dr. Briggs says of him: "Dickinson was the ablest man in the American Presbyterian Church in the colonial period. It is due chiefly to him that the Church became an American Presbyterian Church, and that it was not split into fragments representing and perpetuating the differences of Presbyterians in the mother countries of England, Scotland, Ireland and Wales." He took an active part in establishing the College of New Jersey, the corporate predecessor of Princeton University, and was its first President. Dickinson was born at Hatfield, Mass., and was graduated at Yale in 1706. He received a call to the Independent Church at Elizabethtown, New Jersey, and was ordained in 1709 by the Consociated ministers of Fairfield, Conn., who came on invitation to perform that service.

It therefore appears that his position was originally just like that of other Congregational ministers. His subsequent career was determined by the fact that the existence of the Philadelphia Presbytery provided a basis for ecclesiastical organization that appealed to him. He joined the Presbytery in 1717, and soon after the church of which he was minister put itself under the care of the Presbytery. In 1733 the Presbytery of East Jersey was created and Dickinson became its leading member, which position he also held in the New York Presbytery into which the East Jersey Presbytery was merged.

John Pierson, who was second on the roll of original members, was also a New Englander. He was the son of Abraham Pierson, the first President of Yale College, where he graduated in 1711.

In 1714 he received a call to Woodbridge, N. J., where he was ordained April 27, 1717, by the Presbytery of Philadelphia.

Joseph Houston, the next on the roll, was a Scotch-Irishman who emigrated to New England, whence he removed to the Delaware Bay region. On July 24, 1724, he was taken under the care of the New Castle Presbytery as a probationer, and on October 15 of the same year he was installed as pastor of Elk Church, Md. In or about 1739, he was installed pastor of Wallkill Church, New York.

Among other members of the New York Presbytery who owed their ordination to the Philadelphia Presbytery was Joseph Webb, son of a pastor of the same name at Fairfield, Conn. He was graduated at Yale in 1715, and received a call to Newark, N. J., where he was ordained by the Presbytery of Philadelphia, October 22, 1719.

John Nutman, a native of Newark, graduated at Yale in 1727, was ordained by the Presbytery of Philadelphia in 1730, and settled at Hanover, N. J. Samuel Pumroy was descended from an old Puritan stock of Northampton, Mass. In 1708 he came to Newtown, L. I., as a Congregational minister, but on September 23, 1715, he was admitted to the Philadelphia Presbytery, and in 1717 was one of the three ministers who formed the Presbytery of Long Island. The Church at Newtown to which Mr. Pumroy ministered remained Independent until 1724, when it put itself under the care of the Presbytery. Mr. Pumroy continued in this charge until his death, June 30, 1744.

These instances suffice to show the influence exerted by the Presbytery of Philadelphia in gathering all congenial elements into the Presbyterian Church. Apart from that influence there is little in the antecedents of the ministers forming the New York Presbytery to suggest that they would have preferred Presbyterianism to Congregationalism. Of the sixteen only one, Houston, was of Scotch-Irish nativity. Nearly all of them were from New England. Twelve were graduates of Yale and three of Harvard. The circumstance that determined their adherence to the Presbyterian discipline is to be attributed chiefly to Makemie's foresight in making a timely start of church organization in a strategic position. In population and position Philadelphia then more closely approximated the character of a national capital than any other town in the colonies, and in planting the first Presbytery at that point Makemie associated its growth with the growth of the nation. Demonstrative evidence of this fact is afforded by the speedy appearance of a brood of Presbyteries all mothered by the Presbytery of Philadelphia. All the great organizers of American Presbyterianism were connected either with the Philadelphia Presbytery or with directly affiliated Presbyteries.

Next to the work of Dickinson in structural value was that of the Tennents. The founder of the famous family, William Tennent, was born in Ireland and was a cousin on the mother side of James Logan, Secretary of the Province of Pennsylvania. He married, May 15, 1702, a daughter of the Rev. Gilbert Kennedy, a distinguished Presbyterian minister, who having been ejected from his charge in Girvan, Ayrshire, Scotland, took refuge in Ireland and became minister of Dondonald. He died February 6, 1688. William Tennent was graduated at the University of Edinburgh, July 11, 1695. Notwithstanding the fact that he married into a Presbyterian family, he turned to the Established Church and was ordained by the Bishop of Down as deacon, July, 1704; as priest, September 22, 1706. After becoming a clergyman he is said to have held a chaplaincy in a nobleman's family, but he became unwilling to conform to the requirements of the Established Church and he decided to go to America. He arrived in September, 1716, with his wife, a daughter and four sons, who became ministers. On September 17, 1718, he applied to the Synod of Philadelphia for admission. In so doing he made a statement of his reasons for dissenting from the Established Church, of which he had formerly been a member, being in the main that episcopal government was anti-Scriptural.

It is clearly a fact of great tactical importance that at the time Tennent arrived there was in existence an ecclesiastical organization of which he could become an adherent. Otherwise he might just as readily have become an Independent or a Congregational minister, as happened in so many cases in New England. As it was, his ability as an organizer became of great value to the cause of American Presbyterianism. He settled at East Chester, N. Y., November 22, 1718, and did effective work in spreading Presbyterianism in Westchester County. He removed to Bedford, New York, in May, 1720. In 1721 he took charge of Bensalem and Smithfield in Bucks County, Pa. In 1726 he accepted a call to Neshaminy, where he established the famous Log College, thus becoming, says Dr. Briggs, "the Father of Presbyterian Colleges in America." He died May 6, 1746.

Gilbert Tennent, eldest son of William, was born in the county of Armagh, Ireland, February 5, 1703. He was educated by his father and was licensed as a preacher by the Philadelphia Presbytery in May, 1725. An indefatigable worker and an eloquent preacher, his career is prominent in church history, owing to his vigorous initiative which made a stir wherever he went. A friend of Whitefield, who admired his eloquence, Gilbert Tennent exemplified the same type of fervent and emotional religion, and like Whitefield, he became an itinerant evangelist. After a conference with Whitefield in New Brunswick, in November, 1740, Tennent went to New England, where he preached numerous sermons with marked effect in arousing popular interest. He frequently preached three times a day. His tour included a number of towns in Massachusetts, New Hampshire, Maine and Connecticut. At New Haven he preached seventeen sermons, and a large number of students were drawn into the ministry. He returned to New Brunswick in 1741, and soon became as active in writing as in teaching. In 1744 he removed to Philadelphia and took charge of the Second Presbyterian Church, but he does not appear to have been successful in routine pastoral work, which was probably too restricted a field for his powers. In 1763 he went to Great Britain in company with Samuel Davies to raise funds for the College of New Jersey, in which they had marked success. In 1755 Tennent was again with the Second Church of

Philadelphia, and his labors at this period appear to have been more fruitful in parish results. He died January 23, 1764.

~ William Tennent, brother of Gilbert and second son of the first William Tennent, was born in County Antrim, Ireland, June 3, 1705. He, too, became a distinguished Presbyterian minister. He settled at Freehold, N. J., and like his brother he was active in evangelistic work, visiting Maryland and Virginia in such labors. John Tennent, third son of the first William, was born in County Armagh, Ireland, November 12, 1707. He was licensed September 18, 1729, and in 1730 was ordained by the Philadelphia Presbytery as pastor at Freehold, N. J., in which charge he preceded his brother William. He died April 23, 1732, aged twenty-five. His brother William carried on his pastoral work for him six months prior to his decease. A younger brother, Charles Tennent, born in County Down, May 3, 1711, was also an eminent minister. He was pastor of Whiteday Church under New Castle Presbytery, but in 1763 removed to Buckingham, now Berlin, on the Eastern Shore of Maryland. He died in 1771.

The Tennent family afford an extraordinary instance of hereditary faculty, and their services were of inestimable value in popularizing the Presbyterian type of worship. Dr. Briggs says that "William Tennent is one of the grandest trophies won by Presbyterianism from Episcopacy in the first quarter of the eighteenth century."

Among the early recruits gained by the Synod of Philadelphia were a number of Scotch-Irish clergymen, some coming by way of New England and some direct. Adam Boyd, born at Ballymoney, Ireland, in 1692, came to New England in 1722 or 1723. He followed Craighead to Pennsylvania and was ordained at Octorara September 13, 1724. The Forks of the Brandywine was included in his field until 1734. He spent his life in this region, dying November 23, 1768. He left a widow, five daughters and five sons. The eldest son is said to have entered the ministry but he died young. One of the sons, Adam, went to Wilmington, N. C., where he started the Cape Fear *Mercury*, in 1767. He was a leading member of the Committee of Safety, formed among the Revolutionary patriots of that region. In 1776 he entered the ministry and became chaplain of the North Carolina brigade.

Archibald McCook was received as a student from Ireland by New Castle Presbytery in March 1726, and was licensed September 13, of that year. In 1727 he was sent to Kent in Delaware, his charge embracing several congregations. He was ordained June 7, and died within a few months.

Hugh Stevenson, a theological student from Ireland, was received by the New Castle Presbytery, May 11, 1726. He was licensed September 13, and employed in temporary supply of pulpits until 1728 when he was called to Snow Hill, Md. In 1733, while preaching in Virginia, he experienced treatment of which he made formal complaint to the Synod. The Synod sent a copy to the Church of Scotland with a request that that body use its influence with the British Government to lay "a restraint upon some gentlemen in said neighboring Province as may discourage them from hampering our missionaries by illegal persecutions." In 1739 or 1740 Stevenson opened a grammar school in Philadelphia. He was a teacher of high reputation, but in turning from ministerial work to education he discontinued ministerial labor and fell into some irregularities for which in 1741 he was suspended by the Synod. He died some time before May, 1744.

John Wilson, of whose antecedents nothing is recorded save that he was a minister from Ireland "coming providentially into these parts," was received by the Synod of Philadelphia in 1729. He preached at Lower Octorara and established himself in the favor of the congregation, but in January, 1730, the Presbytery of New Castle received a letter from Armagh Presbytery of such tenor that the Presbytery resolved not to employ him. He was then preaching at New Castle and the congregation stood by him. Robert Gordon, Judge of New Castle County Court, appealed to the Synod in Wilson's behalf, but the Synod upheld the Presbytery. Wilson soon after removed to Boston, and died there January 6, 1733, aged sixty-six. It is supposed that the Rev. John Wilson was his son, who was born in Ulster, and was ordained pastor of the Presbyterian Church in Chester, N. H., in 1734, and who died there, February 1, 1779, aged seventy-six.

Dr. Hodge writing in 1839 gives a list of the ministers who entered the Presbyterian Church from 1729 to 1741, but he states that the records are so imperfect that the list cannot be regarded as complete. He mentions thirty-eight and of these nineteen were from Ireland; the others so far as known being natives of America.

Most of the information we now have about the early ministers of the Presbyterian Church prior to 1760 we owe to the antiquarian zeal of the Rev. Richard Webster, pastor of the Presbyterian Church of Mauch Chunk, Pa., whose writings on the subject were put in shape in 1853 although they were not published until shortly after his death in 1856. Mr. Webster leaves out of account the Scotch-Irish ministers that were absorbed by New England Congregationalism as he is intent upon the history of the Presbyterian Church and the work of her ministry prior to 1760. Out of 200 early ministers mentioned by him there were thirty-three whose place of nativity could not be determined, but of the remainder fifty-five were from Ireland, twenty-six from Scotland, six from England, five from Wales, two from Continental Europe and seventy-three were American born, many of Scotch-Irish ancestry. The Scotch-Irish preponderance is particularly marked in the early period before American schools began to graduate fit candidates for the ministry. The American field long continued to attract ministerial supply from Ulster. Numerous cases are on record of the application to an American Presbytery of a probationer of an Ulster Presbytery indicating that the candidate had prepared for the ministry with a view to going to America for admission. Some defective material got into the American ministry in this way, but the Presbyteries were firm in maintaining discipline and a few Scotch-Irish ministers were deposed for heterodoxy or misdemeanor. One case of the sort became famous owing to the part which Benjamin Franklin took in it. He gave the following account of it in his *Autobiography*:

"About the year 1734 there arrived among us a young Presbyterian preacher named Hemphill, who delivered with a good voice, and apparently extempore, most excellent discourses; which drew together considerable members of different persuasions, who joined in admiring them. Among the rest I became one of his constant hearers, his sermons pleasing me, as they had little of the dogmatical kind, but inculcated strongly the practice of virtue, or what in the religious style are called good works. Those however, of our congregation who considered themselves as orthodox Presbyterians, disapproved his doctrine, and were joined by most of the old ministers, who arraigned him of heterodoxy before the Synod, in order to have him silenced. I became his zealous partisan and contributed all I could to raise a party in his favor and combated for him awhile with some hopes of success. There was much scribbling *pro* and *con* upon the occasion; and finding that though an elegant preacher he was but a poor writer, I wrote for him two or three pamphlets and a piece in the *Gazette* of April, 1735. These pamphlets as is generally the case with controversial writings though eagerly read at the time, were soon out of vogue, and I question whether a single copy of them now exists.

"During the contest an unlucky occurrence hurt his cause exceedingly. One of our adversaries having heard him preach a sermon, that was much admired, thought he had somewhere read the sermon before, or at least a part of it. On searching he found the part quoted at length, in one of the British *Reviews*, from a discourse of Dr. Foster's. This detection gave many of our party disgust, who accordingly abandoned his cause, and occasioned our more speedy discomfiture in the Synod. I rather approved his giving us good sermons composed by others, than bad ones of his own manufacture; though the latter was the practice of our common teachers. He afterward acknowledged to me, that none of those he preached were his own; adding that his memory was such as enabled him to retain and repeat any sermon after once reading only. On our defeat, he left us in search elsewhere of better fortune, and I quitted the congregation never attending it after; though I continued many years my subscription for the support of its ministers."

This minister was Samuel Hemphill, who while a probationer in Ireland acted as supply to the congregation at Burt, propounding doctrines to which exceptions were taken by the Rev. Patrick Vance. After Hemphill went to America Vance wrote to his brother-in-law, an elder at Nottingham, Pa., expressing an unfavorable opinion of Hemphill. Hemphill however presented credentials from the Presbytery of Strabane, Ireland, and was licensed to preach and eventually he settled in Philadelphia as Franklin has described. Although his sermons gave such great satisfaction to Franklin, who was a deist, orthodox Presbyterianism promptly resented his teachings. The Rev. Jedediah Andrews, in a letter written June 14, 1735, gave the following account of the situation:

> "There came from Ireland one Mr. Hemphill to sojourn in town for the winter, as was pretended, till he could fall into business with some people in the country, though some think he had other views at first, considering the infidel disposition of too many here. Some desiring that I should have assistance and some leading men, not disaffected to that way of Deism as they should be,—that man was imposed upon me and the congregation. Most of the best people were soon so dissatisfied that they would not come to the meeting. Free thinkers, deists, and nothings, getting a scout of him, flocked to hear. I attended all winter, but making complaint brought the ministers together, who acted as is shown in the books I send you."

Hemphill, when cited before the Presbytery, asserted that Andrews was actuated by jealousy, because there was always a larger audience when Hemphill preached than when Andrews preached. The ecclesiastical court met April 17, 1735, and the indictment of Hemphill's theology was formulated in a series of articles. Hemphill's mode of defence seems to have been chiefly the making of imputations on the motives of his accusers. He also took the ground that his utterances had been misrepresented, meanwhile displaying reluctance to declare just what he did say and just what he did believe. Sufficient was eventually extracted from him to elicit an unanimous verdict that his teachings were unsound and dangerous and he was suspended from the ministry. Hemphill posed as a martyr, and issued a statement that the commission of the Presbytery which tried him had "no pattern for their proceedings but that hellish tribunal the Spanish Inquisition." The Synod approved the action of the Presbytery and Hemphill sent a communication in which he said: "I shall think you do me a deal of honor if you entirely excommunicate me."

At one time Hemphill had such a following that Presbytery and Synod were the targets of a pamphlet warfare. In the midst of this hubbub came the announcement of Hemphill's systematic plagiarism. The evidence was incontrovertible as the sermons by various authors which he had taken and passed off for his own had been published in England, and he made the mistake of supposing that copies would not get into the American colonies. Franklin, as appears from his own account, continued to uphold Hemphill even after the exposure, but the martyr was now shown to be an impostor and his popularity suddenly collapsed. He moved away and nothing is known of his subsequent career. He was an early example of the clever, plausible sophist, a type that from time to time appears in the ministry, but is better assured of a career in our own time than it was in the pioneer stage of the American church. Although the need of ministers was so great that easy judgment of qualifications would have been a natural tendency, yet the early Presbyterians seem to have been firm in their discipline. Notwithstanding Hemphill's marked success as a popular preacher and the formidable championship that rallied to his support, the Presbytery did not flinch from discharging its duty, and the commission that tried Hemphill was unanimous in its decision. The incident seems worthy of particular detail for perhaps more than any other event it illustrates the courage and loyalty of the founders of the Presbyterian Church of the United States.

CHAPTER XIV

EXPANSION SOUTH AND WEST

The introduction of Presbyterianism in South Carolina was almost coeval with the Chesapeake Bay settlements. The first Presbyterian settlers were Scotch, being part of the migration to America from Scotland that set in after the battle of Bothwell in 1684. A body of twenty-two sailed from Glasgow to Carolina and settled at Port Royal on the Broad River. William Dunlap served as minister to this flock, which eventually dispersed as the place proved unhealthy and the colony broke up. Dunlap returned to Scotland and eventually became Principal of the University of Glasgow.

A number of Puritan ministers from New England went to Carolina and founded churches of the Congregational pattern, but distinctive Presbyterianism again entered the region in 1699, as an accidental consequence of the attempt made to establish a Scotch colony on the Isthmus of Darien. With the breakup of that colony the majority of the emigrants sought refuge in New England, but one of the ministers, Alexander Stobo, was with a party that set sail for Scotland.

The vessel was so damaged by a storm that it made for America and Stobo was landed at Charleston, S. C. The Puritan congregation there had just lost its pastor, John Cotton, who died September 8, 1699. Stobo received a call and he settled with them, remaining there the rest of his life. It was not, however, until the Church had been recruited by Scotch-Irish immigration that Presbyterianism became strong enough to display its characteristic organization in the Carolinas. When the General Assembly was formed three Carolina Presbyteries were represented, Orange, South Carolina and Abingdon. But all three Presbyteries were derived from the activities of the Synod of Philadelphia. New Castle Presbytery, created in 1716 by subdivision of the original Presbytery of Philadelphia, was the parent in 1755 of Hanover

Presbytery, Virginia, out of which were formed Orange Presbytery in 1770 and Abingdon in 1785. South Carolina Presbytery was formed out of Orange Presbytery in 1784.

Organized Presbyterianism was communicated to the South by the ministers who accompanied Scotch-Irish emigration from Pennsylvania southward, moving down the valleys that stretch from Pennsylvania and Maryland into Virginia. Beginning in 1732 a stream of Scotch-Irish emigration poured into the Shenandoah Valley in Virginia and the first Presbyterian minister in that region was probably Samuel Gelston. He was born in the North of Ireland in 1692, and emigrated to America in 1715. After having held a number of charges in Pennsylvania and New York, he seems to have visited Virginia in 1735. Little is known of his labors there except that they were so acceptable that a call for his services was sent to Donegal Presbytery of which he was then a member. In 1736 the Presbytery directed him to supply Pequea church, but in the following spring he notified the Presbytery that he was about to remove from its bounds and was dismissed. No record of his subsequent career seems to have been preserved, although he is said to have lived to the age of ninety.

The records of the Synod of Philadelphia note an application for ministerial supply made in 1719 by "the People of Potomoke," believed to be identical with the congregations of Falling Water and Tuscorara, near the present town of Martinsburg. The Rev. Daniel Magill, who came from Scotland in 1713, was appointed to visit them. He made a stay of several months and reported the following year that he had "put the people into church order." The people desired him to settle as their pastor but he declined the call.

The first minister to settle in Virginia under the jurisdiction of the Synod of Philadelphia was John Craig. He was born in Ireland, September 21, 1710, but was educated in America. He presented himself to Donegal Presbytery in the fall of 1736, was taken on trial the following spring and was licensed August 30, 1738. He was at first employed as a supply in Maryland, but toward the close of 1739 he was sent to Irish Tract and other places in Virginia. He formed two congregations in the south part of what is now Augusta County, Va. In April, 1740, he received a call from what was described as the congregation of the Triple Forks of Shenandoah, but the places where the meeting-houses were situated were known as Augusta and Tinkling Springs. This region, being southwest of the Blue Ridge, was exposed to Indian raids and Braddock's defeat imperiled the safety of the settlement. Craig encouraged his people to stand their ground. The church was fortified, and men brought their rifles and posted sentries when attending service. Through the measures taken the community held together and sustained little loss although Indians prowled in the vicinity.

Craig resigned the pastoral care of Tinkling Springs church in November, 1764, but he remained in charge till his death, April 21, 1774, aged sixty-three. He appears to have had in a marked degree the adaptability and resourcefulness of a pioneer. It is related of him that when asked how he found suitable persons for elders in new settlements, where he organized churches, he replied, "When there were no hewn stone I just took dornicks." When he resigned the Tinkling Springs charge in 1764 he was able to say to the congregation: "Few and poor and without order, were you when I accepted your call; but now I leave you a numerous, wealthy congregation, able to support the Gospel and of credit and reputation in the Church."

Thus far the work of Presbyterian ministers in Virginia had been mainly in the nature of supply to congregations formed by the Scotch-Irish settlers. But a period of active missionary and evangelistic work followed in which the leader was William Robinson. He was of English Quaker ancestry and on coming to America he settled in Hopewell, N. J., as a school teacher. While teaching he also studied at the Log College, so he was a recruit to Presbyterianism made by the Tennents. In the winter of 1742 Robinson went into the Valley of Virginia, traveling southward until he penetrated North Carolina, where he spent the winter enduring hardships that affected his health. He returned along the eastern slope of the Blue Ridge, achieving great success as an evangelist. His missionary tour had a marked effect in spreading Presbyterianism. His aptitude was for evangelistic work rather than for the work of a settled pastor. From Virginia he went to New York State and thence to the Eastern Shore of Maryland, where in 1745 there was a marked revival under his ministrations.

The Synod of New York at its first meeting, September, 1745, considered the situation in Virginia and was unanimously of the opinion that Mr. Robinson was the most suitable person to be sent, and earnestly recommended him to visit that field as soon as his circumstances would permit. Robinson was present at that meeting and probably intended to go, but meanwhile he became interested in a congregation at St. George's, Del., where there had been a revival under his visit, and the last six months of his life was spent in their services. He died August 1, 1746. He bequeathed most of his books to Samuel Davies and left it as a last request that Davies should take up the work in Virginia. The ministry of Davies was the great organizing influence of pioneer Presbyterianism in Virginia, but there were others prior to him in point of time among Robinson's successors.

John Blair, born in Ireland in 1720, educated at the Log College and licensed by the New Side Presbytery of New Castle, was ordained December 27, 1742, as pastor of congregations in Cumberland County, Pa. He visited Virginia soon after Robinson and organized congregations east and west of the Blue Ridge. In 1746 he made another visit to Virginia and again organized a number of congregations. He resigned his pastoral charge in Pennsylvania in December, 1748, owing to Indian invasions. He became associated with his brother, Samuel Blair, in carrying on the school at Fagg's Manor. In 1767 he became Professor of Divinity and Moral Philosophy in the College of New Jersey, Princeton, and for a period acted as President, until Dr. Witherspoon was elected to that office in 1769. Blair resigned and accepted a call to Wallkill, in the Highlands of New York. He died, December 8, 1771.

John Roan, born in Ireland, educated at the Log College, was licensed by the New Side Presbytery of New Castle and sent to Virginia in the winter of 1744. He made trouble by his attacks on the Established Church, and was indicted for libelous utterances. Gilbert Tennent and Samuel Finley interested themselves in his defense and the case broke down, as there was no evidence that he had used the expressions imputed to him. The man who made the information on which the indictment was found practically confessed perjury by fleeing. His Virginia mission finished, Roan settled in Pennsylvania as pastor of the congregations of Derry, Paxton and Mount Joy. Toward the close of his life he again went on extensive missionary tours and at one time spent eight weeks on the South Branch of the Potomac. He died October 3, 1775, and was buried at Derry meeting-house on the Swatara.

William Dean went with Eliab Byram of the Synod of New York to the Valley of Virginia and preached there in 1745–1747. Dean was one of the graduates of Log College, was taken on trial by New Brunswick Presbytery August 3, 1741, was licensed October 12, 1742, and was sent to Neshaminy and the Forks of the Delaware, by which term was designated the country in the angle between the Lehigh River and the Delaware. It was then Indian country but Scotch-Irish settlements had been made in the region. Later he was appointed to supply at the Forks of Brandywine and Pequea. He went to Virginia and as a result of his labors there he received a call from the church at Timber Ridge and Forks of James River, May 18, 1748. Before action was taken on the call he died, July 29, 1748, aged only twenty-nine. Byram, his associate in the Virginia field, was of New England stock and was graduated at Harvard University in 1740. He became minister of Roxiticus, now Mendham, N. J., in October, 1743, under the care of New York Presbytery. His work in Virginia was limited to the tour made with Dean, and although he received a call he declined to settle in Virginia. He joined New Brunswick Presbytery May 22, 1751, and settled at Amwell, June 25. He died before May, 1754.

Samuel Davies, whom Dr. Briggs declares to be "one of the greatest divines the American Presbyterian Church has produced," was born November 3, 1723, in the county of New Castle, now in the State of Delaware, but then in the Province of Pennsylvania. He is supposed to have been of Welsh descent. He lived on a farm and did not attend school until he was ten, learning meanwhile what his mother could teach him. He went to school first to the Rev. Abel Morgan, afterward the Baptist minister at Middletown, N. J. He pursued his studies under the Rev. Samuel Blair, at Fagg's Manor, Chester County, Pa. The influence of Blair and Gilbert Tennent attracted him to the Presbyterian ministry. He was licensed by New Castle Presbytery, July 30, 1746, at the age of twenty-three and ordained an evangelist February 19, 1747. The same year he went to Virginia and in 1748 settled at Hanover as pastor.

At that time there were three Presbyterian ministers in Virginia, Samuel Black, in Albemarle County near Rockfish Gap, of the Blue Ridge; the Rev. John Craig and Alexander Miller in what was then Augusta County, west of the Blue Ridge. These were all Irish born and were connected with the Presbytery of Donegal, belonging to what was then called Old Side. Davies as a member of New Side Presbytery would not count on any assistance from them. Of the situation with which he had to cope Davies himself gave the following account:

> "There are meeting-houses licensed in five different counties in this part of the State, but the extremes of my charge lie 80 or 90 miles apart; and the dissenters under my care are scattered through six or seven different counties... The counties are large, generally 40 or 50 miles in length, and about 20 or 30 in breadth; so that though members may live in one county, it would be impossible for them all to convene at one place, and much more so when they are dispersed through so many counties. Though there are now seven places of worship licensed, yet the nearest to each other are 12 or 15 miles apart; and many have to travel from 10, 15 or 20 miles to the nearest, and from 40 to 60 miles to the other places licensed; nay some of them have from 30 to 40 miles to the nearest place of worship."

Of the effect of his labors the amplest acknowledgment has come from opponents. In Dr. Hawks' history of the Protestant Episcopal Church in Virginia, he mentions Davies as the chief instrument in the upbuilding of Presbyterianism. When he settled in Hanover County "there were not ten avowed dissenters within one hundred miles of him." Inside of three years he had established seven meeting-houses, three in Hanover County, one in Henrico, one in Caroline, one in Louisa and one in Goochland.

Among these houses, some of them forty miles apart, he divided his labors. In addition to being a zealous missionary and an eloquent preacher he was an able man of affairs. He was harassed in his work by a contention that his proceedings were illegal, on the ground that the English Act of Toleration did not extend to Virginia. That position was taken by Peyton Randolph, Attorney-General of Virginia. On one occasion Davies argued the point with him in court. Dr. Hawks remarks: "He was frankly acknowledged to have sustained his cause with great learning and eloquence." It eventually turned out that Davies was in the right on the law of the case. When Davies visited England, in 1753, with Tennent to collect funds for Princeton College, he took the matter up with the Attorney-General, Sir Dudley Rider, and obtained from him an opinion that the English Act of Toleration was the law of Virginia.

Davies returned to Virginia in February, 1755, and resumed his indefatigable labors. There were two months of 1757 in which he travelled 500 miles and preached forty sermons. On August 16, 1758, he was elected President of Princeton, but he doubted whether he should forsake the Virginia field, and recommended Samuel Finley as better qualified than himself. But the trustees reelected him, May 9, 1759, and the Synod of New York and Philadelphia dissolved his pastoral relation. Davies was inaugurated September 26, and applied himself energetically and successfully to the duties of his position but his term was brief. At the close of 1760 a friend, alluding to the sermon expected from Davies on New Year's day, remarked that his predecessor Aaron

Burr had begun the last year of his life with a sermon on Jeremiah, xxviii, 16: "This year thou shalt die." Davies selected the same text, and died a little more than a month later, February 4, 1761.

Davies's picture in Nassau Hall, Princeton University, shows a man of plethoric habit, the ruddiness of his face emphasized by his large wig. Yet in early life he came near dying of consumption. He married October 23, 1746, and on September 15, 1747, his wife was dead with her infant son. His own health was such that it seemed there was nothing more for him to do than to spend freely what was left of it. He went to the Eastern Shore of Maryland, engaged actively in evangelistic work, suffering from fever by night and riding and preaching day and evening in the extremest cold of winter. As it turned out, in thus losing his life he was saving it as he was unwittingly taking what is now known as the fresh air cure. His health had been restored when he went to Virginia and after settling in Hanover he married again, October 4, 1748. When he went to Princeton he became an indoor man. He left off his habit of riding and gave himself up to study, rising with the dawn and continuing his labors till midnight. The ailment of which he died started as a bad cold and then fever set in, ending fatally after an illness of ten days. He was only in his thirty-eighth year.

Although Davies was not himself of Scotch-Irish stock yet his career is so intimately associated with the spread of the Scotch-Irish settlements in the South and Southwest and was such a formative influence that it merits special consideration. For one thing the evidence points strongly to the fact that Davies was the founder of a school of oratory that profoundly affected forensic method in America, whether in the forum, in the pulpit or at the bar. It is known that Patrick Henry as a child used to be taken to hear Davies preach, and in after life he used to say that he had drawn inspiration from Davies for his own oratory, which certainly bears the marks of Davies's style. An extract will be sufficient proof. After Braddock's defeat in 1755 Davies was active in rousing the people to defend the frontier against the French and Indians, and on May 8, 1758, by invitation he preached a sermon to the militia of Hanover County, at a general muster. In this discourse Davies said:

> "Need I inform you what barbarities and depredations a mongrel race of Indian savages and French Papists have perpetrated upon our frontiers? How many deserted or demolished houses and plantations? How wide an extent of country abandoned? How many poor families obliged to fly in consternation and leave their all behind them? What breaches and separations between the nearest relations? What painful ruptures of heart from heart? What shocking dispersions of those once united by strongest and most endearing ties? Some lie dead, mangled with savage wounds, consumed to ashes with outrageous flames, or torn and devoured by the beasts of the wilderness, while their bones lie whitening in the sun, and serve as tragical memorials of the fatal spot where they fell. Others have been dragged away as captives and made the slaves of cruel and imperious savages; others have made their escape, and live to lament their butchered or captivated friends and relations. In short, our frontiers have been drenched with the blood of our fellow-subjects through the length of a thousand miles, and new wounds are still opening. We, in those inland parts of the country are as yet unmolested, through the unmerited mercy of Heaven. But let us glance a thought to the western extremities of our body-politic, and what melancholly scenes open to our view! Now perhaps while I am speaking, now while you are secure and unmolested, our fellow subjects there may be feeling the calamities I am now describing. Now, perhaps, the savage shouts and whoops of Indians and the screams and groans of some butchered family, may be mingling their horrors and circulating their tremendous echoes through the wilderness of rocks and mountains."

Davies had a successor in the Valley of Virginia who perhaps attained even greater fame as an orator, though this was probably due to accidental circumstances rather than to real preeminence. This was James Waddel, who was born at Newry in the North of Ireland in July, 1739, but emigrated with his parents to Pennsylvania while a child. He was educated at the school of Dr. Samuel Finley (later President of the college at Princeton), at

Nottingham, Cecil County, Md. He intended to practice medicine but entered the ministry through Davies's influence. He was licensed in 1762 and in 1764 received a call to Tinkling Springs Church to succeed Craig, who had retired, but declined it in favor of a charge on the Northern Neck, where he remained until his health was broken by the malarial fever prevalent in that region. In 1776, another call having been made by Tinkling Springs Church, he accepted it and his health improved in the mountain air. In 1783 he organized a congregation at Staunton to which he ministered in conjunction with his Tinkling Springs charge, the joint salary being forty-five pounds. A few years later he removed to an estate which he had purchased in Louisa, where he taught a select school. He was a fine classical scholar, and a man of cultivated literary taste. Some of his pupils became men of distinction, such as Governor Barbour of Virginia and Meriwether Lewis, the explorer of the Rocky Mountains. After his removal to Louisa he lost his sight from cataract, but continued to preach, and it was during that period that William Wirt, then a rising lawyer, later Attorney-General of the United States, was thrilled by Waddel's eloquence, and wrote an account of it that has become classic.

Wirt relates that he was traveling through Orange County when his eye "was caught by a cluster of horses tied near a ruinous, old wooden house, in the forest not far from the roadside." Moved chiefly by curiosity he stopped, "to hear the preacher of such a wilderness." On entering he saw "a tall and very spare old man; his head, which was covered with a white linen cap, his shriveled hands and his voice, were all shaking under the influence of the palsy; and a few moments ascertained to me that he was perfectly blind." Evidently there was nothing in the appearance of the preacher to prepare Wirt for what was to follow. He goes on to say: "It was a day of the administration of the sacrament; and his subject, of course, was the passion of the Saviour. I had heard the subject handled a thousand times; I thought it exhausted long ago. Little did I suppose that in the wild woods of America, I was to meet with a man whose eloquence would give to this topic a new and more sublime pathos, than I had ever before witnessed." Wirt gives a vivid account of the effect upon the congregation of the picture drawn by the preacher of the scene of the Crucifixion:

"I began to be very uneasy for the situation of the preacher. For I could not conceive how he would be able to let his audience down from the height to which he had wound them, without impairing the solemnity and dignity of his subject, or perhaps shocking them by the abruptness of the fall. But—no; the descent was as beautiful and sublime as the elevation had been rapid and enthusiastic...

"The first sentence with which he broke the awful silence, was a quotation from Rousseau: 'Socrates died like a philosopher, but Jesus Christ like a God.'

"I despair of giving you any idea of the effect produced by this short sentence, unless you could perfectly conceive the whole manner of the man, as well as the peculiar crisis in the discourse. Never before did I completely understand what Demosthenes meant by laying such stress on *delivery*. You are to bring before you the venerable figure of the preacher; his blindness, constantly recalling to your recollection old Homer, Ossian and Milton, and associating with his performance the melancholly grandeur of their geniuses; you are to imagine that you hear his slow, solemn, well accented enunciation, and his voice of affecting, trembling melody; you are to remember the pitch of passion and enthusiasm to which the congregation were raised; and then the few moments of portentous deathlike silence which reigned throughout the house; the preacher removing his white handkerchief from his aged face (even yet wet from the recent torrent of his tears), and slowly stretching forth the palsied hand which holds it, begins the sentence, 'Socrates died like a philosopher'—then pausing, raising his other hand, pressing them both clasped together, with warmth and energy to his breast, lifting his sightless eyes to heaven and pouring his whole soul into his tremulous voice,—'but Jesus Christ—like a God!' If he had been indeed and in truth an angel of light, the effect could scarcely have been more divine...

"If this description gives you the impression, that this incomparable minister had anything of shallow, theatrical tricks in his manner, it does him great injustice. I have never seen in any other orator such a union of simplicity and majesty. He has not a gesture, an attitude or an accent, to which he does not seem forced by the sentiment which he is expressing. His mind is too serious, too earnest, too solicitous, and at the same time, too dignified, to stoop to artifice. Although as far removed from ostentation as a man can he, yet it is clear from the train, the style, and substance of his thoughts that he is, not only a very polite scholar, but a man of extensive and profound erudition.

"This man has been before my imagination almost ever since. A thousand times, as I rode along, I dropped the reins of my bridle, stretched forth my hand, and tried to imitate his quotation from Rousseau; a thousand times I abandoned the attempt in despair, and felt persuaded that his peculiar manner and power arose from an energy of soul, which nature could give, but which no human being could justly copy…

"Guess my surprise, when on my arrival at Richmond, and mentioning the name of this man, I found not one person who had ever before heard of James Waddel!! Is it not strange, that such a genius as this, so accomplished a scholar, so divine an orator, should be permitted to languish and die in obscurity, within eighty miles of the metropolis of Virginia?"

These rather copious extracts have been given of Wirt's description of a pioneer Scotch-Irish preacher because of the force with which they display the fact that although preachers of his class may have been poor in circumstances and obscure in social position they could be great orators and erudite scholars. At the time Scotch-Irish immigration became a notable influence in the population of the colonies the American seaboard had been settled over a century, and a social elegance had been established in the older capitals vying with that of the old country, whose fashions in life and literature were assiduously copied by provincial coteries. As has already been pointed out Scotch-Irish immigration flowed around and beyond the old settlements into new territory, carrying with the stream an educated clergy whose high attainments were unknown to the centers of American culture. As Mr. Wirt remarked, nobody in Richmond had ever heard of Waddel.

But despite this obscurity Waddel was the exponent of a forensic method that founded a school of oratory and had a marked effect upon literary style. The evidence points strongly to the fact that the Scotch-Irish preachers were the agents by whom heavy prose style derived from England was superseded by the warm, vivid, direct energetic expression of thought and feelings characteristic of American oratory from the time of Patrick Henry down to the present time. The eighteenth century stands out in English literature as a transition period. The luxuriance of Elizabethan forms was trimmed and repressed. Literature was made neat and formal.

In the hands of such masters as Johnson and Gibbon prose style attained a stately elegance that suggests the silk waistcoats and the full bottomed wigs of the period. In the hands of less skillful practitioners it was a style that inclined to ungainly affectations and cumbrous pedantry. Illustrations of these characteristics abound in the works of the Mathers, particularly in Cotton Mather's *Magnalia*. Jonathan Edwards exhibits probably the highest colonial attainment in the classic form of eighteenth century style. Together with precision of form and logical force he combined a pithy directness of expression that was the precursor of the simplicity and ease of nineteenth century prose. But emancipation of pulpit style and political oratory from the artificiality of eighteenth century method was the work of Wesley and Whitefield in England, men whose zeal and emotion needed ampler channels for expression than were afforded by the conventional forms. The Tennents, particularly Gilbert Tennent, substituted the new hortatory method for the old pulpit dissertation, under the direct influence of Whitefield and in close association with him during his American tour. How effective that method was in impressing the feelings and in influencing conduct, we have impressive testimony from Benjamin Franklin, than whom there could be no more prudent and circumspect an observer. In his *Autobiography* he tells in the plain, matter-of-fact, unemotional style characteristic of the man how in spite of himself he had to yield his judgment to the persuasion of Whitefield's eloquence.

The new style, which was in effect a personal harangue, was liable to serious defects. It admitted possibilities of rant and incoherence against which the older method guarded. Criticism on this score was directed against Gilbert Tennent himself. It appears to have been the special work of Davies and his successors to systematize the new method, imparting to it dignity and character, and establishing its artistic canons. In so doing a distinctively American school of oratory was founded, whose best examples vie with the finest passages of literature the world can furnish. But it is also a method that in incapable hands produces the style that has become popularly known as "highfalutin." Tinsel rhetoric, affected emotion and pumped enthusiasm became ordinary adjuncts of public discourse, and dreadful examples of this sort may still be found in the *Congressional Record*. But the fact that the style has degenerated until it is now insufferable does not detract from the merit of the masters who unconsciously originated it, in adapting pulpit method to the needs of the times. With them that style was unaffected, natural and sincere. The literary emancipation in which they were leaders remains as a permanent gain since to it modern prose owes its ease and freedom.

CHAPTER XV

Some Pioneer Preachers

The first settled pastor in North Carolina appears to have been Hugh McAden who was born in Pennsylvania, of Scotch-Irish parentage. He was graduated at Nassau Hall in 1753, was licensed by New Castle Presbytery in 1755, and set out soon after on a missionary tour throughout North Carolina, his journal of which has been preserved. He was in the Valley of the Shenandoah when the news reached him of Braddock's defeat. He made the following entry in his journal:

> "Here it was I received the most melancholly news of the entire defeat of our army by the French at Ohio, the General killed, numbers of the inferior officers, and the whole artillery taken. This, together with the frequent account of fresh murders being daily committed upon the frontiers struck terror to every heart. A cold shuddering, possessed every breast, and paleness covered almost every face. In short, the whole inhabitants were put into an universal confusion. Scarcely any man durst sleep in his own house, but all met in companies with their wives and children and set about building little fortifications, to defend themselves from such barbarian and inhuman enemies, whom they concluded would be let loose upon them at pleasure."

McAden crossed the Blue Ridge with an armed escort, and went southward, holding meetings as he went along. The first religious services by him in North Carolina were held August 3, 1755. Although there was no settled pastor in North Carolina at that time there were already some Presbyterian meeting-houses in which the people used to gather for worship. McAden went from place to place preaching and organizing, using any convenient place for the purpose. He records that at one place he preached in a Baptist meeting-house to a people "who seemed very inquisitive about the way to Zion." At another time he "came up with a large company of men, women and children who had fled for their lives from the Cow and Calf pasture in Virginia, from whom I received the melancholly account that the Indians were still doing a great deal of mischief in those parts, by murdering and destroying several of the inhabitants, and banishing the rest from their houses and livings, whereby they are forced to fly into desert places."

McAden himself was exposed to peril from the Indians in North Carolina, when he extended his missionary tour into the country occupied by the Catawba Indians, south of the river that perpetuates their name. He intended to visit some settlements on Broad River, two young men from which had come to guide him. At one place just as they stopped to get breakfast they were surrounded by Indians, shouting and hallooing, and prying into their baggage. The travelers moved off as fast as possible and the Indians did nothing more than to make noisy demonstrations. Later on they passed a camp of Indian hunters who shouted to them to stop but they pushed on as fast as possible. Not until they had ridden twenty-five miles did they feel it safe to stop and get breakfast. McAden's tour extended into the northwestern section of South Carolina, never previously visited by clergymen. He notes on November 2 that he preached to people "many of whom I was told had never heard a sermon, in all their lives before, and yet several of them had families." McAden relates an anecdote told him of an old man, who said to the Governor of South Carolina, when in those parts in treaty with the Cherokee Indians, that he "had never seen a shirt, been in a fair, heard a sermon or seen a minister." The Governor promised to send a minister, that he might hear one sermon before he died. A minister came and preached; and this was all the preaching that had been heard in the upper part of South Carolina before McAden's visit.

From this country McAden returned to North Carolina, and preaching as he went he reached Virginia and passed through Amelia County to the house of a friend on the James River, at which point his diary abruptly closes on May 9, 1756. McAden returned to South Carolina and became the settled minister of the congregations in Duplin and New Hanover. In 1759 he joined Hanover Presbytery which then included the greater part of Virginia and extended indefinitely southward. After a pastorate of ten years his health became so poor that he resigned his charge and moved to Caswell County, where he resided until his death, June 20, 1781. To the extent that his health permitted he continued preaching up to the close of his career. Two weeks before his death British forces encamped in the grounds about the Red House Church, close to McAden's dwelling. They ransacked his house, destroying many of his private papers. His remains lie in the burial ground of that Church, about five miles from the present town of Milton, N. C.

Presbyterianism in Kentucky as in the Carolinas was introduced by Scotch-Irish influence. Originally Kentucky was regarded as a part of Fincastle County, Virginia. It was set off as a separate county, with a municipal court, in 1776. Among the first settlers such Scotch-Irish names occur as McAfee, McCoun and McGee. The settlers drew their ministerial supplies from the Virginia Synod, the period being so late that as a rule they were American born. Among them however was Robert Marshall, who was born in County Down, Ireland, November 27, 1760. His parents came to Western Pennsylvania in the stream of emigration that flowed strongly just before the outbreak of the War of Independence. He enlisted in the army, although only a youth of sixteen, and took part in six general engagements, one of which was the battle of Monmouth, where he made a narrow escape, a bullet grazing the hair of his head. He kept up his study of mathematics while in the army and after the war began studying for the ministry, being then twenty-three. He was licensed by Redstone Presbytery and entered the Virginia field. He removed to Kentucky in 1791, as a missionary appointed by the Synod. He was ordained June 13, 1793, as pastor of Bethel and Blue Spring Churches.

An early missionary whose activities extended not only into Virginia and North Carolina but also western Pennsylvania and eventually Ohio was Charles Beatty. He was born in County

Antrim, Ireland, some time between 1712 and 1715. He accompanied a party of Scotch-Irish who emigrated to America in 1729, and after a stay in New England made a settlement in what is now Orange County, New York. Although he had received a classical education Beatty became a pedlar and his entrance in the ministry is attributed to an accidental encounter with William Tennent. Beatty happened to call at the Log College while on a trading tour, and as a jocose recognition of its pretensions as an institute of learning used Latin in offering his wares. Tennent replied in Latin, and the conversation developed such evidences of capacity in Beatty that Tennent counselled him to give up his pedlar's business and prepare for the ministry. He pursued his studies at the Log College and was licensed by New Brunswick Presbytery in 1742. He was called to the Forks of Neshaminy, May 26, 1743. In 1754 the Synod sent him to Virginia and North Carolina.

This was not long prior to Braddock's defeat and that event probably interrupted Beatty's Southern labors for he was back again in Pennsylvania in 1755, and acted as chaplain to the forces led by Benjamin Franklin. Franklin had been commissioned by the Governor of Pennsylvania to take charge of the frontier and provide for the defense of the settlers by building forts and establishing garrisons. He recruited a force of 560 and set out for Gnadenhutten, a village settled by the Moravians. Indians had attacked it slaying the inhabitants, and Franklin thought it was important that one of the proposed forts should be erected there. Franklin established his base at Bethlehem, which although in a county now in the tier immediately west of New Jersey was at that time close to Indian country. Detachments were sent out to various points, Franklin himself accompanying one that went to Gnadenhutten. During the march ten farmers who had received from Franklin supplies of ammunition, with which they thought they could defend their homes, were killed by the Indians. Franklin himself had some anxiety as it rained heavily, and he remarked: "It was well we were not attacked in our march, for our arms were the most ordinary sort, and our men could not keep the locks of their guns dry. The Indians are dexterous in contrivances for that purpose which we had not." The first night out from Bethlehem the party took shelter from the rain in a barn, where says Franklin "we were all huddled together as wet as water could make us." The next day they arrived at Gnadenhutten where their first task was to bury the bodies of the massacred inhabitants. Beatty accompanied the troops through these scenes, looking zealously after their welfare. Franklin describes Beatty's activity with sly humor:

> "We had for our chaplain a zealous Presbyterian minister, Mr. Beatty, who complained to me that the men did not generally attend his prayers and exhortations. When they were enlisted they were promised, besides pay and provisions, a gill of rum a day, which was punctually served out to them, half in the morning and the other half in the evening; and I observed they were punctual in attending to receive it; upon which I said to Mr. Beatty, 'It is perhaps below the dignity of your profession to act as a steward of the rum; but if you were only to distribute it out after prayers, you would have them all about you.' He liked the thought, undertook the task, and with the help of a few hands to measure out the liquor, executed it to satisfaction; and never were prayers more generally and more punctually attended."

A fort was erected at Gnadenhutten and soon afterward Beatty left to go into Bucks County and aid in recruiting. His services in that respect were specially valuable as the Scotch-Irish were a leading source of supply for soldiers both in the Indian wars and later in the Revolutionary War. In 1756 the Synod made a dispensation of his services in favor of his service to the Government, but in 1759 when there was another call by the Pennsylvania authorities for his services, the Synod on account of the state of his congregation advised him not to go, but he was permitted to act as chaplain to Colonel Armstrong's regiment.

Beatty's ability and energy made him much in request for missionary work of any kind. In 1760 the Corporation for the Widows' Fund sent him to Great Britain to raise funds and he went with letters of introduction from Davies and others. He was quite successful in this mission, making collections in England and inducing the General Assembly of the Scottish Kirk to order a national collection. After his return to America Beatty engaged in missionary work that carried him through Western Pennsylvania into Ohio. In 1766 the Synod sent Beatty on a missionary tour to the frontiers of the Province. Starting from Carlisle, Pa., in August of that year, he penetrated as far west as the Indian country on the Muskingum River, Ohio, 130 miles beyond Fort Pitt, now Pittsburgh, and he made an encouraging report as to the prospects of missionary work among the Indians. In 1768 Beatty made another visit to Great Britain, this time to put his wife under surgical treatment, but she died soon after landing. Beatty returned to his ministerial labors in America, but a few years later he was again called to solicit funds for the College of New Jersey. In that interest he sailed for the West Indies, but died August 13, 1772, soon after reaching Bridgetown in Barbados.

Another pioneer of Presbyterianism in the West was John Steele, who came to America in 1742, as a probationer from Londonderry Presbytery. He was ordained by New Castle Presbytery, some time before May, 1744. He was sent to the frontier and ministered to a congregation in the Upper West Settlement, now Mercersburg, Franklin County, Pa. This region in the southern part of the central section of the State was then Indian country. Steele, who was a man of courage and determination, put himself at the head of his flock as its leader in war as well as peace. He fortified his church, and if it became necessary to send out a force against the Indians he led it. A captain's commission was issued to him and he held it several years. He spent his life in the western country. In 1768 Penn solicited his aid to make a peaceable settlement with people who had squatted on land in the Youghiogheny region, and Steele visited the country for that purpose, assembling the people and reasoning with them. He died in August, 1779.

Another noted pioneer in the western advance of Presbyterianism was James Finley, who was born in County Armagh, Ireland, in February, 1725, but was educated in America under Samuel Blair at the Fagg's Manor school. He was licensed by New Castle Presbytery and in 1752 was ordained pastor of East Nottingham Church, Cecil County, Md. In addition to pastoral work he engaged in teaching. As lands in the West became open for occupation emigration among Finley's people began on so large a scale that he joined the movement. He crossed the mountains in 1765 and again in 1767. Thirty-four heads of families belonging to Finley's congregation settled in Western Pennsylvania, and the emigrants included three of Finley's sons. He asked for a demission from his charge, that he might follow them, but the congregation was loath to give him up, and the Presbytery refused his application. He appealed to the Synod which dissolved the pastoral relation, May 17, 1782. He was called to Rehoboth and Round Hill, both in the Forks of the Youghiogheny, in the fall of 1784. He was commissioned by the State Government both as Justice of the Peace and as Judge of the Common Pleas. He retained his Youghiogheny charge until his death, January 6, 1795.

Church organization in western Pennsylvania was later than in Virginia for the reason that early emigration from the seaboard tended southward rather than westward. The valleys stretching from middle Pennsylvania and Maryland into Virginia supplied the lines of least resistance upon which the settlement of the interior progressed. Hanover Presbytery in Virginia was organized in 1755; Carlisle Presbytery in central Pennsylvania was not organized until 1765. The first Presbytery organized in western Pennsylvania was Redstone in 1781, which became the parent of Presbyteries in the western country north of the Ohio just as Hanover Presbytery became the parent of Presbyteries in the South and Southwest.

Although Presbyterianism was historically the ecclesiastical form with which the Scotch-Irish stock was originally identified, transplantation to the United States was soon followed by variation. New England Congregationalism was recruited by Ulster emigration. After the Revolutionary War the Protestant Episcopal

Church attracted adherents. The son of James Wilson resigned a judgeship to enter the Episcopal ministry, and Bishop McIlvaine came of a stock that originally belonged to a Scotch-Irish settlement in Bucks County, Pennsylvania. Bishop McKendree, whose labors did much to extend the membership of the Methodist Church, came of Scotch-Irish stock. Alexander Campbell, who in 1827 founded a denomination that now ranks sixth among American ecclesiastical bodies in number of adherents, was born at Shaws Castle, County Antrim, 1786.

CHAPTER XVI

Scotch-Irish Educational Institutions

The fact that originally Presbyterianism was the product of historical research naturally set up standards of scholarship for its ministry. The grounds upon which rested the doctrine of the parity of ministerial orders in the primitive Church were not to be discerned by inward light nor apprehended by emotional fervor. It was a matter calling for historical knowledge, involving familiarity with the languages in which the records of the primitive Church were preserved. Presbyterian ministry thus implied educated ministry from its very nature.

Institutions of learning were therefore a necessary accompaniment of the Presbyterian Church. In Ulster it was the regular thing for a candidate for the ministry to go to Scotland to get a classical education as the foundation of his theological studies. This insistence upon scholarship as a ministerial qualification was sharpened by sectarian tendencies in favor of substituting zeal for knowledge and private inspiration for historical evidence. To fortify the ministry against such tendencies particular attention was paid to education from the earliest times. The records of the Ulster Synod show that the educational qualifications of the ministry received steady care. Conditions in the New World put fresh stress upon the need of an educated ministry. The very freedom found there admitted of vagaries that were repugnant to the orderly instincts of historical Presbyterianism. Zealots appeared who claimed prophetic authority so that they assumed the right to examine ministers as to their opinions and behavior and pass judgment upon their spiritual state. An enthusiast who once had a large following required his followers to give a practical exhibition of their renunciation of idolatry by casting into the flames some ornament or finery in which they had taken pride. A fire was actually kindled for the purpose, and his followers each took off some article of dress or some ornament and tossed it into the flames. A number of religious books which he adjudged heretical were also cast into the fire. Among them was one by the noted Puritan divine Dr. Increase Mather. Dr. Hodge remarks of this period that an "enthusiastical and fanatical spirit ... swept over the New England churches."

Gilbert Tennent, who himself gave countenance to the movement in its early stages, in a letter dated February 12, 1742, remarked that "experience had given him a clear view of the danger of every thing which tends to enthusiasm and divisions in the visible Church." He added: "The sending out of unlearned men to teach others, upon the supposition of their piety, in ordinary cases, seems to bring the ministry into contempt; to cherish enthusiasm, and to bring all into confusion. Whatever fair face it may have, it is a most perverse practice." This conclusion was not reached until after controversies engendered by the situation had disrupted the Church, but in the end the effect was to impress anew the need of an educated ministry and to incite special exertions to supply the means.

As has been set forth in preceding chapters, an educated ministry accompanied the Scotch-Irish settlements in America. But Ireland was so far away and communications were so hard and so slow that America could not depend upon Ulster as a source in the way that Ulster so long depended upon Scotland. It was a comparatively brief and easy matter for a student to go and come between Ulster and Scotland by the short sea-ferry; but if there was to be in America a native born educated ministry, institutions of learning had to be set up. Considerations of this nature had impelled the New England Puritans to found Harvard and Yale. Similar educational activity was evinced by the Ulster Presbyterians when they settled in Pennsylvania. In 1726 William Tennent, an Ulster clergyman for some years resident in America, became pastor of the church at Neshaminy, Bucks County, Pennsylvania. In 1728 James Logan gave Tennent fifty acres of land on Neshaminy Creek "to encourage him to prosecute his views, and make his residence near us permanent." On this tract Tennent put up a school house and as it was built of logs, it was familiarly known as the Log College. But humble as was the building the scholarship it sheltered was sound in quality and ample for the times. No vestige of the building remains but its work goes on.

This foundation, since so famous, passed almost unnoticed at the time. The only contemporary reference appears to be that contained in the journal of George Whitefield, the evangelist, who visited the region during his preaching tours. He made the following quaint entry in his journal for 1739:

"The place wherein the young men study now is, in contempt, called The College. It is a log house, about twenty feet long, and near as many broad, and to me, it seemed to resemble the school of the old prophets, for their habitations were mean; and that they sought not great things for themselves is plain from those passages of Scripture wherein we are told that each of them took a beam to build them a house; and that at the feast of the sons of the prophets, one of them put on the pot, whilst the others went to fetch some herbs out of the field. All that we can say of most of our universities is they are glorious without. From this despised place seven or eight worthy ministers of Jesus have lately been sent forth, more are almost ready to be sent, and the foundation is now laying for the instruction of many others."

Tennent carried on this school almost single-handed. It was said of him that Latin was as familiar as his mother tongue. According to a biographical notice published in 1805, "his attainments in science are not so well known, but there is reason to believe that they were not so great as his skill in language." As a teacher he was singularly successful. He educated for the ministry his four sons who added to the reputation of the family name. Among his pupils were such distinguished men as Samuel Blair, John Rowland, James McCrea, William Robinson, John Blair, Samuel Finley, John Roan, Charles Beatty, Daniel Lawrence and William Dean. Probably no other school ever produced so many eminent men in proportion to the number of its pupils. It was in this way the Log College became progenitor of numerous institutions of learning, and not through any corporate connection. It was the expression of the powers of one individual and did not survive him.

The Log College was only one of a number of schools that were precursors of the Princeton foundation. There was not until 1746, in all the region between Connecticut and Virginia, any institution authorized to confer degrees. But the influx of Ulster clergymen led to the establishing of schools that did valuable work. Samuel Blair, born in Ireland, June 14, 1712, studied for the ministry at the Log College. He was installed pastor of a congregation at Fagg's Manor, Pa., in 1740, where he established a school which produced such men as Samuel Davies, John Rodgers, Alexander Cumming, James Finley, Robert Smith and Hugh Henry. He died in July 5, 1751.

Francis Alison, born in Ireland in 1705 and educated at the University of Glasgow, came to America in 1734 or 1735. On the recommendation of Benjamin Franklin he was employed by John Dickinson of Delaware as tutor for his son, with permission to take other pupils. He is said to have had an academy at Thunder Hill, Md. He was ordained pastor of New London, Chester County, Pa., by New Castle Presbytery in 1737, and in 1743 he started a school there, which the Synod took under its patronage. In 1749 he was invited to Philadelphia to take charge of a school there, which had been founded through subscriptions obtained by Benjamin Franklin. This institution was the germ of the University of Pennsylvania. Among his pupils were Charles Thomson, Secretary of the Continental Congress, and three signers of the Declaration of Independence, Thomas McKean, George Read and James Smith.

Samuel Finley, born in County Armagh, Ireland, in 1715, arrived in Philadelphia, September 28, 1734. He completed his studies at the Log College. In 1741 he was appointed to the care of several congregations, one of which was at Nottingham, Md., where he established a school that became famous. Among his pupils were Governor Martin of North Carolina, Ebenezer

Hazard of Philadelphia, Benjamin Rush and Judge Jacob Rush, Dr. McWhorter of Newark, Dr. Tennent of Abingdon and the famous James Waddel, the blind preacher of Virginia. John H. Finley, Commissioner of Education of the State of New York, is a descendant of the Rev. James Finley, brother of Samuel Finley.

When the movement known as Methodism stirred the Church, chiefly through the preaching of George Whitefield, the controversies engendered by practices attending this movement incidentally put new emphasis upon education as a qualification for the ministry. At the meeting of the Synod of Philadelphia in 1738 the following proposal from the Presbytery of Lewes was adopted by a large majority:

> "That every student who has not studied with approbation, passing the usual course in some of the New England or European Colleges, approved by public authority, shall, before he be encouraged by any Presbytery for the sacred work of the ministry, apply himself to this Synod, and that they appoint a committee of their members yearly, whom they know to be well skilled in the several branches of philosophy and divinity, and the languages, to examine such students in this place, and finding them well accomplished in those several parts of learning shall allow them a public testimonial from the Synod, which till better provision be made, will in some measure answer the design of taking a degree in the College."

In 1739 the order was revised so as to provide that the candidate for the ministry "shall be examined by the whole Synod, or its commission as to those preparatory studies, which we generally pass through at the College, and if they find him qualified, they shall give him a certificate, which shall be received by our respective Presbyteries as equivalent to a diploma or certificate from the College." This action of the Synod was objected to by the Tennents and other adherents of Log College, as it seemed to ignore that institution and to erect a Synodical College. Trouble soon broke out. The New Brunswick Presbytery disregarded the Synod's rule and licensed John Rowland, a Log College graduate.

The Synod declared this proceeding disorderly, admonished the Presbytery and ruled that Rowland was not to be admitted as a preacher until he submitted to the Synodical examination. The Synod at the same time appointed its commission to meet at Philadelphia and "prosecute the design of erecting a school or seminary of learning." Ebenezer Pemberton, Jonathan Dickinson, John Cross and James Anderson were nominated, two of whom were to go to Europe to solicit aid. This design was not carried out at the time, but it traced the lines on which eventually the College of New Jersey was planned.

Underlying the dispute about ministerial qualifications were differences as to church standards and discipline, stirred up by the Methodist movement and particularly by the preaching of George Whitefield. President Ashbel Green, in a historical sketch published in 1822, traced the origin of the College of New Jersey to the rupture of 1741, by which the Synod of Philadelphia was divided and the Synod of New York was organized as a rival body. President Green says:

> "Both Synods, from the time of their separation, made strenuous exertions to educate youth for the Gospel ministry; not only from the laudable desire of extending the blessings of the Gospel to those who, in every direction, were then destitute of them, but also from the less commendable motive of strengthening and extending each its own party. Thus circumstanced and disposed, it was to be expected that the members of the Synod of New York would endeavor to organize their plans of education, in a province where their peculiar views were prevalent and popular. New Jersey was their undisputed territory; and here if anywhere, they might hope to found an institution in which all their wishes might be realized. It happened also that in this Province the ablest champions of their cause, and the man of their Synod who, in all respects, was the best qualified to superintend and conduct the education of youth, had his residence. This was the Rev. Jonathan Dickinson, of Elizabeth Town."

With the probable view of putting Dickinson at the head of

such an institution as could graduate recruits to the learned profession, a charter was obtained from the Province of New Jersey, the official attestation under the Great Seal being made by Acting Governor John Hamilton, of His Majesty's Council, October 22, 1746. This charter was not recorded but its substance is given in an advertisement which appeared in the *Pennsylvania Gazette* of August 13, 1747, concluding with the announcement that the

> "trustees have chosen the Rev. Mr. Jonathan Dickinson president, whose superior Abilities are well known; and Mr. Caleb Smith, tutor of the said college; and that the college is now actually opened, to be kept at Elizabeth Town, till a building can be erected in a more central place of the said Province for the residence of the Students; that all who are qualified for it, may be immediately admitted to an academick education, and to such class and station in the college, as they are found upon examination to deserve; and that the charge of the college to each student, will be Four Pound a year New Jersey money, at Eight Shillings per ounce, and no more."

It appears that the opening of the college thus referred to took place in the fourth week of May, preceding the announcement. Hatfield in his *History of Elizabeth* states that "the first term of the College of New Jersey, was opened at Mr. Dickinson's house, on the south side of the old Rahway road directly west of Race Street." President Dickinson's term of administration was brief, beginning in April, 1747, and closing with his death on October 7, 1747. His educational labors appear however to have been much more extensive than his brief presidency might indicate, as he had previously taken private pupils. It is also certain that his pupils had made very considerable progress, for less than a year after his decease six persons received their Bachelor's degree. In addition to his activities as minister and teacher Dickinson was also a practising physician, in which profession he had considerable reputation.

William Tennent died May 6, 1746. Log College graduates had already joined forces with the men from New York and northern

New Jersey in the formation at Elizabethtown, in September, 1745, of the Synod of New Jersey. This union of forces resulted in the application for a charter for the College of New Jersey. Although there is nothing in the nature of legal succession to the Log College there is a strong tradition of institutional filiation. The two institutions are directly connected through devotion to the same ideals and attachment to the same standards. Both belonged to what was called the New Side; both were in sympathy with the spiritual revival, led by Whitefield. Practical expression of this community of purpose was given by the action of the trustees in associating with themselves some distinguished graduates of the Log College. The trustees named in the original charter were William Smith, Peter Van Brugh Livingston and William Peartree Smith, gentlemen, and Jonathan Dickinson, John Pierson, Ebenezer Pemberton and Aaron Burr, ministers. These seven or any four of them were granted power to select five more trustees and they chose Gilbert Tennent, William Tennent, Samuel Blair, Richard Treat and Samuel Finley, all ministers. Of those five two were sons of the founder of the Log College and all were graduates, except Treat who lived at Abington near the Log College.

What in the beginning differentiated the College of New Jersey from other early schools was not its plant nor its equipment but its high purpose and broad policy. Its founders sought to establish an institution of higher learning not as a denominational agency but as an educational foundation from which all the learned professions would benefit. The original charter provided that no person should be debarred "on account of any speculative principles of religion," and this policy was maintained from the first.

The original charter was not recorded and has disappeared, although its substance is known from the published announcements of the trustees. Its legality was open to suspicion, and the arrival of Governor Belcher in the Province afforded a happy opportunity of procuring a new charter. Jonathan Belcher, son of a member of the Royal Council in Massachusetts, was born in 1681, and was graduated at Harvard in 1699. His father then sent him to

Europe to complete his education and he remained abroad six years, during which time he became known to the Princess Sophia and her son, afterward King George II, an acquaintance which eventually led to public honors. After his return to Boston he lived there as a wealthy and public spirited merchant. He was appointed a member of the Council and in 1722 the Massachusetts Legislature sent him to England as agent of the Province. In 1730 the King appointed him Governor of Massachusetts and New Hampshire. He held this position for eleven years making enemies who resorted even to forgery to discredit his administration. On being superseded he went to England and vindicated his character and conduct so effectually that he was restored to royal favor and promised the first vacant Governorship in America. The vacancy occurring in New Jersey, he was sent to that Province, arriving in 1747 and remaining the rest of his life. As "Captain General and Governor in Chief of the Province of New Jersey, and territories thereon depending in America, and Vice Admiral of the same," he lived in a style and practised a hospitality befitting the dignity of his titles. He promptly interested himself in the affairs of the nascent College of New Jersey and actively exerted his influence to make it worthy of its title. Not long after his arrival he sent the following letter to his cousin William Belcher in England:

> Sr.—This is a fine Climate and Countrey of Great plenty tho' but of Little profit to a Governour. The inhabitants are generally rustick and without Education. I am therefore attempting the building up of a College in the province for Instructing the youth in the Principles of Religion in good Literature and Manners and I have a Reasonable View of bringing it to bear.
>
> I am Sr
> Your Friend and Very humble servant
> J. BELCHER.
>
> BURLINGTON, N. J.
> Sept. 17, 1747.

Governor Belcher granted a new charter, which passed the seal of the Province on September 14, 1748. The preamble sets forth that "the said Petitioners have also expressed their earnest Desire that those of every religious Denomination may have free and equal Liberty and Advantages of Education in the said College, any different Sentiments in Religion notwithstanding." Under this charter the lay trustees were made equal in number to those who were clergymen and its undenominational character was firmly established.

At the time of the granting of the second charter the Rev. Aaron Burr was the Acting President of the College which after President Dickinson's death had been removed to Newark. The formal election of Mr. Burr to the presidency did not take place until November 9, 1748, at a meeting of the trustees in Newark. On the same day the first commencement was celebrated with much ceremony, although the graduating class numbered only six. A set of laws for the government of the college, probably prepared by President Burr, was adopted by the trustees at this time. The high standard of education already set up is attested by the following provisions: "None may be expected to be admitted into College but such as being examined by the President and Tutors shall be found able to render Virgil and Tully's Orations into English; and to turn English into true and grammatical Latin; and to be so well acquainted with Greek as to render any part of the four Evangelists in that language into Latin or English; and to give the grammatical connection of the words."

During the ten years of President Burr's administration the infant college surmounted the difficulties that confronted the struggling little school in which it had its beginning, and became established in its permanent home. Its early years undoubtedly owed much to the hearty support of Governor Belcher. Named in the charter as the first member of the Board of Trustees, he was an active member, attending the meetings of the board and interesting himself in the success of the enterprise. At the meeting in Newark, September 27, 1752, he made an address in which he said that for the present there was no prospect of aid from friends in Great Britain, but urged: "In the meantime I think it our duty, to exert ourselves, in all reasonable ways and measures we can, for the aid and assistance of our friends nearer home; that we may have wherewith to build a house for the accommodation of the students, and another for the President and his family. And it seems therefore necessary that, without further delay, we agree upon the place where to set those buildings."

In 1751 the trustees had voted in favor of New Brunswick upon the strength of expectations that were not realized. The trustees now turned to Princeton and in response to Governor Belcher's appeal it was voted, "That the College be fixed at Princeton upon Condition that the Inhabitants of sd. Place secure to the Trustees that two Hundred Acres of Woodland, and that ten Acres of clear'd land; which Mr. Sergeant view'd; and also one thousand Pounds proc. Money." The allusion is to Jonathan Sergeant, the treasurer of the board, to whom the land had been shown that the Princeton people proposed to give to the college. The conditions were complied with to the satisfaction of the board, and the business of collecting funds was taken in hand. At a meeting of the board in Burlington, May 23, 1753, a committee was appointed "to draw up an address in the name of the trustees, to his Excellency Governor Belcher, humbly to desire that he would use his influence in Europe, recommending the affair of the College by the gentlemen appointed to take a voyage there to solicit benefactions for it." The two gentlemen referred to were the Rev. Gilbert Tennent of Philadelphia and the Rev. Samuel Davies, then in Hanover County, Va. They went on their mission with strong credentials and recommendations from Governor Belcher and were able to collect sufficient funds to enable the trustees to proceed with the erection of the main building. Ground was broken on July 29, 1754. Before the building was occupied Governor Belcher presented the college with his library, comprising 474 volumes, many of them highly valuable. His dead of gift, after a catalogue of the books, goes on to say that they are given "together with my own picture at full length, in a gilt frame, now standing in my blue chamber; also one pair of globes, and ten pictures in black frames, over the mantelpiece in my library room, being the heads of the Kings and Queens of England; and also my large carved gilded coat of arms." The trustees voted an address of thanks, concluding with this proposal:

> "As the college of New Jersey views you in the light of its founder, patron and benefactor, and the impartial world will esteem it a respect deservedly due to the name of *Belcher*; permit us to dignify the edifice now erecting at Princeton, with that endeared appellation, and when your Excellency is translated to *a house not made with hands eternal in the heavens*, let BELCHER HALL proclaim your beneficent acts, for the advancement of Christianity, and the emolument of *the arts* and *sciences*, to the latest ages."

To this address Governor Belcher made a reply in which he said that it had seemed to him "that a seminary for religion and learning should be promoted in this Province; for the better en-lightening of the minds and polishing the manners, of this and the neighboring colonies." Hence "this important affair, I have been, during my administration, honestly and heartily prosecuting, in all such laudable, ways and measures as I have judged most likely to effect what we all aim at." In conclusion he said:

> "I take a particular grateful notice, of the respect and honour you are desirous of doing me and my family, in calling the edifice lately erected in Princeton by the name of Belcher Hall; but you will be so good as to excuse me, while I absolutely decline such an honour, for I have always been very fond of the motto of a late grand personage, *Prodesse quam conspici*. But I must not leave this without asking the favor of your naming the present building Nassau Hall; and this I hope you will take as a further instance of my real regard to the future welfare and interest of the college, as it will express the honor we retain, in this remote part of the globe, to the immortal memory of the glorious King William the third, who was a branch of the illustrious house of Nassau."

In accordance with this recommendation the trustees, at their meeting in Newark, September 29, 1756, voted "that the said

edifice be in all time to come, called and known by the name of
Nassau Hall." Thus it was that the College of New Jersey received
the name by which it was best known. In fact its corporate title
was rarely used.

⸱ The building was ready for occupancy in the fall of 1756 and
in that year the students, then about seventy in number, moved
from Newark into their new quarters. Governor Belcher did
not live to witness the prosperity of Nassau Hall as he died at
Elizabeth, August 31, 1757, aged seventy-six. His body was taken
to Cambridge, Mass., for burial. He was a fine example of the
educated Puritan gentleman, combining dignity of manners, refinement of taste and stately hospitality with sincere piety. He was
Governor of Massachusetts when Whitefield visited that Province
in 1740, and he showed the eloquent preacher marked respect. He
not only attended Whitefield's meetings in Boston but followed
him as far as Worcester, and urged him to continue his faithful
instructions sparing neither ministers nor rulers. Belcher's picture in the faculty room of Princeton University is a half length,
showing a gentleman in all the elegance of attire of his period,
full bottomed wig, lace ruffles and a red vest. The handsome face
is rather long, with firmly moulded, strong features, expressive of
energy and resolution. The present picture is not the one he gave
to the college but is a copy of a portrait. It is now one among a
number of portraits of Princeton worthies and does not indicate
the distinction given to him in the hall as arranged in 1761, the
year in which the royal portrait arrived. The hall then had a gallery
at one end, and at the other end was a stage for use in the public
exhibitions of the students. On one side was the full length portrait
of George II, and on the other side was a like portrait of Governor
Belcher, with his family arms above it, carved and gilded. These
fittings and adornments were ravaged by the alternate occupancy
of the contending armies during the Revolutionary War, the library
presented by Governor Belcher being also a sufferer. What survived
was consumed in a fire, on March 6, 1802, which destroyed all of
Nassau Hall except the bare walls.

The chief source of the funds for the erection of Nassau Hall was the collection made in Great Britain by Tennent and Davies, who went out in 1753 and returned in the following year. The Presbyterians both in England and Scotland made contributions liberal for the times; and Ulster attested its own direct interest by making special effort to raise money for the New Jersey college. In view of the necessitous condition of the Ulster people and clergy at that period the action taken is a marked evidence of the close tie between Ulster and American Presbyterianism. As the official record of this event does not appear in the church histories, it has been transcribed from the Minutes of the General Synod of Ulster, in session at Antrim, Thursday, June 27, 1754, as follows:

> "A Petition was presented to this Synod by the Rev'd M^r. Gilb^t Tennent in the name of the Synod of N. York, & the Trustees of the infant Colledge of N. Jersey, & many of the Inhabitants of the neighbouring Provinces representing that as they had laid a foundation for a Colledge & Seminary of learning, w^c they apprehend may be of important service to the Interests of Religion & Learning: & as they are not able to carry this design to such perfection as is necessary to answer the exigencys of Church & State in these parts of His Majesties Dominions: they therefore humbly supplicate for such assistance as this Synod shall think proper, particularly one Sab. days Collection in the several Congregations subject to this Synod w^t previous intimation for s^d. Collection. The Synod Judging the above s^d Seminary to be of great importance to the promotion of the Interests of Religion & Learning in several Provinces of N. America, unanimously granted the Petition: & ordered that public Collections be made in all the Congregations under their care, some time before the first of Novr. next, in ye meantime recommending it to all the Members of this Synod, to excite by proper exhortations their several societies to this important Charity."

This is an exceptionally long minute to appear upon the Synod's records. In addition to its earnest recommendation the Synod appointed a collector in each Presbytery, to receive and transmit the contributions. The circumstances of the people were then such that it was very difficult to get money for any purpose, but the Synod was persistent in its efforts. At the meeting of the General Synod, June 24, 1755, the following minute was entered upon the records:

> "There has been very little done by the Pbys in the affair of the Charity to the College in N. Jersey, as appointed at last Synod. This Synod renews the recommodation, & enjoins the several Minrs to represent it, in the warmest manner to their Congregations: & to pay their Collections to the Gentlemen formerlie appointed, before the first of Novr. next."

At the meeting in 1756 the matter is again mentioned with the remark that "as some B^n. here made contributions for that purpose the Synod is well pleased with them." There is no record of the exact amount obtained through these collections, but the entire amount raised in Ireland was about 500 pounds; in Scotland, over 1,000 pounds; in England, about 1,700 pounds. It is remarkable that with such pressing needs in the home field the Ulster Synod should have taken such an active interest in a far distant enterprise. This may be attributed to a consciousness that the Church in America was a transplantation of the Church of Ulster. Princeton is undoubtedly a Scotch-Irish educational foundation made upon their cherished principle that what makes for learning and scholarship makes for Presbyterianism.

Princeton was the fourth college to be established in the colonies, Harvard in 1638 being the first, William and Mary in Virginia coming second in 1691, Yale third in 1701 and then Princeton in 1746. It was very advantageously situated and from the first drew attendance from all the region south of New England. A record of the commencement exercises of September, 1764, in President Finley's time, has been preserved from which it appears that they were mainly in Latin with the exception of "an English forensick Dispute," concerning which President Finley noted that it had been introduced because "it entertains the English part of the Audience; tends to the cultivation of our native Language, and has been agreeable on former occasions; which I presume are sufficient apologies for continuing the custom." President Finley was a Scotch-Irishman, a native of County Armagh, Ulster. The tenor of his note on the admission of an English feature into the exercises shows that he instinctively assumed that Latin was the proper language of scholarship.

Mortality was very marked among the early Presidents of Princeton, Dickinson, the first President, did not live to see the first commencement. His successor, Burr, held the office for ten years, and it was during his administration that the college was securely established in Princeton. In the next nine years Jonathan Edwards, Samuel Davies and Samuel Finley died, each while President of the University. The vacancy created by Finley's death July 17, 1766, was not filled for two years, during which time the Rev. William Tennent, Jr., acted as President. He was put in charge of that office by the vote of the trustees at their meeting June 25, 1766, at which time President Finley was disabled from performing its duties by the illness of which he soon afterward died. Mr. Tennent, the second son of the founder of the Log College, was pastor of the Presbyterian church at Freehold, about twenty-three miles from Princeton, so he could extend his activities to cover both places. A charter member of the Board of Trustees, he had always taken an active interest in the management of the college.

In 1768 John Witherspoon, D.D., LL.D., of Paisley, Scotland, yielded to repeated solicitations and came to America to become the sixth President of the College of New Jersey. Witherspoon's administration is of special importance as it extended from 1768 to 1794, covering the whole period of the Revolutionary War and the formation of the national Government through the adoption of the Constitution of the United States. In those events through advantage of position and through Witherspoon's personal ability and influence Princeton played a great part. Witherspoon was the son of a minister whose parish was about eighteen miles from Edinburgh. He was educated at the University of Edinburgh where he distinguished himself for his scholarship. From Beith where he was first settled as a pastor he was called to the large and flourishing town of Paisley, where his labors established for him such a reputation that he received numerous calls, among them one to Dublin, Ireland, and one to Rotterdam, Holland. When called by the trustees of the College of New Jersey to its presidency, he at first declined owing to his wife's extreme aversion to leaving Scotland; but when the call was reiterated he accepted, moved by the conviction that it was an opportunity of service that ought not to be rejected. Witherspoon threw himself into the cause of American learning and American liberty with his whole heart and will. Not only did his administration enlarge the scholarship and augment the instruction of Nassau Hall but the active part which Witherspoon soon took in politics gave a distinction to Princeton that had important results. His public activities hurt as well as helped, for some youth from Tory families passed by Princeton to go to Yale, but on the other hand there were New England students who passed by Harvard and Yale to go to Princeton. The result was that the College of New Jersey became more of a national institution than any other American college during the colonial period, and it became a school of statesmanship for the forming of the nation. Gaillard Hunt, in his *Life of James Madison*, has made an instructive analysis of Princeton influence in the Revolutionary period. In discussing the reasons why James Madison of Virginia went to Princeton rather than William and Mary College in his own State, Mr. Hunt says:

> "He had the advantage of broader surroundings than would have been possible if he had completed his education elsewhere in America; for William and Mary was a local college, and so were Harvard and Yale, with few students coming from any other colony than the one in which each was situated. At the College of New Jersey, on the other hand, every colony was represented among the students; and while New Jersey had a few more than any other one colony, she had not a fourth part of all the students, the actual number being, when Madison entered, only nineteen Jerseymen out of eighty-four students. Of the twelve students who graduated with Madison only one, Charles McKnight, afterward distinguished in the medical department of the army of

the Revolution, came from New Jersey. Chief among Madison's companions in his own class were Gunning Bedford of Delaware, Hugh Henry Brackenridge of Pennsylvania, and Philip Freneau of New York."

﹢ To this unique position of Princeton must be attributed its preponderating influence in the formation period of American history. Before Witherspoon's time Nassau Hall did its part in turning out men qualified for political eminence. Richard Stockton, a member of the first graduating class, was a member of the Continental Congress of 1776–1777 and a signer of the Declaration of Independence. Prior to the accession of Witherspoon in 1768 the College of New Jersey graduated 301 students of whom the majority entered the ministry, but there were many who turned to law and politics and became eminent in public life. Eighteen graduates of this period became members of the Continental Congress. Men of such national reputation as Samuel Livermore of New Hampshire, Joseph Shippen, Jr., of Pennsylvania, Alexander Martin of North Carolina, Joseph Reed of Pennsylvania, Benjamin Rush of Pennsylvania, William Paterson of New Jersey, Oliver Ellsworth of Connecticut and Luther Martin of Maryland were graduated during this period. With the accession of Witherspoon the trend of the times began to shift the interest of the students strongly to public affairs. In the twenty-six years of his incumbency 469 young men were graduated of whom only 114, or less than a quarter, became clergymen. Of the 230 graduates from 1766 to 1776, twelve became members of the Continental Congress, twenty-four became members of the Congress of the United States, three Justices of the Supreme Court, one Secretary of State, one Postmaster-General, three Attorney-Generals, one Vice-President of the United States and one President.

﹢ The most critical period of our history was the formation of the national Government, the fruit of the constitutional convention of 1787. Of its fifty-five members thirty-two were of academic training, including one each from London, Oxford, Glasgow,

Edinburgh and Aberdeen, five from William and Mary, one from the University of Pennsylvania, two from Columbia, three from Harvard, four from Yale and nine from Princeton. Moreover those nine included the leaders of the convention. They were as follows, the graduation class to which each belonged being bracketed after the name: Alexander Martin (1756) of North Carolina, William Paterson (1763) of New Jersey, Oliver Ellsworth (1766) of Connecticut, Luther Martin (1766) of Maryland, William Churchill Houston (1768) of New Jersey, Gunning Bedford, Jr., (1771) of Delaware, James Madison (1771) of Virginia, William Richardson Davie (1776) of North Carolina, and Jonathan Dayton (1776) of New Jersey. With these should be named Edmund Randolph of Virginia who studied at Princeton although he did not graduate.

James Madison was the wheelhorse of the federal movement. Although the Virginia plan in which representation was based on population was submitted by Randolph, it was inspired by Madison. The Jersey plan, based on the principle of State equality, was devised by Paterson. The great controversies of the convention were over the issue raised by these two plans. Ellsworth and Davie took a leading part in arranging the compromise that finally ended the dispute, the small States being accorded equal representation in the Senate, while in the House representation was based upon population. Madison was active and influential at every stage of the proceedings, and he assisted in putting the final touches to the Constitution as he was a member of the committee on style. To his Princeton training may be attributed the fact that such a complete record of the work of the convention has been preserved. Gaillard Hunt's *Life of James Madison* is the most exact and authoritative biography. He remarks that Madison went to the convention with carefully prepared notes on Government. "They were the results of profound study begun twenty years before at Princeton and continued unremittingly." We learn from Madison himself that he derived from his Princeton experience the motive of this exceptional industry. In the introduction of his journal of convention proceedings, which he left for publication after his death, he says:

> "The curiosity I had felt during my researches into the history of the most distinguished confederacies, particularly those of antiquity, and the deficiency I found in the means of satisfying it, more especially in what related to the process, the principles, the reasons and the anticipations, which prevailed in the formation of them, determined me to preserve, as far as I could, an exact account of what might pass in the Convention...
>
> "In pursuance of the work I had assumed, I chose a seat in front of the presiding member, with the other members on my right and left hands. In this favorable position for hearing all that passed, I noted in terms legible and in abbreviations and marks intelligible to myself, what was read from the chair or spoken by the members; and losing not a moment unnecessarily between adjournment and reassembling of the Convention, I was enabled to write out my daily notes during the session, or within a few finishing days after its close."

That is to say he took notes of convention proceedings in the same way and by the same method that he had become accustomed to at Princeton in attending lectures in his course of study.

In addition to the Princeton graduates who were members of the constitutional convention of the United States there were at least thirty-six Princeton graduates who took part in State constitutional conventions including those of New Hampshire, Vermont, Massachusetts, Connecticut, New York, New Jersey, Pennsylvania, Virginia, North Carolina, South Carolina, Georgia and Kentucky. Such a wide distribution is signal evidence of the national scope of Princeton influence.

Besides this close association of Princeton with the organization of American independence the accidents of the Revolutionary War invested Princeton with distinctive historical interest. Nassau Hall was pillaged and wrecked during the war, and since then it has been burned out twice, but it was so well built that the original walls form part of the present structure, a tablet upon which gives the following record:

> "This building erected in 1756 by the College of New Jersey, and named Nassau Hall in honor of King William III, was seized by British forces for military purposes in 1776 and retaken by the American army January, 3, 1777. Here met from June 30, 1783, until November 4, 1783, the Continental Congress, and here August 26, 1783, General Washington received the grateful acknowledgments of the Congress for his services in establishing the freedom and independence of the United States of America."

Elias Boudinot of New Jersey, a Princeton trustee, was President of Congress in 1783. As a special compliment to the college Congress adjourned to attend the commencement exercises of that year, and General Washington was present. At the meeting of the Board of Trustees on the same day a committee was appointed to request General Washington:

> "to sit for his picture to be taken by Mr. Charles Wilson Peale of Philadelphia.—And, ordered that his portrait when finished be placed in the hall of the college in the room of the picture of the late King of Great Britain, which was torn away by a ball from the American artillery in the battle of Princeton."

This portrait now hangs in Nassau Hall in the same frame that had formerly contained the picture of George II. The college familiarly known as Nassau Hall in its earlier days was later known generally by its place name of Princeton, its legal title as the College of New Jersey being used only on formal occasions. In October, 1896, on the 150th anniversary of the founding of the college the present title of Princeton University was assumed.

CHAPTER XVII

The Spread of Popular Education

Everywhere along the track of Scotch-Irish emigration into the South and West institutions of learning sprang up in the making of which the influence of Princeton was marked since the younger institutions naturally drew upon it for supplies of scholarship. In this way Princeton has had a numerous progeny. The first of the brood was Hampden Sidney College, Virginia. It was founded in 1774, with the active support and approval of Hanover Presbytery and the site was fixed in Prince Edward County at a point convenient for the Scotch-Irish settlements in Virginia and North Carolina. The Rev. Samuel Stanhope Smith of the class of 1769, tutor at Princeton 1770–1773, was the first President of Hampden Sidney. The college was opened during the Revolutionary year, 1776, and soon a military company was organized among the students, John Blair Smith, Jr., being captain. He was a Princeton graduate of the class of 1773, and was a young brother of President Smith. The members of this military company wore purple hunting shirts as a uniform. A number of them became officers in the army and others enlisted as common soldiers. Samuel Stanhope Smith left Hampden Sidney to become Professor of Philosophy at Princeton in 1779. In 1795 he became President of that college, continuing in that office until 1812, when he resigned. His brother succeeded him in the presidency of Hampden Sidney, occupying that position from 1779 to 1789. The influence of Hampden Sidney throughout the South was strongly marked. In the period before the Civil War more teachers were graduated from it than from any other institution in the South.

The selection of a site for Hampden Sidney convenient to the Scotch-Irish settlements in North Carolina established that institution in the southeastern portion of the State. The first academy in the region known as the Valley was founded in 1776 in a log house at Timber Ridge, Rockbridge County, through the efforts of the Hanover Presbytery. The school was named Liberty Hall, and it was conducted by the Rev. William Graham, a Princeton graduate of the class of 1773. This institution, which was chartered in 1772, was endowed by General Washington in 1796. In that year the Legislature of Virginia, as a mark of its appreciation of Washington's public services, voted to him one hundred shares of stock in the James River improvement then in progress. Unwilling to accept the present for his own use, Washington conveyed it to Liberty Hall. To perpetuate the memory of his kindness the trustees by unanimous vote changed the name to Washington Academy; from it the present Washington and Lee University has developed.

In 1768 Joseph Alexander, a Princeton graduate of the class of 1760, was ordained pastor of the Sugar Creek Congregation, a few miles from the present town of Charlotte, N. C. He opened there the first classical school in the upper part of Carolina. He was the founder of Liberty Hall, from which developed Queens College, which eventually became the University of North Carolina. The second classical school in upper North Carolina was founded by David Caldwell, a Princeton graduate of the class of 1761. After serving as a missionary in Virginia and North Carolina he settled as pastor of the congregations in Buffalo Creek and at Alamance. He fixed his residence in what was then Rowan County but is now in Guilford County. It is claimed for his school that it brought more men into the learned professions than any other individually conducted academy in the same period of time, the list including five Governors, about fifty ministers and a large number of physicians and lawyers. Caldwell was a member of the convention of 1776 which framed the State Constitution of North Carolina. He suffered many privations and hardships during the Revolutionary War in the course of which his house was plundered and his library destroyed, while he lay in hiding in the woods. He continued his pastoral labors until 1820 when the infirmities of extreme old age compelled him to retire but he lived until 1824 lacking only about seven months of a century when he died.

Samuel Doak, a Princeton graduate of the class of 1775, was the first minister to settle in Tennessee. His parents emigrated from Ulster to Pennsylvania whence they emigrated to Augusta County, Va. After graduating at Princeton, Doak became a tutor in Hampden Sidney college while he was preparing for the ministry. Being licensed by Hanover Presbytery he preached in Virginia for a short period and then removed to Tennessee, where he eventually settled as pastor of a congregation on Little Limestone, in Washington County. He built a church, put up a log schoolhouse and in 1785 opened a school which was incorporated in 1788 as the Martin Academy. It was the first school of classical learning in the Mississippi Valley. In 1795 the institution was incorporated as Washington College. He continued as President until 1818, when he resigned in favor of his son, the Rev. John M. Doak, M.D., and removed to Bethel. Here he opened an academy to prepare youth for college, and under his son Samuel W. Doak this school grew into Tusculum College.

Hezekiah Balch, a Princeton graduate of the class of 1766, was licensed by Donegal Presbytery, Pa. His ministerial labors took him into Tennessee where he founded a school from which Greenville College developed. Samuel Carrick, who went from Virginia to Tennessee about the same time, organized a church at Knoxville, and founded a school which grew into Blount College. The educational beginnings of Kentucky were due to Scotch-Irish emigration from Virginia. The Rev. David Rice, a Princeton graduate of the class of 1761, was one of the founders of Transylvania Seminary in 1783, which began operations in 1785, under Mr. Rice's care in his own house, at or near the present site of Danville, Kentucky. This was the first school opened in the State. In 1788 the seminary was removed to Lexington, where it had a troubled career. What was known as free thought or liberalism had an aggressive championship in Kentucky at that period. The leaders managed to get control of the corporate organization of the Seminary, and reorganized it in accord with their views.

In 1794 the Presbytery of Transylvania proceeded to establish another school, Mr. Rice appearing before the Legislature in behalf of the Presbytery. A charter was granted for the Kentucky Academy which was opened at Pisgah. Collections were taken up in its behalf and among the contributors was President Washington. The Kentucky Academy was soon in a sound and prosperous condition. Meanwhile the institution at Lexington suffered so much in reputation and attendance that peace overtures were made from those in control there, and on petition of both boards in 1798 the Legislature passed an act amalgamating the two institutions under the title "Transylvania University." This institution eventually fell under management so obnoxious to its founders that the Synod again took action and in 1824 Centre College was founded at Danville.

The westward movement of Scotch-Irish settlement, like the southward, was marked by the erection of schools. In 1781 the population in the region of Pennsylvania west of the mountains was still small and scattered but Redstone Presbytery was organized and the founding of schools began. Three of the early clergymen, Thaddeus Dod, John McMillan and Joseph Smith opened schools in their own houses or in the immediate neighborhood, in the usual fashion of which Tennent's Log College on the Neshaminy was the prototype. Dod was a Princeton graduate of the class of 1773. In 1782 he put up a building on his own farm in which he opened a school. It continued in operation for three years and a half, during which time a number of students were prepared for the ministry. The sale of the farm led to the closing of the school, which occurrence transferred a number of pupils to a school opened in 1785 by Joseph Smith, a Princeton graduate of the class of 1764, pastor of the Buffalo and Cross Creek congregations. Owing to failing health, Mr. Smith was able to conduct the school only a few years, and most of the pupils then went to the "Log Cabin" school of Dr. John McMillan, at Chartiers. McMillan was a Princeton graduate of the class of 1772. He first visited the Western country as a missionary in 1775, but he did not settle until 1778, when he took charge of the congregations of Chartiers and Pigeon Creek, in Washington County.

It is in dispute whether Dod's school or Smith's or McMillan's was prior in point of time, but they were all nearly coeval, and it is certain that the Log Cabin Academy was the only pioneer school that survived. From it issued a progeny of famous educational institutions. In 1787 a charter was obtained for Washington Academy, mainly through the influence of Dr. McMillan and his two elders, Judges Allison and McDowell, then members of the Legislature. The original list of trustees embraced all of the settled Presbyterian ministers west of the Monongahela. It was not until 1789, that the Academy went into operation at Washington, Pa., under the presidency of Thaddeus Dod, who had agreed to take the position temporarily. The institution lacked equipment and eventually the burning of the court house, in which classes met, caused a suspension of operations. In 1791 another academy was founded in Canonsburg, Dr. McMillan taking a leading part in the movement. In later years, Dr. McMillan in giving an account of his own school at Chartiers said: "I collected a few who gave evidence of piety, and taught them the Latin and Greek languages some of whom became useful and others eminent ministers of the Gospel. I had still a few with me when the academy was opened at Canonsburg, and finding I could not teach and do justice to my congregation, I immediately gave it up and sent them there." The Canonsburg school was incorporated in 1794, and in 1802 it was chartered as Jefferson College, under the presidency of John Watson, a Princeton graduate of the class of 1797. Washington Academy, which was suspended in 1791, was shortly afterward reopened, and after struggling along for years under difficulties it developed such strength that on March 28, 1806, it received a charter as Washington College. There were then two colleges occupying the same field and appealing to the same sources of support. Neither was able to make satisfactory progress and in 1865 they were united under one management as Washington and Jefferson College. A few years later the operations of the college were all concentrated at Washington, Pennsylvania.

Dickinson College at Carlisle, Pa., was founded in great measure by the Scotch-Irish Presbyterians of Cumberland and neighboring counties in Pennsylvania. Chartered in 1783, it was named after John Dickinson, President of the Executive Council of the State. Its first President was the Rev. Charles Nesbit of Montrose, Scotland, and the other members of the faculty were of Scotch-Irish ancestry. After Dr. Nesbit's death in 1804 the institution languished through lack of means and in 1833 the Methodist Episcopal Church obtained control of the institution, which has prospered under the patronage of that great denomination.

The early educational foundations in Western Pennsylvania have had an illustrious progeny, among them being Western University at Pittsburgh, Allegheny College at Meadville, Franklin College at New Athens, Ohio, which got its first President from Jefferson College; Western Reserve College at Hudson, Ohio; Wooster University, Wayne Co., Ohio; besides numerous academies. Throughout the middle West as in South and Southwest the course of Scotch-Irish settlement is marked by educational foundations.

Although the influence of Princeton was most strongly manifested in the South and West, it is distinctly marked in one great northern institution, Brown University, originally Rhode Island College. The college was the outcome of a movement started by the Philadelphia Baptist Association, whose agent was James Manning, a Princeton graduate, born in Elizabethtown, N. J., October 22, 1738. He made a tour of the Southern colonies, but finally decided in favor of a Rhode Island location. He was the first President of the college, which was opened at Warren in 1764, but was removed to Providence six years later. The first of the college buildings erected in Providence was University Hall, which was in general a copy of Nassau Hall at Princeton.

With the growth of the country in population and the blending of the Scotch-Irish with the general mass of American citizenship the influence of that particular element while still strongly operative becomes less distinctly traceable. In the early period the influence of Princeton is as strongly marked as the fertilizing effects of the rise of the Nile, but progress is now sustained by so many influences and is carried on through so many channels that it is no longer possible to distinguish particular sources in American education. It is however clear enough that Scotch-Irish emigration carried with it a scholarly activity that laid the foundations of popular education throughout the South and West. Ample recognition of Princeton influence is given in the histories of education in the various States issued by the United States Bureau of Education.

CHAPTER XVIII

The Revolutionary Period

Although in the eighteenth century the ocean made a vast separation in space between the two countries, the sense of political communion between Ireland and America was very close. They had interests in common that excited strong political sympathy. Both were dependencies of the British Crown; both resented the claims of the English Parliament to legislate for them, particularly in the matter of taxation; both were addicted to constitutional arguments on such subjects, and an issue of the kind in either country attracted close attention in the other. The active part which the Scotch-Irish took in the American Revolution was a continuation of popular resistance to British policy that began in Ulster. In 1771 the counties of Antrim and Down were thrown into disorder by rackrenting practices of landlords, in which the Marquis of Donegal, an absentee landlord, took the leading part; as leases expired he made exactions for renewal so exorbitant that the total is estimated at $500,000. The tenant farmers were utterly unable to pay so they were dispossessed, losing the value of their improvements. What is known as the Steelboy insurrection resulted. Its subsidence was attributed by the English historian Lecky

> "to the great Protestant emigration which had been long taking place in Ulster. The way had been opened, and the ejected tenantry, who formed the Steelboy bands and who escaped the sword and the gallows, fled by thousands to America. They were soon heard of again. In a few years the cloud of civil war which was already gathering over the colonies burst, and the ejected tenants of Lord Donegal formed a large part of the revolutionary armies which severed the New World from the British Crown."

In 1771 Benjamin Franklin visited Dublin where he conferred with some of the leaders of the Irish National party, at that time a Protestant organization. "I found them," he wrote, "disposed to be friends of America, in which I endeavored to confirm them with the expectation that our growing weight might in time be thrown into their scale, and by joining our interests with theirs, a more equitable treatment from this nation [England] might be obtained for themselves as well as for us." Franklin recommended that if possible an exception should be made in favor of Ireland in carrying out the non-importation agreement of the American colonies. This was found to be impracticable but the Continental Congress was sufficiently concerned about the matter to make an apology. The address to the people of Ireland, adopted on July 28, 1775, declared:

> "Permit us to assure you, that it was with the utmost reluctance we could prevail upon ourselves to cease our commercial connexion with your island. *Your* Parliament had done us no wrong. *You* had ever been friendly to the rights of mankind; and we acknowledge with pleasure and gratitude, that *your* nation has produced patriots, who have nobly distinguished themselves in the cause of humanity and America. On the other hand we were not ignorant that the labor and manufactures of Ireland, like those of the silkworm, were of little moment to herself; but served only to give luxury to those who *neither toil nor spin*. We perceived that if we continued our commerce with you, our agreement not to import from Britain would be *fruitless*, and were, therefore, compelled to adopt a measure to which nothing but absolute necessity would have reconciled us. It gave us, however, some consolation to reflect, that should it occasion much distress, the fertile regions of America would afford you a safe asylum from poverty, and, in time, from oppression also; an asylum, in which many thousands of your countrymen have found hospitality, peace and affluence, and become united to us by all the ties of mutual interest and affection."

Benjamin Franklin was a member of the Committee on Trade appointed by the Continental Congress in 1775. Its report submitted on October 2, 1775, set forth that:

> "The Cessation of the American Trade with Ireland originated

in Policy dictated by Principles of self Preservation and may be attended with Distress to a People who have always manifested a Noble Regard to the Rights of Mankind and have ever been friendly to these much injured Colonies."

The committee then recommended that the non-intercourse agreement be relaxed to the extent that "our Friends and Fellow Subjects in Ireland should be admitted to take Flax seed from these Colonies in Exchange for all such Powder and other military Stores and woolen Yarn of their Manufacture as they shall bring to America."

This attitude of good will was cordially reciprocated in Ireland and it was manifested in the Irish Parliament, notwithstanding the controlling influence assiduously maintained by the English Government. Usually the address to the Throne at the opening of Parliament passed unopposed but at the session of October, 1775, an amendment was proposed and was warmly advocated, strongly urging the necessity of "conciliatory and healing measures for the removal of the discontent which prevails in the colonies." The amendment was defeated by ninety-two to fifty-two. Harcourt, then the viceroy of Ireland, was much displeased by the vigor with which the amendment was supported, particularly since more than half of the members abstained from voting. Many of these owed their seats to government influence, and therefore felt themselves precluded by the received code of parliamentary honor from voting against the Ministers. Hence their abstention indicated American sympathies and made the Government victory merely nominal. In his report to the English Government Harcourt wrote that: "The Opposition to the King's Government in this country … are daily gaining strength upon this ground." He added that "the Presbyterians in the North (who in their hearts are Americans) are gaining strength every day." In a later report Harcourt complained of "the violent opposition made by the Presbyterians to the measures of Government" and he described them as "talking in all companies in such a way that if they are not rebels, it is hard to find a name for them."

It can hardly be doubted that the political ideas derived from Irish experience and poured into the colonies by Ulster immigration exerted a powerful influence in moulding American institutions. The principles involved were however but the staples of the English constitutional system. The chief objects of the Irish National party, during the period of Protestant ascendency, were short Parliaments, secure tenure of judicial authority, and a habeas corpus act. In those things no more was sought than England enjoyed. The struggle was against peculiar privations to which Ireland was subject. The duration of a Parliament in England was limited to seven years; in Ireland there was no limit and a Parliament had been known to continue for thirty-three years. In England judges held office during good behavior; in Ireland, at the pleasure of the Crown. The writ of habeas corpus was not allowed in Ireland, although it was the ordinary privilege of the subject in England.

As early as 1768 the English Government made a concession on the Parliament issue by approving a bill limiting the term to eight years, but the Ministers did not yield on the other points until Ireland was up in arms and they were powerless to resist. The English Government then yielded to Ireland what it had refused to America. The old system of commercial restriction was abolished, the writ of habeas corpus was granted, the permanent tenure of judicial authority was established, and the legislative independence of Ireland was acknowledged. All those concessions were results of the American war. It does not fall within the province of this work to trace the history of Ulster since this period. It may be noted however that the most determined opposition to English rule over Ireland, up to the period when England and Ireland were united under the jurisdiction of one legislature, the Parliament of the United Kingdom, came from Ulster. The United Irishmen movement, which was the prelude to the rebellion of 1798, started in Belfast, and the chief strength of the rebellion was in Ulster. The union of Ireland with England was originally intensely unpopular in Ulster, but with the removal of commercial disabilities and with enlarged opportunities of trade, Ulster has become so reconciled to the union that it has been a centre of violent opposition to the movement in favor of home rule for Ireland.

The particular source of the ideas that presided over American constitution making was the political experience of English dependencies during the eighteenth century. Scotland, Ireland and the American colonies had the same general grievances and the same general attitude of constitutional protest against English policy. It is a significant circumstance that James Boswell, although indulging an almost abject admiration of the massive old Tory, Dr. Samuel Johnson, could not follow him in antipathy to the American colonists. Boswell's own Toryism could not escape modification through his Scottish environment. Such considerations make intelligible the extraordinary political career of Dr. John Witherspoon, brought from Scotland in 1768, to become President of the College of New Jersey. He was a member of the New Jersey Provincial Congress in 1776; member of the Continental Congress, 1776–83; signer of the Declaration of Independence, 1776; member of the New Jersey Senate, 1780; member of the New Jersey Assembly, 1783; member of the New Jersey constitutional convention, 1789. These political activities he combined with incessant activity as an educator and continual occupation as a clergyman. In one of his political articles he observed that "a man will become an American by residing in the country three months." The constitutional ideas which the Americans asserted in opposition to the policy of the British Ministry they brought with them whether they came from England, Scotland or Ireland. But the general conviction was intensified among the Scotch-Irish by deep resentment of the injuries they had sustained from English rule. "They went," says the English historian Lecky, "with hearts burning with indignation, and in the War of Independence they were almost to a man on the side of the insurgents."

Hence it was noted early in the American struggle that the Scotch-Irish were peculiarly energetic, united and formidable in their opposition to British policy. John Hughes, who was appointed Distributer of Stamps for Pennsylvania, in a report under date of October 12, 1765, said:

> "Common justice calls upon me to say, the body of people called Quakers, seemed disposed to pay obedience to the Stamp Act, and so do that part of the Church of England and Baptists, that are not some way under Proprietary influence. But Presbyterians and Proprietary minions spare no pains to engage the Dutch and lower class of people, and render the royal government odious."

In September, 1765, writing to Benjamin Franklin, then in England, Hughes remarked: "When it is known that I have received my commission, I fancy I shall not escape the storm of Presbyterian rage." At that time Franklin himself was inclined to submit to the Stamp Act.

Joseph Galloway, than whom there could be no better informed witness, held that the underlying cause of the American Revolution was the activity and influence of the Presbyterian interest. Galloway was an eminent Philadelphia lawyer and an intimate friend of Benjamin Franklin, who on going to England as agent of the Province left his private and public papers in Galloway's charge. Galloway entered the Provincial Assembly in 1757, continuing a member until the Revolution. From 1766 to 1774 he was the Speaker of the Assembly. He was a member of the first Continental Congress in 1774, and was active in the measures taken to obtain redress of colonial grievances. He was not however willing to go to the length of actual rebellion and when the Declaration of Independence was issued he went over to the Loyalist side. He went to England in 1778 where he was active in spreading information about the American situation, advocating redress of grievances and a settlement of differences between the mother country and the colonies. Galloway's course can not be attributed to self-interest, as in maintaining his English allegiance he abandoned estates which were estimated to be worth £40,000. He never returned to America. In 1788 his property was confiscated by the Pennsylvania Legislature, but a large portion was eventually restored to his daughter.

Galloway, whose attitude to the English Government was that of the candid friend, held that it was the Presbyterians who supplied to colonial resistance a lining without which it would have collapsed. In testimony before a committee of the House of Commons in 1779 he declared that at the beginning of the revolt not one-fifth of the people "had independence in view" and that in the army enlisted by the Continental Congress "there were scarcely one-fourth natives of America,—about one-half Irish, the other fourth were English and Scotch."

In 1780 Galloway published in London his *Historical and Political Reflections*, in which he gave the inside history of the American revolt. His account is too important and significant to be summarized, and a verbatim extract is given in Appendix E. According to Galloway the revolt derived its formidable character from the organized activity of the Presbyterians. His use of the term includes the New England Congregationalists, but the creation of an organization of continental scope he expressly imputes to the leadership of the Pennsylvania Presbyterians who were mostly Scotch-Irish.

This is a view of the origin of the American war quite different from that which has been adopted by popular history, too intent upon dramatic effects to give much consideration to what is going on behind the scenes to produce those effects. But Galloway speaks from abundant personal observation of the springs of action and the purpose of his argument is such as to repel any suspicion as to the sincerity of his opinion. He is arguing in favor of redressing the legitimate grievances of the American colonies, holding that in this way the revolt may be ended and peace restored. Analyzing the situation from this point of view he could have no disposition to exaggerate obstacles to the policy he was commending, and his point is that although what he calls the Presbyterian faction is an implacable element, yet by judicious measures it may be so isolated and its influence so restricted that it will be unable to maintain the struggle for independence. He said:

> "Sincerely disposed, as the greater part of the people in America are, to be more firmly united with Great Britain on constitutional principles, is it not much to be lamented, that the British legislature, seeing the defect in its constitutional authority over the Colonies and knowing that it is the great foundation of their discontent, have not taken it into their serious consideration, and adopted the measure most proper for removing it? Had this been done in the beginning of the opposition to the authority of Parliament, the republican faction must have been destitute of the means by which they have inflamed the minds of the Americans, and led them to a revolt. But I am not fond of dwelling on past errors, further than is necessary to amendment. It is not now too late, arid perhaps all circumstances considered, this is the most proper time for doing it."

His opinion is strongly corroborated by the wide diffusion of Loyalist sentiment in the colonies, the accessible facts in regard to which are collated in Sabine's *American Loyalists*. Of the thirty-seven newspapers published in the colonies in April, 1775, seven or eight were openly Loyalist, and twenty-three championed the Whig interest, but no less than five went over to the Loyalist side during the war. A distinguished New Jersey Loyalist declared that "most of the colleges had been the grand nurseries of rebellion" but he may have been unduly impressed by his proximity to Princeton, which was a centre of Whig influence under the presidency of Witherspoon. Upward of one hundred and fifty persons educated at Harvard or some other institution of learning were among the Loyalists. In a number of Massachusetts towns, among them Marshfield, Freetown, Worcester and Sandwich, the Loyalists were strong enough to form associations to oppose the Whigs. In Boston itself the opponents of the Whigs, known as "the Protesters," were upward of one hundred and they included eminent citizens. When the British evacuated Boston upward of 1100 Loyalists left at the same time. Sabine says: "Of members of the council, commissioners, officers of the customs and other officials there were 102; of clergymen 18; of inhabitants of country towns, 105; of merchants and other persons who resided in Boston, 213; of farmers, mechanics and traders, 382."

In New York State Tories were so numerous that in some counties Whigs were hard to find. In New Jersey the Tories were strong enough to wage war upon the Whigs, and to perpetrate dreadful outrages. In parts of North Carolina the Tories so far outnumbered the Whigs as to ravage their estates long before any British troops entered the State. General Green estimated that some thousands had been killed in South Carolina in fighting between the Whigs and the Tories, and he declared that "if a stop cannot be soon put to these massacres, the country will be depopulated." Some twenty-nine or thirty regiments or battalions of American Loyalists were regularly organized, armed and officered. In an address to the King from American Loyalists presented in 1779 it was declared that their countrymen then in his Majesty's army "exceeded in number the troops enlisted [by Congress] to oppose them." At the time of Cornwallis's surrender at Yorktown a part of his army was composed of native Americans, and failing to obtain special terms for them in the articles of capitulation, he availed himself of the privilege of sending a ship northerly without molestation, to convey away the most noted of them. Sabine computes that the number of American Loyalists who took up arms for the British could not have been less than twenty thousand.

With such sharp division of sentiment among the colonists it was clearly a factor of inestimable importance that there existed what Galloway designates as the "union of Presbyterian force." It supplied a systematic influence that in the circumstances was probably decisive. The forensic leadership of American resistance was mainly supplied by the older settled portions of the colonies in which the governing class was of English origin, but it could not have been successful without such organized popular support as was supplied through the Ulster settlements in the colonies.

The most dispassionate and balanced account of the Revolutionary War is that contained in Lecky's *History of England in the Eighteenth Century.* The great English historian repeatedly calls attention to the direct connection between Ulster emigration to America and the successful vigor of American resistance. The Scotch-Irish were no more forward in protests against British policy than the mass of the population during the period of agitation and controversy before the fighting began. They met in their frontier settlements and passed resolutions, but that was what the colonists were doing all over the country; and they were apparently following in the wake of an agitation started by the seaboard cities, which naturally made common cause with Boston, since if that port might be closed by the British Parliament any other port might be made to suffer likewise. It was, however, rather remarkable that an issue of such a character should have roused frontier settlements as it did. and secured the prompt adherence of the leading men. The bill closing the port of Boston went into operation June 1, 1774. A meeting held at Carlisle, Cumberland County, Pennsylvania, July 12, was presided over by John Montgomery, of Irish nativity. The resolutions adopted were of the usual tenor at the meetings of this period, condemning the proceedings of the British Ministry and favoring the united action of the colonies to obtain redress of grievances. Three deputies were chosen to a provincial convention and among them was James Wilson, born in Scotland, who became a member of the Continental Congress, was a signer of the Declaration of Independence, was an active and influential member of the constitutional convention of 1787, and eventually a justice of the Supreme Court of the United States. The other deputies, both born in Ireland, were William Irwin, who became a general, and Robert Magaw, who became a colonel, in the army of the Revolution.

The historian Bancroft notes as a striking coincidence that on the day on which Lord Chatham was making his peace proposals to the House of Lords, January 20, 1775, the people of a remote frontier settlement, "beyond the Alleghenies, where the Watanga and the forks of the Holston flow to the Tennessee" were meeting to make formal protest against British policy. They were, says Bancroft, "most of them, Presbyterians of Scotch-Irish descent." They passed resolutions in favor of united action and appointed a Committee of Safety.

The American revolt began as a movement to enforce redress of grievances. Imputations that the movement aimed at independence were resented as libels rendering their utterers liable to be called to account by the local Committee of Safety. It was not until the news came, early in May, 1776, that the British Government was using Hanoverian and Hessian soldiers, that the opposition to independence succumbed. In the struggle to commit Congress to that decisive step the Scotch-Irish influence was active and effective, but in this respect the truth of history has been somewhat obscured by a vehement controversy that has gone on about a document known as the Mecklenburg Declaration of Independence. The legend is that at a meeting of settlers, mainly Scotch-Irish, in Charlotte, Mecklenburg County, N. C., on May 20, 1775, resolutions were adopted renouncing all allegiance to the British Crown and declaring the American people to be free and independent. The document was first brought to public notice in 1819 and its authenticity while energetically asserted has been strongly impugned. Those interested in the details will find a complete record in William Henry Hoyt's work with that subject title. Even were the Mecklenburg Declaration authentic it would possess merely antiquarian interest rather than historical importance for no recognition of such action or mark of its influence appears in the records of the times. There is however recorded action taken by a Mecklenburg County Convention on May 81, 1775, which is of such signal importance as marking the beginning of American independence that it is given in its entirety in Appendix F.

These resolutions practically constitute a state of political independence. Crown authority is annulled, provincial authority under the direction of Congress is substituted, and it is declared that no other authority is in existence. Such language asserts independence, and the resolutions then go on to make provision for giving practical effect to the decision by arranging for the collection of taxes, the administration of justice and the public defense. Resolutions providing for organized opposition to British policy were abundant at this period, but the Mecklenburg County Convention was the first to announce independence. The leaders in the meeting were Thomas Polk, an ancestor of President Polk; Abraham Alexander and Ephraim Brevard, and the movement derived its strength from the Scotch-Irish settlers while the opposition came from other elements of the community. Governor Martin, the royalist Governor of the Province, in a dispatch of August 28, 1775, to the home Government, mentions that "a considerable body of Germans, settled in the County of Mecklenburg," had forwarded to him "a loyal declaration against the very extraordinary and traitorous resolves of the Committee of that County." The Mecklenburg Resolves were not only the first to make a virtual declaration of independence but they also indicated the course that had to be followed to attain independence, namely, the setting up of a system of government independent of Crown authority. The institutions of colonial government were rooted in Crown authority, and they served as intrenchments for the opposition to independence. As a matter of fact it became necessary to revolutionize colonial government before the Declaration of Independence could be carried through Congress. The Mecklenburg Resolves were the first step in this direction, and proclaimed a policy that nearly a year later was adopted by Congress. On May 10, 1776, Congress voted:

> "That it be recommended to the respective assemblies and conventions of the United Colonies, where no government sufficient to the exigencies of their affairs has been hitherto established, to adopt such government as shall in the opinion of the representatives of the people, best conduce to the happiness and safety of their constituents in particular and America in general."

This action was completed on May 15 by the adoption of a preamble which pursues the some line of argument adopted in the Mecklenburg Resolves, namely, that since the American colonists had been excluded from the protection of the Crown "it is necessary that the exercise of every kind of authority under the said Crown should be totally suppressed." The language differs; the argument is the same.

At the time Congress took this decisive step delegates from Pennsylvania, New Jersey, New York, Delaware and Maryland were under instructions to vote against independence. Pennsylvania was the keystone of the conservative opposition. The action of Congress on May 15 marks the beginning of the movement that overthrew the colonial charter and substituted State government. In this struggle Scotch-Irish influence was strongly manifested. A petition from Cumberland County was presented to the Assembly on May 22, requesting the withdrawal of the instructions given to the Congressional delegates. On May 25 the City Committee of Philadelphia issued a call for a conference of County Committees with a view to holding a convention to reconstitute the Government. The call was signed by Thomas McKean, chairman. He was born at Londonderry, Pa., March 19, 1734, the son of William and Laetitia (Finney) McKean, both natives of Ireland. Thomas McKean was a leader of the Whig party in the Pennsylvania Assembly. He became a member in 1765 and was reelected consecutively for seventeen years. At the time when as chairman of the City Committee he started the movement for a convention to remodel the State Government the Assembly, based upon an inequitable apportionment and chosen by narrowly limited suffrage, was controlled by the conservatives. The Quakers had issued an address expressing "abhorrence of all such writings and measures as evidence a desire and design to break off the happy connection we have hitherto enjoyed with the kingdom of Great Britain." The County Committee of Philadelphia opposed any change in the existing status. The western counties had sent Whig representatives to the Assembly. The city of Philadelphia, which had four members, had elected three Conservatives and one Whig, after a close contest. The Assembly was strongly disinclined to rescind its instructions against independence. Threats were made to Congress that if it made a declaration of independence the delegates from the middle colonies could retire and possibly those colonies might secede from the Union. But the Congressional leaders were now assured of popular support and the movement for independence steadily advanced.

At this juncture Joseph Reed threw his influence in favor of rescinding. He was born, August 27, 1741, at Trenton. New Jersey, of Scotch-Irish ancestry, his grandfather emigrating from Carrickfergus. The family were well to do, and Joseph received a thorough education. He was graduated at Princeton, after which he studied law under Richard Stockton of New Jersey and was admitted to the bar in 1763. He went to London to complete his legal studies, and from December, 1763, to the spring of 1765 was a student in the Middle Temple. Returning to America he settled in Philadelphia to practice his profession. When the news arrived in May, 1774, of the bill closing the ports of Boston, Reed in conjunction with the Scotch-Irishman, Charles Thomson, and Thomas Mifflin, of Quaker ancestry, issued a call for a mass meeting of protest. From that time on he was active and prominent as a champion of colonial rights. When Washington took the field Reed accompanied him as his military secretary, and thereafter remained his close friend and correspondent.

In 1776 Reed was a member of the Pennsylvania Assembly. Both he and Thomson were classed as Moderates. While both were prominent Whigs, both were in favor of working with and through the Assembly. While the movement in favor of independence was advancing Reed was exerting his influence to bring the Assembly into accord. Congress was sitting in Philadelphia and the leaders were in close touch with the Pennsylvania situation. On June 7 Richard Henry Lee of Virginia moved in Congress his resolution for independence, and on June 8 the Pennsylvania delegation voted against it five to two. On June 14 the Assembly adopted cautiously worded resolutions, framed by a committee of which Reed was a member, which in effect rescinded the previous instructions and authorized the delegates to use their discretion in "adopting such other measures as shall be judged necessary." On July 2 the vote of Pennsylvania was recorded in favor of independence, the delegation standing three to two, two members absenting themselves to facilitate this result. As soon as Pennsylvania was committed to independence Reed rejoined Washington as his adjutant-general, to which position he was appointed by Congress on June 5, at Washington's request.

Charles Thomson, whose name frequently appears in the records of the times as a man of sound judgment and of great influence, is one of the most interesting characters of the period. He was born in Maghera, County Derry, Ireland, November 29, 1729. While on his way to America with his father and three brothers, the father died at sea. An elder brother already settled in America was the only person the boys could look to for aid. Charles attracted the attention of Dr. Francis Alison, who took him into his Academy at New London, Pa., and gave him such a good education that he became principal of the Friends' Academy at New Castle, Del. He had marked success as a teacher and also attracted notice through his writings upon public affairs. He took an active interest in the welfare of the Indians, and in 1756 the Delawares adopted him into their tribe bestowing upon him the name of "Man of Truth." A marked trait of Thomson's character was self-abnegation. While from the first active in the cause of American liberty he was interested in results rather than in his personal distinction and his activity was mainly behind the scenes. By a fortunate accident a letter of his has been preserved that gives a specimen of his address as a political tactician and a view of inside politics in the revolutionary period.

In 1774, when the news of the British port bill arrived, and Reed, Thomson and Mifflin were laying plans to commit Pennsylvania to joint action with the other colonies, it was deemed of supreme importance to secure the cooperation of John Dickinson, who was of Quaker stock and had great influence with that element of the population, which if no longer dominant was still weighty. It was therefore arranged to create an opportunity for Dickinson to appear in a moderate and conciliatory attitude. Thomson himself, in an account which he wrote in later years as an act of justice to Dickinson, says:

> "It was agreed that his friend who was represented as a rash man should press for an immediate declaration in favor of Boston and get some of his friends to support him in the measure, that Mr. D——— should oppose and press for moderate measures, and thus by an apparent dispute prevent a farther opposition and carry the point agreed on."

Thomson himself took the part of "the rash man." A meeting of leading citizens was held in the City Tavern. Reed addressed the assembly "with temper, moderation, but in pathetic terms." Mifflin spoke next "with more warmth and fire."

Thomson then "pressed for an immediate declaration in favor of Boston and making common cause with her." The room was hot, Thomson had scarce slept an hour for two nights and he fainted and was carried into an adjoining room. Dickinson then addressed the company. As soon as Thomson recovered he returned to the meeting and took an active part in its proceedings. Upon his motion it was decided that a committee should be appointed to voice the sense of the meeting. Two sets of nominees were proposed but the matter was compromised by accepting them all as the committee. As a result of this management the movers in the business got all they desired. Thomson relates:

> "The next day the Committee met and not only prepared and sent back an answer to Boston but also forwarded the news to the southern colonies accompanied with letters intimating the necessity of a Congress of delegates from all the colonies to devise measures. [In furtherance of this it was] necessary to call a general meeting of the inhabitants of the City at the State House. This required great address. The Quakers had an aversion to town meetings and always opposed them. However it was so managed that they gave their consent, and assisted in preparing the business for this public meeting, agreed on the persons who should preside and those who should address the inhabitants."

There is a touch of humor in the selection of the classical scholar Thomson, a noted educator, in which capacity he was widely known and respected by the Quakers, to act the part of "the rash man." It was shrewdly calculated to impress the conservative portion of the community with the need of associating themselves with the movement in order to moderate it.

Although Thomson's influence was chiefly exerted in shaping action, leaving the front of the stage to others, his ability was well known. John Adams characterized him as "the Sam Adams of Philadelphia, the life of the cause of liberty." In 1774, when the Continental Congress was first constituted, his assistance was sought and without any effort on his part he was installed in the important position of Secretary of Congress. He refused to accept any salary the first year, but he found that in addition to his ordinary duties his services were so much in request for consultation and advice that his work absorbed his time and strength, and in order to provide for his family he had to accept compensation. He continued to serve as Secretary of Congress all through the Revolutionary War, and afterward until the Constitution of the United States was adopted. He resigned in 1789. His modesty, tactfulness and unselfishness made him very popular with the members, and in this way he wielded a great but unobtrusive influence. When the Count de Rochambeau arrived in America in 1780 in command of the body of regulars sent by France, he had with him as a chaplain Abbe Robin. As a result of Robin's observations of Thomson's work in Congress he remarked that "he was the soul of that political body."

One effect of the kindliness of Thomson's character must ever be deeply regretted by historians as it caused a great and irreparable loss. During his secretaryship, which covered the whole existence of the Continental Congress, he accumulated material which he embodied in a historical account; but eventually he destroyed it for fear that its publication should give pain to the descendents and admirers of some of the notables of the Revolutionary period. The reason seems inadequate for so great an offense against the truth of history. Sufficient consideration for personal feelings could have been displayed by sealing the documents for publication at some future period. It was, however, a characteristic display of self-ab-negation for there can be no doubt that Thomson himself took an important part in promoting the adoption of the Declaration of Independence. As Secretary of Congress he was in constant touch with the advocates of that measure. As a leader of the Whig party of Pennsylvania he was active in promoting measures to bring that State in line with the movement. But with the destruction of his manuscript the details are lost. Their preservation would be par-ticularly desirable as regards the promulgation of the Declaration of Independence, the curt entries of the official record being in-sufficient to prevent a rank growth of fiction. Independence was actually declared on July 2, 1776, by the adopting of a resolution, "that these United Colonies are, and of right, ought to be, Free and Independent States; that they are absolved from all allegiance to the British Crown, and that all political connexion between them, and the State of Great Britain, is and ought to be, totally dissolved." This resolution was a report from the Committee of the Whole, which report is in the handwriting of Charles Thomson. Writing to his wife the next day, John Adams said: "The second day of July, 1776, will be the most memorable *epocha* in America… It ought to be commemorated as the day of deliverance by solemn acts of devotion to God Almighty."

But the commemoration settled on the Fourth of July, as that was the day when Congress made its action public. It was the prac-tice of Congress in arriving at an important conclusion to appoint a committee to propose a preamble. This course was followed with respect to the Declaration of Independence and as Lee had been called to his home by the illness of his wife Jefferson became chair-man of the committee which was appointed in anticipation of the passage of the resolution. Jefferson draughted the document which was adopted on July 4, and on the same day Congress directed that copies should be sent "to the several assemblies, conventions and committees or councils of safety, and to the several commanding officers of the Continental troops; that it be proclaimed in each of the United States and at the head of the army." In pursuance of this resolution, Secretary Thomson sent a copy to the printer, a Scotch-Irishman named John Dunlap. The printer's copy is lost, but presumably was in the writing of Thomson, who used the broadside print received back from Dunlap as part of the record by wafering it in the proper place in the journal. The only signatures were those of John Hancock, President; and Charles Thomson, Secretary. One of the printed copies was sent to the Committee of Safety in Philadelphia which directed that it should be publicly proclaimed at the State House Monday, July 5. This meeting was the first public demonstration over the passage of the Declaration.[5] The copy of the Declaration to which signatures of

---

[5]   Dr. Herbert Friedenwald in his monograph on *The Declaration of Independence*, ascribes the legend of the ringing of the Liberty Bell, when the Declaration was adopted, to "the fertile imagination of one of Philadelphia's early romancers, George Lippard." The story was first published in a work entitled *Washington and his Generals or Legends of the Revolution*, by George Lippard; Philadelphia: G. B. Zeiber & Co., 1847. It is written in a style of turgid melodrama, disregarding the actual facts.

In giving a fancy picture of the debate in Congress on July 4 Lippard says: "Then the deep-toned voice of Richard Henry Lee is heard swelling in syllables of thunder-like music." But as a matter of fact Lee was not present, having left Philadelphia on June 13, because of sickness in his family. On July 4 he was attending the Virginia convention. Lippard relates how "a flaxen-haired boy, with laughing eyes of summer blue" waited at the door of Congress for a message to be given by "a man with a velvet dress and a kind face." Meanwhile in the belfry stood "an old man with white hair and sunburnt face," anxiously waiting for the message that the Declaration of Independence had been adopted. He was almost in despair when "there among the crouds on the pavement stood the blue-eyed boy, clapping his tiny hands, while the breeze blowed his flaxen hair all about his face. And then swelling his little chest, he raised himself tiptoe, and shouted, a single word—*Ring!*"

This account, which by its style and matter plainly announces itself to be fiction, is the original version of the ringing of the Liberty Bell. It has since been taken into popular history and the mythical legend was

members of Congress were attached was engrossed on parchment under a resolution adopted July 19, 1776. It was presented to Congress August 2, and was signed by members present. Other signatures were appended later. Some of those who subsequently signed were not members of Congress when the Declaration was adopted and some who were members at that time never did sign.

Robert R. Livingston of New York, who was a member of the committee to draft the Declaration of Independence, appears in Trumbull's famous picture of the signers, but his name does not appear on the list, as he was absent when the actual signing took place.

Dr. Zubly of Georgia had been detected in correspondence with the Crown Governor of the Province, and took flight. Congress requested John Houston, a Georgia delegate of Scotch-Irish ancestry who was an ardent supporter of the movement for independence, to follow Zubly to counteract his plots. Owing to his absence on this service his name does not appear among the signers.

The name of Thomas McKean of Pennsylvania did not appear on the list of signers as first published, and he did not append his signature until some time in 1781.

The explanation of such circumstances is that the adoption of the Declaration of Independence was a means to an end, and the leaders were too intent upon that to concern themselves at the time about the formalities that have since become so precious to popular history. McKean was active in Congress in support of the adoption of the Declaration, and as chairman of the Philadelphia City Committee he took a leading part in overthrowing the Pennsylvania opposition to independence. At the same time he was raising troops to strengthen General Washington's forces then in New Jersey. Upon the same day the Declaration was adopted, Congress appointed a committee to confer with the Pennsylvania Committee of Safety on the subject, and the conference took place

widely propagated through the Centennial Exhibition of 1876, in which year a new edition of Lippard's work was issued and vigorously pushed.

on July 5. As a result McKean left for the scene of war as colonel of a regiment, so he was absent when the Declaration came up for signatures on August 2, 1776.

The annual celebration of July 4, as Independence Day, started the following year. A letter preserved in the *North Carolina Records*, written from Philadelphia, July 5, 1777, notes that at the celebration on the preceding day "a Hessian band of music which were taken at Princeton performed very delightfully, the pleasure being not a little heightened by the reflection that they were hired by the British court for purposes very different from those to which they were applied."

Of the fifty-six signers, three were natives of Ireland, Matthew Thornton of New Hampshire and James Smith and George Taylor of Pennsylvania. All three were probably from Ulster, although that fact is not of record in the case of Smith and Taylor. Two signers, James Wilson and John Witherspoon, were natives of Scotland. Two were natives of England, Button Gwinnett and Robert Morris. Francis Lewis of New York was born at Llandaff, Wales. Forty-eight of the signers were American-born, five of them of Irish ancestry, Carroll, Lynch, McKean, Read and Rutledge. But of these only McKean and Rutledge were of Ulster derivation. Lynch's people came from Connaught, Read's from Dublin and Carroll's from King's County, in central Ireland. Two signers, Hooper and Philip Livingston, were of Scotch descent. Four, Jefferson, Williams, Floyd and Lewis Morris, were of Welsh descent. John Morton, one of the Pennsylvania signers, was of Swedish stock. Thirty-six of the American born signers were, so far as known, of English ancestry. Combining these data we have the following apportionment: English thirty-eight, Irish eight (including five of Ulster ancestry), Scotch four, Welsh five, Swedish one.

CHAPTER XIX

The Birth of the Nation

The extensive participation of the Scotch-Irish in the Revolutionary War has been generally set forth in preceding chapters. Consideration of particulars shows how vitally important was the support of that element. Its military traditions and its tenacity of character were specially valuable in the discouraging circumstances under which American resistance was kept up. There was much to dishearten and even to repel patriotic sentiment in the way in which the war was conducted and there were periods when it seemed that the cause would collapse from its own weakness. There was one such period soon after the Revolutionary War was fairly started.

The actual beginning of hostilities was a casual explosion. The battle of Lexington, April 19, 1775, was brought on by an expedition sent out by General Gage to destroy some military stores collected by the Americans at Concord. The British troops accomplished their purpose but the countryside rose against them and on their way back they were sniped at from behind hedges, walls and farm buildings, so that they sustained heavy losses. The battle of Bunker Hill, June 17, 1775, was brought on by the attempt of the British commander to strengthen his position by occupying an eminence commanding Boston harbor. The Americans heard of his intention, slipped in ahead of him during the night and threw up some earthworks. The engagement that ensued illustrated both the strength and the weakness of American volunteers and militia.

The Americans, long accustomed to meeting frontier perils, had a general familiarity with firearms, the use of which among the middle and lower classes of England was almost unknown, owing to the game laws and to the sheltered condition of their lives. Hence American militia excelled in marksmanship even when confronted with the regular troops of England. But the Americans were without the discipline that keeps troops steady and obedient to command. Their instinct was to look out for themselves and if the notion seized them that the issue was turning against them they were likely to break precipitately. At Breed's Hill a force of about 1,500 men endured for hours the fire from British ships in the harbor, and then repulsed two attacks made by a superior force of British regulars. But they gave way before the third attack, largely owing to the fact that their ammunition had run out. The troops on Bunker Hill, seeing the retreat from Breed's Hill, could not be held in line, although General Putnam stormed, implored, raged and pleaded. The English gained the field, but at such a heavy cost in killed and wounded as to open their eyes to the fact that the Americans were really formidable foes, and seldom if ever has any other battle made such a favorable impression for the defeated side.

So far, however, the warfare was really on a tiny scale, and the British troops in Boston were so encompassed by a hostile population that only defective organization on the American side enabled them to hold their ground so long as they did. It was not until after the battle of Bunker Hill that Washington was appointed commander-in-chief of the American forces. His correspondence from the American camp at Cambridge gives a picture of continual vexation and perplexity as to the material from which he was seeking to fashion an army. The British in Boston remained quiescent until Washington was ready to move. On the night of March 4, 1776, Washington made their position untenable by occupying Dorchester Heights. The British, then numbering about 7,600, got into their ships and sailed for Halifax. But this small force had held Boston for eleven months, after all the country around had risen in revolt with help coming from the other colonies.

The Boston campaign hardly belongs to the strategy of the Revolutionary War. It was essentially an insurrection with which the British forces were not strong enough to cope and before which they retreated. General Washington himself thought that if they had used their opportunities energetically it might have gone hard with his command, but allowance must be made for the doubts and uncertainties which beset the British general, confronted not by an avowed public enemy but by fellow subjects having eminent support even in the British Parliament. It was not until after the Boston campaign that the business of suppressing American resistance was seriously taken in hand as a military problem. The center of operations then shifted from Boston never to return, and in view of the prominence of Massachusetts in the transactions bringing on the war her actual experience of its stress was remarkably small.

The little army which General Howe took with him from Boston to Halifax in March, 1776, he transferred from Halifax to New York harbor in the following June and on July 8 he established his camp on Staten Island. Reinforcements soon arrived on an English fleet commanded by his brother, Admiral Howe, and additional reinforcements were obtained through troops withdrawn from Virginia, South Carolina and the West Indies, making his total force about 30,000 strong.

Field operations by the British opened on August 22, with the landing of troops on Long Island. The American army was defeated at the battle of Long Island, August 27; and again at the battle of Harlem Plains, September 16, and again at the battle of White Plains, October 28, 1776. Washington saved the remnant of his army by crossing the Delaware River into Pennsylvania, but his situation seemed almost desperate. His letters during this period complain bitterly of the character of the officers and men with whom he was expected to defend his country. Writing to his brother on November 19, 1776, Washington said: "The different States, without regard to the qualifications of an officer, are quarreling about the appointments, and nominate such as are not fit to be shoeblacks, from the local attachments of this or that member of Assembly." Joseph Reed, who was Washington's adjutant-general throughout the campaign of 1776 in New York and the Jerseys, wrote that "a spirit of desertion, cowardice, plunder, and shrinking from duty when attended by fatigue or danger, prevailed but too generally through the whole army."

Washington's difficulties were greatly aggravated by the wide-spread disaffection to the American cause which existed in all the middle colonies and was particularly strong in Pennsylvania where many people had been alienated by the revolutionary subversion of the charter Government. After he had crossed the Delaware he wrote to a friend, "We are in a very disaffected part of the Province, and between you and me I think our affairs are in a very bad condition; not so much from the apprehension of General Howe's army as from the defection of New York, the Jerseys and Pennsylvania." The capture of Philadelphia seemed so imminent that Congress fled to Baltimore.

The Pennsylvania revolution was mainly the work of the Scotch-Irish element of the population, but it was not approved by all the Scotch-Irish. Charles Thomson always regarded it as an untoward event that hurt much more than it helped the American cause. Close study of the period in our own time has on the whole corroborated Thomson's views. Paul Leicester Ford concludes a minute account of the revolution that overthrew the charter institutions of Pennsylvania with this statement of the consequences:

> "The price paid is hard to compute. The division in the State had far reaching results. It prevented Washington from receiving the full aid of the most important State of the Union at Long Island, at White Plains and in the campaign of the Jerseys. It alienated the richest city and the best grain and beef region from the American cause. It made Tories of many and rendered Howe's eventual occupation of Philadelphia almost the occupation of a friendly country. It so weakened the Government of Pennsylvania that for months, at the most critical period of the war, it not only was powerless to aid the Continental side but had actually to rely on the Congress for support. It created a lawlessness in the people that led to riots and confusion equalled in no other State, to the mutiny of the Pennsylvania line, the driving of Congress from Philadelphia and the later civil insurrections. Finally it built up a powerful 'popularist' party, opposed to commerce, to sound finance and to federal union, that for many years hung like a dead weight on all attempts tending to advance those measures."

But if the Scotch-Irish were mainly responsible for these consequences by outrunning public opinion in general by their radical measures, they retrieved the situation by their staunch loyalty to the American cause. As soon as Washington had crossed the Delaware he was in touch with the Scotch-Irish settlements in Bucks and Northampton Counties and felt the sustaining influences of active popular support. Clothing and blankets were collected by committees of citizens for the use of his soldiers. The Rev. John Rosbrugh, pastor of the Presbyterian Church at Allen and Lower Mount Bethel, Northampton County, raised a company and brought it to join the Continental army. The patriotic clergyman was killed by the enemy a few weeks later. More important even than the direct aid was the assurance of protection against surprise by volunteer scouts in every direction. The Scotch-Irish farmers could be depended upon to watch the roads and convey prompt intelligence of a movement in any quarter.

With his base of operations thus made secure Washington was in a position to conceive and execute the brilliant exploits by which he gained military renown in the crisis. The initiative was Washington's own. On December 14 he wrote to Governor Trumbull of his purpose "to attempt a stroke upon the forces of the enemy, who lie a good deal scattered," in the hope that success would "rouse the spirits of the people, which are quite sunk by our late misfortunes." The particular stroke actually attempted appears to have been due to the suggestion of Reed, who wrote from Bristol, N. J., December 22, 1776, giving detailed information of the location of the British forces, and asking, "Will it not be possible, my dear general, for your troops, or such part of them as can act with advantage, to make a diversion, or something more, at or about Trenton?" He went on to urge that "our cause is desperate and hopeless, if we do not take the opportunity of the collection of troops at present, to strike some stroke." On receipt of this letter Washington at once sent for Reed to come to his headquarters and the arrangements were made for the attack upon the Hessians at Trenton on the night of Christmas. The stroke was completely successful. The Hessians were defeated and their commander was mortally wounded. Washington having secured his prisoners re-crossed the Delaware and resumed his former position in Bucks County.

Meanwhile Reed was active in getting information of the position of the enemy and on December 28 he was able to send to Washington an account of conditions offering an opportunity for another stroke. Washington at once set the troops in motion and on the 30th he reoccupied Trenton. The General directed Reed, who was a Princeton graduate and knew the country well, to make a reconnoissance. Reed at once set out accompanied by six horsemen, members of the Philadelphia city troop—John Dunlap, James Hunter, Thomas Peters, William Pollard, and James and Samuel Caldwell. This little detachment performed a remarkable exploit, thus related by Reed:

> "We met with little success on our way, or in the immediate vicinity of Princeton, to which we had approached within three miles. The ravages of the enemy had struck such terror that no rewards would tempt the inhabitants, though otherwise well disposed, to go into Princeton on this errand. But it being fully resolved not to return while there was a chance of success, it was concluded to pass on, and even to go round Princeton, expecting that in the rear they would be less guarded. As we were passing slowly on, almost within view of the town, a British soldier was observed passing from a barn to the dwelling house without arms. It being supposed that he was a marauder two of our party were sent to bring him in, but they had scarcely set out before another was seen, and then a third, when orders were given for our whole party to charge. This was done, and the house surrounded. Twelve British soldiers, equipped as dragoons, and well armed, their pieces loaded, and having the advantage of the house, surrendered to seven horsemen, six of whom had never before seen an enemy."

Reed returned to headquarters with these and other prisoners the same evening. The British began to concentrate against Washington's position in Trenton and began an attack on January

2, 1777. He decided to make a forced march during the night and attack the British in Princeton. This movement brought on the battle of Princeton, in which the British were signally defeated.

The effect of these brilliant successes upon the fortunes of war was far greater than the actual gains would indicate. Congress returned to Philadelphia and adopted measures for reorganizing the army. The Jerseys were practically abandoned by the British. The English historian Lecky says that "a fatal damp was thrown upon the cause of the Loyalists in America from which it never wholly recovered."

The British Government planned a campaign in 1777 which if successful would have cut the theatre of war in two. General Burgoyne, who had served with distinction in the war in Portugal, was in command of the British forces in Canada. The plan was that he should move southward to the Hudson, and in cooperation with General Clinton, stationed in New York, and General Howe, stationed in Philadelphia, hold the line of the Hudson, severing New England from the rest of the country. The southern part of the campaign was carried out according to the design. Clinton held New York and Howe was able to occupy Philadelphia after defeating General Washington at the battle of Brandywine. Meanwhile Burgoyne was pushing southward. He drove the Americans out of their fortifications at Ticonderoga and during their retreat inflicted upon them crushing defeats, the remnants that escaped fleeing in the direction of Albany. Affairs seemed in a desperate state, when the New Hampshire authorities appealed to John Stark to take charge of the defense of that State.

Stark's career is finely illustrative of the military aptitude implanted in the Scotch-Irish by their Ulster training and by their frontier experience in America. Born in Londonderry, N. H., in 1728, he experienced Indian captivity in his boyhood and gained a knowledge of the interior that enabled him to act as a scout for an expedition sent into the Indian country in 1753. In 1755 he was commissioned lieutenant of a company stationed at Fort Edward. While this company was upon an expedition it was attacked in overpowering numbers by the French and Indians, and all the superior officers were killed or wounded, so that the command devolved upon Stark. He managed the retreat so skillfully that he was successful in reaching Fort George with his men, bringing all his wounded. He was at once commissioned captain and served throughout the French War, gaining a high reputation as a cool and intrepid tactician.

It was only natural that a man of his military experience and ability should be prominent in the Revolutionary War. At the outbreak of hostilities he received a colonel's commission and raised a regiment almost in a day. That regiment formed the left of the American line at the battle of Bunker Hill, and covered the retreat. After the evacuation of Boston Colonel Stark with his regiment was sent to New York which he assisted in fortifying. The following spring he took part in the Canadian campaign, at the close of which he joined Washington in New Jersey, a few days before the battle of Trenton, in which engagement he commanded the van of the right wing. Although his efficiency in the New Jersey campaign was generally recognized he was passed over in the promotions made by Congress, while colonels whom he outranked became brigadiers. Stark resented the slight so deeply that he resigned his commission and retired to his New Hampshire farm. As it turned out this retirement was the prelude to a most important military service.

In response to the call of his State he formed an independent corps, the strength of which was largely drawn from the Scotch-Irish settlements. Stark had stipulated that he should not be subject to any orders save from his own State. He refused to recognize orders reaching him from the commander of the Continental troops opposing Burgoyne. This discord seemed to Burgoyne to afford a good opportunity for striking a blow, but the actual result was a severe reverse that was the beginning of the end of his campaign.

Burgoyne dispatched a well appointed force to attack Stark's independent corps which, being composed of volunteers and State militia, seemed to be an easy prey. The only uniformed troops in Stark's command were the Green Mountain rangers who wore hunting frocks with green facings. On August 13, 1777, Stark received word that Indian scouts acting for the British had appeared twelve miles from Bennington, Vt., and he began preparations at once. The British commander took position upon high ground, made intrenchments and mounted two pieces of ordnance. During the fifteenth there was skirmishing which had the effect of driving off the Indian scouts. Meanwhile Stark made a shrewd plan of attack, involving a feint diverting attention from the main assault. The attack was completely successful. The British were driven out of their intrenchments, although the Americans had not a single cannon to support their attack. The British fled abandoning their baggage and artillery.

It was rather a characteristic incident of American warfare at this period that the battle was nearly lost after it had been won. With the retreat of the British the Americans dispersed to collect plunder. Reinforcements sent by Burgoyne came up, arresting the retreat and renewing the battle. Stark had difficulty in holding his position. At the nick of time fresh troops arrived from Bennington and by their aid Stark kept up the battle which was fought with obstinacy until sunset when the enemy finally broke and fled. Among the numerous prisoners made by the Americans was the British commander who was badly wounded and died soon afterward. Although known as the battle of Bennington the action really took place about seven miles distant in New York territory, two miles west of the Vermont boundary. Congress now appointed Stark a brigadier-general, and he served until the close of the war, when he retired, declining all public office. He lived to be ninety-four, dying at Manchester, N. H., May 2, 1822.

The battle of Bennington led to the failure of Burgoyne's campaign. His line of march was flanked by a tier of Scotch-Irish settlements, from which volunteers and militia poured into the American camp. The spirit of the soldiers was animated by Stark's victory and Burgoyne at last found himself in a position from which he could neither advance nor retreat. All his communications were cut off and he was hopelessly outnumbered. On October 17, 1777, Burgoyne surrendered his entire command. The event practically decided the issue of the struggle for it secured the French alliance. Previously the French Government had been undecided but when the news reached Europe the American commissioners were notified that France was now ready to acknowledge and support American independence.

The carrying on of the war with France so occupied the British Government that operations in America languished for several years. In June, 1778, the British evacuated Philadelphia, and although they still held New York, no systematic American campaign was undertaken until 1780, when the Southern States became the theatre of operations. Clinton, with forces sent from New York, landed in the vicinity of Charleston, South Carolina, in March, 1780, and although the American garrison made an obstinate defense it was at last, on May 12, obliged to capitulate. Soon after Clinton returned to New York, leaving Cornwallis to prosecute the war. What followed is like the story of Burgoyne's campaign, over again, with a similar turning point.

On August 16, 1780, the American army under General Gates was defeated by Cornwallis, near Camden, S. C., and its organization was shattered. Two days later Tarleton routed Sumter at Fishing Creek. American resistance for the time was crushed out except in the western section where Scotch-Irish settlements were thick. Cornwallis detached Major Patrick Ferguson with a force of regulars and Tories, to scour the country west of the Wateree, beat back the Mountain Men, as the frontiersmen were called, and rally the Loyalists. Major Ferguson came of the same stock as those who were soon to end his career, up to this time one of brilliant promise. He was born in Scotland, son of the eminent jurist James Ferguson, and nephew of Lord Elibank. He served with the army in Flanders when only eighteen years old. He came to America with his regiment in 1777 and was active in the battle of the Brandywine in September of that year. He was engaged in operations on the Hudson in 1779, establishing his reputation as an able and energetic officer. At the siege of Charleston in 1780 he so distinguished himself that he received special mention from the commander-in-chief.

As Ferguson moved toward the mountain country, Colonel Charles McDowell of Burke County, North Carolina, put himself in communication with Colonel John Sevier of Washington County, and Colonel Isaac Shelby of Sullivan County. Expresses were sent out along the western tier of settlements for help and nearly 1,400 men responded to the call. The largest contingent came from Washington County, Virginia, under Colonel William Campbell, who took the general command in the engagement that followed. Campbell's father was one of the Scotch-Irish settlers in Augusta County, Virginia, and William was born there in 1745. In 1767 he settled in Washington County, where he became a justice of the peace, a militia officer and a leading man of affairs. He married a sister of Patrick Henry.

Learning of the concentration of force against him, Ferguson occupied a strong position on King's Mountain. He had over eleven hundred men in his force, in part regulars and in part Loyalist militia. The position was stormed by the Americans, who not only drove the British from their lines but also cut off their retreat. Ferguson fought with conspicuous gallantry, repeatedly leading charges upon the American lines, but his men fell rapidly under the deadly accuracy of the frontiersmen's fire, and at last he too was shot dead. This disheartened the defense, and the officer upon whom the command devolved raised the white flag, and surrendered his entire force, October 7, 1780.

Colonel Campbell received votes of thanks from the Virginia Legislature and the Continental Congress, while Washington sent him a congratulatory letter. He was appointed brigadier-general but while in the service he contracted a fever of which he died in 1781.

Colonel Charles McDowell who was active in the arrangements for collecting the frontiersmen was the son of Joseph McDowell, an Ulster emigrant who arrived in America in 1730. Charles McDowell was not present at the battle of King's Mountain. When the frontier militia colonels came together, it was a question who should take command, and it was finally settled that McDowell should proceed to headquarters and have a general officer detailed to take over the command which meanwhile should be held by Campbell. In McDowell's absence the militia from Burke and Rutherford Counties, North Carolina, were led by his brother, Major Joseph McDowell. Another brother, William, also fought in the battle. Joseph McDowell led a force of his Mountain Men at the battle of Cowpens, January 17, 1781. In 1788 he was a member of the North Carolina constitutional convention and in 1792 he was elected a member of Congress.

King's Mountain and Cowpens were fatal to the plans of the British. At the end of the campaign they held no part of the Carolinas except the country immediately round Charleston. Additional British troops were landed in Virginia, and Cornwallis, marching from the Carolinas, effected a junction and took charge of the entire force. He experienced Burgoyne's fate, as he had to surrender with his whole army on October 19, 1781. This virtually ended the Revolutionary War. When the news reached England there was a change of Government and the new Ministry negotiated liberal terms of peace.

Both Bennington and King's Mountain showed that the British thrust was stopped when it met the solid resistance of the Scotch-Irish settlements along the frontier. These events marked the turning point of the British campaign both in the North and in the South. Such exploits by local militia do not become intelligible until one considers how military aptitude was instilled in the Scotch-Irish by Ulster training and American experience.

A signal example of this aptitude is presented by the career of Henry Knox. Born in Boston, July 25, 1750, of County Antrim stock, he took an ardent interest in military affairs from his boyhood. At the age of eighteen he was a member of a military company and when the Boston Grenadier Corps was organized he was chosen second in command. Meanwhile he was engaged in the book trade and he became proprietor of a shop much frequented by the officers of the British garrison and also by ladies of literary tastes. In this way he became acquainted with Miss Lucy Flucker. His marriage with her on June 16, 1774, made a stir in Boston society, as her father, Provincial Secretary under Gage, and a high Tory, had more ambitious plans for his daughter and was opposed to the match. Most of her friends thought she had sacrificed her prospects in life and they were confirmed in this belief when Knox rejected the efforts of General Gage to attach him to the Loyalist side. His vigorous personality, together with his active interest in military affairs, made him such a marked man that when he decided to to go to the American camp he had to slip out of Boston in disguise. After placing his wife in safe quarters at Worcester he joined the American forces.

At the battle of Bunker Hill Knox acted as a staff officer, reconnoitring the British movements. During the campaign that followed he was active in planning and constructing works of defense for the various positions held by the Americans. His ability as a military engineer and as an artillerist attracted attention and obtained General Washington's esteem. On November 17, 1775, although Knox was only twenty-five years old, he was commissioned colonel of the only artillery regiment in the Continental Army. He served throughout the war with distinction, enjoying the steady confidence and friendship of Washington. He took part in all the important engagements down to the siege of Yorktown, his arrangements for which were such that Washington reported to the President of Congress that "the resources of his genius supplied the deficit of means."

Knox reached the grade of major-general in 1782, and in 1785 he was appointed by the Continental Congress to the office of Secretary of War, which he continued to hold under General Washington after the national Government was organized under the Constitution. He was also Secretary of the Navy, the two portfolios being then united. He retained office until the close of

1794 when he withdrew from public life, retiring to an extensive estate in Maine, upon which he created and built up the town of Thomaston. He had here a fine library, part of it in the French language, and he was living the life of a hospitable country magnate when he died suddenly in his fifty-seventh year. It was a singular fate for a man who had escaped the perils of so many battlefields, for he choked to death on a chicken bone.

The War Department also owes much to the administrative genius of another Scotch-Irishman whose career presents a marked example of hereditary faculty. Among the early emigrants from Ulster to the Cumberland Valley, Pennsylvania, was John Armstrong. Some time before 1748 he settled in Carlisle and became a surveyor under the Proprietary Government. He took a leading part in organizing the settlers to repel Indian raids and was commissioned a colonel of militia. He was also a justice of the peace and was active and energetic in the discharge both of his military and of his civil functions. In 1755 he led a force of about two hundred and eighty frontiersmen against the Indian settlement at Kittanning, about twenty miles northeast of Fort Duquesne. Although Colonel Armstrong was severely wounded in the engagement, he completely routed the Indians and destroyed their stronghold, to the great relief of the frontier settlements. In 1758 he commanded a body of troops in the vanguard of the army with which General Forbes retrieved Braddock's defeat and captured Fort Duquesne. During this campaign he formed an acquaintance with Washington which ripened into lifelong friendship. He was a leader in the protest against the closing of the port of Boston in 1774 and was a member of the Committee of Correspondence appointed to concert measures of joint action by the colonies. His commission as brigadier-general in the Continental Army bears date March 1, 1776, and in 1777 he appears as a major-general in command of the Pennsylvania troops at the battle of Brandywine. In that year he left the regular army, his action being due to some grievance, but he did not abandon the cause. At the battle of Germantown he commanded the

Pennsylvania militia. In 1778–1780, and also in 1787–1788, he was a member of Congress. His election was warmly recommended by General Washington, who recognized the value of having one of his military knowledge in the governing body. He died March 9, 1795, aged seventy-five years.

John Armstrong, Jr., born at Carlisle, November 25, 1758, was a student at Princeton when the Revolutionary War broke out, and he left his books to become an aide on the staff of General Mercer. When Mercer received his mortal wound at the battle of Princeton Armstrong bore him off the field. After the death of Mercer Armstrong joined the staff of General Gates and was with him in the campaign that culminated in the surrender of Burgoyne at Saratoga. In 1780, when he was only twenty-two years old, he was made adjutant-general of the southern army, but owing to an attack of illness served only a short time in that position. He rejoined the staff of General Gates, continuing in that capacity until the end of the war.

Upon the close of the war Armstrong entered public life in which he rose rapidly. He filled successively the offices of Secretary and adjutant-general of Pennsylvania, and in 1787 he was elected to Congress. In 1789 he married a sister of Chancellor Livingston, and removed to that State. Early in the next year he was chosen United States Senator from New York, serving until 1804 when he entered the diplomatic service. He was Minister to France and Spain until 1810, when he returned to the United States. When the War of 1812 began he was appointed brigadier-general and placed in command of the district of New York. In March, 1813, he was called to the Cabinet as Secretary of War.

Armstrong's career as Secretary of War ended in apparent failure. The blame for American defeats was laid upon him and the British invasion of Washington was the finishing stroke, forcing him out of the Cabinet and retiring him to private life. The verdict of history is nevertheless in his favor as disinterested consideration of the case shows that he was the victim of circumstances that he tried to remedy, accomplishing results of permanent value. The bane of the army has been and still is government by Congressional committees. Armstrong selected officers for their merits, disregarding Congressional influence to an extent that excited a malignant opposition which pursued him relentlessly until it compassed his downfall. The chief authority for this period of our national existence is Henry Adams's *History of the United States*. While charging Armstrong with defects of temper and manners, the historian says:

> "Whatever were Armstrong's faults, he was the strongest Secretary of War the Government had yet seen. Hampered by an inheritance of mistakes not easily corrected, and by a chief [Madison] whose methods were non-military in the extreme, Armstrong still introduced into the army an energy wholly new... The energy thus infused by Armstrong into the regular army lasted for half a century."

The confidence with which he inspired the army was one of the causes of his downfall. He was charged with aiming at a military domination of the Government. His action in issuing a major-general's commission to Andrew Jackson aggrieved General Harrison and his friends and was at the time regretted by President Madison. The opposition to Armstrong became so strong that Madison dismissed him from office. He lived for nearly thirty years afterward but he never again accepted public office. He published a number of treatises on military and agricultural topics; and he prepared a military history of the Revolution, which from his intimate knowledge of the subject would doubtless have been a work of great value, but unfortunately the manuscript was destroyed by fire.

Andrew Jackson, the recognition of whose military genius by Armstrong was based upon his behavior in the Creek Indian War, splendidly vindicated Armstrong's judgment by his conduct of the southern campaign and his brilliant victory at New Orleans. His career is a well known instance of the military aptitude of the Scotch-Irish strain in American citizenship.

- The origin of all the officers of the Revolutionary army cannot be determined with sufficient accuracy to admit of any statistical exhibit, but Scotch-Irish of Ulster nativity were so numerous that a provision of the Constitution of the United States was drawn so as to meet their case. When the qualifications for membership in the House of Representatives were considered in the convention it was in question whether natives only should be eligible or else how long a term of citizenship should be a prerequisite. In the course of the debate Wilson of Pennsylvania remarked that "almost all the general officers of the Pennsylvania line of the late army were foreigners," and he mentioned that three members of the Pennsylvania delegation in the convention, he himself being one, were not natives. The term was finally fixed at seven years, which admitted to Congressional eligibility the generation that participated in the Revolutionary War, whether native born or not. The immigrants thus provided for were mainly Scotch-Irish.

In the formation of the Constitution of the United States no racial or denominational influence can be traced. Such claims have been made but they belong rather to political mythology than to serious history. The breach in the continuity of political development due to the circumstances of the American struggle precipitated the States into constitution-making with unsatisfactory results. The character of the new State Governments was distrusted and their behavior viewed with dismay by the statesmen under whose leadership American independence had been achieved. Such feelings energized the movement for a strong national Government whose outcome was the Convention of 1787 and the framing of the Constitution of the United States. The winding and shifting of individual activity on the issues arising during the formative period sustain no relation to racial origins or to denominational attachments, but cut across them with entire facility. The debates of the Convention show that the accident of hailing from a small State or a large State had more to do with a delegate's course than any other consideration.

- The Scotch-Irish supplied leaders both for and against the adoption of the Constitution. The movement for liberalizing the Constitution, extending the suffrage, and substituting popular election of the President for choice by the Electoral College derived its strongest support from the Scotch-Irish element of the population, and it triumphed in the national Government under the leadership of Andrew Jackson.

CHAPTER XX

A Survey and an Appreciation

From time to time objections have been raised to the term "Scotch-Irish." In his *Dutch and Quaker Colonies*, John Fiske says:

"The name Scotch-Irish is an awkward compound, and is in many quarters condemned. Curiously enough, there is no one who seems to object to it so strongly as the Irish Catholic. While his feelings toward the 'Far-Downer' are certainly not affectionate he is nevertheless anxious to claim him with his deeds and trophies, as simply Irish, and grudges to Scotland the claim to any share in producing him. It must be admitted, however, that there is a point of view from which the Scotch-Irish may be regarded as more Scotch than Irish. The difficulty might be compromised by calling them Ulstermen, or Ulster Presbyterians."

The *Century Magazine* for September, 1891, contained an article by Henry Cabot Lodge on "The Distribution of Ability in the United States," in which he classified the Scotch-Irish as a distinct race-stock. This was the subject of criticism, in replying to which he said:

"I classified the Irish and the Scotch-Irish as two distinct race-stocks, and I believe the distinction to be a sound one historically and scientifically… The Scotch-Irish from the North of Ireland, Protestant in religion and chiefly Scotch and English in blood and name, came to this country in large numbers in the eighteenth century, while the people of pure Irish stock came scarcely at all during the colonial period, and did not immigrate here largely until the present century was well advanced."

The term does not matter so much as the thing signified. That there is a particular breed of people in the North of Ireland introduced there by the Ulster Plantation, is indisputable. In that region itself the term Ulster Scot seems to be preferred as an appellation. The people there habitually regarded and spoke of themselves as belonging to the Scottish nation, and the term appears in Ulster documents. The term Scotch-Irish is also ancient, being the designation used in the Scottish universities for the students resorting to them from Ulster. Their Scottish character was fully recognized, but at the same time they were not of Scotland, so the Ulster student was registered as *Scoto-Hibernus*.

When Ulster emigration to America became noticeable it was a common practice in the colonies to speak of the arrivals as Irish. As they certainly came from Ireland the designation could not be wholly disowned, yet the arrivals strongly objected to being described as Irish. They regarded themselves as Scottish people who had been living in Ireland. The circumstances were such as naturally to engender the term Scotch-Irish, which is a sufficiently accurate description of a distinct race-stock. It is true that the Ulster Plantation was designed to be English rather than Scotch, but for reasons set forth in preceding chapters, the Plantation became a Scottish settlement into which the English ingredient was absorbed. Ulster emigration to America was distinctly Scotch-Irish in its composition. The use of the term is therefore not only justifiable but is required by accuracy of statement.

The use of that or some corresponding term is forced upon historians because it is impossible to tell the story of the American nation with any completeness without considering the Scotch-Irish. That is how John Fiske came to make the mention already cited. He was speaking of early emigrants from Germany, and he tells how some "pressed onward and spread along the Appalachian frontier." In pursuing this particular theme the truth of history compels him to bring in the Scotch-Irish, although rather abruptly. He remarks: "Here they [the Germans, from the Rhenish Palatinate] have played an important part, usually in association with a race of men of still more vigorous initiative, the so-called Scotch-Irish." And then he proceeds to give a brief account of the Ulster Plantation and Ulster emigration to the colonies as an essential feature of American history. Mr. Fiske computed that "between 1730 and 1770 more than half the Presbyterian population of Ulster came to America, where it formed more than one-sixth part of our entire population at the time of the Declaration of Independence."

Theodore Roosevelt experienced the same necessity of considering Scotch-Irish influence, in his *Winning of the West*. The leaders in national expansion were the backwoods mountaineers. He says that "the dominant strain in their blood was that of the Presbyterian Irish—the Scotch-Irish as they were often called." He remarks that "it is doubtful if we have wholly realized the importance of the part played by that stern and virile people, the Irish whose preachers taught the creed of Knox and Calvin"; and he declares that "the West was won by those who have been rightly called the Roundheads of the South, the same men, who, before any others, declared for American independence."

The fact has not been duly observed that upon every computation of numbers Scotch-Irish immigration far exceeded all other Puritan immigration. The Massachusetts immigration of Puritan Independents about which so much has been written, was comparatively small, as may be seen by the figures of the colonial historian Hutchinson, given in Chapter VI. of this work. He estimated the total arrivals at 21,200 men, women and children up to 1640 after which until Scotch-Irish immigration began more people left New England than arrived there. It was not until after the extensive infusion of Scotch-Irish blood that New England developed traits since regarded as characteristic. This fact is incidentally displayed by the considerations which Charles Francis Adams notes in his *Massachusetts—Its Historians and Its History*. He points out that the intellectual influence and literary distinction of New England are late developments. That section was once characterized by such mental sterility and moral insensibility that he designates the years from 1637 to 1760 as the glacial period. Then began the political activity that made Massachusetts prominent in the Revolutionary period; but the associations of literary culture now attaching to New England were not established until the first quarter of the nineteenth century.

Even upon such a restricted view of history as that which makes it simply a narrative of events the Scotch-Irish can not be left out. When history performs its proper function of tracing the causes which form national character and decide national destiny, the Scotch-Irish factor becomes prominent. Since American history has improved in scientific character and in philosophic spirit, it is noticeable that there has been increasing recognition of the importance of the Scotch-Irish contribution to American nationality. There are considerations, some of which will now be instanced, that indicate that this recognition will be still more enlarged in the future.

As the events of the Revolutionary period are reduced to scale, the more disproportionate they seem in relation to the vast results. In all history there appears to be no parallel instance of the founding of a great nation as an incident of controversies over constitutional principles. Insurrection and revolt were nothing new in the experience of England, but whatever the particular conclusion, the national sovereignty emerged stronger than before. It was very difficult for English statesmen to admit the idea that American independence was an actual possibility, and even after the fact was formally recognized the notion was long held that it would surely be transient. The American cause was throughout most of the Revolutionary period in a precarious state. There were sharp divisions of sentiment among the people, and the Government of the improvised confederation was never able to command even the limited resources within its jurisdiction, or to act with steady vigor. The more one studies the details of the struggle the more remarkable appears the successful issue. It seemed little less than a miracle to Washington himself, when he calmly reviewed it in later days. The affair remains a mystery until the effect of the Ulster migration is considered. Here is a factor, whose extent and activity puts it foremost in any scientific study of cause and effect. If, as Mr. Fiske computes, the Scotch-Irish population must have amounted to one-sixth of the entire population at the time of the Declaration of Independence, and remembering that they were all hot for independence while everywhere else there were streaks of cold or lukewarm feeling, there can be hardly any question as to where lay the decisive influence.

In the opinion of Lecky, who is with justice regarded as the most impartial historian of this period, the issue of the Revolutionary War once rested upon the action of the Pennsylvania line, whose "privates and non-commissioned officers consisted chiefly of immigrants from the North of Ireland." Lecky remarks, "no troops in that army had shown themselves more courageous, more patient, and more devoted." But their pay was a whole year in arrears; they were left nearly naked and destitute of provisions; their complaints had not received attention, and early in 1781 they rebelled. Although some officers were killed or wounded in attempting to suppress the mutiny, the force stuck together and acted as a disciplined body. They left camp at Morristown, about 1,300 strong, with their muskets and six field-pieces; and marched to Princeton, apparently with the intention of proceeding to Philadelphia.

The situation caused great alarm. Lecky remarks that "in the weak condition of the American forces such a body, if it had gone over to the English, might have turned the fortunes of the war." The English commanders had hopes that this might be accomplished, and there was much to encourage them for many deserters from the American army had already gone over to the British camp. But the Scotch-Irish were not of that sort. Sir Henry Clinton sent confidential messengers with offers of amnesty and payment of all arrears due them, leaving it entirely to them whether they would render military service or be discharged. The offers were rejected, the emissaries were arrested and sent to the American camp to be dealt with as spies. The mutineers kept together as a disciplined body, committed no depredations and proclaimed their loyalty to the American cause and their readiness to resume service as soon as their grievances were redressed. The affair was finally settled by a partial satisfaction of their just demands. Congress was delighted at getting out of so serious a difficulty, and a purse of one hundred guineas was made up for those who had delivered up the British emissaries. But the men who had gone to such extreme lengths to force the payment of what was due them, now refused to accept the present of money, saying that they had only done their duty. The whole affair was characteristically Scotch-Irish.

The logic of the American controversy has not worn well, and at present deeper reasons are sought for the conflict than those assigned at the time. It is now regarded as having its source in the fact that the colonies had outgrown their tutelage, and that a nationality was developing, which, to get its breath and live its life, had to burst its bonds. The manifestation of this incipient nationality was a sudden phenomenon, and it corresponds to the great increase of American population through Ulster emigration. Prior to that the colonies had been separated by intense antipathies. Now a marked unifying and nationalizing influence makes its appearance, together with an energetic movement toward territorial expansion. Prior to the Ulster emigration the population of the colonies had been stagnant and, in New England especially, even tended to decline. The Scotch-Irish immigration changed that and set in motion forces of national expansion whose attainments soon exceeded the bounds that colonial imagination dared to think possible. So late as 1775 the poetic fancy of Philip Freneau was satisfied with this modest anticipation:

> The time shall come when strangers rule no more,
> Nor cruel mandates vex from Britain's shore;
> When commerce shall extend her shortened wing,
> And her rich freights from every climate bring;
> When mighty towns shall flourish free and great,—
> Vast their dominions, opulent their state;
> When one vast cultivated region teems
> From ocean's side to Mississippi's streams.

American settlements extended beyond the Mississippi in the poet's own lifetime. Freneau died in 1832. Missouri was admitted as a State in 1821. This rapidity of national expansion beyond

all early expectation is a direct consequence of Scotch-Irish immigration, and is unaccountable until that factor is considered.

· This national expansion was accompanied by an industrial
development quite as remarkable for the rapidity of its process.
An economic transformation took place in which Scotch-Irish
immigration was an influential factor. It has been noted that the
development of manufactures in the first distinctively Scotch-Irish
settlements in America, was so great as to excite the anxious concern of English officials in Maryland. When Ulster immigration
poured into New England the culture of the potato, practically
unknown there before, was introduced. Spinning and weaving
were widely diffused by the same agency. In the three years prior
to 1774, the number of Ulster weavers who had emigrated to
America was officially computed in England to be not less than
ten thousand. The rapid rise of manufactures in the first part of the
nineteenth century was a development prepared mainly through
Scotch-Irish influence. New England, the dominant interest in
which had been navigation, experienced an industrial revolution.
Important developments took place wherever the Scotch-Irish
settled. The invention of the reaper, which has created a vast
American industry and has worked a revolution in agricultural
conditions, was an incident of Scotch-Irish occupation of the
Valley of Virginia. Cyrus McCormick made his great invention
by improving a mechanism originally devised by his father as a
labor-saving contrivance in the work on his Rockbridge County
farm.

The industrial history of Pennsylvania is a wonderful record
of Scotch-Irish achievement. Conditions there were such as to
give special stimulus to the racial capacity and at the same time
to provide rich material for its exercise.

· The particular history of each of the leading industries of that
great State is crowded with Scotch-Irish names. The movement
to the interior characteristic of Scotch-Irish immigration developed an interest in agencies of transportation, which was strongly
manifested in the improvement of water-ways even before the

Revolutionary War. One of the early commissioners appointed to remove obstructions to river traffic was Colonel Ephraim Blaine, grandfather of James G. Blaine. When the steam-engine was invented the importance of applying it to navigation was strongly impressed by the extent of river traffic. Robert Fulton, who successfully accomplished this with the aid of Chancellor Livingston, was born in Lancaster County, Pennsylvania, in 1765, of Scotch-Irish ancestry. The building of canals and railways, was powerfully stimulated by needs created through Scotch-Irish settlement of the Western country, and Scotch-Irish names figure abundantly in such enterprises. The list of the chief officers of the Pennsylvania Railroad from its inception to the present day presents very much the character of a Scotch-Irish dynasty.

The influence of Scotch-Irish immigration in establishing and propagating the Presbyterian Church in the United States is generally recognized. But its influence upon American religious life is of far wider scope. Almost from the time Scotch-Irish immigration began, the old identification of Ulster Scot and Ulster Presbyterian began to fail. For reasons heretofore presented in this work there was a large leakage from Presbyterianism to Congregationalism in New England, which section was, and still is, stony ground for Presbyterianism. At the same time Congregationalism has not shown proportionate gains. But even out of New England the strength of the Presbyterian Church is far from being commensurate with the strength of the Scotch-Irish element of the population and its diffusion throughout the United States. The case recalls the old fable of the traveler and his cloak, which he held tight during the storm but laid aside when the sun came out. The Scotch-Irish strain has participated in the religious variation that has been so marked in the United States. The Puritan movement originally aimed at reformation, not sectarianism. The actual consequences involve multiplication of agency with dissipation of energy quite opposed to the original intention. The final judgment of history upon the value of that movement will depend largely upon the solution of the problems raised by existing ecclesiastical conditions.

Early in our national history interest in popular education became noted as a distinctive American characteristic. School facilities for the masses of the people certainly did not figure in the institutional equipment inherited by America from England, in which respect the latter has not been a leader among nations. In this field the effect of Scotch-Irish immigration has been distinct and indubitable. The high rank speedily attained by the United States for literacy of citizenship must be ascribed to that stream of influence. There was no more familiar figure in American society in the formative period than the Scotch-Irish schoolmaster. Everywhere one hears of him in the early records.

In tracing this particular influence to its original source one must turn not only to Ulster but beyond it to Scotland. To this day the American school system has a Scottish stamp, and American Universities have still a closer resemblance to the Scotch than to the English. Exactly why it was that Scotland originally developed its peculiar zeal for popular education is not quite clear. While the Reformation had much to do with it, that crisis did not originate it. Three great Scottish universities were founded before the Reformation. In the fifteenth century interest in popular education was as distinctively characteristic of Scotland as interest in art was of Italy. The hereditary jurisdiction then exercised in Scotland by the landlord class was doubtless one source of this interest. This is indicated by the remarkable law enacted in 1496 by the Scotch Parliament requiring all persons and freeholders of substance, under pain of a heavy fine, to send their eldest sons to school until they had obtained a competent knowledge of Latin and sufficient familiarity with jurisprudence to distribute justice among their people. The statesmen of the Reformation built upon the existing educational foundations and enlarged their scope. In 1560 John Knox proposed an elaborate system of national education. A system of parochial schools, imitated from Geneva, was established during the seventeenth century. The system was accompanied by arrangements for special aid to deserving students which, according to Lecky, "brought the advantage of University education within the range of classes wholly excluded from it in England." Although the material welfare of the people was "considerably below the average standard in England, the level of intelligence among them was distinctly higher, the proportion of national faculties called into active exercise was distinctly great-er than in any other part of the empire." This judgment of the English historian necessarily includes Ulster, since both ecclesi-astically and educationally that was a Scottish annex.

The foregoing pages contain numerous particulars showing the educational intimacy of Ulster and Scotland. A striking evidence of the general literacy of the people of Ulster is supplied by the petition to Governor Shute in 1717 signed by 322 persons, nearly all of the signatures being in fair autograph. Only eleven of the signers had to make their marks. Nowhere in England at that time would so little illiteracy have been found in so large a body of poor people planning to emigrate to better their condition. And wherever the Scotch-Irish went the establishment of schools was one of their first cares. As has been pointed out, education was a necessary incident of their ecclesiastical system, and concern for education was a deeply implanted race instinct, abundantly manifested in their history. To the activity of that characteristic the remarkably prompt and rapid spread of popular education throughout America is to be mainly attributed.

Generally in new settlements professional vocation does not set in until after the community is well rooted. The first call is for the artificer, and this class of employment usually absorbs the energies of the first generation. But among the Scotch-Irish the aptitude for scholarship was so strong that almost from the first this stream of immigration brought recruits to all the learned professions. John Rutledge who arrived in South Carolina about 1735, became a practicing physician in Charleston. Two sons were distinguished lawyers, one becoming a signer of the Declaration of Independence, the other a member of the constitutional conven-tion of 1787 and eventually justice of the Supreme Court of the United States. James McHenry, after whom the fort was named whose bombardment inspired the Star Spangled Banner, was surgeon to the Fifth Pennsylvania battalion in the Revolutionary War. He was a delegate from Maryland to the constitutional convention of 1787 and was Secretary of War during Washington's second term, continuing under Adams. The Breckinridge family of Kentucky, which has produced numerous clergymen, military officers, lawyers and statesmen, is derived from Alexander Breckinridge who emigrated from Ulster to Pennsylvania in 1728 and a few years later settled in Augusta County, Virginia.

In preceding chapters numerous particulars have been given showing the influence of the Scotch-Irish schools in recruiting the Presbyterian ministry with men of sound scholarship. The effect upon the legal profession was almost as strongly marked. This profession became strong and influential in the colonies at an early date. Recruits to it were numerous from all the Scotch-Irish settlements. The importance of this element has been specially marked in Pennsylvania and in the settlement of the West. John Bannister Gibson, born at Carlisle, November 8, 1780, Chief Justice of Pennsylvania from 1827 to 1851, is regarded by students of jurisprudence as one of the greatest jurists America has produced. The rapidity with which legal and political institutions, in advance of provision by central authority, were erected in the interior of the national domain, is an extraordinary occurrence that is hardly intelligible until one considers the character of the Scotch-Irish immigration that was the dominating influence in the westward movement of population. So many Scotch-Irish lawyers were prominent in public affairs in the formative period of the West that any attempt to give particulars would transcend the bounds of a general history.[6]

---

[6] The report of the Pennsylvania Scotch-Irish Society for 1898 contains a paper by the Hon. John B. McPherson of Dauphin County, now a member of the United States Circuit Court of Appeals for the Third Circuit, giving particulars of the strength of the Scotch-Irish element in the Pennsylvania judiciary. An address by Governor James E. Campbell of Ohio, contained in the report of the Scotch-Irish Congress of 1890,

With the growth of the nation and the blending of its elements complications of heredity increase and the race dominant in particular cases may be brought into question. The Scotch-Irish in America have never organized on racial lines.

Their social and political activities have mixed freely and spread freely through the general mass of American citizenship. Hence when one turns from the collective aspect of the case to genealogical particulars one enters a region of controversy. An instance is supplied by the various classifications made of the racial origins of Presidents of the United States. Whitelaw Reid's examination of the subject is carefully done. According to it Andrew Jackson, James K. Polk, James Buchanan, Andrew Johnson, Chester A. Arthur and William McKinley are of Ulster ancestry. General Grant has Scotch ancestry on his father's side, Scotch-Irish on his mother's side. Benjamin Harrison, Grover Cleveland and Theodore Roosevelt have Scotch-Irish ancestry on the mother's side. The paternal ancestry of James Munroe and Rutherford B. Hayes goes to Scotland direct. Since Mr. Reid's book was published, the Presidency has been attained by Woodrow Wilson, whose presumably authorized biography in *Who's Who* states that he is Scotch-Irish on both sides. Mr. Reid gives a long roll of distinguished Americans of Scotch-Irish ancestry.[7]

---

gives many particulars of the prominent part taken by the Scotch-Irish in organizing and developing the Western States.

[7] A great mass of information is contained in the published proceedings of the Scotch-Irish Society of America, organized in 1889, under the presidency of Robert Bonner of New York. Its first congress was held at Columbia, Tennessee, in May, of that year. Subsequently congresses were held at Pittsburgh, Louisville, Atlanta, Springfield, Ohio, Des Moines, Lexington, Va., Harrisburg, Knoxville, and Chambersburg, Pa. Ten volumes of proceedings were issued by this Society, making an expressive exhibit of the achievements of the Ulster breed in America.

The only Scotch-Irish Society known now to exist is the Pennsylvania Scotch-Irish Society, which was organized in the fall of 1889 as a branch of the National Society. It holds annual meetings, the transactions of which are published in a series of reports containing much information on Scotch-Irish history.

Whatever questions be raised as to the controlling heredity in particular cases there can be no question that there is a distinct Scotch-Irish type of frame and physiognomy. It is well known and easily recognized. The long chin gives a characteristic square effect to the lower part of the face. One may notice it in the pictures of Woodrow Wilson as in the pictures of Andrew Jackson. And the race character is as persistent as the physical type. Professor Heron's description of the distinguishing characteristics of the Ulster Scots is applicable also to their kinsmen, the Scotch-Irish in America:

"An economy and even parsimony of words, which does not always betoken a poverty of ideas; an insuperable dislike to wear his heart upon his sleeve, or make a display of the deeper and more tender feelings of his nature; a quiet and undemonstrative deportment which may have great firmness and determination behind it; a dour exterior which may cover a really genial disposition and kindly heart; much caution, wariness and reserve, but a decision, energy of character, and tenacity of purpose, which, as in the case of Enoch Arden, 'hold his will and bear it through'; a very decided practical faculty which has an eye on the main chance, but which may co-exist with a deep-lying fund of sentiment; a capacity for hard work and close application to business, which, with thrift and patient persistence, is apt to bear fruit in considerable success; in short, a reserve of strength, self-reliance, courage and endurance, which, when an emergency demands (as behind the Walls of Derry), may surprise the world."

The activity and influence of that race have a securely established importance among the factors of American history.

APPENDIX A

Ireland at the time of the Plantation

Documents illustrative of the condition of Ireland at the time of the Ulster Plantation will be found in a volume of the Carisbrooke Library published by George Routledge & Sons, London and New York, entitled "*Ireland under Elizabeth and James*," edited by Professor Henry Morley of University College, London. Accounts by Edmund Spenser, Sir John Davies and Fynes Moryson are included. Moryson, born in Lincolnshire in 1566, obtained a fellowship at Cambridge University. In 1589 he obtained leave of absence for travel until July, 1600. He spent ten years in foreign travel and his account of his observations has been republished in recent years under the title of *Shakespeare's Europe*. In 1600 he went to Ireland, where his brother was Vice-President of Munster. Moryson was a plodding, unimaginative writer, and his works now possess no interest save as records of fact in which respect they have great documentary value. The following is extracted from his account of Ireland:

"The fields are not only most apt to feed cattle, but yield also great increase of corn. I will freely say that I observed the winter's cold to be far more mild than it is in England, so as the Irish pastures are more green, and so likewise the gardens all winter-time, but that in summer, by reason of the cloudy air and watery soil, the heat of the sun hath not such power to ripen corn and fruits, so as their harvest is much later than in England. Also I observed that the best sorts of flowers and fruits are much rarer in Ireland than in England, which notwithstanding is more to be attributed to the inhabitants than to the air; for Ireland being often troubled with rebellions, and the rebels not only being idle themselves, but in natural malice destroying the labors of other men, and cutting up the very trees or fruit for the same cause or else to burn them, for these reasons the inhabitants take less pleasure to till the ground or plant trees, content to live for the day, in continual fear of like mischiefs. Yet is not Ireland altogether destitute of these flowers and fruits, wherewith the County of Kilkenny seems to abound more than any other part. And the said humidity of the air and land making the fruits for food more raw and moist, hereupon the inhabitants and strangers are troubled with looseness of the body, the country disease. Yet for the rawness they have an excellent remedy by their *Aqua Vitae*, vulgarly called Usquebaugh, which binds the belly and drieth up moisture more than our *Aqua Vitae*, yet inflameth not so much. Also inhabitants as well as strangers are troubled there with an ague which they call the Irish ague, and they who are sick thereof, upon a received custom, do not use the help of the physician, but give themselves to the keeping of Irish women, who starve the ague, giving the sick man no meat, who takes nothing but milk and some vulgarly known remedies at their hand.

"Ireland after much blood spilt in the civil wars became less populous, and as well great lords of countries as other inferior gentlemen laboured more to get new possessions for inheritance than by husbandry and by peopling of their old lands to increase their revenues; so as I then observed much grass, therewith the island so much abounds, to have perished without use, and either to have rotted or in the next springtime to be burnt, less it hinder the coming of new grass. This plenty of grass makes the Irish have infinite multitudes of cattle, and in the heat of the last rebellion the very vagabond rebels had great multitudes of cows, which they still, like the nomades, drove with them whithersoever themselves were driven, and fought for them as for their altars and families. By this abundance of cattle the Irish have a frequent though somewhat poor traffic for their hides, the cattle being in general very little, and only the men and greyhounds of great stature. Neither can the cattle possibly be great, since they eat only by day, and then are brought at evening within the bawns of castles, where they stand or lie all night in a dirty yard without so much as a lock of hay; whereof they make little, for sluggishness, and that little they altogether keep for their horses. And they are thus brought in by nights for fear of thieves, the Irish using almost no other kind of theft, or else for fear of wolves, the destruction thereof being neglected by the inhabitants, oppressed with greater mischiefs, they are so much grown in number as sometimes in winter nights they will come to prey in villages and the suburbs of cities. ...

"In cities passengers may have feather beds, soft and good, but most commonly lousy, especially in the highways, whether they came by their being forced to lodge common soldiers or from the nasty filthiness of the nation in general. For even in the best city, as at Cork, I have observed that my own and other Englishmen's chambers, hired of the citizens, were scarce swept once in the week, and the dust then laid in a corner, was perhaps cast out once in a month or two. I did never see any public inns with signs hanged out, among the English or English-Irish; but the officers of cities and villages appoint lodgings to the passengers, and perhaps in each city they shall find one or two houses where they will dress meat, and these be commonly houses of Englishmen, seldom of the Irish, so these houses having no signs hung out, a passenger cannot challenge right to be entertained in them, but must have it of courtesy and by entreaty.

"The wild and (as I may say) mere Irish, inhabiting many and large provinces, are barbarous and most filthy in their diet. They scum the seething pot with an handful of straw, and strain their milk taken from the cow with a like handful of straw, none of the cleanest, and so cleanse, or rather more defile, the pot and milk. They devour great morsels of beef unsalted, and they eat commonly swine's flesh, seldom mutton, and all these pieces of flesh, as also the entrails of beasts unwashed, they seethe in a hollow tree, lapped in a raw cow's hide, and so set over the fire, and therewith swallow whole lumps of filthy butter. Yea (which is more contrary to nature) they will feed on horses dying of themselves, not only on small want of flesh, but even for pleasure; for I remember an accident in the army, when the Lord Mountjoy, the Lord Deputy, riding to take the air out of the camp, found the buttocks of dead horses cut off, and suspecting that some soldiers had eaten that flesh out of necessity, being defrauded of the victuals allowed them, commanded the men to be searched out, among them a common soldier, and that of the English-Irish, not of the mere Irish, being brought to the Lord Deputy, and asked why he had eaten the flesh of dead horses, thus freely answered, "Your Lordship may please to eat pheasant and partridge, and much good do it you that best likes your taste; and I hope it is lawful for me without offence to eat this flesh, that likes me better than beef." Whereupon the Lord Deputy, perceiving himself to be deceived, and further understanding that he had received his ordinary victuals (the detaining whereof he suspected, and purposed to punish for example), gave the soldier a piece of gold to drink in usquebaugh for better digestion, and so dismissed him.

"The foresaid wild Irish do not thresh their oats, but burn them from the straw, and so make cakes thereof; yet they seldom eat this bread, much less any better kind, especially in the time of war. Whereof a Bohemian baron complained who, having seen the Courts of England and Scotland, would needs, out of his curiosity, return through Ireland in the heat of the rebellion; and having letters from the King of the Scots to the Irish lords then in rebellion, first landed among them in the furthest north, where in eight days' space he found no bread, not so much as a cake of oats, till he came to eat with the Earl of Tyrone; and after obtaining the Lord Deputy's pass to come into our army, related this their want of bread, to us as a miracle, who nothing wondered thereat. Yea, the wild Irish in time of greatest peace impute covetousness and base birth to him that hath any corn after Christmas, as if it were a point of nobility to consume all within those festival days. They willingly eat the herb Shamrock, being of a sharp taste, which, as they run and are chased to and fro, they snatch like beasts out of the ditches.

"Neither have they any beer made of malt or hops, nor yet any ale, no, nor the chief lords, except it be very rarely. But they drink milk like nectar, warmed with a stone first cast into the fire, or else beef broth mingled with milk. But when they come to any market town, to sell a cow or horse, they never return home till they have drunk the price in Spanish wine (which they call the King of Spain's daughter) or in Irish usquebaugh, and till they have outslept two or three days' drunkenness. And not only the common sort, but even the lords and their wives, the more they want this drink at home the more they swallow it when they come to it, till they be as drunk as beggars.

"Many of these wild Irish eat no flesh but that which dies of disease or otherwise of itself, neither can it scape them for stinking. They desire no broth, nor have any use for a spoon. They can neither seethe artichokes nor eat them when they are sodden. It is strange and ridiculous, but most true, that some of our carriage horses falling into their hands, when they found soap and starch carried for the use of laundresses, they, thinking them to be some dainty meats, did eat them greedily, and when they stuck in their teeth cursed heartily the gluttony of us English churls, for so they term us. They feed most on white meats, and esteem for a great dainty sour curds, vulgarly called by them Bonaclabbe. And for this cause they watchfully keep their cows, and fight for them as for religion and life; and when they are almost starved, yet will they not kill a cow except it be old and yield no milk. Yet will they upon hunger, in time of war, open a vein of the cow and drink the blood, but in no case kill or much weaken it. A man would think these men to be Scythians, who let their horses blood under their ears and for nourishment drink their blood; and indeed, as I have formerly said, some of the Irish are of the race of Scythians, coming into Spain and from thence into Ireland. The wild Irish, as I said, seldom kill a cow to eat, and if perhaps they kill one for that purpose, they distribute it all to be devoured at one time; for they approve not the orderly eating at meals, but so they may eat enough when they are hungry, they care not to fast long...

"These wild Irish never set any candles upon tables—what do I speak of tables? since indeed they have no tables, but set their meat upon a bundle of grass, and use the same grass as napkins to wipe their hands. But I mean that they do not set candles upon any high place to give light to the house, but place a great candle made of reeds and butter upon the floor in the midst of a great room. And in like sort the chief men in their houses make a great fire in the midst of the room, the smoke whereof goeth out at a hole in the top thereof. An Italian friar coming of old into Ireland and seeing at Armagh this their diet and the nakedness of the women, is said to have cried out:

> "Civitas Armachana, civitas vana,
>   Carnes crudae, mulieres nudae."

> "Vain Armagh city, I thee pity,
>   Thy meat's rawness and women's nakedness."

"I trust no man expects among these gallants any beds, much less feather beds and sheets, who, like the Nomades removing their dwellings according to the commodity of pastures for their cows, sleep under the canopy of heaven, or in a poor house of clay, or in a cabin made of the boughs of trees and covered with turf, for such are the dwellings of the very lords among them. And in such places they make a fire in the midst of the room, and round about it they sleep upon the ground, without straw or other thing under them, lying in a circle about the fire, with their feet towards it. And their bodies being naked, they cover their heads and upper parts with their mantles, which they first make very wet, steeping them in water of purpose; for they find that when their bodies have warmed the wet mantles, the smoke of them keeps their bodies in temperate heat all the night following. And this manner of lodging not only the mere Irish lords and their followers use, but even some of the English-Irish lords and their followers when, after the old but tyrannical and prohibited manner vulgarly called coshering, they go, as it were on progress, to live upon their tenants till they have consumed all the victuals that the poor men have or can get."

APPENDIX B

The Scottish Undertakers

The first list of Scottish applicants for Ulster allotments was completed by September 14, 1609. The following is the list as given in volume VIII of the official edition of the Register of the Privy Council of Scotland:

ADAMSON, JAMES, brother of Mr. William Adamson of Graycrook [Craigcrook]: *surety*, Andrew Heriot of Ravelston: 2,000 acres.

AITCHISON, HARRY, in Edinburgh: *surety*, Mr. James Cunningham of Mountgrennan: 2,000 acres.

ALEXANDER, ROBERT, son of Christopher Alexander, burgess of Stirling: *surety*, his said father: 1,000 acres.

ANDERSON, JAMES, portioner of Little Govan: *surety*, John Allison in Carsbrig: 1,000 acres.

ANDERSON, JOHN, burgess of Edinburgh: *surety*, Thomas Anderson, burgess there.

BELLENDEN, JOHN, son of the late Justice-Clerk Sir Lewis Bellenden: *surety*, Sir George Livingstone of Ogilface: 2,000 acres.

BELLENDEN, WILLIAM, also son of the late Sir Lewis Bellenden: *surety*, Mr. John Hart, younger, in the Canongate: 2,000 acres.

BORTHWICK, DAVID, chamberlain of Newbattle: *surety*, George Thorbrand, burgess of Edinburgh: 2,000 acres.

BROWN, JOHN, in Gorgie Mill: *surety*, Harry Aikman, in Brumehouse: 2,000 acres.

CARMICHAEL, DAVID, son of James Carmichael of Pottishaw: *surety*, Mr. John Ross, burgess of Glasgow: 1,000 acres.

COLQUHOUN, MR. MALCOLM, burgess of Glasgow: *surety*, Alexander Colquhoun of Luss: 2,000 acres.

COUTTS, ROBERT, of Corswoods: *surety*, John Coutts, skinner, burgess of Edinburgh: 1,000 acres.

CRANSTOUN, NATHANIEL, son of Mr. Michael Cranstoun, minister of Cramond: *surety*, Robert Wardlaw in Edinburgh: 1,500 acres.

CRAWFORD, DANIEL, goldsmith in Edinburgh: *surety*, George Crawford goldsmith there: 1,000 acres.

CRAWFORD, DAVID, son of Andrew Crawford of Bedlair: *surety*, Robert Montgomery of Kirktown: 2,000 acres.

CRAWFORD, JAMES, goldsmith, burgess of Edinburgh: *surety*, Archibald Hamilton of Bairfute: 2,000 acres.

CRAWFORD, ROBERT, of Possil: *surety*, John Montgomery of Cokilbie: 2,000 acres.

CRICHTON, ABRAHAM, brother of Thomas Crichton of Brunstone: *surety*, said Crichton of Brunstone: 2,000 acres.

CRICHTON, THOMAS, of Brunstone: *surety*, Mr. James Cunningham of Mountgrennan: 2,000 acres.

CUNNINGHAM, ALEXANDER, of Powton: *surety*, George Murray of Broughton: 2,000 acres.

CUNNINGHAM, JOHN, of Raws: *surety*, James Guidlet in Strabrock: 2,000 acres.

DALYRYMPLE, JAMES, brother of Dalyrymple of Stair: *surety*, George Crawford, younger of Auchincorse: 2,000 acres.

DOUGLAS, GEORGE, of Shiell: *surety*, Douglas of Pumpherston: 2,000 acres.

DOUGLAS, JAMES, of Clappertoun: *surety*, George Douglas of Shiell: 1,000 acres.

DOUGLAS, WILLIAM, son of Joseph Douglas of Pumpherston: *surety*, his said father: 2,000 acres.

DUNBAR, ALEXANDER, of Egirness: *surety*, George Murray of Broughton: 2,000 acres.

DUNBAR, JOHN, of Avach, *surety*, David Lindsay, Keeper of the Tolbooth of Edinburgh: 2,000 acres.

FINLAYSON, MR. JOHN, heir apparent of Killeith: *surety*, John Dunbar of Avach: 2,000 acres.

FORRES, JOHN, in Dirleton: *surety*, Walter Ker of Cocklemill: 2,000 acres.

FORSTER, WILLIAM, in Leith: *surety*, John Forster in Edinburgh: 1,000 acres.

FOWLER, WILLIAM, merchant-burgess in Edinburgh: *surety*, James Inglis, skinner, burgess of Edinburgh: 2,000 acres.

GUIDLET, JAMES, in Strabrock: *surety*, John Cunningham of Raws: 2,000 acres.

HAMILTON, CLAUD, of Creichness: *surety*, Archibald Hamilton of Bairfute: 2,000 acres.

HAMILTON, GEORGE, of East Binnie: *surety*, Mr. Edward Marshall, clerk of commissary of Edinburgh: 2,000 acres.

HAMILTON, ROBERT, of Stanshouse: 2,000 acres.

HAMILTON, ROBERT, son of the late Gilbert Hamilton: *surety*, Gavin Hamilton of Raploch: 2,000 acres.

HEPBURN, ALEXANDER, of Bangla: *surety*, Sir Robert Hepburn of Alderstoun: 2,000 acres.

HOME, ROBERT, of Blackhills: *surety*, Mr. John Home of Swansheill: 2,000 acres.

INGLIS, THOMAS, younger of Auldliston: *surety*, James, Lord Torphichen: 1,000 acres.

IRVING, ROBERT, at the mill of Cowie: *surety*, Edward Johnston, younger, merchant in Edinburgh: 2,000 acres.

JOHNSTONE, JOHN, bailie of Water of Leith: *surety*, Daniel Coutts in Dairy Mill: 2,000 acres.

KER, WALTER, of Cocklemill: *surety*, John Forres in Dirleton: 1,500 acres.

LAUDER, ALEXANDER, son of William Lauder of Bellhaven: *surety*, his said father: 2,000 acres.

LINDSAY, MR. JEROME, in Leith: *surety*, David Lindsay, keeper of the Tolbooth of Edinburgh: 2,000 acres.

LINDSAY, MR. ROBERT, in Leith: *surety*, George Smailholm in Leith: 2,000 acres.

LIVINGSTON, SIR GEORGE, of Ogilface: *surety*, John Crawford of Bearcrofts: 2,000 acres.

LOCKHART, STEPHEN, of Wicketshaw: *surety*, Thomas Weir of Kirktoun: 2,000 acres.

MCCLELLAN, HERBERT, of Grogrie: *surety*, George Murray of Broughton: 2,000 acres.

MCCULLOCH, JAMES, of Drummorell: *surety*, George Murray of Broughton: 2,000 acres.

McGILL, M. SAMUEL, burgess of Glasgow: *surety*, Robert Gray, brother of Patrick, Lord Gray: 2,000 acres.

MAC WALTER, PARLANE, of Auchinvennell: *surety*, Alexander Colquhoun of Luss: 2,000 acres.

MARJORIBANKS, THOMAS, son of Thomas Marjoribanks of Ratho: *surety*, John Marjoribanks, apparent of Ratho: 2,000 acres.

MELDRUM, JOHN, brother of the Laird of Seggie: *surety*, Ramsay of Balmonth: 2,000 acres.

MELVILLE, JAMES, son of John Melville of Raith: *surety*, James Melville of Fodinche: 2,000 acres.

MONTGOMERY, ROBERT, of Kirktown: *surety*, Robert Crawford of Possill: 2,000 acres.

MOWBRAY, WILLIAM, son of John Mowbray of Groftangry: *surety*, his said father: 2,000 acres.

MURE, JAMES, portioner of Both-Kenner: *surety*, Cuthbert Cunningham, provost of Dumbarton: 2,000 acres.

MURRAY, GEORGE, of Broughton: *surety*, Alexander Dunbar of Egirness: 2,000 acres.

ORROCK, CAPTAIN DAVID: *surety*, Lord Ochiltree: 2,000 acres.

PONT, MR. TIMOTHY, minister: *surety*, Alexander Borthwick of Nether Laich: 2,000 acres.

PURVES, THOMAS, in Bald: *surety*, John Purves, cordiner in Edinburgh: 1,000 acres.

RAMSAY, ALEXANDER, brother of Thomas Ramsay of Balmonth: *surety*, Meldrum of Seggie: 2,000 acres.

ROSS, MR. JOHN, burgess of Glasgow: *surety*, James Carmichael of Pottishaw: 1,500 acres.

SMAILHOLM, GEORGE, in Laith: *surety*, Mr. Robert Lindsay in Leith: 2,000 acres.

STEWART, HARRY, of Barskimming: *surety*, Lord Ochiltree: 2,000 acres.

STEWART, JAMES, of Rossyth: *surety*, William Stewart of Dunduff: 2,000 acres.

STEWART, ROBERT, uncle of Lord Ochiltree: *surety*, said Lord Ochiltree: 2,000 acres.

STEWART, ROBERT, of Robertoun: *surety*, William Stewart of Dunduff: 2,000 acres.

STEWART, ROBERT, in Edinburgh: *surety*, William Stewart of Dunduff: 2,000 acres.

STEWART, WILLIAM, of Dunduff: *surety*, Lord Ochiltree: 2,000 acres.

TARBET, JAMES, servitor to the Earl of Dumfermline: *surety*, Thomas Inglis, younger of Auldliston: 1,000 acres.

THORBRAND, ALEXANDER, son of George Thorbrand, burgess of Edinburgh: *surety*, his said father: 1,500 acres.

WATSON, MR. JAMES, portioner of Sauchton: *surety*, John Watson, portioner of Sauchton: 2,000 acres.

WATSON, JOHN, portioner of Sauchton: *surety*, James Crawford, goldsmith, burgess of Edinburgh: 2,000 acres.

WEIR, THOMAS, of Kirktoun: *surety*, Stephen Lockhart of Wicketshaw: 2,000 acres.

WILKIE, JOHN, burgess of Edinburgh: *surety*, James Murray, burgess there: 2,000 acres.

WOOD, ANDREW, brother of John Wood of Galstoun: *surety*, his said brother: 2,000 acres.

THE SECOND LIST

The Scottish Undertakers who were actually granted allotments in Ulster were those on the list made up in 1610 by the King and his English Privy Council sitting in London. The following schedule is taken from Vol. IX of the Register of the Privy Council of Scotland:

UNDERTAKERS FOR 3,000 ACRES EACH

LUDOVIC STEWART, Duke of Lennox (in Donegal County).

JAMES HAMILTON, Earl of Abercorn (in County Tyrone).

ESME STEWART, Lord D'Aubigny, brother of the Duke of Lennox (in County Cavan).

MICHAEL, BALFOUR, Lord of Burley (in County Fermanagh).

ANDREW STEWART, Lord Ochiltree (in County Tyrone).

Undertakers for 2,000 Acres Each

JOHN CLAPEN (in County Tyrone).
SIR JAMES CUNNINGHAM, of Glengarnock (in County Donegal).
SIR JAMES DOUGLAS (in County Armagh).
SIR ALEXANDER HAMILTON (in County Cavan).
SIR CLAUD HAMILTON (in County Tyrone).
SIR JOHN HOME (in County Fermanagh).
SIR ROBERT MACLELLAN, of Bomby (in County Donegal).

Undertakers for 1,500 Acres Each

———— BALFOUR, Younger of Montquhany (in County Fermanagh).
SIR THOMAS BOYD (in County Tyrone).
WILLIAM FOWLER (in County Fermanagh).
JAMES HAIG (in County Tyrone).
ROBERT HAMILTON (in County Fermanagh).
SIR ROBERT HEPBURN, late Lieutenant of the King's Guard in Scotland (in County Tyrone).
GEORGE MURRAY, of Broughton (in County Donegal).
WILLIAM STEWART, brother of Lord Garlies (in County Donegal).
SIR JOHN WISHART of Pitarro (in County Fermanagh).

Undertakers for 1,000 Acres Each

HENRY AITCHINSON (in County Armagh).
ALEXANDER AUCHMUTIE (in County Cavan).
JOHN AUCHMUTIE (in County Cavan).
WILLIAM BAILLIE (in County Cavan).
JOHN BROWN (in County Cavan).
———— CRAWFORD, of Liefnoreis (in County Tyrone).
JOHN CRAIG (in County Armagh).
ALEXANDER CUNNINGHAM, of Powton (in County Donegal).
CUTHBERT CUNNINGHAM (in County Donegal).
JAMES CUNNINGHAM (in County Donegal).
JOHN CUNNINGHAM, of Granfield (in County Donegal).
SIR JOHN DRUMMOND, of Bordland (in County Tyrone).
ALEXANDER DUNBAR (in County Donegal).
JOHN DUNBAR (in County Fermanagh).

WILLIAM DUNBAR (in County Cavan).
JAMES GIBB (in County Fermanagh).
SIR CLAUD HAMILTON (in County Cavan).
CLAUD HAMILTON (in County Armagh).
GEORGE HAMILTON (in County Tyrone).
ALEXANDER HUME (in County Fermanagh).
WILLIAM LAUDER (in County Armagh).
BARNARD LINDSAY (in County Tyrone).
JOHN LINDSAY (in County Fermanagh).
ROBERT LINDSAY (in County Tyrone).
ALEXANDER MACAULAY, of Durling (in County Donegal).
JAMES MACCULLOCH (in County Donegal).
SIR PATRICK M'KIE (in County Donegal).
———— MONEYPENNY, of Kinkell (in County Fermanagh).
JOHN RALSTON (in County Cavan).
GEORGE SMAILHOLM (in County Fermanagh).
JOHN STEWART (in County Donegal).
ROBERT STEWART, of Haltoun (in County Tyrone).
ROBERT STEWART of Robertoun (in County Tyrone).
SIR WALTER STEWART, of Minto (in County Donegal).
WILLIAM STEWART, of Dunduff (in County Donegal).
JAMES TRAIL (in County Fermanagh)
PATRICK VAUS (in County Donegal).

APPENDIX C

The Making of the Ulster Scot

By the Rev. Professor James Heron, D.D., of The Assembly's College, Belfast, Ireland.

As to the parts of Scotland from which the Ulster settlers came there is no controversy, and they may be indicated in a sentence or two. As we gather from such records as the Hamilton and Montgomery MSS., Hill's account of the Plantation, the State Calendars, Commissioners' Reports in the "Carew MSS.," Pynnar's "Survey," and other contemporary documents, the districts of Scotland which supplied the Ulster colonists of the seventeenth century may be grouped conveniently under three heads—namely:

WHENCE THEY CAME

(1) Galloway and the Scottish counties included in the ancient kingdom of Strathclyde—Dumbartonshire, Ayrshire, Renfrewshire, Lanarkshire, and Dumfriesshire;

(2) The counties around Edinburgh—Edinburghshire, Haddingtonshire, and Berwickshire; and

(3) The district lying between Aberdeen and Inverness, corresponding to the ancient province of Moray.

It should be noted here, however, that a certain portion of Scotland was expressly excluded from the privilege (if it was a privilege) of sharing in the Ulster Plantation. It was made a necessary condition that the colonists, both of the higher and lower ranks, must have been "born in England or *the inward parts of Scotland*." This restriction of authorised Scottish settlers to those born in "the inward parts" of the country was evidently designed to exclude Argyllshire and the Isles; that is to say, the Scottish Dalriada, the parts of Scotland inhabited by Celts from Ireland. It was manifestly for the express purpose of excluding them that the restriction referred to was made. They were not the sort of people that were wanted.

Now, let us trace the history of the several regions named, note the successive races by whom they were occupied, the numerous invasions, the incessant conflicts, the devastations and colonisations they passed through, and the probable outcome as regards the blood, race, and moral quality of the residue. A superficial view on a perfunctory survey of the history might be quite misleading. As the history reaches back far so as to touch even prehistoric tracts of time, and as the events and movements to be observed, even within the historic period, are often involved and complex, and extend over more than a thousand years, both patient study and a fair share of trained insight and of the historic imagination are requisite to realise those movements in their operation and outcome. In the present brief statement of the case I can only attempt to place before you the elementary facts of a somewhat difficult problem, and thus put you in a position to judge for yourselves. And for obvious reasons I have though it better, as far as possible, to state the facts in the words of recognised historians rather than in my own.

THE PICTS

As a necessary preliminary, however, to our consideration of the districts I have named, some notice must be taken of the Picts, who held almost the whole of the country we now call Scotland when it begins to emerge into the light of history. A keen controversy as to the racial connection of the Picts, in which the Scottish historians, Pinkerton and Chalmers, toward the end of the eighteenth century, were the chief protagonists, raged for many years, Pinkerton maintaining that they were Teutons, and his opponent arguing with equal vigour that they were Celts. Sir Walter Scott, in his tale of the "Antiquary," has a most amusing skit on that controversy. At the dinner-table of Monkbarns a sharp debate arises between the Antiquary and Sir Arthur Wardour on this very question, who were the Picts? Mr. Oldbuck asserts with

Pinkerton that they were Goths, while Sir Arthur asseverates quite as strenuously with Chalmers that they were Celts. The discussion, like many a similar one, gets more heated as it proceeds, till at length the combatants lose their temper, and Sir Arthur rises from the table in high dudgeon and "flounces out of the parlour." Dr. Hill Burton, in his "History of Scotland," describes the controversy between Pinkerton and Chalmers as quite inconclusive. In fact, the verdict of the latest and best modern experts is that both were wrong, and that the Picts were neither Celts nor Teutons! Dr. Skene, writing more than a generation ago, held that they were Celts; but I suppose the highest living authority on the subject is Sir John Rhys, Principal of Jesus College, Oxford, and Professor of Celtic in Oxford University, and Sir John Rhys, led by philological, ethnological, and topographical considerations, affirms that "the most tenable hypothesis may be said to be that the 'Picts' were non-Aryan, whom the first Celtic migrations found already settled" in the country. "The natural conclusion is," he says, "that the Picts were here before the Aryans came; that they were in fact the aborigines." He adds that "it is not too much to say that the theory of the non-Aryan origin of the Pictish language holds the field at present" ("The Welsh People," pp. 13–16). The judgment of the late eminent Professor of Celtic Philology in the University of Berlin, Professor Zimmer, coincides with that of Rhys. His opinion is that "Pict" was the Roman translation of the name given to the aborigines by the British and Irish Celts. And I see that Dr. Macewen, in the volume of his "History of the Church in Scotland," which has just appeared—a work of very careful research and scholarship—adopts this view. Note, then, that, according to such distinguished experts as Sir John Rhys and Professor Zimmer, of Berlin, the original inhabitants of the greater part of North Britain, including the aborigines of Galloway and of the North of Scotland from the Firth of Forth to the Pentland Firth, and by the Romans called "Picts," were not Celts.

I. We turn now, then, to the first of the three groups of districts I have named as having supplied a very large number of

Ulster colonists—namely, Galloway and the Northern portion of the ancient British kingdom of Strathclyde, which included the modern counties of Dumbartonshire, Renfrewshire, Lanarkshire, Ayrshire, and Dumfriesshire.

GALLOWAY

(1) As to Galloway, the remarks just made with regard to the Pictish aborigines have to be kept in mind. Even in the time of Bede we find here a people called by him "Niduari Picts," and at a still later time known as "Galloway Picts."[8] According to Sir John Rhys they were neither Goidelic nor Brythonic Celts, but non-Aryan aborigines, who had been subdued by the Celts, and had adopted the language of their Celtic invaders. When they were subjugated by a Celtic people, and became in a measure Celticised, is quite uncertain. In Strathclyde also, embracing the counties I have mentioned, there appears to have been a considerable substratum of Pictish aborigines. But overlying them, and constituting the dominant element in the population, were the Britons, or Brythonic Celts, who formed the British kingdom of Strathclyde. They were in close kinship with the Welsh. That, then, is the first thing to be noted with regard to this region—that prior to the coming of the Romans, and later, Galloway is chiefly populated by Pictish aborigines, and Strathclyde by Britons, who were Brythonic Celts, akin to the Welsh.

(2) The second fact to which I have to direct your notice is the invasion of North Britain by the Romans. The Roman occupation began in the year 80 of our era, continued till 410, and left, without doubt, some lasting effects. The six campaigns in which Agricola sought to subdue North Britain, and the numerous campaigns of later Roman invaders, laid waste the country, and exterminated a considerable proportion of a population which was already sparse, for the forests, moors, and marshes were then

---

[8]   See Life of St. Cuthbert, chap. XI, sec. 18. The designation "Niduari" appears to be derived from the river Nith, which bounded Galloway on the east.

extensive; while in the course of the three centuries of the Roman occupation there would be more or less intermarriage with the Britons, and some infusion of Roman, or at least foreign blood. Remains of Roman camps have been found in various places. We hear of one (at Bar Hill), where, with a cohort of auxiliaries from Germany, about a thousand settlers continued to live for nearly half a century. Dr. Macewen, in his recent "History of the Church in Scotland" (p. 18) says that with the Picts and Britons there was "blended a mongrel, half-foreign element, the residue of the Roman population. This element is difficult to explain in its relations to native life, but it is extremely historical both in itself and in its influences." He describes the people even at this early date as "the hybrid inhabitants of Strathclyde"; while Dr. Zimmer points out that Patrick in his letter to Coroticus speaks of the subjects of Coroticus in Strathclyde as being of both British and Roman descent.

(3) We have next to record the influx into the whole province of Galloway and Strathclyde of a Teutonic people. In the words of Skene "Galloway was for centuries a province of the Anglian kingdom of Northumbria" ("Celtic Scotland," Vol. I., p. 311); and the same is true of Strathclyde also. Bede informs us, for example, that in the year 603 Aethelfrid, king of Northumbria, "ravaged the Britons more than all the great men of the Angles. He conquered more territory from the Britons, either making them tributory or expelling the inhabitants, and planting Angles in their places, than any other king" ("Eccl. Hist.," B. I., c. 34). Mark the policy of the Northumbrian king, as described by Bede, of "expelling the inhabitants and planting Angles in their places"—a policy which seems to have been pursued by his successors. Bede also states that Oswald, another Northumbrian king (635–642), "brought under his dominion all the nations and provinces of Britain"; and that his brother and successor, Oswiu, even extended his realm ("Eccl. Hist.," B. III., c. 6). As Mr. Andrew Lang puts it: "Oswiu dominated Strathclyde and Pictland up to the Grampians, the English element for the time extending itself, and Anglicising

more and more the Scotland that was to be" (Article on "Scotland" in "Encycl. Britan."). Under Ecgfrid, Oswin's successor, they tried to throw off the yoke of servitude, but Ecgfrid "made so great a slaughter of them that two rivers were almost filled with their bodies, and those who fled were cut to pieces" (Eddi's "Life of Wilfrid," c. 19). A century later, in 756, "the successes of Eadbert reduced the fortunes of the Britons in this quarter of the lowest ebb," and Cunningham and Kyle were taken possession of, with Alclyde itself, the bulwark of the North Britons (Robertson's "Scotland Under Her Early Kings," Vol. I., p. 18). By the repeated ravages, slaughter, and expulsion of the native Britons, they must have been immensely reduced in number, while the possession and domination of the province for so long a period by a Teutonic people, whose policy it was to "expel the natives and to plant Angles in their stead," cannot but have added a large and powerful Teutonic element to a population already much reduced and mixed with other than Celtic ingredients.

THE SCANDINAVIAN INVASION

(4) But we come now to another Teutonic invasion which must have still more profoundly affected them—the seizure and occupation of both Galloway and Strathclyde by the Scandinavians. There is a record in the Ulster Annals to the effect that in 822 "Galloway of the Britons was laid waste with all its dwellings and its Church." But in 870 again both Strathclyde and Galloway were devastated by the terrible Northmen; Alclyde was taken and demolished, and many captives and much booty carried away. And the chronicler, Symeon of Durham, records another desperate invasion of the same territories by the Danes in 875, when they laid waste the country and "made great slaughter" of the inhabitants; and this is confirmed by the Ulster Annals. Referring to the same incursion in his "History of the County of Ayr" (p. 15), Paterson says that they "laid waste Galloway and a great part of Strathclyde," and that thus harassed by the insatiable Northmen, many of the inhabitants "resolved on emigrating to Wales. Under Constantin, their

chief, they accordingly took their departure… The Strathclyde kingdom was, of course, greatly weakened by the departure of their best warriors, and it continued to be oppressed both by the Scots and the Anglo-Saxon princes." "And with the retreating emigrants," says Robertson, "the last semblance of independence departed from the Britons of the North" ('Scotland Under Her Early Kings,' Vol. I., p. 54). But in 944 we find the Danes, Ronald and his sons, in possession of Galloway, and continuing in possession till the end of the century, when the Danes are displaced by the Norwegians, who remain in occupancy till the end of the next century (see Sir Herbert Maxwell's "History of Dumfries and Galloway," p. 48; Skene's "Celtic Scotland," and the "Annals of the Four Masters"). "From the end of the ninth century," says Rait, "Norse settlements continued for 300 years. The districts of Dumfriesshire and Galloway, all of the Western islands, the West coast of the Firth of Clyde northwards, and the coasts from Caithness and Sutherland to the Moray Firth were deeply affected by the influx of a Scandinavian population" (Rait's "Scotland," p. 7). As was inevitable, these Northmen left their mark deep on Galloway and Strathclyde, and added a strong Teutonic ingredient to the population. "It is plain," says Sir Herbert Maxwell, "from the place names of Norse origin scattered through the stewartry and the shire that there was a permanent Scandinavian settlement there" ("History of Dumfries and Galloway," p. 88).

"A sure and certain test of a colonisation of this description," says Robertson, "is afforded by the topography of the districts occupied, the 'caster' and 'by' invariably marking the presence of the Northmen not only as a dominant, but as an actually occupying class." He then proceeds to give clear evidence of such colonisation by the Northmen in the South-West of Scotland. Sir Herbert Maxwell also refers to "the remains of Scandinavian occupation preserved in the place-names of the South-West. Many hills," he says, "bear the title 'fell'—the Norse 'fjall'—as in 'Fell a' Barhullian' in Glasserton parish, or disguised as a suffix, as in 'Criffel.' The well-known test syllable, 'by,' a village, farm, or dwelling, so characteristic of Danish rather than of Norse occupation, takes the place in southern districts which 'bolstadr' holds in northern. 'Lockerby,' the dwelling of Locard or Lockhart; Canonby and Middleby in Dumfriesshire, Busby, Sorby, and Corsby in Wigtonshire are instances in point. 'Vik,' a creek, or small bay, gives the name to Southwick (sand-vik = sandbay), and 'n'es,' a cape, appears in Sinniness (south point), and Borness (burgh or fort point). Pastoral occupation is implied in Fairgirth (sheep-fold)… Tinwald, like Dingwall in the North, is the Assembly-field, and Mouswald the Mossfield" (Maxwell's "Dumfries and Galloway," pp. 44, 45). A Norwegian writer, quoted by Mackerlie, states that "the language of the Lowlands of Scotland is so much like that of Scandinavia that the Scottish seamen wrecked on the coasts of Jutland and Norway have been able to converse without difficulty in their mother-tongue with the people there."

In short, nothing in Scottish history is more certain than that a very large infusion of Danish and Norse blood has been given to the people of Galloway and Strathclyde. In view of the repeated devastation and depopulation of the country by war and by emigration of the natives, and the large influx and colonisation by Scandinavians, that infusion must have been very large indeed.

THE NORMANS AND SAXONS

(5) But we have to notice in the next place the greatest revolution of all in the history of this region, and of nearly all Scotland, the revolution caused by the influx of Saxons and Normans.

"Through the troubles in England consequent on the Danish and Norman invasions," says Dr. Hume Brown, a "succession of Saxon settlers crossed the Tweed in search of the peace they could not find at home. In itself this immigration must have powerfully affected the course of Scottish history; but under the Saxon Margaret and her sons the southern influence was directed and concentrated with a deliberate persistence that eventually reduced the Celtic element to a subsidiary place in the development of the

Scottish nation." And here it is most important to take note of and to carry in our memory the emphatic statement of Dr. Hume Brown with regard to the district under consideration when the Saxon and Norman colonisation began. "From all we know of Strathclyde and Galloway previous to the time of the Saxonised and Normanised kings" (Dr. Brown says) "extensive districts must have consisted of waste land" ("History of Scotland," Cambridge Historical Series, pp. 50, 89).

The movement which began under Malcolm II. (1005–1034) went on on a still larger scale in the time of Malcolm Canmore (1057–1093). He had long resided as an exile at the Court of Edward the Confessor, and had become thoroughly English in sentiment and sympathy. It was in his time that the Norman Conquest took place, and had a profound influence on the history of Scotland—an influence which appears not only in the copious inflow of Englishmen into Scotland, but in the gradual transformation of Scottish society and Scottish institutions. "The form in which the Conquest was first felt in Scotland," says Dr. Hill Burton, "was by a steady migration of the Saxon people northward. They found in Scotland people of their own race, and made a marked addition to the predominance of the Saxon and Teutonic elements" (Hill Burton's "History of Scotland," Vol. I., p. 373).

On the death of their king at Hastings, Edgar the Atheling had been chosen by the English people to succeed him, but he and his mother and two sisters, driven from England by the Conqueror, took refuge at the Court of Malcolm Canmore. And not only the Royal family, but "many of the Saxons fled into Scotland," says Cunningham, "to escape from their Norman masters… From this period," he adds, "we find a stream of Saxon and Norman settlers pouring into Scotland. They came not as conquerors, and yet they came to possess the land. With amazing rapidity, sometimes by Royal grants, and sometimes by advantageous marriages, they acquired the most fertile districts from the Tweed to the Pentland Firth; and almost every noble family in Scotland now traces from them its descent. The strangers brought with them English civilisation" (Cunningham's "Church History of Scotland," Vol. I., p. 105). Edgar's sister, Margaret, who became Malcolm's queen, was an able and ambitious, as well as an intensely religious woman after the Roman fashion, bent on the predominance of the English interest and of the English, that is, of the Roman Church. In 1070 Malcolm, her husband, made a raid into England, harried Cumberland, and carried back with him to Scotland as captives large numbers of young people of both sexes. "So great was the number of these captives," says the chronicler, Symeon of Durham, "that for many years they were to be found in every Scottish village, nay, in every Scottish hovel. In consequence, Scotland became filled with menservants and maidservants of English parentage; so much so that even at the present day," says Symeon, writing in 1120, "not only is not the smallest village, but not even is the humblest house to be found without them." "And besides the Saxons, many of the Norman nobility, dissatisfied with the rule of the Conqueror, retired to Scotland, where they were encouraged by every mark of distinction that could be heaped upon them" (Paterson's "History of the County of Ayr," Vol. I., p. 18). After referring to Symeon's testimony, Dr. Macewen adds that "in the next half-century there arrived with the monks a stream of settlers engaged in trade and agriculture, who frequented the towns or markets which were usually established in the vicinity of monasteries. According to another chronicler, William of Newburgh, all the inhabitants of Scottish towns and burghs were Englishmen" ("History of the Church in Scotland," Vol. I, pp. 172, 173). It is certainly not going too far to say, as Mr. Andrew Lang does, that "the long reign of Malcolm Canmore intensified the sway of English ideas, and increased the prepotency of the English element" (Article on "Scotland" in "Encyclop. Brit.").

And the policy of Malcolm was followed by his successors. Of his son Edgar (1097–1107) we are informed that "he welcomed the stream of settlers who poured into Scotland in ever-increasing volume," while Edgar's brother, Alexander I. (1107–1124) "did his utmost to Anglicise both Church and State to the north of the Forth."

It was, however, by David I. (1124–1153), who has been called "the maker of Scotland," that more was done in the way of Anglicising, Teutonising, and revolutionising that country than by any of his predecessors. And now it is by Norman rather than by Saxon agency and influence that the revolution is effected. Instead of describing in my own words the change that was now wrought, I think it better here, for obvious reasons, to put before you the statements of Dr. Hume Brown in his "History of Scotland." "When during the reign of David the Eastern Lowlands became the heart of his dominions," he says, "the future course of Scotland may be said to have been determined; it was then finally assured that the Teutonic races were to be the predominating force in fashioning the destinies of the country." "It was during David's reign that the Norman element attained such a predominance as to become the great formative influence in the Scottish kingdom." "The dominating fact of the period is the extensive assignment of lands within the bounds of Scotland to men of Norman, Saxon, or Danish extraction. Wherever these strangers settled they formed centres of force, compelling acceptance of the new order in Church and State by the reluctant natives… This gradual apportionment of lands by successive kings had begun at least in the reign of Malcolm Canmore; but it was David who performed it on a scale which converted it into a revolution." As examples of what was done Dr. Hume Brown notices the grant of Annandale to de Bruce, of Cunningham in Ayrshire to de Moreville, and of Renfrew, with part of Kyle, to Fitzalan; but these are only specimens of a colonisation which took place on a most extensive scale. Referring to Strathclyde, Lothian, and the East country north of the Forth, Dr. Hume Brown proceeds—"In the case of these three districts, the revolution was at once rapid and far-reaching. Following the example of his fellows elsewhere, the Southern baron planted a castle on the most advantageous site on his new estate. With him he brought a body of retainers, by whose aid he at once secured his own position, and wrought such changes in his neighborhood as were consistent with the conditions on which the fief had been granted. In the vill or town which grew up beside his castle were found not only his own people, but natives of the neighbourhood who, by the feudal law, went to the lord with the lands on which they resided. ... In the East country to the north of the Forth a change in nomenclature is a significant indication of the breach that was made with the old order" ("History of Scotland," Vol. I., pp. 88, 89, 90). "Of the nation itself, it may be said," Dr. Brown adds, "that the Teutonic element had now the preponderating influence in directing its affairs. The most valuable parts of the country were in the hands of men of Norman and Saxon descent, and the towns owed their prosperity to the same people" (p. 131).

THE FLEMISH ADVENT

So much with regard to the Saxons and Normans, who, for more than a century and a half, continued to flood Scotland, and to make the race predominant in the country.

(6) But the entrance of yet another Teutonic element has now to be recorded. "One great cause of the wealth and prosperity of Scotland during these early times," says the well-known historian, Mr. Fraser Tytler, "was the settlement of multitudes of Flemish merchants in the country, who brought with them the knowledge of trade and manufactures, and the habits of application and industry. In 1155 Henry II. banished all foreigners from his dominions, and the Flemings, of whom there were great numbers in England, eagerly flocked into the neighbouring country, which offered them a near and safe asylum. We can trace the settlement of these industrious citizens during the twelfth and thirteenth centuries in almost every part of Scotland, in Berwick, in St. Andrews, Perth, Dumbarton, Ayr, Peebles, Lanark, Edinburgh, and in the districts of Renfrewshire, Clydesdale and Annandale, in Fife, in Angus, in Aberdeenshire, and as far north as Inverness and Urquhart" (Tytler's "History of Scotland," Vol. II., c. iii., § 4).

Try now to realize the transformation which in the course of more than 1,000 years of eventful history—of repeated slaughterings, emigrations, and colonizations—the inhabitants of Galloway and Strathclyde have undergone. We have, first of all, as aborigines the Picts, who were not Celts, but who continued to survive in considerable numbers. We have next the British, or Brythonic, Celts, akin to the Welsh, who subjected, but did not expel the Picts. We have the numerous Roman campaigns against the British, in which large numbers of the latter were slain or carried captive, and in the course of a Roman occupation of 300 years' duration the addition of more or less of a Roman element. We have next for a long period measured by centuries its possession and domination by the Teutonic Northumbrians, an immense reduction of the number of the native inhabitants by war, captivity, and actual emigration, and the settlement there of many Angles. We have, then, its capture and occupation by the Northmen, and a powerful addition of Danish and Norse blood to the population. Most important of all, we have for a period of more than a century pouring into the country a continuous stream of Saxon and Norman colonists, who, in conjunction with other Teutonic settlers, soon took the upper hand and became predominant. And finally, we have the inflow of a multitude of Flemings, who were also Teutons.

There was unquestionably in "the remains of the old Midland Britons" a Celtic element, which, however, through inter-marriage and fusion of the races in the twelfth and thirteenth centuries, soon ceased in the Lowlands to be a separate and appreciable quantity. By that inter-marriage race distinctions were obliterated, and the Scottish people of the Lowlands amalgamated and consolidated into a compact unity, in which the Celtic element had become decidedly exiguous. As Mr. Andrew Lang puts it: "A Dumfries, Ayr, Renfrew, Lanark, or Peebles man, as a dweller in Strathclyde, has some chance of remote British (Brython) ancestors in his pedigree; a Selkirk, Roxburgh, Berwickshire, or Lothian man is probably for the most part of English blood" (Article on

"Scotland" in "Encycl. Britannica").

"Since the twelfth age," says Father Innes, "We have no further mention of the Walenses or Welsh ["the remains of the old Midland Britons"] in those parts as a distinct people, they being insensibly so united with and incorporated into one people with the rest of the inhabitants of that country, that in the following age they appeared no less eclipsed or vanished than if they had left the country." "Thence come," he adds, "the expressions of the preface to the Chartulary of Glasgo, that the remains of the old Britons or Welsh in the Western parts of Scotland had been by the invasions and ravages of the Picts, Saxons, Scots, and Danes forced to leave the country" ("Critical Essay on the Ancient Inhabitants of the Northern Parts of Britain or Scotland," Book I., c. ii., p. 41, in Vol. VIII. of the "Historians of Scotland"). Father Innes is recognized as one of the most learned, best informed, and accurate of Scottish historians.

THE SECOND TERRITORY

II. We turn now to the second territory, including Edinburghshire, Haddingtonshire, and Berwickshire, which provided a considerable number of the Ulster colonists of King James's Plantation. These are all named in the records as having supplied not a few of the Ulster undertakers and settlers. Now, the whole district from the Tees to the Forth, embracing these counties, was early taken possession of by a Teutonic people. Prior even to 449, a tract of country south of the Forth had received a considerable settlement of Frisians, a Teutonic race. But under a leader of the Angles called Ida an English kingdom was founded there in 547 called the kingdom of Bernicia. Later, with Deira added, it became the kingdom of Northumbria, consisting of a thoroughly Teutonic people, Angles or English both in blood and speech. Later still, Northumbria was taken by the Northmen, who added another powerful ingredient to the Teutonic blood of the people there, which was still further strengthened by two causes already noticed—first, by the immigration of the discontented refugees who followed Edgar, the Atheling, from England on the invasion of the Normans, and, secondly, by the numerous captives carried into Scotland by Malcolm Canmore.

By the victory of the Scottish King, Malcolm II., over Northumbria at Carham in 1018, the whole territory from the Tweed to the Forth, containing the counties named, was ceded to Malcolm. This cession of what was now called Lothian was one of the most momentous and epoch-making events in Scottish history, for it added a rich, fertile, Teutonic, and English-speaking province to the Scottish kingdom, which before long became the central and predominating influence in the nation. "It involved nothing less than the transference to another race of the main destinies of a united Scottish people," and the Anglicising of all Lowland Scotland (Hume Brown, p. 43).

But what I ask you very particularly to notice is that the people occupying that region of Lothian, which sent a very considerable number of colonists to Ulster, were Angles or English, so that it is quite certain that the Ulster immigrants from that area were to all intents and purposes of purely Teutonic blood. "The annexation of Lothian," says Paterson, "occupied for centuries chiefly by the Angles, brought them into closer contact with the inhabitants of the adjacent districts, while a body of Saxons actually effected a settlement in Kyle and Cunningham… The many Saxons brought into Scotland by Malcolm Canmore … must have tended greatly to disseminate a language already constituting the vernacular tongue of the East Coast from the Forth to the Tweed. … In the next, or Anglo-Saxon period, the growth of the Scottish dialect can be still more distinctly traced" ("History of County of Ayr," Vol. I., pp. 16, 17).

PICTLAND

III. We pass finally to that wide territory north of the Forth, known in early times as Pictland, and which gave many emigrants to Ulster. It is known that a good many years later than the actual Plantation under King James, a large number of people came from the region that lies between Aberdeen and Inverness, the ancient province of Moray. In a curious book of "Travels" by Sir William Brereton, the author states that in July, 1635, he came to the house of Mr. James Blare, in Irvine, Ayrshire, who informed him that "above 10,000 persons have within two years last past left the country wherein they lived, which was betwixt Aberdine and Ennerness, and are gone for Ireland; they have come by one hundred in company through this town, and three hundred have gone hence together, shipped for Ireland at one tide." Now, what is the previous history of that province of ancient Moray, lying between Aberdeen and Inverness, from which they emigrated? It was originally inhabited by Picts, a non-Celtic people. But its later history is noteworthy.

It was one of the territories which the Northmen took possession of and made their own. In 875 Thorstein the Red, a Danish leader, added Caithness, Sutherland, Ross, and Moray to his dominions. Later the same territory was seized by the Norse jarl, Sigurd, who ruled over it till his death at the battle of Clontarf, when he was succeeded by his son Thorfinn, so that for a long period it was practically a province of Norway. Skene says that the Mormaers and men of Moray "had as often been subject to the Norwegian earls as they had been to the Scottish kings." It is known that, occupying that province for so long a series of years, the Northmen added a strong Norse element to the blood of the residents; while it was the scene of many conflicts which must have greatly diminished the native population.

But another vigorous Teutonic ingredient was still to be given to it. The old province of Moray was one of those specially favoured by a large and liberal Norman colonization. The Mormaer of Moray and his brother in 1130 took advantage of David's absence in England to raise a force hostile to the king's interest, and they were defeated with heavy loss—the "Annals of Ulster record that 4,000 of the Morebh were slain," "and so complete was the victory," says Dr. Hume Brown, "that the district of Moray was definitely attached to the Scottish Crown, and its lands divided among the Normans, and such of the natives as the king could trust" ("History of Scotland," Vol. I., p. 76). He adds that it "was largely colonized by Norman settlers." Another rising was attempted in 1162 under Malcolm IV., "who," we are informed, "expelled very many of the rebellious inhabitants of Moray, and planted new colonists in their place, chief among whom were the Flemings or natives of Flanders" ("Critical Essay," &c., by Thos. Innes, M.A., p. 102). In those 10,000 emigrants who went to Ulster from this region there may have been some infusion of Pictish blood, but it is probable that by that time its main ingredient was Teutonic.

VARIETY OF RACES

In the rapid survey I have given the thing that most strikes one is the great variety of races that have combined to produce the Lowland Scot, whether he resides on the other side or on this side of the Channel. Pict and Celt, Roman, Frisian, Angle, and Saxon, Dane and Norwegian, Norman and Fleming—ten different nationalities—have all gone to the making of him. It is not to any one constituent, but to the union and combination in himself of such a great variety of vigorous elements that he owes those distinctive traits and qualities which distinguish him from other men. If you ask what proportion the Celt bears to the other nationalities which have united in the amalgam which we call the "Ulster Scot," my own impression is that the Angle and the Saxon, the Dane and the Norwegian, the Norman and the Fleming, all of which have gone to his formation, when taken together, make a combination by which, I imagine, the Celt in him is overpowered and dominated. That is my impression, but you can gauge the justice of it by the facts which I have placed before you. And the course of the subsequent history seems to justify this view. It is significant that, after the amalgamation of the races to which I have referred, the people of the Lowlands should be habitually regarded and spoken of as Sassenachs, and the Highlanders of the West as Celts. After the Teutonisation of the former, and the fusion of the races, and when the unabsorbed Celtic population was confined mainly to the Western Highlands and Islands, it was almost inevitable that there should be a determined and final struggle on the part of the latter to maintain, if not their predominance, at least their independence. Such a decisive struggle actually occurred at the famous and desperate battle of Harlaw in 1411. Donald, Lord of the Isles, a Celtic chieftain, with many Highland chiefs at the head of their clans, and an army of 10,000 men, set out to seize Aberdeen, bent on making himself master of the country as far south as the Tay, when he was met at Harlaw by the Earl of Mar, son of "the wolf of Badenoch," defeated in "one of the bloodiest battles ever fought in Scotland," driven back to his fastnesses, and compelled to make submission. By both Highland and Lowland historians the battle of Harlaw is described as "a decisive contest between the two races," the Saxon and the Celt. The authors of "The Clan Donald" assert that "Donald's policy was clearly to set up a Celtic supremacy in the West"; and Dr. Hume Brown affirms that "as a decisive victory of the Saxon over the Celt," the battle of Harlaw "ranks with the battle of Carham in its determining influence on the development of the Scottish nation," and in "ensuring the growth of a Teutonic Scotland" ("History of Scotland," Vol. I., p. 206).

Sir Walter Scott was more than a mere writer of romance. From his early years he had given special interest and continued attention to antiquarian pursuits, and to the past history of his country, an interest which appears in the historical cast and character of so many of his tales. It is true he wrote under a personal bias against the men of the Covenant, but that he was exceptionally familiar with antiquarian lore, and had an intimate knowledge of the past history of Scotland is beyond question. Now, Sir Walter Scott habitually represents the Lowlanders as "Saxons" (which he uses as an equivalent for "Teutons") and the Highlanders as Celts. In the "Fair Maid of Perth," for example, the Booshalloch says to Simon the Glover from Perth, "These are bad manners which he [the young Celtic Highland chief] has learned among you Sassenachs in the Low Country." Then at the desperate combat on the North

Inch of Perth between the warriors of the two Highland Clans, Clan Qubele and Clan Chattan, when the latter discovered the absence through funk of one of their heroes: "Say nothing to the Saxons of his absence," said the chief, MacGillie Chattanach; "the false Lowland tongues might say that one of Clan Chattan was a coward." To the great literary artist, the Lowlanders are to all intents and purposes "Saxons." Was an antiquarian expert, such as Scott was, likely to put into the mouth of a Highland chief what he believed to be a gross historical blunder?

But Scott is not alone in this representation. I have given the statements of Dr. Hume Brown, the Historiographer Royal of Scotland, and Professor of Ancient Scottish History and Palaeography in Edinburgh University. I shall only trouble you with the deliberate judgment of another modern historian, who has traversed the whole field of Scottish history. "The Scots, originally Irish," says Mr. Andrew Lang, "have given their name to a country whereof, perhaps, *the greatest part of the natives are as English in blood as they are in speech*" ("History of Scotland," Vol. I., p. 87).

IN CONCLUSION

The exact proportion of the Celt in the Lowland Scotsman or the Ulsterman it is now impossible to measure with precision. It is the fact that so many different races have united in producing him—that the blood not only of the Pict and the Celt, but of the Frisian, the Angle, and the Saxon, the Norwegian and the Dane, the Norman and the Fleming, all intermingled, is flowing in his veins—that seems to me the main thing to be noted in the making of him, the secret to which he owes the distinguishing features in his character. What are they? To summarize them in a sentence, are they not something like these? An economy and even parsimony of words, which does not always betoken a poverty of ideas; an insuperable dislike to wear his heart upon his sleeve, or make a display of the deeper and more tender feelings of his nature; a quiet and undemonstrative deportment which may have great firmness and determination behind it; a dour exterior which may cover a really genial disposition and kindly heart; much caution, wariness, and reserve, but a decision, energy of character, and tenacity of purpose, which, as in the case of Enoch Arden, "hold his will and bear it through;" a very decided practical faculty which has an eye on the main chance, but which may co-exist with a deep-lying fund of sentiment; a capacity for hard work and close application to business, which, with thrift and patient persistence, is apt to bear fruit in considerable success; in short, a reserve of strength, self-reliance, courage, and endurance which, when an emergency demands (as behind the Walls of Derry), may surprise the world.

APPENDIX D

Statement of Frontier Grievances

"We, Matthew Smith and James Gibson, in behalf of ourselves and his Majesty's faithful and loyal subjects, the inhabitants of the frontier countries of Lancaster, York, Cumberland, Berks, and Northampton, humbly beg leave to remonstrate and lay before you the following grievances, which we submit to your wisdom for redress.

"First, We apprehend that as Freemen and English subjects, we have an indisputable title to the same privileges and immunities with his Majesty's other subjects who reside in the interior counties of Philadelphia, Chester, and Bucks, and, therefore, ought not to be excluded from an equal share with them in the very important privilege of legislation; nevertheless, contrary to the Proprietor's charter and the acknowledged principles of common justice and equity, our five counties are restrained from electing more than ten Representatives, viz., four for Lancaster, two for York, two for Cumberland, one for Berks, and one for Northampton; while the three counties and City of Philadelphia, Chester, and Bucks, elect twenty-six. This we humbly conceive is oppressive, unequal, and unjust, the cause of many of our grievances, and an infringement of our natural privileges of Freedom and equality; wherefore, we humbly pray that we may be no longer deprived of an equal number with the three aforesaid counties, to represent us in Assembly.

"Secondly, We understand that a bill is now before the House of Assembly, wherein it is provided that such persons as shall be charged with killing any Indians in Lancaster County, shall not be tried in the County where the act was committed, but in the Counties of Philadelphia, Chester, or Bucks. This is manifestly to deprive British subjects of their known privileges, to cast an eternal reproach upon whole counties, as if they were unfit to serve their county in the quality of jurymen, and to contradict the well-known laws of the British nation in a point whereon life, liberty, and security essentially depend, namely, that of being tried by their equals in the neighborhood where their own, their accusers, and the witnesses' character and credit, with the circumstances of the fact, are best known, and instead thereof putting their lives in the hands of strangers, who may as justly be suspected of partiality to as the frontier counties can be of prejudices against Indians; and this, too, in favor of Indians only, against his Majesty's faithful and loyal subjects. Besides it is well known that the design of it is to comprehend a fact committed before such a law was thought of. And if such practices were tolerated, no man could be secure in his most valuable interest. We are also informed, to our great surprise, that this bill has actually received the assent of a majority of the House, which we are persuaded could not have been the case, had our frontier counties been equally represented in Assembly. However, we hope that the Legislature of this Province will never enact a law of so dangerous a tendency, or take away from his Majesty's good subjects a privilege so long esteemed sacred by Englishmen.

"Thirdly. During the late and present Indian War, the frontiers of this Province have been repeatedly attacked and ravaged by skulking parties of the Indians, who have with the most savage cruelty murdered men, women, and children, without distinction, and have reduced near a thousand families to the most extreme distress. It grieves us to the very heart to see such of our frontier inhabitants as have escaped savage fury with the loss of their parents, their children, their wives, or relations, left destitute by the public, and exposed to the most cruel poverty and wretchedness, while upwards of an hundred and twenty of these savages, who are with great reason suspected of being guilty of these horrid barbarities, under the mask of friendship, have procured themselves to be taken under the protection of the Government, with a view to elude the fury of the brave relatives of the murdered, and are now maintained at the public expense. Some of these Indians, now in the barracks of Philadelphia, are confessedly a part of the Wyalusing Indians, which tribe is now at war with us, and the others are the Moravian Indians, who, living with us under the cloak of friendship, carried on a correspondence with our known enemies on the Great Island. We cannot but observe, with sorrow and indignation, that some persons in this Province are at pains to extenuate the barbarous cruelties practiced by these savages on our murdered brethren and relatives, which are shocking to human nature, and must pierce every heart but that of the hardened perpetrators or their abettors; nor is it less distressing to hear others pleading that although the Wyalusing tribe is at war with us, yet that part of it which is under the protection of the Government, may be friendly to the English, and innocent. In what nation under the sun was it ever the custom that when a neighboring nation took up arms, not an individual should be touched but only the persons that offered hostilities? Who ever proclaimed war with a part of a nation, and not with the whole? Had these Indians Disapproved of the perfidy of their tribe, and been willing to cultivate and preserve friendship with us, why did they not give notice of the war before it happened, as it is known to be the result of long deliberations and a preconcerted combination among them? Why did they not leave their tribe immediately, and come among us before there was ground to suspect them, or war was actually waged with their tribe? No, they stayed amongst them, where privy to their murders and revenges, until we had destroyed their provisions, and when they could no longer subsist at home, they come, not as deserters, but as friends, to be maintained through the winter, that they may be able to scalp and butcher us in the spring.

"And as to the Moravian Indians, there are strong grounds at least to suspect their friendship, as it is known they carried on a correspondence with our enemies on the Great Island. We killed three Indians going from Bethlehem to the Great Island with blankets, ammunition, and Provisions, which is an undeniable proof that the Moravian Indians were in confederacy with our open enemies; and we cannot but be filled with indignation to hear this action of ours painted in the most odious and detestable colors, as if we had inhumanly murdered our guides, who preserved us from perishing in the woods, when we only killed three of our known enemies, who attempted to shoot us when we surprised them. And, besides all this, we understand that one of these very Indians is proved, by oath of Stinson's widow, to be the very person that murdered her husband. How, then, comes it to pass that he alone, of all the Moravian Indians, should join the enemy to murder that family? Or can it be supposed that any enemy Indians, contrary to their known custom of making war, should penetrate into the heart of a settled country to burn, plunder, and murder the inhabitants, and not molest any houses in their return, or ever to be seen or heard of? Or how can we account for it, that no ravages have been committed in Northampton County since the removal of the Moravian Indians, when the Great Cove has been struck since? These things put it beyond doubt with us that the Indians now at Philadelphia are his Majesty's Perfidious enemies, and, therefore, to protect and maintain them at the public expense, while our suffering brethren on the frontiers are almost destitute of the necessaries of life, and are neglected by the public, is sufficient to make us mad with rage, and tempt us to do what nothing but the most violent necessity can vindicate. We humbly and earnestly pray, therefore, that those enemies of his Majesty may be removed as soon as possible out of the Province.

"Fourthly. We humbly conceive that it is contrary to the maxims of good policy, and extremely dangerous to our frontiers, to suffer any Indians, of what tribe soever, to live within the inhabited parts of this Province while we are engaged in an Indian war, as experience has taught us that they are all perfidious, and their claim to freedom and independency puts it in their power to act as spies, to entertain and give intelligence to our enemies, and to furnish them with provisions and warlike stores. To this fatal intercourse between our pretended friends and open enemies, we must ascribe the greatest of the ravages and murders that have been committed in the course of this and the last Indian war. We, therefore, pray that this grievance be taken under consideration and remedied.

"Fifthly. We cannot help lamenting that no provision has been hitherto made, that such of our frontier inhabitants as have been wounded in defence of the Province, their lives and liberties, may be taken care of, and cured of their wounds at the public expence. We, therefore, pray that this grievance may be redressed.

"Sixthly. In the late Indian war, this Province, with others of his Majesty's colonies, gave rewards for Indian scalps, to encourage the seeking them in their own county, as the most likely means of destroying or reducing them to reason, but no such encouragement has been given in this war, which has damped the spirits of many brave men, who are willing to venture their lives in parties against the enemy. We, therefore, pray that public rewards may be proposed for Indian scalps, which may be adequate to the dangers attending enterprizes of this nature.

"Seventhly. We daily lament that numbers of our nearest and dearest relatives are still in captivity among the savage heathen, to be trained up in all their ignorance and barbarity, or to be tortured to death with all the contrivances of Indian cruelty, for attempting to make their escape from bondage; we see they pay no regard to the many solemn promises they have made to restore our friends who are in bondage amongst them. We, therefore, earnestly pray that no trade may hereafter be permitted to be carried on with them until our brethren and relatives are brought home to us.

"Eighthly. We complain that a certain society of people in this Province, in the late Indian War, and at several treaties held by the King's representatives, openly loaded the Indians with presents, and that J. P., a leader of the said society, in defiance of all government, not only abetted our Indian enemies, but kept up a private intelligence with them, and publicly received from them a belt of wampum, as if he had been our Governor, or authorized by the King to treat with his enemies. By this means the Indians have been taught to despise us as a weak and disunited people, and from this fatal source have arose many of our calamities under which we groan. We humbly pray, therefore, that this grievance may be redressed, and that no private subject be hereafter permitted to treat with, or carry on a correspondence with, our enemies.

"Ninthly. We cannot but observe with sorrow, that Fort Augusta, which has been very expensive to this Province, has afforded us but little assistance during this or the last war. The men that were stationed at that place neither helped our distressed inhabitants to save their crops, nor did they attack our enemies in their towns, or patrol on our frontiers. We humbly request that proper measures may be taken to make that garrison more serviceable to us in our distress, if it can be done.

"N. B.—We are far from intending and reflection against the commanding officer stationed at Augusta, as we presume his conduct was always directed by those from whom he received his orders.

"Signed on behalf of ourselves, and by appointment of a great number of the frontier inhabitants.

"MATTHEW SMITH,
"JAMES GIBSON

"February 13th, 1764."

APPENDIX E

Galloway's Account of the American Revolt

The following is extracted from *Historical and Political Reflections*, by Joseph Galloway; London: 1780:

In the beginning of the year 1764, a convention of the ministers and elders of the Presbyterian congregations in Philadelphia wrote a circular letter to all the Presbyterian congregations in Pennsylvania, and with it enclosed the proposed articles of union. The reasons assigned in them are so novel, so futile, and absurd, and the design, of exciting that very rebellion, of which the congregationalists of New England, and the Presbyterians in all the other Colonies are at this moment the only support, is so clearly demonstrated, that I shall make no apology for giving them to the Reader at full length, without any comment:

The Circular Letter and Articles of "Some Gentlemen of the Presbyterian Denomination," in the Province of Pennsylvania.

Philadelphia, March 24, 1764.

Sir, The want of union and harmony among those of the Presbyterian denomination has been long observed, and greatly lamented by every public-spirited person of our society. Notwithstanding we are so numerous in the province of Pennsylvania, we are considered *as nobody*, or a body of very little strength and consequence, so that any encroachments upon our *essential* and *charter privileges* may be made by evil-minded persons who think that they have little fear from *any opposition* that can be made to their measures by us. Nay, some denominations openly insult us as acting without plan or design, quarreling with one another, and seldom uniting together, even to promote the most salutary purposes: And thus they take occasion to misrepresent and asperse the whole body of Presbyterians, on the account of the indiscreet conduct of individuals belonging to us.

It is greatly to be wished that we could *devise some plan* that would cut off even the least grounds for such aspersions, that would enable us to prevent the bad conduct of our members, and that would have a tendency *to unite us more closely together; so that, when there may be a necessity to act as a body*, we may be able to do it whenever we may be called *to defend our civil or religious liberties and privileges*, which we may enjoy, or to obtain *any of which we may be abridged*.

"A number of gentlemen in this city, in conjunction *with the clergymen* of our denomination here, have thought the enclosed plan may be subservient to this *desirable purpose*, if it be *heartily* adopted and prosecuted by our brethren in this province, and three lower counties; and in this view we beg leave to recommend it to you. It cannot possibly do any hurt to us, and it will beyond doubt make us a more *respectable body*. We therefore cannot but promise ourselves your hearty concurrence from your known public spirit, and desire to assist anything that may have a tendency to promote the *union and welfare of society*, and the general good of the community, *to which we belong*.

We are yours, &c."

The Plan or Articles

Some gentlemen of the Presbyterian denomination, having seriously considered the necessity of *a more close union among ourselves*, in order to enable us to act as a body with unanimity and harmony &c. have unanimously adopted the following plan viz.:

1st, That a few gentlemen in the city of Philadelphia with the ministers of the Presbyterian denomination there, be chosen to correspond with their friends in different parts, *to give and to receive advices, and to consult what things may have a tendency to promote our union and welfare, either as a body*, or as we are connected together in particular congregations, so far as it will consist with our duty to the best of Kings, and our subjection to the laws of Government.

2d, That a number of the most prudent and public-spirited persons in each district in the province, and those lower counties, be chosen *with the ministers* in said districts, to correspond in like manner with one another, and with the gentlemen appointed for this purpose in Philadelphia; or

3d, That the same be done in each congregation or district where there is no minister; a neighboring minister meeting with them as oft as it is convenient and necessary.

4th, That a person shall be appointed in each committee thus formed who shall sign a letter in the name of the committee, and to whom letters shall be directed, who shall call the committee together, and communicate to them what advice is received, that they may consult together what is best to be done.

5th, That one or more members be sent by the committee in each county or district, yearly or half-yearly, to *a general meeting of the whole body*, to consult together what is necessary for the advantage of the body, and to give their advice in any affairs that relate to particular congregations; and that on stated meeting of said delegates be on the last Tuesday of August yearly.

6th, That the place of the general meeting be at Philadelphia or Lancaster, on the last Tuesday of August, 1764.

7th, That each committee transmit to the committee in Philadelphia their names and numbers, with what alterations may at any time be made in them.

8th, That the committee in town consist of ministers of the Presbyterian denomination in this city, and Mr. Treat, together with

Mess.	Samuel Smith	Mess.	T. Montgomery
	Alex Huston		Andrew Hodge
	George Brian		John Redman
	John Allen		Jed Snowden
	William Allison		Isaac Snowden
	H. Williamson		Robert Harris
	Thomas Smith		Wm. Humphreys
	Sam Purviance		John Wallace
	John Merse		T. Macpherson
	H. McCullough		John Bayard
	P. Chevalier, jun.		John Wikoff
	Isaac Smith		William Rust
	Charles Petit		S. Purviance, jun.
	William Henry		

In consequence of this letter, an union of all the Presbyterian congregations immediately took place in Pennsylvania and the Lower Counties. A like confederacy was established in all the Southern Provinces, in pursuance of similar letters wrote by their respective conventions. These letters were long buried in strictest secrecy. Their design was not sufficiently matured, and therefore not proper for publication. Men of sense and foresight, were alarmed at so formidable a confederacy, without knowing the ultimate extent of their views; however, at length, in the year 1769, the letters from the conventions of Philadelphia and New York were obtained and published.

A union of Presbyterian force being thus established in each Province, these projectors then took *salutary steps* (as they were called in a letter from one of the Committee at Philadelphia to his friend) to get the whole Presbyterian interest on the *Continent* more firmly united. These steps ended in the establishment of an annual Synod at Philadelphia. Here all the Presbyterian congregations in the *Colonies* are represented by their respective ministers and elders. In this Synod all their general affairs, political as well as religious, are debated and decided. From hence their orders and decrees are issued throughout America; and to them as ready and implicit obedience is paid as is due to the authority of any sovereign power whatever.

But they did not stop here; the principal matter recommended by the faction in New England, was an union of the *congregational and Presbyterian interest* throughout the colonies. To effect this, a negotiation took place which ended in the appointment of a standing committee of correspondence with powers to communicate and consult, on all occasions, with a like committee appointed by the congregational churches in New England. Thus the Presbyterians in the Southern Colonies who while unconnected in their several congregations, were of little significance, were raised into weight and consequence, and a dangerous combination of men, whose principles of religion and polity were equally averse to those of the established Church and Government was formed.

United in this manner throughout the Colonies, those republican sectaries were prepared to oppose the Stamp Act, before the time of its commencement, and yet sensible of their own inability without the aid of others, no acts or pains were left unessayed to make converts of the rest of the people; but all their industry was attended with little success. The members of the Church of England, Methodists, Quakers, Lutherans, Calvinists, Moravians, and other dissenters were in general averse to every measure which tended to violence. Some few of them were, by various arts, and partial interests, prevailed on to unite with them! and those were either lawyers or merchants, who thought their professional business would be affected by the act, or bankrupt planters, who were overwhelmed in debt to their British factors. But the republicans, predetermined in their measures, were unanimous. It was these men who excited the mobs, and led them to destroy the stamped paper; who compelled the collectors of the duties to resign their offices, and to pledge their faith that they would not execute them; and it was these men who promoted, and for a time enforced the non-importation agreement and by their personal applications, threats, insults, and inflammatory publications and petitions, led the Assemblies to deny the authority of Parliament to tax the Colonies, in their several remonstrances.

APPENDIX F

THE MECKLENBURG RESOLVES

Charlotte-Town, Mecklenburg County, May 31, 1775.

This day the Committee of this county met, and passed the following Resolves:

WHEREAS by an Address presented to his Majesty by both Houses of Parliament, in February last, the American colonies are declared to be in a state of actual rebellion, we conceive, that all laws and commissions confirmed by, or derived from the authority of the King or Parliament, are annulled and vacated, and the former civil constitution of these colonies, for the present, wholly suspended. To provide, in some degree, for the exigencies of this country, in the present alarming period, we deem it proper and necessary to pass the following Resolves, viz.

I—That all commissions, civil and military, heretofore granted by the Crown, to be exercised in these colonies, are null and void, and the constitution of each particular colony wholly suspended.

II—That the Provincial Congress of each province, under the direction of the great Continental Congress, is invested with all legislative and executive powers within their respective provinces; and that no other legislative or executive power, does, or can exist, at this time, in any of these colonies.

III—As all former laws are now suspended in this province, and the Congress have not yet provided others, we judge it necessary, for better preservation of good order, to form certain rules and regulations for the internal government of this county, until laws shall be provided for us by the Congress.

IV—That the inhabitants of this county do meet on a certain day appointed by this Committee, and having formed themselves into nine companies, (to wit) eight in the county, and one in the town of Charlotte, do chuse a Colonel and other military officers, who shall hold and exercise their several powers by virtue of this choice, and independent of the Crown of Great-Britain, and former constitution of this province.

V—That for the better preservation of the peace and admin-istration of justice, each of those companies do chuse from their own body, two discreet freeholders, who shall be empowered, each by himself and singly, to decide and determine all matters of controversy, arising within said company, under the sum of twenty shillings; and jointly and together, all controversies under the sum of forty shillings; yet so as that their decisions may admit of appeal to the Convention of the Select-Men of the county; and also that any one of these men, shall have power to examine and commit to confinement persons accused of pettit larceny.

VI—That those two Select-Men, thus chosen, do jointly and together chuse from the body of their particular company, two persons properly qualified to act as Constables, who may assist them in the execution of their office.

VII—That upon the complaint of any persons to either of these Select-Men, he do issue his warrant, directed to the Constable, commanding him to bring the aggressor before him or them, to answer said complaint.

VIII—That these eighteen Select-Men, thus appointed, do meet every third Thursday in January, April, July, and October, at the Court-House, in Charlotte, to hear and determine all matters of controversy, for sums exceeding forty shillings, also appeals; and in cases of felony, to commit the person or persons convicted thereof to close confinement, until the Provincial Congress shall provide and establish laws and modes of proceeding in all such cases.

IX—That these eighteen Select-Men, thus convened, do chuse a Clerk, to record the transactions of said Convention, and that said clerk, upon the application of any person or persons aggrieved, do issue his warrant to one of the Constables of the company to which the offender belongs, directing said Constable to summons and warn said offender to appear before the Convention, at their next sitting, to answer the aforesaid complaint.

X—That any person making complaint upon oath, to the

Clerk, or any member of the Convention, that he has reason to suspect, that any person or persons indebted to him, in a sum above forty shillings, intend clandestinely to withdraw from the county, without paying such debt, the Clerk or such member shall issue his warrant to the Constable, commanding him to take said person or persons into safe custody, until the next sitting of the Convention.

XI—That when a debtor for a sum below forty shillings shall abscond and leave the county, the warrant granted as aforesaid, shall extend to any goods or chattels of said debtor, as may be found, and such goods or chattels be seized and held in custody by the Constable, for the space of thirty days; in which time, if the debtor fail to return and discharge the debt, the Constable shall return the warrant to one of the Select-Men of the company, where the goods are found, who, shall issue orders to the Constable to sell such a part of said goods, as shall amount to the sum due: That when the debt exceeds forty shillings, the return shall be made to the Convention, who shall issue orders for sale.

XII—That all receivers and collectors of quit-rents, public and county taxes, do pay the same into the hands of the chairman of this Committee, to be by them disbursed as the public exigencies may require; and such receivers and collectors proceed no further in their office, until they be approved of by, and have given to, this Committee, good and sufficient security, for a faithful return of such monies when collected.

XIII—That the Committee be accountable to the county for the application of all monies received from such public officers.

XIV—That all these officers hold their commissions during the pleasure of their several constituents.

XV—That this Committee will sustain all damages that ever hereafter may accrue to all or any of these officers thus appointed, and thus acting, on account of their obedience and conformity to these Resolves.

XVI—That whatever person shall hereafter receive a commission from the Crown, or attempt to exercise any such commission heretofore received, shall be deemed an enemy to his country, and upon information being made to the Captain of the company in which he resides, the said company shall cause him to be apprehended, and conveyed before two Select-Men of the said company, who upon proof of the fact, shall commit him, the said offender, to safe custody, until the next sitting of the Committee, who shall deal with him as prudence may direct.

XVII—That any person refusing to yield obedience to the above Resolves, shall be considered equally criminal, and liable to the same punishment, as the offenders above last mentioned.

XVIII—That these Resolves be in full force and virtue, until instructions from the Provincial Congress, regulating the jurisprudence of the province, shall provide otherwise, or the legislative body of Great-Britain, resign its unjust and arbitrary pretentions with respect to America.

XIX—That the eight militia companies in the county, provide themselves with proper arms and accoutrements, and hold themselves in readiness to execute the commands and directions of the General Congress of this province and this Committee.

XX—That the Committee appoint Colonel Thomas Polk, and Doctor Joseph Kenedy, to purchase 300 lb. of powder, 600 lb. of lead, 1000 flints, for the use of the militia of this county, and deposit the same in such place as the Committee may hereafter direct.

Signed by order of the Committee,

EPH. BREVARD, Clerk of the Committee.

LIST OF AUTHORITIES CONSULTED

ADAIR, P. A True Narrative of the Presbyterian Church in Ireland.

ADAMS, H. History of the United States.

ALEXANDER, S. D. The Presbytery of New York, 1738 to 1888.

American Archives.

AVERY, E. M. History of the United States.

BAGWELL, R. Ireland Under the Stuarts.

BANCROFT, G. History of the United States.

BLENERHASSETT, T. A Direction for the Plantation of Ulster.

BOLLES, A. Pennsylvania: Province and State.

BOLTON, C. K. Scotch-Irish Pioneers in Ulster and America.

BOWEN, L. P. The Days of Makemie.

BRIGGS, C. A. American Presbyterianism.

BURKE, E. Account of the European Settlements in America.

BURY, J. B. Life of St. Patrick.

Calendar of State Papers. America and West Indies.

——, Carew Manuscripts.

——, Ireland.

CALVIN, J. Institutes of the Christian Religion.

Cambridge Modern History.

CAMPBELL, C. History of Virginia.

CARSON, J. The Cahans Exodus.

CHALMERS, G. Political Annals of the present United Colonies.

CHAMBERLAIN, M. John Adams and Other Essays.

CHAMBERS, G. Irish and Scotch Early Settlers of Pennsylvania.

COLLINS, V. L. Princeton.

CRAIGHEAD, J. G. Scotch and Irish Seeds in American Soil.

Centenary Memorial of the Planting and Growth of Presbyterianism in Western Pennsylvania.

DAVIDSON, R. History of the Presbyterian Church in the State of Kentucky.

DAVIS, W. W. H. History of Bucks County, Pennsylvania.

DAY, S. Historical Collections of the State of Pennsylvania.

DODDRIDGE, J. Settlement and Indian Wars of Virginia and Pennsylvania.

DOYLE, J. A. The English in America.

DWIGHT, N. The Lives of the Signers.

EGLE, W. H. History of Pennsylvania.

Encyclopaedia Brittanica.

ETTING, F. M. Independence Hall.

FALKINER, C. L. Illustrations of Irish History and Topography.

FISHER, S. G. The Making of Pennsylvania.

FISKE, J. The Dutch and Quaker Colonies in America.

FOOTE, W. H. Sketches of Virginia.

——, Sketches of North Carolina.

FRANKLIN, B. Works Edited by J. Sparks.

FRIEDENWALD, H. The Declaration of Independence.

GARDINER, S. R. History of England.

GORDON, T. F. History of Pennsylvania.

GRAHAM, G. W. and A. The Mecklenburg Declaration of Independence.

GREEN, A. Discourses Delivered in the College of New Jersey.

GREEN, A. S. Irish Nationality.

GREEN, S. S. The Scotch-Irish in America.

HANNA, C. A. The Scotch-Irish.

——, The Wilderness Trail.

HAMILTON, W. F. and others. History of the Presbytery of Washington.

HARTING, J. E. Extinct British Animals.

HAWKS, F. L. Contributions to the Ecclesiastical History of the United States.

HENDERSON, T. F. Scottish Vernacular Literature.

HERON, J. A Short History of Puritanism.

HEWATT, A. Historical Account of the Rise and Progress of the Colonies of South Carolina and Georgia.

HICKSON, M. Ireland in the Seventeenth Century.

HILL, G. The Plantation in Ulster.

HODGE, C. Constitutional History of the Presbyterian Church in the United States.

HOLMES, A. The Annals of America.

HOWARTH, O. J. R. A Geography of Ireland.

HOWE, G. History of the Presbyterian Church in South Carolina.

HOWE, H. Historical Collections of Virginia.

HOYT, W. H. The Mecklenburg Declaration of Independence.

HUTCHINSON, T. History of Massachusetts Bay.

JOHNSTON, A. Connecticut. Journals of the Continental Congress.

KERCHEVAL, S. History of the Valley of Virginia.

KERNOHAN, J. W. Two Ulster Parishes.

KILLEN, W. D. Ecclesiastical History of Ireland.

LANG, A. History of Scotland.

LANMAN, C. Biographical Annals of the United States Civil Government.

LECKY, W. E. H. History of England in the Eighteenth Century.

LEE, F. B. New Jersey as a Colony and a State.

LINCOLN, C. H. The Revolutionary Movement in Pennsylvania.

LIVINGSTON, E. B. The Livingstons of Livingston Manor.

LOSSING, B. J. Pictorial Field Book of the Revolution.

MACAULAY, T. B. History of England.

M&RSQUO;CRIE, T. Autobiography and Life of Robert Blair.

MCILVAIN, J. W. Early Settlements in Maryland.

MAYER, B. Logan and Cresap.

MICHAEL, W. H. The Declaration of Independence.

MORGAN, L. H. Ancient Society.

MORLEY, H. Ireland Under Elizabeth and James I.

MYERS, A. C. The Immigration of the Irish Quakers into Pennsylvania.

NEAL, D. The History of the Puritans.

NEVIN, A. Churches of the Valley.

——, Encyclopaedia of the Presbyterian Church.

——, Men of Mark of Cumberland Valley, Pennsylvania.

PALFREY, J. G. History of New England.

PARKER, E. L. History of Londonderry.

PENHALLOW, S. History of the Wars of New England with the Eastern Indians.

Pennsylvania Archives.

Pennsylvania Scotch-Irish Society. Reports beginning 1890 and continued since.

PERRY, A. L. The Scotch-Irish in New England.

Presbytery of Carlisle. Centenary Memorial.

Princeton University General Catalogue 1746–1906.

PROUD, R. History of Pennsylvania.

Records of the General Synod of Ulster.

REED, W. B. Life and Correspondence of Joseph Reed.

Register of the Privy Council of Scotland.

REID, J. S. The History of the Presbyterian Church in Ireland.

REID, W. The Scot in America and the Ulster Scot.

ROBERTS, W. H. One Hundred Years of the Presbyterian Church in America.

ROOSEVELT, T. The Winning of the West.

SABINE, L. American Loyalists.

Scotch-Irish Society of America. Ten volumes of proceedings of the Congress held annually, 1889–1901 inclusive.

SHARPLESS, I. A Quaker Experiment in Government.

SHEAFER, P. W. Historical Map of Pennsylvania.

SLOANE, W. M. Princeton in American History.

SMITH, S. History of the Colony of New Jersey.

SPENCE, I. Early History of the Presbyterian Church.

STEWART, A. A Short Account of the Church of Christ.

STEWART, G. B. Centennial Memorial English Presbyterian Congregation, Harrisburg, Pa.

STILLÉ, C. J. The Life and Times of John Dickinson.

SULLIVAN, J. History of the District of Maine.

SWOPE, G. E. Big Spring Presbyterian Church.

TRAILL, H. D. Social England.

———, Lord Strafford.

TURNER, D. K. History of Neshaminy Presbyterian Church.

TYLER, M. C. The Literary History of the American Revolution.

WALPOLE, C. G. The Kingdom of Ireland.

WATSON, J. F. Annals of Philadelphia and Pennsylvania.

WEBSTER, R. History of the Presbyterian Church in America.

WEEDEN, W. B. Economic and Social History of New England.

WILLIAMS, J. R. The Handbook of Princeton.

WILLIAMSON, W. D. A History of the State of Maine.

WINSOR, J. Narrative and Critical History of America.

Winthrop Papers. Massachusetts Historical Collections, Sixth series.

WIRT, W. Letters of the British Spy.

WOODBURN, J. B. The Ulster Scot.

YOUNG, A. Tour in Ireland.

YOUNG, R. M. Old Belfast.

ZIEGLER, J. L. History of Donegal Presbyterian Church.

INDEX

Printed in Great Britain
by Amazon